Palestine Inside Out

Palestine Inside Out

An Everyday Occupation

SAREE MAKDISI

W. W. NORTON & COMPANY

*New York * London*

For information about permission to reproduce selections from this book,
write to Permissions, W. W. Norton & Company, Inc.,
500 Fifth Avenue, New York, NY 10110

For information about special discounts for bulk purchases,
please contact W. W. Norton Special Sales at specialsales@wwnorton.com or 800-233-4830

Manufacturing by RR Donnelley, Harrisonburg
Book design by Chris Welch
Production manager: Julia Druskin

Library of Congress Cataloging-in-Publication Data

Makdisi, Saree.
Palestine inside out : an everyday occupation / Saree Makdisi.
p. cm.
Includes bibliographical references and index.
ISBN 978-0-393-06606-7 (hardcover)
1. Arab-Israeli conflict—1993– 2. Israel—Politics and government—1993–
3. Israeli West Bank Barrier. 4. Military occupation—West Bank.
5. Palestinian Arabs—West Bank. 6. Palestinian Arabs—Gaza Strip. I. Title.
DS119.76.M3395 2008
956.95'3044—dc22

2008001293

W. W. Norton & Company, Inc.
500 Fifth Avenue, New York, N.Y. 10110
www.wwnorton.com

W. W. Norton & Company Ltd.
Castle House, 75/76 Wells Street, London W1T 3QT

1 2 3 4 5 6 7 8 9 0

Then every man of every clime,
That prays in his distress,
Prays to the human form divine,
Love Mercy Pity Peace
—*William Blake*

For Ussama and Karim, my brothers

Contents

MAPS

AUTHOR'S NOTE

The first time I saw Palestine, I was too young to understand what I was seeing. I was with my parents and brothers on the banks of the Dead Sea in Jordan, and someone pointed across the sea to the hills on the other side. "That's Palestine," I was told, "and beyond those hills lies Jerusalem." I remember trying to squint to see if I could make out Jerusalem, though I was not sure what to look for exactly, nor how to know if I had seen it.

The first time I can remember hearing the word "Palestine," I was even younger. In a geography class in school in Beirut, where I grew up, there was a country with a funny name wedged in on the map between Lebanon, Syria, Jordan, Egypt, and the Mediterranean. Filastin al-Muhtalla: Occupied Palestine. Since I was far too young to have any idea what "Occupied" meant, and nobody at the school taught us what it meant, I thought it was kind of an odd name for a country to have. Why would they call it al-Muhtalla, I wondered? All the other countries had much simpler names: Lubnan, Suriyya, Urdun. Filastin al-Muhtalla stood out.

Many more years would pass before I saw Palestine again. This happened in the early 1990s when I was visiting then-Israeli-occupied southern Lebanon with my brother Ussama. The high point of our trip was a drive through the beautiful southern Lebanese countryside. As we wound our way along the hills and valleys, we soon found ourselves at the border with Israel.

We were at a point on the border where the high ground belongs to Lebanon. Standing alongside a pockmarked, battered, and shell-scarred bit of road in a devastated ruin of a Lebanese village, we looked across the border and down into what looked like Switzerland or Holland: neat, orderly houses, well-cultivated squares of farmland, swimming pools. We couldn't see any people, however. It was another world from the world of war we lived in. We gazed down, and I remember thinking "So that's Israel." Israel had become such an abstraction in my head that it was strange to look down at the place itself.

But it couldn't have been more than a few seconds after thinking to myself "So that's Israel" that I startled myself with the observation "And that's Palestine, too." And indeed there it was: the Filastin al-Muhtalla of my schoolboy days. "That land, over there, is in a sense what this war is all about," I thought to myself. "There is Palestine: look at it."

Since then, I have been to Palestine several times. I have studied its history, familiarized myself with recent and current events, and developed a thorough enough understanding of its people and their cause to be emboldened to write and speak about them in public. Writing about Palestine is not what I do for a living, though. I teach English literature, and most of my time is taken up with my teaching, reading, or writing about eighteenth- and nineteenth-century poems and novels. Much of my literary scholarship is concerned with the play of language and politics, exploring, for example, the ways in which the English Romantic poets William Wordsworth and William Blake conveyed the immense revolutionary upheavals of their own time in literary works such as *The Prelude* or *Songs of Innocence and of Experience*. I have become especially interested in the ways in which language can be used to express, suppress, or alter the understanding of political and historical events.

My scholarly interests have served me well in reading and writing about the Israeli-Palestinian conflict, in which the interplay of language and politics has a special, almost unique, importance. Whether the barrier that Israel is constructing in the West Bank is conveyed as a "wall" or a "fence"; whether Israeli housing units in the occupied ter-

ritories are described as "neighborhoods," "settlements," or "colonies";
whether various personalities or movements are represented as "moderate" or "extremist"; whether violence directed against civilians is thought
of as "terrorism" or "collateral damage": all these distinctions are both
linguistic and political. Simple word choices both express and—more
importantly—generate political effects. Language and politics are inseparable in the Israeli-Palestinian conflict, and it is virtually impossible to
understand what is happening without paying particular attention to the
ways in which language is used.

My interest in Palestine is not only linguistic and scholarly, of
course. I have very strong feelings about the Palestinian experience
and cause. But my feelings are not motivated simply by a sense of
belonging to the people, for my sense of belonging—to any group or
people—has always been rather complicated. My mother is Palestinian; but my father is Lebanese. I was born in Washington; so I am
an American, in addition to being Lebanese and Palestinian. I spent
the first few years of my life in the United States, before my family moved to Lebanon; so I arrived in the Arabic-speaking world as
a native speaker of English. I grew up in a Christian family; but in
a largely Muslim neighborhood of Beirut. I returned to the United
States for my final year of high school; but as a war-weary Beiruti. I
went to college and graduate school at American universities, and my
teaching career has been spent in the States, but I have also lectured
at universities around the world. I have, in short, become far too used
to being an outsider ever to feel entirely comfortable as an "insider"
identifying completely with any group or nation.

The long and awful war in Lebanon, during which I grew up, taught
me to regard any kind of group identification with what I think is a
healthy degree of skepticism. Like so many others, I have shared in the
experience of being a Lebanese who has been shelled by Lebanese; a
Palestinian shot at by Palestinians; an Arab who has come under Arab
fire; an American who has been bombed by American-made weapons.
My experience of war inoculated me against nationalism of any kind, and
brought home to me the truth of Dr. Johnson's dictum that "patriotism is
the last refuge of a scoundrel." But the main thing I learned from the war
was that war is unjust, no matter who is pulling the trigger, and that, as

my parents taught me, we owe it to each other as human beings to speak out against injustice.

What draws me to Palestine, then, is neither nationalism nor patriotism, but my sense of justice, my refusal to remain silent in the face of injustice, my unwillingness to just go on living my life—and enjoying the privileges of a tenured university professor—while trying to block out and ignore what Wordsworth once called the still, sad music of humanity.

—S. M., November 2007

| Palestine | Inside | Out |

Israel and the Occupied Territories. Courtesy of United Nations Cartographic Section.

One morning in early September 2006, Sam Bahour, a Palestinian businessman happily settled with his wife and two daughters in the West Bank town of al-Bireh, was informed by the State of Israel, by way of the Palestinian Authority, that within a month he must leave—leave his family, his home, and the successful businesses that he had started up and cultivated against all the odds imposed by a life under military occupation. He was also told that he need not bother trying to return; he would be barred from doing so.

The announcement was delivered to him by a Palestinian Authority civil servant, who in turn had received the order from the Israeli government facility in the Jewish settlement of Beit El, which administers Israel's military occupation of the West Bank. Even as he was grappling with what he had been handed, Sam couldn't help reflecting on the irony that the Israeli soldier who had signed the order telling him to leave was sitting behind a desk in an office built on land that had been illegally expropriated from Palestinian families in al-Bireh. One of the families was Sam's own.

Sam was born in Ohio. Like any Palestinian born outside of Palestine, Sam can't move back just because he wants to. Even to return to the

West Bank, which, like the Gaza Strip and East Jerusalem, is not part of Israel (all three are Palestinian territories captured by Israel in the 1967 War and held ever since), he has to obtain Israeli permission. He was counting on being able to obtain that permission when, in that fleeting moment of optimism in the early 1990s with the Oslo peace process still in its infancy, he, like thousands of other Palestinians, made the decision to abandon an easy life in the American suburbs and return to his ancestral land. By bringing home their education, their commitments, their wealth, and their business acumen, Palestinians like Sam hoped to contribute to the emergence of a viable Palestinian state alongside Israel. But the only way to or from al-Bireh is through Israeli-controlled borders, and entry requires Israeli permission.

Sam's wife, Abeer, was born in the West Bank and was listed on the territory's official population registry, so the couple was eligible to apply for family unification, which, if approved, would give Sam the right to reside permanently with Abeer in al-Bireh. Yet although Sam and Abeer were seeking permission to live on Palestinian land, their application would have to be processed and approved by Israel, which, despite the nominal return of parts of the West Bank to Palestinian self-rule, retains complete control over the population registry (as well as borders, water, airspace, taxation, and other vital matters)—and hence the sole authority to permit the issuance of all Palestinian identity cards, the keys to life in the occupied territories.

Sam and Abeer's application for family unification has been pending since 1994.

In the meantime, Sam, like thousands of other Palestinians with foreign passports, has been coming and going on temporary visas that he has had to renew every three months, sometimes less, by leaving Israel and reentering on his American passport. This has been in keeping with Israel's own regulations, according to which only a person who is physically present in the occupied territories may be added to the population registry—and ultimately granted an identity card—if and when an application for family unification is actually approved. The only way to be physically present is to enter on a temporary permit, leave when it expires, and enter again on a new visa. This procedure, and all the coming and going it entailed, was always a hassle, not to mention a financial burden, but at least it enabled Sam and Abeer to settle down and start a family, while Sam also started three companies—one of which, Paltel, became a major player in the telecom sector, and is now the largest private-sector employer in the West Bank. Their two daughters, Areen and Nadine, have lived in al-Bireh all their lives.

And so, every three months, more or less, for thirteen years, Sam would either apply for a visa extension or he'd simply leave the country and return on a new visa.

Then, in the summer of 2006, Sam left and returned as usual. This time, however, he was granted only a one-month visa at the border. Toward the end of the month, he applied via the Palestinian Authority to the Israeli administrative post at Beit El to request the usual three-month extension. He was granted only a one-month extension to the visa in his U.S. passport—which was overwritten, in Arabic, Hebrew, and English handwriting, "LAST PERMIT," meaning that he need not bother to apply for another extension, as none would be forthcoming. Sam argued, protested, and appealed. Finally, after weeks of agony, he was able to take on a temporary assignment with an international organization, through which he was able to obtain a three-month permit after all (but only after being forced to leave the country to pick up his new visa at the Israeli embassy in Jordan). This allowed Sam's family to remain intact for another few weeks at least. But he would have to begin the process all over again a couple of months later.

Sam's is by no means a unique case. Another Palestinian-American, a senior director of the largest investment fund in the West Bank—who has personally invested over $300 million in the occupied territories—was twice denied reentry in July 2006. So was the local distributor for Procter & Gamble and Philip Morris. Zahi Khouri, who holds the franchise for Coca-Cola in the West Bank, was granted a one-week visa, and had to scramble for an extension as well. And these are the lucky few: educated members of the urban middle class, or influential businessmen with good connections. Most Palestinians are not so well connected.

Amal al-Amleh, for example, has been unable to see her children for years. Her youngest child, Arwa, was only ten months old when Amal crossed the Jordan River to visit her infirm father in Jordan. When she tried to return to the West Bank, the Israeli soldiers at the Allenby Bridge denied her request for a temporary permit to rejoin her husband, Muhammad, and their children. Though she is Palestinian, Amal was born in Jordan; Muhammad is a West Bank native. They, too, had been waiting for their family unification application to be approved. Now Amal can only speak to her kids on the phone. She can't get back in, and Muhammad—barely able to support his children, his parents, and his wife in Jordan—can't afford to take time off from work to take the kids to visit their mother. Though she is only a few miles away, they are growing up without her.

Hundreds of Palestinians, having left as usual on their quarterly visa cycles, have been denied entry at various Israeli border posts. According to the Israeli human rights organization B'Tselem, 120,000 Palestinian applications for family unification have been pending since 2000. All across the West Bank, thousands of Palestinian families are facing the same dilemma. Once their visas run out, they, too, may have to face the choice of either leaving behind lives, homes, jobs, ancestral villages, and the living communities to which they have done their best to contribute despite years of war, occupation, curfew, and siege—or splitting up, the native-born family members staying behind, and the foreign-born ones leaving for an uncertain future. Article 16 of the U.N.'s Universal Declaration of Human Rights recognizes that "men and women of full age, without any limitation due to race, nationality or religion, have the right to marry and found a family," and that "the family is the natural and fundamental group unit of society and is entitled to protection by society and the State." But, as a recent B'Tselem report puts it, the result of the new Israeli policy is "the forced break-up of the family unit."

The Declaration of Human Rights also says (in Article 13) that "no one shall be subjected to arbitrary arrest, detention or exile," and that "everyone has the right to leave any country, including his own, and to return to his country." At the very end of December 2006, the Israeli government, facing mounting international pressure to alter its new approach to Palestinians living in the West Bank with temporary visas, relented, and issued new orders to its military commanders. Visa renewals would once again be permitted, under the same circumstances as before. "The 'LAST PERMIT' stamp has been cancelled," the Israeli ministry of defense announced. "People who have this stamp on their passport may leave the area, and their return will not be prevented solely on the basis of this stamp." Under the new Israeli orders, Palestinians can renew visitor visas for up to a year at a time, for a maximum of twenty-seven months, "during which time the visitor must receive a West Bank and Gaza identity card, without which they would have no legal basis to remain," as the World Bank notes in its May 2007 report on the Palestinian economy. "There also remains considerable uncertainty whether a person will be allowed entry even with a valid visitor's visa." Since Israel has the power to reject family unification applications (or to approve them in what the Israeli government considers "a special benevolent act"), because it alone controls the population registry on the basis of which West Bank and Gaza identity cards may be issued, it remains Israel alone that will determine the disposition of all these individual and family cases at the end of twenty-seven months. A study cited by the World Bank report estimates that some 17 percent of West Bank families are affected by Israel's family unification policies.

The Israeli soldiers, administrators, and bureaucrats who had been denying visas or visa extensions to Palestinians with foreign passports did not have anything personally against the families that they were pushing to the edge of dissolution. They were just doing their job—setting into practice a policy that was formulated by their superiors higher up along the military, and ultimately the political, chain of command. Although the conflict between Israelis and Palestinians is usually given international media coverage only during episodes of large-scale physical violence, such violence is still the exception rather than the rule, especially in towns like al-Bireh, Ramallah, and Bethlehem, the communities surrounding Palestinian East Jerusalem. The overwhelming majority of the daily encounters between Israel and the Palestinians occur in those everyday places where Israeli policy becomes Palestinian reality—where a politically charged vision, having assumed the neutral and technical language of administrative procedures and bureaucratic regulations, is played out in government offices, at roadblocks and checkpoints, and in planning applications; housing permits; citizenship, identity and residency documents—and, of course, visa stamps.

Encounters like the mediated one between Sam Bahour and the Israeli soldier-administrators in Beit El may not be spectacular: since they occur on an individual and intimately personal scale, they are usually played out silently and invisibly. But, since they are the very tissue and fabric of which Israel's military occupation is made, they cumulatively set the stage for the more overt acts of violence surrounding them. Such violence does not always assume the form of large-scale combat. Much more often, the Israeli project of claiming land and, whenever possible, clearing it of Palestinians, takes place in an endless chain of small, invisible, almost— but not quite—banal episodes, the background music of the occupation, whose real significance only becomes apparent when it is cumulatively assessed. According to Amnesty International, there are about 5,000 Israeli military orders regulating Palestinian life in the occupied territories. In many cases, a Palestinian cannot work, travel, study, tend crops, transport goods, dig for water, start a business, obtain medical care—or even visit relatives in the next town—without obtaining the appropriate permission from the Israeli authorities. And, beyond that, her life is subject to an ever-changing and unpredictable web of curfews, checkpoints, roadblocks, ditches, walls, fences, closures, whose very randomness helps keep Palestinians off-balance. This is not to mention the formidable set of permanent physical obstacles in the form of sprawling Jewish settlements, and a road network for the Jewish settlers, built on Palestinian land, to which Palestinians are denied access.

The result of Israel's military hyperregulation of everyday life has been catastrophic for the Palestinians, as the May 2007 World Bank report makes clear. While the Jewish settlements in the West Bank and East Jerusalem—all of them implanted in violation of international law—enjoy growth rates exceeding those of Israel itself, Palestinian towns and villages are slowly being stifled. While Jewish settlers move across the occupied territories with total freedom, the combination of physical obstacles and the bureaucratic pass system imposed by the Israeli army on the territories' Palestinian population has not only permanently separated the Palestinians of the West Bank from those of Gaza, East Jerusalem, and Israel (movement among which is forbidden for all but a tiny minority), it has also broken up the West Bank into three distinct sections and ten internal enclaves within those sections. Almost half of the West Bank is in effect off-limits to most of its Palestinian residents; to move from one part of the remaining territory to another, Palestinians must apply for a permit from the Israelis. Frequent bans are imposed on movement into or out of particular enclaves (the city of Nablus, for example, has been under siege since 2002), or on whole segments of the population (e.g., unmarried men under the age of thirty-five). And all permits are summarily invalidated when Israel declares one of its comprehensive closures of the West Bank, at which point the entire Palestinian population stays home. There were seventy-eight such days in 2006.

"The practical effect of this shattered economic space," the World Bank report concludes, "is that on any given day the ability to reach work, school, shopping, healthcare facilities and agricultural land is highly uncertain and subject to arbitrary restriction and delay." Given the circumstances, it is hardly any wonder that two-thirds of the Palestinian population had, by mid-2006, been reduced to absolute poverty (with incomes of less than $2 a day), or that a third of the Palestinians in the occupied territories, and 80 percent of those in Gaza, have been made dependent for their day-to-day survival on aid handouts from international relief agencies.

Israel says that these measures are necessary for the protection of its citizens from Palestinian attacks, which have killed hundreds of Israeli civilians since the start of the second intifada in 2000. Palestinians say that such attacks and other, legitimate, forms of resistance are generated by the occupation, which has killed thousands of Palestinians since 2000; that without the occupation there would be no resistance; and that the surest way for Israel to ensure its own security would be for it to adhere to international demands that it end the occupation. Human rights organizations and United Nations agencies acknowledge that Israel has the right to protect its citizens, but point out that military occupations are regulated by international law. They also point out that, as long as Israel remains in occupation of the Palestinian territories—even if doing so is itself a violation of U.N. Security Council resolutions calling on it to withdraw—it is subject to the legal obligations that come with occupation.

The Fourth Geneva Convention of 1949, to which Israel is a signatory, spells out precisely what an occupying power can and cannot do. "Protected persons are entitled, in all circumstances, to respect for their persons, their honor, their family rights, their religious convictions and practices, and their manners and customs," according to Article 27 of the Convention. Outrages upon personal dignity; extrajudicial executions; torture; violence to life and person; hostage-taking; coercion to extract information; reprisals; individual or mass transfers of population; settlement and colonization; the wanton destruction of private or public property; collective punishment—these are all specifically forbidden by the Convention. Yet U.N. and human rights reports make it clear that they are all also routine aspects of Israel's occupation policy. "The Israeli authorities have responded to the *intifada* and the killing of Israeli civilians by killing Palestinians at demonstrations, checkpoints and borders, and by shelling residential areas and police stations," warned a report published by Amnesty International in 2001. "In the name of security, hundreds of Palestinian homes have been demolished and Palestinians barred from traveling along certain roads in the Occupied Territories. All Palestinians in Israel's Occupied Territories—more than three million people—have been collectively punished." Moreover, according to the Geneva Convention, an occupying power has the obligation to ensure the well-being of the occupied people, their medical care, freedom of movement, access to food, water, work, and educational institutions: obligations that Israel has not fulfilled.

These regulations are designed in part to prevent abuses and in part to discourage any country from undertaking an occupation in the first place—or, if it does, letting it last any longer than absolutely necessary, for international law conceives of military occupations as short-term affairs. Israel's occupation of the West Bank, Gaza, and East Jerusalem has lasted for more than four decades. Rather than denying that it violates the Geneva Conventions, Israel claims that they do not apply to the occupied territories: a position dismissed by the U.N. Security Council and the International Court of Justice. Israel maintains its pressure on the Palestinian population not simply for its own security, then, but because such pressure has for four decades enabled it to maintain control over the territories—and, quite simply, because it encourages Palestinians to leave.

By the end of October 2006, foreign consulates had received almost 50,000 applications from Palestinians seeking to emigrate from the West Bank for good. There are fears that tens of thousands more are poised to follow on their heels, including a substantial proportion of the educated middle class, and a disproportionately large number of Palestinian Christians. For the Palestinians, a people already fragmented and dispersed, this would be a catastrophe. But every Palestinian who can—for whatever reason—be induced to leave the occupied territories is one Palestinian fewer for Israeli planners and politicians confronting what they candidly refer to as "the demographic problem," or in other words the ratio of Jewish to non-Jewish inhabitants of land held by the Jewish state.

There is a "problem" because only half the residents of the land under Israeli control (that is, Israel within its pre-1967 borders, plus the Palestinian territories captured in 1967) are Jewish. Faced with the choice of either genuinely relinquishing control over territory it would otherwise have liked to retain—because it comes with too many non-Jews on it—or formally annexing that territory, and hence granting their residents citizenship—which would mean further diluting the proportion of Jewish to non-Jewish citizens of the state—Israel has stalled, and it has remained stalled for two-thirds of its existence as a state. Israel does not want the people of the occupied territories, but it does want their land. That is the nature of the demographic "problem" facing Israel: how can it keep the land that it wants, without the people that come with it; and how can it continue to claim to be the Jewish state, when half the people over whom it rules are not Jewish?

Israel's demographic anxieties are no secret. They are proclaimed in newspaper headlines and on the evening news. They are explicitly used to justify current government policy as set in place by Ariel Sharon and reaffirmed by his successor Ehud Olmert—the stated objective of which is the separation of Jews from non-Jews. "The Jews have one small country, Israel, and must do everything so that this state remains a Jewish state in the future as well," Sharon argued in making the case for his policy of ethnic separation from the Palestinians who live on the land that Israel controls. "There is no intention of hurting anyone here; there's merely a correct and important intention of Israel being a Jewish state with a massive Jewish majority. That's what needs to be done, and that's exactly what we're doing." The same demographic concerns are bluntly asserted by the intellectual architects of Israeli government policy. Professor Arnon Sofer of Haifa University, who advised the Sharon government, estimates that 400,000 Palestinians left the West Bank between 1948 and 1967. "This is what will happen after separation," he has said, referring to the current government policy to separate Jews from non-Jews in Israel and the occupied territories. "If a Palestinian cannot come into Tel Aviv for work, he will look in Iraq, or Kuwait, or London. I believe that there will be movement out of the area." Like other Israelis, Sofer refers to this as "voluntary transfer."

"Transfer" is a concept that has a long and established history in Israel; it is a euphemism referring to the removal or expulsion of the indigenous, non-Jewish, population of Palestine. Only 20 percent of the population of Israel within its pre-1967 borders today is Palestinian because hundreds of thousands of Palestinians were forced from their homes—or "transferred"—during the creation of Israel in most of what had been Palestine in 1948, and forcibly prevented from returning to their homes afterward, despite their moral and legal right to do so (as affirmed, for example, by United Nations General Assembly Resolution 194, in 1949, and by the Universal Declaration of Human Rights). Having captured what remained of Palestine after 1948 during the 1967 War—that is, the West Bank, Gaza, and East Jerusalem—Israel once again found itself taking control of land with a population it did not want. But what had been possible in 1948—large-scale forcible expulsion—has seemed more difficult to carry out since 1967; hence the shift in Israeli strategy from outright expulsion to the "voluntary transfer" of the Palestinian population.

While the "voluntary transfer" of Palestinians from the occupied territories is an unstated objective of current Israeli government policy (as Sofer makes clear), compulsory transfer is still the openly declared objective of prominent Israeli political parties—parties that hold significant numbers of seats in the Israeli parliament and have served (or serve today) in the Israeli government. One such party, Moledet, which was founded by one-time cabinet minister Rehavam Ze'evi, declares openly (on its English-language Web site, for example) that "The Land of Israel," which, as far as it is concerned, includes the West Bank, Gaza, and East Jerusalem, "belongs to the Nation of Israel and only to the Nation of Israel." The party supports the formal annexation of the occupied territories and the permanent removal of their Palestinian population. Pending a formal population transfer, it says, measures—including the prevention of work—should be taken that will "encourage them to immigrate [sic] to other countries." The right-wing National Union bloc, which incorporates Moledet, currently holds nine seats in the Israeli parliament, compared with the twelve seats held by Likud, the most prominent opposition party. It does not hold any cabinet posts in the current Israeli government, but it held posts in the previous government, and the one before that. Ze'evi himself, who compared Palestinians to "lice" and "cancer," served as minister of tourism in Ariel Sharon's first government. He was assassinated by a Palestinian gunman in 2001.

At exactly the same time in September 2006 as Sam Bahour and hundreds of other Palestinians were scrambling to renew their permits to stay with their families on their land, the Israeli member of parliament Effie Eitam (one of the National Union bloc's politicians) took to the airwaves to declare not only that Israel would never leave the occupied territories, but that something had to be done about their population. "It's impossible with all of these Arabs, and it is impossible to give up the territory," Eitam argued. "We will have to expel the great majority of the Arabs of Judea and Samaria," he added, using the official biblical-sounding Israeli terminology for the West Bank. Eitam's comments caused an outcry among Israel's more liberal politicians, but his position is hardly as extreme within the Israeli context as they made it seem. The National Union has run an effective series of electoral campaigns. Its leaders have served in Israeli governments. They are hardly a fringe group (Ze'evi, for example, was a product of the mainstream Labor party).

Avigdor Lieberman's Yisrael Beiteinu party achieved a stunning success in the March 2006 Israeli elections by running on a platform of which the central plank was the territorial transfer—the removal—of Palestinians living not in the occupied territories, but in Israel itself: the state of which they are citizens. "They have no place here," he told his supporters at a rally; "they can take their bundles and get lost." Alongside the supposedly dovish Labor Party, Yisrael Beiteinu is now part of Prime Minister Olmert's ruling coalition, and Lieberman himself is deputy prime minister of Israel. The irony is that Lieberman was born in a remote province of the former Soviet Union, and the people he wants to remove from the country were born in the land to which he came as a twenty-year-old Russian-speaking foreigner. But he is Jewish; they are not.

And that, again, is the point. None of the rules and regulations that impede Palestinian life in the occupied territories (or Israel itself) apply to Israeli Jews who want to live there, or, for that matter, to any Jews at all. Israeli law considers all Jews members of the "nation" of which Israel claims to be the state, and hence eligible for instant citizenship, not to mention residency rights—rights that it denies to Palestinians like Sam Bahour. Palestinians are not members of the Jewish nation, and hence, even if some Palestinians have citizenship in the State of Israel, they are denied the benefits that accrue only to the members of the nation (and are handled by officially designated "national institutions" like the Jewish National Fund).

According to the State of Israel, there is no such thing as a specifically Israeli nationality because, as the High Court of Justice expressed it in a ruling in the early 1970s, "there is no Israeli nation separate from the Jewish people. The Jewish people is composed not only of those residing in Israel but also of Disaspora Jewry." Various military regulations specifically enable rights for foreign, non-Israeli Jews—those who are "eligible to immigrate to Israel in accordance with the Law of Return"—that are denied to native Palestinians, including, for example, freedom of access to certain "closed military areas." And the ability of foreign-born Jews to move into homes in the West Bank and East Jerusalem—as almost half a million settlers have done—is greatly encouraged by Israel, while the right of Palestinians like Sam Bahour to return to their family land in the occupied territories is severely limited, and refused altogether in the case of Palestinian land and homes inside Israel itself. Israeli government policies directly facilitate—and are directed by—the view that Jews have an exclusive entitlement to all the "Land of Israel." Palestinians are routinely denied building permits, and their homes are frequently demolished—but there are government incentives making it easier for Jewish individuals and families to buy or rent space in the settlements built in the occupied territories. Palestinian schools are underfunded, frequently closed, students and teachers alike having to run a gauntlet of curfews and checkpoints just to get to class—but there are generous government subsidies for schools in the Jewish settlements. Israel has illegally withheld hundreds of millions of dollars of tax receipts that it collects on behalf of the Palestinian Authority—but there are huge tax breaks for Jews who elect to settle in the occupied territories. When they are open at all, Palestinian roads are constantly blockaded and interrupted, undermined and washed away—but there are special roads reserved for the exclusive use of Jewish settlers, making their commute to jobs in Israel much easier. There is a formidable Israeli military presence restricting life for the Palestinians precisely in order to guarantee the safety of Jewish settlers. There is one legal and administrative system applied to the Jewish population of the occupied territories—Israeli civil law—and another—military law—applied to the Palestinian population.

At heart, the conflict between Israel and the Palestinians is actually very simple. It is not about religion. It is not about security. It is not about terrorism. It is about land. Or, to be more precise, it is a struggle that, as the late Israeli sociologist Baruch Kimmerling put it, is driven by two mutually exclusive impulses within Zionism, with "one Zionist imperative—to possess the largest possible amount of sacred land—contradicting the other Zionist imperative—to ensure a massive Jewish majority inhabiting a land that was preferably free of all Arabs." The problem for Zionists is—and has always been—that the land that they want comes with non-Jews already on it. When the Zionist program got underway in earnest in the early twentieth century, Palestinian Arabs constituted 93 percent of the population of the land that immigrant European Zionists wanted to transform into a Jewish state. As the settlement program now enters its terminal phase, non-Jewish Palestinian Arabs still constitute the majority in the land that is militarily occupied by Israel and settled by Jews but has not yet (officially) been made part of the Jewish state. Acting on the desire for land occupied by others is a necessarily violent activity, and it has always been. No people in the history of the world has ever gone away just because another people wanted them to.

"Any native people—it's all the same whether they are civilized or savage—views their country as their national home, of which they will always be the complete masters," wrote Vladimir Jabotinsky, the father of Revisionist Zionism, in a prophetic 1923 essay entitled "The Iron Wall." "Compromisers in our midst attempt to convince us that the Arabs are some kind of fools who can be tricked by a softened formulation of our goals, or a tribe of money grubbers who will abandon their birth right to Palestine for cultural and economic gains. I flatly reject this assessment of the Palestinian Arabs. Culturally, they are 500 years behind us, spiritually they do not have our endurance or our strength of will, but this exhausts all of the internal differences. We can talk as much as we want about our good intentions; but they understand as well as we what is not good for them. They look upon Palestine with the same instinctive love and true fervor that any Aztec looked upon his Mexico or any Sioux looked upon his prairie." Jabotinsky's point was quite simple. If, he argues, "every indigenous people will resist alien settlers as long as they see any hope of ridding themselves of the danger of foreign settlement," the point is not that the Zionists should abandon their project to transform Palestine into a Jewish state: the point is that that project can only be effected by the uncompromising subjugation of the will of the Palestinians. "Zionist colonization, even the most restricted, must either be terminated or carried out in defiance of the will of the native population. This colonization can, therefore, continue and develop only under the protection of a force independent of the local population—an iron wall which the native population cannot break through. This is, *in toto*, our policy toward the Arabs. To formulate it any other way would only be hypocrisy."

For Jabotinsky, writing in the 1920s, the iron wall was merely a metaphor. But Israel has in the past few years built a number of actual iron walls—barriers of concrete and steel—surrounding Palestinian communities in the occupied territories. And the policy that Jabotinsky outlined in merely theoretical terms in 1923, over two decades before the war for Palestine even began in earnest, has become reality in 2008, exactly as he said it should. This book explains how that happened—and how, in view of what has happened, the conflict can be brought to a peaceful and just resolution.

Outsides

1

Mohammad Jalud lives in the small village of Izbat Jalud, just south of Qalqilya in the West Bank. He has been eking out a living by farming a small plot of land, growing tomatoes and cucumbers and other crops. Until recently, it took him ten minutes to walk from his house to the plot of land that he owns just to the west of the village. In September 2003, the immense wall (I will use the terminology adopted by the International Court of Justice in its 2004 Advisory Opinion) that Israel had started building in the West Bank reached the Qalqilya region. The wall skirted the very edge of the built-up part of Izbat Jalud, cutting off the town from much of its most valuable farmland to the west.

The Israelis had built a gate in the wall that could enable access to the other side, but the gate was not open to Palestinians.

To reach his crops, Mohammad had to start traveling several miles along the wall to the gate at Azun Atma, which was open to Palestinians. For a couple of months, he was able to go south to Azun Atma, cross through the gate there, and then go back north on the other side of

Israel's West Bank wall, Qalqilya. Photo by author.

the wall to reach his land—just across from the Izbat Jalud gate, which remained closed to him. What had once been a ten-minute walk to his land now involved at least an hour, assuming there was no delay coming and going through the gate at Azun Atma. But at least, for now, he could get to his crops.

For most of its length, the wall is built not on the border, the 1949 Armistice Line that had until 1967 separated Israel from the West Bank, but rather inside—often miles inside, and in certain places almost halfway into—the occupied territory itself (see map, p. 336). Almost 10 percent of the West Bank's most fertile land will eventually be absorbed into the gap that Israel has opened between the 1967 border and the wall: an area to which the Israelis refer as the "seam zone."

In October 2003, the Israelis classified the "seam zone"—which, if the wall is built as currently projected, will ultimately enclose some 60,000 Palestinians in forty-two villages and towns—as a closed military area. "Facing the special security circumstances in the area and the need to take the necessary steps in order to prevent terrorist attacks and the exit of attackers from the areas of Judea and Samaria to the state of Israel," wrote General Moshe Kaplinsky that month, "I hereby declare that the seam zone is a closed area." Henceforth, according to General Kaplinsky's orders, "No person shall enter the seam zone or stay in it."

General Kaplinsky's orders—reiterating Israel's standard protocol for orders declaring a closed military area—explicitly exempt Israelis. And the orders specifically define "Israeli" not only as a citizen or resident of Israel, but also as "one who is eligible to emigrate to Israel in accordance with the Law of Return." So, as of October 2003, Mohammad Jalud couldn't access his own land without applying for a permit from the Israeli authorities; but Jews from Latvia and Moldova could, if they wanted to, because they are eligible for the Law of Return; Palestinians are not.

Israeli military regulations, pursuant to General Kaplinsky's orders, specify up to a dozen different kinds of permits that Palestinian farmers who live on the east side of the wall need to apply for in order to access and work on their land on the west side. A complex series of bureaucratic and administrative hurdles needs to be cleared for each permit.

The main hurdle involves proving that one actually *has* land on the other side of the wall. This is easier said than done. For one thing, Palestinian farming depends heavily on traditional practices and relations to the land. Often, whole families, rather than individuals, maintain plots of productive land. In such cases, for as far back as anyone can remember, the ownership of agricultural land was passed from generation to generation through traditional methods that never required documentation in the modern sense; families and communities just *knew* whose land was whose. Superimposed on the traditional system of tracking land ownership was the Ottoman Land Code of 1858, which classified large swathes of fertile land as *miri* lands. Although the Sultan was recognized as the ultimate (nominal) owner of *miri* land, the Ottomans' complex tax system granted to farmers, in return for paying a tax on the crops grown there, the right to possess, sell, and inherit actively cultivated *miri* land—as long as there was no break in cultivation for more than a certain number of years, in which case the land reverted to the ownership of the Sultan.

With the demise of the Ottoman Empire and the institution of the British Mandate in Palestine in 1922, a systematic effort was made to modernize landholding, including formally registering *miri* land ownership—freed from the Sultan at last—and assigning it to specific individuals or families.

This program of modernization was continued after 1948 when the West Bank came under Jordanian rule following the destruction of Palestine and creation of Israel and the eventual annexation of the West Bank by Jordan, in April 1950. But the process was slow; by the time the West Bank fell to the Israelis in 1967, only about a third of the land had been formally registered, and most of that was in urban areas.

The Israelis immediately suspended the process of formally registering land ownership when they took over the territory. They also issued a number of military orders based on their reinterpretation of the 1858 Ottoman Land Code, which, on their reading, granted to the Israeli military command the authority to assume the former power of the Sultan and to take possession, in the name of the state, of hundreds of thousands of dunums (1,000 square meters, or about a quarter of an acre each) of not-yet-registered *miri* lands, even if they were already cultivated. Many a Palestinian farmer did not find out until it was far too late to do anything about it that the plot that his family had been tending for generations had been declared "state land" by Israel and was henceforth off-limits to him. The Israeli human rights organization B'Tselem notes that even if Israel had followed the Ottoman Land Code to the letter, and not declared private property to be state property, its treatment of properly identified state land has also been improper. "State-lands are public property, belonging to the lawful residents of the West Bank," B'Tselem notes. "The role of the occupying power, i.e., the State of Israel, as the temporary substitute of the sovereign, is to administer the public land for the benefit of that public, or, alternatively, to meet its [short-term] military needs in the occupied territory. Rather than acting this way, Israel, since it started taking control of those state-lands, has completely denied the Palestinians their right to use these lands, and has allocated them exclusively for the establishment and expansion of Jewish settlements." For, along with land seized for "military needs" and land expropriated for "public use"— which, all together, amounted to almost half of the entire territory—such land was immediately made available for Jewish colonization and settlement. A widely cited report published in 2006 by the Israeli organization Peace Now found that, as of November 2006, privately held Palestinian land—not state land—accounted for some 40 percent of the land used for Jewish settlement in the West Bank. Even according to Israel's own laws (let alone international law), the construction of settlements on privately held land is illegal.

Today the built-up areas of the Jewish settlements in the West Bank account for no more than 2 percent of the territory's surface area. But, according to B'Tselem, through a variety of Israeli bureaucratic procedures, the settlements actually exert administrative control over some 42 percent of the West Bank's surface area. And according to a report published by the U.N. Office for the Coordination of Humanitarian Affairs (UN-OCHA) in July 2007, almost 40 percent of the West Bank is now taken up by Israeli infrastructure, including roads, settlements, and military outposts.

As B'Tselem points out, Israel's actions are in violation of the Hague Convention Respecting the Laws and Customs of War on Land as well as the Fourth Geneva Convention, which are the key international legal documents regulating the disposition of militarily occupied territory. The Geneva Convention, for example, expressly prohibits the "destruction by the Occupying Power of real or personal property belonging individually or collectively to private persons, or the state, or to any other public authorities, or to social or co-operative organizations." It also forbids "individual or mass forcible transfers, as well as deportations of protected persons from occupied territory to the territory of the Occupying Power or to that of any other country," and stipulates that "the Occupying Power shall not deport or transfer parts of its own civilian population into the territory it occupies." Israel has tried to claim that the Geneva Conventions do not apply to the Palestinian territories it occupies, but this claim has been dismissed not only by international legal scholars but also by a series of U.N. Security Council resolutions affirming the applicability of the Conventions to the Israeli occupied territories. "*Affirming once more* that the Geneva Convention relative to the protection of Civilian Persons in Time of War, of 12 August 1949, is applicable to the Arab territories occupied by Israel since 1967, including Jerusalem," Security Council Resolution 465 of 1980, for example, reiterates that "all measures taken by Israel to change the physical character, demographic composition, institutional structure or status of the Palestinian and other Arab territories occupied since 1967, including Jerusalem, or any part thereof have no legal validity and that Israel's policy and practices of settling parts of its population and new immigrants in those territories constitute a flagrant violation of the Geneva Convention relative to the Protection of Civilian Persons in Time of War and also constitute a serious obstruction to achieving a comprehensive, just and lasting peace in the Middle East." More recently, in its Advisory Opinion of July 2004 ("Legal Consequences of the Construction of a Wall in the Occupied Palestinian Territory"), the International Court of Justice in The Hague also unanimously reaffirmed the applicability of the Geneva Conventions to the Israeli-occupied territories and added that all of the agreements (notably the Oslo Accords) entered into by the Israelis and Palestinians since 1993 "have done nothing to alter" the fact that "all these territories (including East Jerusalem) remain occupied territories and Israel has continued to have the status of occupying power."

None of these findings and rulings has made any difference to the way in which Israel administers its occupation of the West Bank. Its regulations, rather than those of international law, are the ones to which the Palestinian population is held accountable (even when, as with the case of Jewish settlement on privately owned land, Israeli actions violate Israel's own laws, there is little Palestinians can do to seek redress). And when it comes to land west of the wall, those regulations require that a Palestinian prove to the satisfaction of the Israeli authorities that a given plot of land is his.

It is often extremely difficult for a Palestinian to do so. Even if some ancestor did obtain a tax certificate from the Ottoman Empire, or register the land with the British or the Jordanians, the Israelis apply the most stringent criteria to his application for a permit to enter the "seam zone." Papers are often incomplete or inconsistent, especially given the fact that the legal documentation of West Bank land has gone through various conflicts and upheavals, including two world wars, and passed through the hands of countless municipal offices in four different political entities (the Ottoman Empire, Britain, Jordan, Israel). If a Palestinian farmer's land was misregistered, or if there are errors in the original registration, or if the original owner had died or moved overseas, or if there are any questions about inheritances or divisions of land among or within or between families, or any questions about bills of sale, or titles, then the application for a permit will be suspended until all the legal difficulties can be sorted

out. In the meantime, Israel will retain control of and access to the land
in question.

In a number of cases, a Palestinian landowner has been able to prove
that he does indeed have a claim on the land, only for the Israelis to
declare that the land in question may be his, but that it does not lie on
the west side of the wall after all. Eid Ahmed Yassin, for example, lives in
al-Ras, a small village near Qalqilya. He and his family own and farm 110
dunums, or about 28 acres, of land in the "seam zone" west of the wall,
but still in the West Bank. Eid submitted several applications to the Israelis for a permit in order to access his land, all of which were turned down.
Finally, with the help of a coalition of human rights organizations, he
applied again and was granted a permit in late 2004. When that permit
expired in early 2005, he reapplied and was again rejected. This time his
application was returned, overwritten with Hebrew handwriting asserting
that his property does not exist west of the wall. He can see and point
to his land, his trees, his crops, from a nearby hilltop. But neither he nor
the al-Ras municipality possess one of the official Israeli maps indicating
the exact location of the plots of land listed in their taxation documents
(through which he was able to establish ownership). Since Israel prints
and controls the maps, he has no way to prove that the land specified on
a piece of paper is the land that has now been enclosed on the other side
of the wall.

This is not just Eid's problem. According to the municipality, 90 percent of al-Ras's land is located west of the wall. In February 2005, 120
applications for permits to access land west of the wall were submitted to
the Israelis by farmers in al-Ras. By April, only seven had been approved,
all for elderly people. In June, another three permits were granted, for
children aged ten to fifteen. Their parents' applications were rejected.
Between June and September, one more person was granted a permit. In
anticipation of the autumn's crucial olive harvest, al-Ras's farmers submitted 180 applications to the Israelis in the late summer. One in three
was granted. For an impoverished agricultural community, this was a
catastrophe.

Thus, even if a landowner is granted a permit to access his land, his
immediate family may not be, so he may not have anyone to help him
plow, sow, weed, water, or harvest his crops. And even if various mem-

bers of the family are granted permits, seasonal day laborers will almost certainly be turned down—laborers on whom the farmer depends at peak moments of the production cycle, such as the annual olive harvest, when, traditionally, up to half the Palestinian population would take time off from other occupations to help out. Tenant farmers, spouses, day laborers, grandchildren—all along the length of the wall, about half of these have had their permit applications denied. By mid-2005, almost 40 percent of the permits submitted by Palestinians to access farmland on the west side of the wall were being rejected by the Israeli authorities (a figure that would rise to more than 80 percent by November 2007, by which time Israel was granting permits only to some 18 percent of those who used to work land west of the wall). Two-thirds of the rejections are handed down because the applicant can't prove to Israel's satisfaction that he or she owns land, or has a direct relationship to the landowner.

Mohammad Jalud, however, had cleared all these hurdles. Shortly after November 2003, when the Israelis institutionalized the "seam zone" permit system, Mohammad was able to obtain the two permits he needed to get to his land. The Israeli army allowed him to use its patrol road to cover the distance from the Azun Atma gate back up to where his plot of land lies, near the still-closed Izbat Jalud gate; any other route would have taken him too close to the settlement of Oranit. (The wall had also obliterated the previous road and path system, so farmers often had to cross through each other's fields to get to their own land). Mohammad was not, however, allowed to bring his tractor. He would have to carry his farm tools himself for the long walk on the west side of the wall, and he would have to carry his produce back out on his back. He could buy a donkey, but the donkey would need a permit too—and that would involve a whole separate set of applications.

Mohammad persevered. He kept going with the hour-long journey, tending his crops, looking after the irrigation, fertilization, and so on. Then the gate opening and closing times got more erratic. The Israelis started opening the gates for twenty minutes to an hour three times a day, not always in a punctual and timely manner. Even if he had only an hour or two of work to do, Mohammad would have to commit to four or five hours on the other side of the wall, waiting for the gate to reopen so he could leave the "seam zone." And after any security incident, no matter how distant, the Israelis would seal all the gates and keep them closed for days or weeks. At the peak of the olive harvest season in 2003, for example, the Israeli army sealed all the gates in the wall near Qalqilya— in response to a bombing in Haifa, about forty miles away on the coast.

Then, in mid-2004, the Israelis decided to open the Izbat Jalud gate: the one close to Mohammad's home and fields. That would cut his daily commute down considerably. But when he tried to get through the gate at Izbat Jalud, the Israeli soldiers manning the gate told him that his permit was for the gate at Azun Atma. He could not cross through at Izbat Jalud. Then, making his way down to the Azun Atma gate, he was informed by the Israeli soldiers there that he could no longer use that gate because the army would no longer allow him to use the patrol road to reach his land. The reason, they said, was that another, more direct route, through the Izbat Jalud gate, was now open to him.

For much of the summer of 2004, Mohammad couldn't get to his land. He applied for another permit. In August, the new permit came through—but it once again restricted him to the Azun Atma gate. He made an official request to the Israelis to change his gate assignment to the Izbat Jalud gate. In February 2005, at last, he received a new per- mit. But it also assigned him to the Azun Atma gate. Cut off from his crops on the other side of Israel's wall, Mohammad had to start work- ing as a day laborer just to make ends meet. He made further requests and entreaties, and, finally, in September 2005, he was granted a permit allowing him access to the Izbat Jalud gate. It had been over a year since he'd tended his land.

He lost a year's worth of crops, but at least he was able to save his land—for now. According to Israel's interpretation of the Ottoman land laws, *miri* land that is not actively cultivated for a certain amount of time (even if its cultivation is being actively and forcibly prevented) reverts to state ownership.

OCCUPATION BY THE NUMBERS

- Length of West Bank–Israel border: 196 miles
- Projected length of West Bank wall: 437 miles
- Projected proportion of wall built on border: 20 percent

- Length of wall in and around East Jerusalem: 104 miles
- Length built on internationally recognized border near Jerusalem: 3 miles
- Percentage of West Bank surface area, including enclaves in and near East Jerusalem, cut off by the wall: 12
- Amount of land expropriated for construction of the wall: 8,750 acres
- Number of gates built into the wall: 67
- Number open on a daily basis to Palestinians (with appropriate permits): 19
- Percentage of Palestinian agricultural land planted with olive trees: 45
- Percentage of Palestinian population that participates in annual olive harvest: 50
- Number of olive trees in occupied territories: 9 million
- Number inaccessible or access restricted after construction of wall: 1 million
- Number burned, uprooted, or bulldozed by Israeli army from 2000 to 2005: 465,945
- Percentage of Palestinian families not permitted to access their land in "seam zone" in northern West Bank: 82
- Palestinian communities in "seam zone" with 24-hour access to emergency medical care: 1
- Palestinians living in "seam zone" upon its completion: 60,500
- Palestinians living in Jerusalem cut off from the city by the wall: 63,000

2

Mohammad Jalud's story is typical rather than exceptional. Half a million Palestinians live within less than a mile from the wall in the West Bank. All of their lives have been severely disrupted. Whole towns have been cut off from some of their richest and most productive land, devastating the local farming-based economy. Almost half the workers in the area around Qalqilya, for example, are dependent on agriculture for their day-to-day subsistence, yet more than 80 percent of farming families there are unable to reach their lands west of the wall. Mohammad Salim, a farmer from Jayyus, also near Qalqilya, tells a story much like Mohammad Jalud's. He and his seven brothers inherited a 6-acre patch of land from their father, on which they have olive and citrus trees, in addition to growing vegetables in greenhouses. The brothers worked their land together, as they had been doing since the 1960s, until the wall went up in their area in 2003, after which they had to obtain permits from the Israelis to access their crops. In October that year, Mohammad's brothers were granted permits; but he, his wife, and his sons were not. He reapplied in January 2004, and again in February, and again in March. Each time he was refused, though no reason was given. He suspects, however, that he is being singled out for a reason. "On 5 January 1998," he explains, "Israeli authorities arrested my son, Ma'an, in Qedumim on charges of theft. Ma'an was later killed in a car accident that occurred when the army was moving him from detention in Qedumim to a detention site inside Israel [in violation of the Geneva Convention]. I should note," he adds, "that farming is the sole source of income for myself and my family."

Abdel-Latif Odeh, another farmer near Qalqilya, faces similar circumstances. His house is only about 200 feet from the wall, on the eastern side; he can see his land, on the western side, from his house, but can only get to it by crossing through the gate at Ras Atiya, for which he has a permit. "From there," he explains, "I continue on to the Habla junction, and then to the Jal'ud intersection. Then I go to Khirbet al-Salman, and then another eight kilometers [five miles] by car and two kilometers by foot, because there is no paved road or dirt path to get to the land. It takes me about two hours to get to my land. If there are delays at the gate, it can take three or four hours. As a result, whenever I want to work my land, I end up spending most of my time just getting to and from it. Many farmers, including my brother, Rafik Ibrahim el-A'araj, have abandoned their fields because of the difficulties in reaching them." Indeed, for every Mohammad Salim or Mohammad Jalud or Abel-Latif Odeh, there are thousands of others like them. The U.N. estimates that some 15,000 people have already been displaced because of the hardships associated with life in the shadow of the wall, and this number is likely to rise into the tens of thousands in the coming years. To give one example: the village of Jubara, near Tulkarm in the northern West Bank, "used to have a vibrant economy with 10 poultry farms and numerous greenhouses," but, according to one U.N. agency, "these businesses have shut down or are floundering." Unemployment in Jubara now stands at 90 percent. A report published by UN-OCHA in November 2007 revealed that in the area around Qalqilya, some 1,800 farming families do not have an able-bodied member with a permit to access land west of the wall.

The disruption affects more than work, for all the other rhythms of day-to-day life have been severely affected. Abdel-Latif's village, Daba'a, for example, is cut off from vital resources by the wall. The village's high school students have to attend classes in schools in Habla or in Qalqilya itself, and that requires passing through gates in the wall. Teenage boys are frequently harassed by the Israeli soldiers manning the gates. Students have missed exams because of the gates' erratic opening hours, or because of delays or the routine hassles in crossing. Matters are hardly much better for elementary school children. "We have only one school in the village," Abdel-Latif explains, "and it has a large teaching staff. Most of the teachers live on the other side of the barrier and need permits to get to the school. The dependence on permits disrupts the school's functioning. When the permits expire, it often takes a long time to get them renewed. In the meantime, classes are canceled and the children are unable to continue their lessons." Even the normal social lives of Palestinian families living near the wall have been disrupted. To have friends or relatives from neighboring villages over for tea or a meal, Abdel-Latif has to apply for permits for them, which takes time, and success is by no means certain. Only a quarter of the guests invited to his son Ibrahim's wedding in the village were given permits by the Israelis to attend.

And, as with education and socializing, so with health care. The largest hospital in the region around Qalqilya is in Qalqilya itself, access to which is cut off from fields and villages in the "seam zone" to the west of the wall when the gates are closed. Under such circumstances, any emergency can quickly escalate into a life-threatening situation. Mu'atasem Omar recounts an accident involving a tractor that flipped over in the fields west of the wall, trapping his cousin, Adel, underneath. Mu'atasem and a

Schoolchildren passing through gate, near Tulkarm. Courtesy UN-OCHA.

friend were able to get another tractor to winch the overturned one and free Adel, who had been badly injured. They brought a car to the scene, bundled Adel in, and rushed to the nearest gate, at Azun Atma (the one Mohammad Jalud had been given a permit for). The gate was closed. "We got out of the car and called to the soldiers who were in the guard tower," Mu'atasem recalls; "I shouted to them in Hebrew that we had a person in the car who had been injured in an accident and that we had to rush him to the hospital. Qusai [his friend], who speaks Hebrew better than I do, explained Adel's condition to the soldier. Through a small window in the tower, one of the soldiers ordered us to move away from the gate. Qusai and I insisted and again asked the soldiers to open the gate so that we could take Adel to the hospital." The Palestinians kept calling to the Israeli soldiers to open the gate, but to no avail. "After about an hour and five minutes had passed," Mu'atasem continues, "three soldiers came out of the tower and went over to the car. They saw Adel and realized that he had to get to the hospital. One of the soldiers asked what happened. We explained about the accident, and one of the soldiers opened the

gate. All told, the soldiers delayed us for about an hour and ten minutes."
Twenty minutes later, they were at al-Aqsa Hospital in Qalqilya. Adel
died shortly afterward, of internal bleeding.

Reviewing the wall's impact on the inhabitants of the West Bank as
well as the legal status of Israel's occupation in general, the International
Court of Justice was unequivocal in its 2004 Advisory Opinion. "The
Court is of the opinion that the construction of the wall and its associated
régime impede the liberty of movement of the inhabitants of the Occupied Palestinian Territory," it declared. "They also impede the exercise
by the persons concerned of the right to work, to health, to education
and to an adequate standard of living as proclaimed by the International
Covenant on Economic, Social and Cultural Rights and in the United
Nations Convention on the Rights of the Child." The court concluded
that "Israel accordingly has the obligation to cease forthwith the works
of construction of the wall being built by it in the Occupied Palestinian
Territory, including in and around East Jerusalem. Moreover, in view of
the Court's finding . . . that Israel's violations of its international obligations stem from the construction of the wall and from its associated
régime, cessation of those violations entails the dismantling forthwith
of those parts of that structure situated within the Occupied Palestinian
Territory, including in and around East Jerusalem." The Court added that
Israel also has the obligation "to return the land, orchards, olive groves
and other immovable property seized from any natural or legal person
for purposes of construction of the wall," and to make reparations for the
damage done.

The wall has not been dismantled since the International Court's Advisory Opinion; it has been extended. Expropriated property has not been
returned; more has been confiscated. The Israeli government, backed
by the Israeli High Court, dismissed the International Court's Advisory
Opinion, saying that Israeli security was at stake. After the Israeli government finally admitted, in early 2006, that the wall was designed in effect
to annex most of the Jewish settlements in the West Bank, and to mark
Israel's hitherto undeclared eastern border (in defiance of international
law), rather than merely for security purposes, the Israeli High Court
publicly rebuked the government for having misled it. That, too, made no
difference. And if the Israeli government's official plans for the wall are

bad enough, what the Israeli army actually builds on the ground is often even worse than that, and sometimes in defiance of specific government and even High Court orders. According to Haggai Alon, a senior advisor in the Israeli Ministry of Defense, the Israeli army has a will of its own in the occupied territories. It can do, or not do, just what it pleases, often in cooperation with Jewish settlers in the West Bank. This, says Alon, is "the greatness of military rule. It [the army] can simply refrain from doing: it can refrain from enforcing the law on the settlers and it can refrain from allowing the Palestinians to move around. In the entire story of violations of the law in the territories, the spirit of the commander is the determining factor. It is stronger than any law or procedure."

"The Wall that Israel is presently building largely in Palestinian territory is clearly illegal," the U.N.'s Special Rapporteur on Human Rights, John Dugard, wrote in his January 2007 update on the human rights situation in the occupied territories. That same month, the Israeli government announced plans to shift the route of the barrier another three miles deeper into the West Bank in order to incorporate two more Jewish settlements. A recent study funded by the New Israel Fund and the British embassy in Tel Aviv, and cited by the World Bank in its May 2007 report on the Palestinian economy, found that the current route of the wall "almost totally ignores the daily needs of the Palestinian population," that it cuts employment for Palestinians, isolates farmers from markets, causes "particularly serious damage" to residents' medical needs, that it undermines social and family life—and that "there has been no meaningful change in the system of considerations guiding the [Israeli] planners."

All these rulings and reports (in addition to those by the U.N., human rights organizations, journalists, academics, and others) have made no difference to the Israeli planners for the simple reason that the fracturing and division of Palestinian territory—which is the defining feature of the wall—is a long-standing feature of the Israeli occupation going back to 1967, rather than an innovation introduced with the wall itself. The wall, in other words, is only one manifestation of an underlying process that preexisted it by decades, namely, the Israeli project to break up and isolate Palestinian spaces from each other, while unifying and tying together the Jewish-Israeli spaces of Israel and the occupied territories. So although the wall has had a devastating impact on Palestinian life all along the West Bank, it needs to be understood as an effect rather than a cause—and the real problem that needs to be addressed isn't the wall as such, but rather the occupation. For wherever you look in the West Bank, you will find the same logic at work, by which the space of Palestinian existence is fragmented and broken up, while that of the Jewish-Israeli existence in the West Bank and East Jerusalem is unified. Almost wherever they go, Palestinians run into the physical and geographical limits of their day-to-day existence.

ONE WEEK OF OCCUPATION: UN-OCHA WEEKLY BRIEFING, 2–8 MAY 2007

- 2 May: The IDF [Israeli army] closed 'Anata checkpoint due to construction near the checkpoint.
- 3 May: Palestinians from the town of Adh Dhahiriya (Hebron) along with international activists opened the closure at the entrance of the town on Road 60. The opening was reclosed by the IDF after two hours.
- 3–8 May: Despite an Israeli High Court ruling of 14 December 2006 dictating the dismantling of the Road Barrier along Road 317, the Road Barrier is still present and no attempts to remove it have been carried out. Rather, the IDF have closed some of the gaps Palestinian herders used to use to reach their lands.
- 4 May: Israeli settlers from the Gush Etzion area prevented landowners from the town of Al Khadr from accessing their land located to the west of Road 60.
- 5 May: The IDF closed the road between Yasouf and Iskaka villages (Salfit) by an earth mound. However, Palestinians managed to bypass the earth mound the next day.
- 5 May: The IDF closed Jaljoulia checkpoint for two hours because of a suspicious object found at the checkpoint.
- 5 May: The IDF imposed curfew on Deir Qaddis village (Ramallah) between 13:30 and 16:00 hours following the shooting of an Israeli guard of a gas station near the village.
- 5 May: The IDF imposed curfew on Iskaka village (Salfit) for 12

hours after a Molotov cocktail was reportedly thrown at an Israeli vehicle travelling to Ariel.

- 5 May: The IDF entered Al Lubban ash Sharqiya secondary school for girls (Nablus) and ordered the teachers to put the Palestinian flag down. When the teachers refused, the IDF brought the flag down by force.

- 5 May: The IDF forced the students of Iskaka mixed elementary school (Salfit) to leave the school early because of the curfew that was imposed on the village.

- 5–8 May: Long queues and delays were reported at Al Badhan checkpoint north of Nablus. On 7 May the IDF used tear gas to control hundreds of Palestinians waiting at both sides of the checkpoint.

- 6 May: The IDF imposed curfew on Yasouf village (Salfit) for 12 hours after a Molotov cocktail was reportedly thrown at an Israeli vehicle travelling to Ariel.

- 6 May: The IDF forced the students of the schools in Yasouf (Salfit) (one mixed elementary school, one secondary school for girls and one secondary school for boys) to leave their schools early because of the curfew that was imposed on the village.

- 6 May: The IDF closed Za'atara checkpoint for one hour because of a suspicious object found at the checkpoint.

- 7 May: The IDF closed Beita vegetable market (off Road 60) for three hours. According to the IDF, stones were thrown from the area earlier the same day.

- 8 May: The IDF closed Beita vegetable market (off Road 60) for three hours. According to the IDF, stones were thrown from the area earlier the same day.

ONGOING INCIDENTS

- Since 29 April 2007, the IDF closed the southern entrance of Qaryut village with an earth mound. The road connects the village with Road 60 and the water filling point for the village. Palestinians are now forced to take a long detour to reach the filling point.

- Since 28 March 2007, the IDF closed Shave Shomron checkpoint for all Palestinians, ambulances, UN and international organisations.

• The IDF continues to close the gate at the northern entrance of Kafr ad Dik.

3

The West Bank road network is one of the Israeli army's most effective closure mechanisms. For Palestinians, roads have come to represent and embody paralysis rather than movement. Roads, like the wall itself, have come to mark one of the limits of their existence.

There are two independent road networks in the West Bank: one for the use of Jewish settlers and the other for indigenous Palestinians (see map, p. 337). The 1,000 miles of roads designated for the use of Jewish settlers are wide, well paved, well lit; they allow uninterrupted movement between Israel and the far-flung network of settlements deep inside the West Bank. In many cases, the Israeli road network in the West Bank incorporates the key thoroughfares that used to tie Palestinian towns and cities to each other. West Bank Palestinians are now blocked from accessing much of what had once been their primary road network by a system of closures and checkpoints imposed by the Israeli army. Elsewhere, the Israelis have built new roads that deliberately deviate from Palestinian communities, so they are referred to as bypass roads. The Israeli army calls these "sterile" roads because they are "uncontaminated" by Palestinians. The army has cleared about 200 feet on either side of these roads as additional "sanitary margins," where Palestinians cannot build, tend, cultivate, or grow anything.

Although one aim of the Israeli bypass roads in the West Bank is to facilitate movement among the Israeli settlements and between the settlements and Israel, they also have the effect of interrupting Palestinian movement. Because they cannot be crossed, or even approached, by Palestinians, the bypass roads and the cleared zones on either side—which amount to undulating ribbons of territory the width of two or three football fields—are like borders; they encircle entire Palestinian communities and cut villages and towns off from each other. As the Israeli architect

Eyal Weizman points out, the Israeli road scheme emphasizes the profound contradictions of Israeli policy in the West Bank, where, as he puts it, two separate geographies inhabit the same landscape. The Jewish parts of the West Bank, he explains, are seamlessly incorporated into Israel: Jewish settlers enjoy continuous and uninterrupted travel along the road network reserved for them. The Palestinian parts of the West Bank, on the other hand, are fractured and broken and fragmented into shards of territory cut off from each other. For Jewish settlers, roads *connect*; for Palestinians, they *separate*. The result, according to Weizman, is an Escher-like representation of geography.

In order to develop their network of bypass roads, the Israelis have confiscated and razed about 31 square miles of Palestinian land, most of it formerly agricultural. Combined with the confiscation, clearing, razing, bulldozing, and uprooting of fertile land during the construction of the wall or military operations—or simply as forms of collective punishment directed at entire communities—the resulting damage has been devastating to Palestinian farmers. But because the destruction is routine, it generally takes place out of the view of the global media. The weekly reports maintained by UN-OCHA provide a sense of the scale of the damage. Here is a sample taken from the weekly OCHA briefing of 30 June to 6 July 2004:

> Approximately 300 olive trees belonging to Palestinian farmers were uprooted by Jewish settlers near the villages of Farata and Kfar Thulth, near Qalqilya; according to the Israeli army, the trees were planted on "state land" and therefore "lacked permission." The Israeli army destroyed one acre of olive trees along road 585 near Ya'abad, in the northern West Bank. The army uprooted 60 olive trees besides road 443 that had belonged to families in Beit Sira; it claimed that children and youths used the trees as cover to throw stones and a Molotov cocktail; the villagers deny this. The army began leveling land belonging to families in Beit Ta'amir and Za'atar, near Bethlehem, to continue the expansion of the Za'atara bypass road on the east side of Bethlehem. The army cut down more than 300 olive trees to clear a line of sight near the Tarqumiya checkpoint near the village of Beit Kahil, close to Hebron.

Since they are off-limits to Palestinians, the bypass roads and other roads to which Palestinians are denied access serve in effect as a network of virtual walls. The Palestinian town of Salfit, for example, is a major administrative and commercial center for dozens of villages in its surrounding area, but because one of the entrances to the Jewish settlement of Ariel branches off the main road approaching Salfit from the north, the army has sealed off that road to Palestinians. As a result, the residents of Salfit's dependencies to the north, instead of crossing a bit more than a mile to reach the town, now have to make a 12-mile detour, to the north, east, and south, before approaching Salfit from the opposite direction. A journey that ought to take five minutes, for basic grocery shopping, to get to school, or to visit relatives, could now take an hour—over the broken, discontinuous and poorly maintained roads set aside for the Palestinian population.

4

Unlike the roads used by Jewish settlers, the roads that Israel sets aside for Palestinians (that is, the territory's secondary and tertiary roads) are improperly illuminated, and often unpaved. Sometimes they consist of no more than gravel trails, or ancient horse and donkey tracks. Often, when a Palestinian road comes across one of the roads reserved for Jewish settlers, it is cut off. At such junctures, a Palestinian must abandon his road and his vehicle and scramble across the bypass road on foot. Such crossings are violations of Israel's military regulations and are dangerous: those who attempt them can be arrested, or even shot at by soldiers or the heavily armed Jewish settlers. At a minimum they are subject to harassment.

For Yasser Alian, a laborer from the village of 'Aba, near Jenin in the northern West Bank, worrying about crossing a bypass road is a daily occurrence. One such road cuts right through his village. Two of Yasser's children, Abdel Karim, seven, and Suleiman, eight, go to a school in the other part of the village, and so have to cross the bypass road to get to school, which is about a mile away, near where the bypass road intersects with the road leading into the village. "There are soldiers on that road, and

Palestinian road meets Israeli bypass road, West Bank. Photo by author.

in the intersection near the school all the time," Yasser explains. "There have been incidents where the soldiers chased the kids, threw teargas canisters at them and yelled at them. These incidents have had serious effects on my kids. They are afraid to walk to school and often ask me to come with them. In many cases, the soldiers won't let the kids cross the road and they can't get to the school." As a result, Abdel Karim and Suleiman frequently miss classes. Sometimes the soldiers let the kids cross to school but not back home, so that they have to take an 18-mile detour all the way around the nearby Jewish settlements to get back home.

Yasser recalls a time when his sons begged him to walk them to school. "Other kids from the village who were on their way to school joined us. There was an APC [an Israeli army armored personnel carrier, a tracked armored vehicle similar to a tank] in the intersection near the school. When we came up to it, one of the soldiers peered out of it and called me. He ordered me to lift up my shirt to check if I had any weapons or explosives. He then demanded my ID card. I walked over to him and gave him my ID. He ordered me to walk away and wait at a distance of about 30 feet from the APC. There were two more people that the soldiers had detained there. When the soldier ordered me to stop, my son

Palestinians wait at entrance to blockaded village, West Bank. Photo by author.

Abdel Karim began to cry and tried to walk back home. I tried to cheer him up and told him to carry on to school with his friends. He left crying. The soldiers detained me for about twenty minutes and then ordered me to go back." The kids made it to school all right. On a different occasion, however, another APC was blocking the road so the kids couldn't get home from school. "The soldiers wouldn't let them cross and held them up for about two hours. The Red Cross and the Palestinian District Coordination Office intervened and negotiated with the Israeli army, but the soldiers still wouldn't let them cross the bypass road. They had to take a bus and drive for about 30 kilometers [18 miles], around Ganim and Kadim [nearby Jewish settlements]."

Often, when the army finds a path used by Palestinians to cross one of the roads designated for Jewish settlers, it constructs a roadblock (often simply a pile of stones and rubble) to cut it off. Palestinians then find a new opening and exploit it for as long as they can, before the army finds it and cuts it off, too. Access to virtually every town and city in the West Bank is also restricted by Israeli army roadblocks, gates or earth mounds. At the entrances to most villages, one can see Palestinians waiting near the local roadblock for rides that may or may not be coming. Education,

Tunnel for Palestinians beneath Israeli bypass road, West Bank. Photo by author.

shopping, health care—all must be attended to locally now. Emergency medical attention usually has to be brought to the patient, rather than the other way around.

In order to complete the separation of the Israeli and Palestinian road network in the West Bank, Israel is planning a system of bridges and tunnels that will link the fragmented Palestinian areas while allowing Jewish traffic to cut through the West Bank on "sterile" roads. The Israeli army likes this idea because in the future it will be possible to stop communication between Palestinian areas simply by closing a few of these bridges and tunnels.

In the meantime, the donkey tracks and ancient shepherds' trails of the hills and valleys of the West Bank have become the new Palestinian highways. According to B'Tselem, only 7 percent of Palestinian private cars are permitted by Israel to circulate within the West Bank (let alone to enter Israel or Jerusalem or cross to Gaza). So, Palestinian circulation between towns in the West Bank is generally allowed only on public transport, typically buses and minivans. Palestinians are allowed to drive their own cars within their towns and cities, but taking a private car beyond one's own village requires obtaining two separate permits, one for the driver and one for the car.

Forced off the primary road by Israeli regulations, a Palestinian vehicle is stranded on a dirt road. Courtesy UN-OCHA.

Obtaining such a permit is time-consuming and also very expensive—about $450 a year, which is far beyond the reach of the average Palestinian. Moreover, obtaining a transport permit from the Israelis can involve being recruited as an informer, or running the risk of being refused a permit because one refuses to collaborate with the occupation. This fits into a broader system of Israeli pressure on Palestinians to collaborate. "Since 1967, there is no one in the [occupied] territories who has requested a service or permit of some kind from the Military Government who did not receive an offer from the GSS [General Security Service, i.e., intelligence service] to act as a collaborator in return for his request being fulfilled," one Palestinian collaborator told the Israeli human rights organization B'Tselem; "that is the nature of the occupation." A recent B'Tselem investigation concluded, for example, that "Israel, through the General Security Service (GSS), uses its authority to revoke work permits of Palestinians from the Occupied Territories as a means to pressure them into cooperating with the GSS." Since the Israelis know that Palestinians are dependent for their day-to-day survival on employment that only a permit makes possible, there is always a large pool of potential informants who can be coerced into service (in violation of the Geneva Conventions). A worker who has been denied a permit is often approached by a GSS agent who offers "assistance" in return for information about activity or particular people in his neighborhood or village. "If the worker refuses," B'Tselem reports, "the authorities take his permit and tell him to return after a certain period of time 'to determine whether the situation has changed.' "

A Palestinian truck driver who lives in the West Bank city of Ramallah explains what it's like to be pressured in this way. He had been supporting his family with a decent wage by moving goods around the West Bank, which required obtaining the necessary permits from the Israelis. In March 2004, he applied to have his permit to drive around the West Bank renewed and was rejected because the Israeli intelligence service had placed a block on his file. In order to clear the block and have his permit reissued, he was told he would have to meet a certain Captain Rasmi from the GSS. He arrived to meet this Rasmi at 8 A.M. on 28 March 2004. After a long delay, Rasmi finally appeared.

> He asked where I worked, and if I was having trouble crossing the checkpoints. I said that I have some problems. Then he said, "What would you think if I were to give you a permit to enter Israel, and not just one to move around within the West Bank?" I told him that I didn't want a permit to enter Israel, but only one for inside the West Bank. He insisted. "With a permit to enter Israel, you could move around easily, and your employer would like you better." I told him that I don't need a permit to enter Israel. He continued to try and convince me. "What would you think if I were to give you a cellular phone and you would tell me what you see when you drive along the roads?" Then, I realized that he wanted me to collaborate with the Israeli intelligence services. I immediately refused, and told him that that was the job of the police. He threatened me, and said that the police can't erase the security grounds for rejection which appear next to my name in the computer, that I should think it over, and that he was available whenever I wanted. He tried to give me his telephone number, but I refused to take it. Then he demanded that

I give him my telephone number. He said, "If you want some help from me, you can help me as well." He gave me back my ID card and I left. It was about 1:00 P.M.

However, now that he no longer had one of the valuable permits to drive his truck around the West Bank, he was of much less use to his employer, who cut his wages. He filed petitions with the Israeli authorities, who told him again that there was a "security" block on his file and that his permit would not be renewed without the approval of the GSS. A month later, he again applied for a permit and was again told that to clear the "security" block he would have to see Captain Rasmi.

He took me to the same room where I had been the previous time, and he sat down next to me. He asked me, "Well, did you think about it?" I replied, "I don't want anything other than a permit to move about inside the West Bank. I do not want a permit to enter Israel." He asked me about a relative of mine who was in prison in Israel. He asked how we were related. I told him that the man is my brother-in-law, my wife's brother. "Captain Rasmi" said, "We don't want to give you the permit because of your relationship to him. He is very dangerous to Israel." I asked him if someone should have to suffer because of what a relative of his does. I asked, "What do I have to do with that?" He replied, "Maybe he asked you to help him?" I told him that I never visited him in prison. He said that he knew that, but maybe I got letters from him. Then he asked, "Why are you being so stubborn in your refusal to cooperate with me. You are not the first, and won't be the last, to cooperate with me." "I don't want to cooperate," I said. "Captain Rasmi" said that we were not having a pleasant meeting. He suggested that we meet wherever I wanted, whether in Jerusalem or anywhere else. He said that I would enjoy the meeting. I told him, "I am not happy now and I don't want to sit with you." He said, "As you wish. Your name will remain on the computer." I did not give in, and said I would go to a lawyer. He said, "It's a waste of money to pay a lawyer, because nobody will pay any attention to your case." Around 1:30 P.M., I left.

His permit was not renewed. His employer has threatened to cut his wages even further. He supports a family of nine, including his elderly mother.

5

Even if a Palestinian obtains a permit to move around the West Bank, she is still subject to the grid of gates, roadblocks, and checkpoints that the Israeli army maintains throughout the West Bank. As of October 2007, there were, according to the U.N., 561 fixed or permanent obstacles in the West Bank: trenches, metal gates, concrete blocks, earth mounds, walls, barriers, and checkpoints, all of which are designed to disrupt or prevent altogether the circulation of Palestinian traffic—and none of which interfere with the free movement of the West Bank's Jewish population. In addition, there were, as of October 2007, 69 "flying" or randomly located military checkpoints blocking the movement of Palestinians in the West Bank. Of the permanent obstacles, too, checkpoints pose the greatest difficulties for Palestinians because they are manned by Israeli troops. Even under the best circumstances, they represent a major hassle. Merely in order to carry out their day-to-day lives, Palestinians have to submit to searches, questions, interrogations, and the often arbitrary behavior of Israeli soldiers.

For Laila Shqeirat, the difficulties imposed by such checkpoints are a matter of everyday life. Laila lives in the village of Sheikh Saad, just at the edge of East Jerusalem, but works as a school inspector inside the city. She is normally able to obtain and renew a three-month permit allowing her to enter Jerusalem in order to work. There is an Israeli checkpoint at the junction connecting the village to Jerusalem. Even though she has a valid permit, the Israeli soldiers there usually demand that Laila use a different entrance to Jerusalem, specifically the checkpoint at al-Zaitun. "It is almost impossible to get to that checkpoint," Laila says. "I have to go via a long dirt path and then, full of dust, I have to find public transportation, which is not always available in al-Sawahrah al-Sharqiyah, to get to the al-Zaitun crossing. And when I cross at that point, there is no public transportation, and I have to take a taxi, which costs twenty-five shekels [$6]. I can't pay that sum day after day. If I go this way, it would cost me sixty shekels a day [$15], and if I go via the Sheikh Saad checkpoint, it

Traffic jam at checkpoint, West Bank. Photo by author.

costs me fourteen shekels [$3]." Laila recalls a day when she was able to get through the nearer checkpoint only to be caught by an Israeli patrol. "I got to the checkpoint at around 7:00 A.M. I showed my permit to the policeman at the entrance to the village. He checked it and let me pass. I got onto a bus. After it drove a few meters, a Border Police jeep blocked its way, and the police ordered the driver to go back to the checkpoint. We went back to the checkpoint and the police told the passengers to get out. They checked our identity cards and our permits. I explained to the officer that I had a valid permit and that I had crossed the checkpoint after the policeman checked the permit. The officer told me, 'I'll take away your permit.' I was the only one the police held, and they kept me there until about 11:30. I sat there in the sun all the time. I didn't go to work that day, both because of the delay and because I had developed a headache. I was almost sick when I went home."

Nor are the difficulties only a matter of getting to work. "The checkpoint also makes it hard for us to obtain medical services," Laila explains. Sheikh Saad has no medical clinic; the closest one is al-Jinan, which is around 150 feet from the entrance to Sheikh Saad. "Even though it is close, and even though my husband and I have permits to enter Israel, the police at the checkpoint do not let us cross," she says. "Our son Khaled, who is seven years old, has a medical problem. Rather than undergo surgery, he gets injections. We bought the syringe and the medicine on our own and a few weeks ago my husband wanted to take him to the clinic in Jabel al-Mukaber to get the shot. My husband told the policeman at the checkpoint that he had a permit to enter Israel, but the policeman threatened to break the syringe he had with him, and did not let him pass." This disrupts the everyday routine of life as well: even such mundane activities as grocery shopping become major logistical challenges. Laila recounts an occasion when she had done some grocery shopping in Jerusalem. "When I got to the entrance to Sheikh Saad, I called my husband to come and help me carry the goods home. The policemen at the checkpoint did not let him cross even a few meters to enable him to help me. They told him to go via the al-Zeitun crossing, and to get to me from there, which meant traveling 12 miles rather than walking 30 feet. A young [Palestinian] guy with an Israeli ID card was there, and he saw me arguing with the policeman. He took my things and brought them to my husband."

In addition to the hassle and humiliation they can impose on Palestinian travelers, Israeli checkpoints also open and close at random intervals. Palestinian traffic will stall completely if a checkpoint closes, or refuses to admit traffic from a certain direction. Such arbitrary closures can last for hours or days. Since travel from one part of the West Bank to another usually requires passage through several such checkpoints, a routine trip can quickly turn into a living nightmare of waiting and immobility.

Not only are all possessions subject to search; at various checkpoints (especially the ones near major cities) no vehicles are allowed through at all: everyone has to leave one vehicle, cross through the checkpoint on foot, and find another vehicle on the other side. Those kinds of checkpoints are surrounded by scenes of chaos and confusion: massive, slow-moving traffic jams of taxis, cars, buses, minivans, and trucks, some trying to find a place to park; others, to get out of the parking spaces they had been wedged into; still others, just to get through the mess. Hundreds of people end up milling about: women, crying children, men carrying boxes and suitcases, farmers carrying crates, merchants carrying loads of material, all trying to find cars or buses or trucks to their final destinations—or, more likely than not, simply to their next destination on a chain of such

Qalandia checkpoint, West Bank. Courtesy UN-OCHA.

checkpoints, each of which entails disembarkation, reembarkation, and further hassles and delays.

Standing 200 yards from the Israeli army checkpoint at Huwwara, near Nablus, Farid Subuh, a thirty-nine-year-old father of two, explains how his day has gone so far. He sells vegetables in Nablus; normally, he goes alone, but on this day his wife and kids came with him:

> I left my house at around 5:00 A.M. My wife, Nu'am, and my children, Suleiman, age 7, and Muhammad, age 6, came with me. I took my family to Nablus that morning in order to get the children clothes for school. We drove through the Huwwara checkpoint. When we got there, one of the soldiers checked my papers and my ID card and let us through. I drove toward the central vegetable market and sold my vegetables. When I finished, we went to get clothes and school supplies. When we finished shopping, we got back in the car and started driving home. We got to the Huwwara checkpoint at around 8:00 A.M. I noticed

Road leading to checkpoint, Nablus. Photo by author.

that the soldiers who let me go through earlier to Nablus had been replaced. I stopped the car in front of the checkpoint, and the commander, who had tags on his arms, told me to show him my ID. I gave him my ID card and the special permit I got from the Israeli DCO which allows me to drive my car through the checkpoint. The commander checked my papers and then told me to park by the concrete blocks near the checkpoint. After I parked, the commander took my keys and said to me: "You have to wait." He also told me and my wife and kids to stand by the checkpoint. About an hour later, I went over to him to see if there was some sort of problem because of which he wasn't letting us through. The commander said there was no problem, but that I wasn't allowed to pass today. I told him I had crossed the checkpoint earlier in order to go to Nablus to sell my vegetables and that now I wanted to go home. The commander said: "Don't argue. Today, you're not allowed to pass." He then told me to stand on the side of the road with my family. I know Hebrew, so we spoke in Hebrew. At around 9:30 A.M., my children got hungry and wanted breakfast. My wife decided to ask the com-

mander to let us through. He told her, in bad Arabic, that she
and the kids could go through but that I couldn't cross with my
car. My wife told him that we had passed through the checkpoint
earlier and that we are a family. She asked him why he was trying
to separate us, and why he wants them to leave their breadwin-
ner at the checkpoint. The commander yelled at my wife, saying:
"Hush. Go away, before I get mad." He pointed toward Nablus.
About ten minutes later, I went up to him again. I said: "Stop
tormenting us. I have to get home. My kids are crying from hunger and boredom." The commander said: "Take your papers and
your keys." He told me to park the car on the side of the road and
then took my keys. He gave me the keys and papers back and told
me to go back to Nablus. He told me not to try to come to the
checkpoint again. I said: "Take pity on me. Stop this suffering,"
but he motioned me to leave the checkpoint. I stayed put and
asked him: "Why did you let me through in the morning if you're
not going to let me go back home?" He told me: "I didn't let you
through." He told one of the soldiers who was at the checkpoint

Huwwara checkpoint, West Bank. Courtesy UN-OCHA.

to write down my license plate number and inform the soldiers
not to let me through the checkpoint again. I left the checkpoint
and went back to Nablus to buy food for the children. From there
I went to the 'Awarta checkpoint, which is about a kilometer away
from the Huwwara checkpoint. When I got there, I asked the
soldiers to let me through. They said I had to go to the Huwwara checkpoint because only trucks pass through at the 'Awarta
checkpoint. Now, I'm standing about 200 meters [656 feet] from
the Huwwara checkpoint and I don't know what to do. I'm considering going back to Nablus and sleeping in a hotel.

For Palestinians, Israeli army checkpoints are, at best, an extraordinary imposition on the conduct of everyday life. But things at these
checkpoints can rapidly deteriorate from the boring and the insulting to
the physically injurious and life-threatening. Abdallah Khamis was once
also caught at the same checkpoint where Farid Subuh and his family
had been detained for so long. Abdallah, his wife, and two of their children (aged two and three) had been visiting relatives; their path home
took them via the Huwwara checkpoint. There they found about seven
hundred people already in line. The Israeli soldiers were letting people
through one at a time. Although he is thirty-one, Abdallah and his family
got into the queue reserved for men over forty, women, and children; with
a long wait ahead of them, his wife wanted help with their restless tod-
dlers, and anyway they wanted to stay together as a family. After a three-
hour wait in the line, their turn finally came. "I handed over my identity
card to the soldier who was checking ID cards," Abdallah explains:

> He looked at it and then he said to me, in Hebrew, "Go back." I
> told him that I can't go back because I always pass from that line.
> He replied, "Go back." I told him, in Arabic, "Then I'll go through
> the parallel line through which the men less than forty cross." He
> said, "Go back," and pointed to the end of the line. There were
> more than four hundred people in line. I told the soldier, "My wife
> cannot cross here by herself with the two children." The soldier
> pushed my wife with his hand, and I grabbed his hand. He tried
> to push her again. He and another soldier who was standing there

grabbed me. One child was in my arms. The soldier took him from me and put him on the ground. One of them told me, in Arabic, "Go to the pen for those who are detained." I told him, "I am not going anywhere. I am going to my house." They tried to bind my hands with plastic cuffs, and I resisted. Suddenly, one of the soldiers grabbed me by the ears while another soldier smashed my head on a concrete partition-wall. Another soldier hit me on the back of my head with his rifle butt. He hit me again on my neck. They punched and kicked me. By now there were seven or nine soldiers. They all hit me with their hands, kicked me and cursed at me. I don't know where they came from. The beating continued for about five minutes. I tried to protect my head and neck from their fists. Then I didn't feel anything and lost my balance. I didn't know what was happening to me any more. My wife screamed and cried, and my children cried. She tried to get the soldiers off me, and one of them pushed her by the throat. Then one of the soldiers grabbed me by the throat and led me to the area where Palestinians are held. I did not lose consciousness, but the many blows I suffered completely disoriented me. The two soldiers who beat me in the beginning punched and kicked me all over my body. The first soldier was light-skinned, thin, short, around 1.65 meters [5 feet 5 inches] tall, around 23–26 years old. He wore sunglasses, had two stripes on his shoulder, and had freckles. The other soldier was tall, full-bodied, with a slight paunch, and dark skin. He spoke to me in Hebrew and after he cuffed me, he said, "You'll stay with us tonight, and we'll show you what we'll do. . . . You'll regret this."

Separated from his family, Abdallah was held for several hours longer, threatened with various further punishments, and finally released at about midnight.

Stories of the beating and abuse of Palestinians at Israeli army checkpoints are very common. Human rights organizations as well as the U.N. have compiled exhaustive reports on checkpoint abuses: people being threatened by Israeli soldiers; people being forced to strip naked; people being intimidated, pushed around, and beaten. Here is a partial list of testimonies made available by B'Tselem: Border police officer

severely beats three Palestinians at a flying checkpoint next to 'Ajjul village, May 2007; IDF soldiers beat and abuse Muhammad Jabali, Huwwara Checkpoint, March 2007; Israeli soldier beats Shadi Shatareh
at Jit Checkpoint, 9 November 2006; Soldiers abuse Tha'ir Muhsen
near the Beit Iba checkpoint, 26 August 2006; IDF soldiers beat Shadi
Mahmud, throw eggs on him, and damage his car, Ramin Plain, August
2006; IDF soldiers beat 17-year-old at a surprise checkpoint, January
2006; IDF soldiers order taxi driver and passengers to undress in public
and detain them for hours wrapped in nylon sheets, 'Araba area, September 2005; IDF soldiers beat Palestinian ambulance driver and medic
at checkpoint near Ofra settlement, January 2004; Beit Furik Village,
Nablus District: IDF soldiers beat Muhammad Hanani and bury him
under dirt and stones, September 2003; Huwwara Checkpoint, Nablus
District: IDF soldiers force woman in labor out of ambulance and beat
driver, August 2003.

Indeed, Israeli army checkpoints often do not distinguish among the

Palestinians being processed through Israeli checkpoint, West Bank. Courtesy UN-
OCHA.

Palestinians whose movements they hold up. An investigation published by the World Health Organization published in 2005 found that sixty-one Palestinian women gave birth at Israeli army checkpoints between September 2000 and December 2004. Thirty-six of those babies died shortly after birth due to complications that could not be attended to in the mud and dirt on the sides of roads. Many seriously wounded people have died while waiting in lines at Israeli checkpoints, or simply while kept waiting by soldiers on routine interdiction patrols, or as a result of other unnecessary delays imposed by Israeli soldiers. Mahmoud Yaqub, a taxi driver from the region around Tulkarm in the northern West Bank, recalls rushing to the home of a kidney patient, Mohammad Kheiri, to take him to the hospital in Nablus, the biggest city nearby. "When I saw him, I realized that he was indeed in serious condition," Mahmoud recalls:

He was all swollen and had trouble breathing. While on our way to the Deir Sharaf checkpoint, he constantly complained of pain, and often put his hand on his head and scratched himself. I drove toward the Deir Sharaf checkpoint via the dirt road that bypasses the roadblock near Ramin. Because of that roadblock, which is composed of piles of dirt and concrete blocks, we have to drive along dirt paths, which adds another twenty minutes or so to the trip. After about thirty minutes, I got onto the main road and continued toward the Deir Sharaf checkpoint. After about five hundred meters [1,640 feet], at the junction with the Kedumim-Shavey Shomron bypass road, I saw an army jeep. Two soldiers were inside and another was standing on the road next to the jeep. When I was about fifty meters [164 feet] from the jeep, the soldier signalled me to stop. I stopped and asked Muhammad to take his medical documents and my identity card to the soldier and ask him to let us pass so that we could get to the hospital in Nablus. Muhammad walked over to the soldier, with the documents in his hands. It was apparent that his illness even made it hard for him to walk. The soldier took the documents and told him to get back into the taxi and wait. The soldier handed the documents to one of the soldiers who was sitting inside the jeep. In the meantime, we waited in the taxi. Muhammad was constantly complaining about the pain, and I soon felt that he was going to die from the great pain he was in. After waiting for thirty minutes, and because of Muhammad's serious medical condition, I decided to get out of the taxi and ask the soldiers to let me pass, or to give me back my identity card and Muhammad's medical documents so that I could take him to the hospital in Tulkarm. But the second that I opened the door, the soldier aimed his weapon at me and ordered me to stay inside the car. I shouted at him in Arabic that the passenger is in a very serious condition and is liable to die, but he motioned to me to stay in the car. I had no choice but to do as he said. Five minutes later, the soldier who was standing outside got into the jeep, and the three of them drove toward Kedumim with our identity cards and the medical documents. I didn't know what to do. I thought that they might arrange it so that we could pass and would return in a few minutes, so I waited with the hope that they would return quickly. Muhammad continued to complain that he was in pain. I was in a quandary. I did not want to leave without our identity cards and Muhammad's medical documents. Because of the many army checkpoints in the area, traveling without our identity cards would have been dangerous. Besides, I hoped that the soldiers would return in a few minutes. About two hours passed before the jeep returned. It was already 11:00 A.M. One of the soldiers got out and motioned that one of us should go over to him. I asked Muhammad to summon his strength and go to them, hoping that they would see how bad his condition was and would let us pass. Muhammad barely was able to get to them. When he did, they gave him the documents and told him to turn around and go back. I heard him beg and tell them that he is dying. The soldier told him to leave immediately. Muhammad got back into the taxi, and I turned around and rushed to the hospital in Tulkarm [where dialysis is unavailable]. As we drove, I felt that he was going to die in the taxi. It took an hour to get to the hospital. I took Muhammad into the emergency room. By now, his condition was critical. He received preliminary treatment in the emergency room. The physician told me that he had to go immediately to al-Watani Hospital, in Nablus, for dialysis treatment. He said that Muhammad would die if he did not receive the treatment. Muhammad got into the hospital

ambulance, and a physician accompanied him. The hospital's director contacted the District Coordination Office to coordinate the
passage of the ambulance. At this stage, I left the hospital. At night,
I was told that Muhammad had died after arriving at the hospital in
Nablus.

Many Israeli soldiers have come forward to express their doubts about
the purpose of the closure system that they enforce in the West Bank, and
especially about the routine maintenance of checkpoints. For one thing,
soldiers complain that a typical shift on checkpoint duty lasts for twelve
hours, which they find exhausting. "There are two typical responses to
the fatigue," one soldier notes. "There are those who check less carefully
and there are those whose 'fuse' is shortened and for any small thing they
will decide not to let people pass." Apart from the question of fatigue,
this soldier is convinced that the only function of his checkpoint is "to
put pressure on the Palestinian population. Officers explicitly told me
that the checkpoint has no security value and was meant to harass the
population." Another soldier agrees. "The idea is to make life hard for
the Palestinian citizenry. There is no operational objective" to the checkpoints. "Even the soldier with the best intentions, who is on guard at the
checkpoint from 8 A.M. to 8 P.M., in the heat, will reach a breaking point."
He continues:

> The heat and fatigue affect the ability to treat them [Palestinians]
> one way or another. You sit in the shade, and then have to get up,
> motion for a car to approach and examine it. Sometimes you wait ten
> minutes until you motion to a car to approach but sometimes it takes
> an hour or two, simply because you don't have the strength to get up
> and search them. It creates huge traffic jams. On an average morn-
> ing, when things are going quickly, people will wait four or five hours
> in line. In other places you can often wait from 4 A.M. to 2 P.M. The
> commander at the checkpoint can arbitrarily decide not to allow the
> passage of someone with a permit, or let someone without a permit
> pass through. A commander at the checkpoint can decide that some-
> thing is not to his liking and confiscate a permit or certificate of any
> kind—it happens a lot and quite arbitrarily. The issue of passage of

merchandise is also arbitrary: Sometimes they are permitted to pass goods through "back-to-back" [unloading the goods from one truck and loading onto another] and sometimes the commander decides not to let them through. Anyone who shows up after the checkpoint is closed will have to wait until the morning, even if he was detained at another checkpoint or for any other reason.

"I was ashamed of myself the day I realized that I simply enjoy the feeling of power," another Israeli soldier says of his checkpoint duties:

I don't believe in it: I think this is not the way to do anything to anyone, surely not to someone who has done nothing to you, but you can't help but enjoy it. People do what you tell them. You know it's because you carry a weapon. Knowing that if you didn't have it, and if your fellow soldiers weren't beside you, they would jump on you, beat the shit out of you, and stab you to death—you begin to enjoy it. Not merely enjoy it, you need it. And then, when

Qalandia checkpoint, West Bank. Courtesy UN-OCHA.

someone suddenly says 'No' to you, what do you mean no? Where do you draw the chutzpah from, to say no to me? Forget for a moment that I actually think that all those Jews [i.e., the settlers] are mad, and I actually want peace and believe we should leave the territories, how dare you say no to me? I am the Law! I am the Law here! And then you begin to understand that, it makes you feel good. I remember a very specific situation: I was at a checkpoint, a temporary one, a so-called strangulation checkpoint, it was a very small checkpoint, very intimate, four soldiers, no commanding officer, no protection worthy of the name, a true moonlighting job, blocking the entrance to a village. From one side a line of cars wanting to get out, and from the other side a line of cars wanting to pass, a huge line, and suddenly you have a mighty force at the tip of your fingers, as if playing a computer game. I stand there like this, pointing at someone, gesturing to you to do this or that, and you do this or that, the car starts, moves towards me, halts besides me. You come here, you go there, like this. You barely move, you make them obey the tip of your finger. It's a mighty feeling. It's something you don't experience elsewhere. You know it's because you have a weapon, you know it's because you're a soldier, you know all this, but it's addictive.

Checkpoints, and the system of closure as a whole, may be made better or worse according to which particular Israeli soldiers are on duty at each checkpoint at a given time, how long they have been on duty, and what kind of mood they happen to be in. But just as the system itself was not devised by the soldiers who actually enforce it, what it reflects isn't the goodness or badness of those soldiers but rather a political logic that exists beyond them as individuals.

CHECKPOINT UPDATE FROM UN-OCHA
WEEKLY BRIEFING, 28 MARCH–3 APRIL 2007

- **Qalandiya (near Ramallah)** Open for internationals, Jerusalem blue ID holders and Palestinians with West Bank IDs. Only drivers of vehicles and their family members are allowed through inside the vehicle. Passengers, both West Bank ID holders and Jerusalemites, have to cross through the pedestrian lanes. As of 10 December, Israeli private Security Guards are present at the checkpoint at a second line behind the IDF for extra random security checks. Long delays during the morning and evening rush hours are being reported at the pedestrian lane on daily basis.

- **Ni'lin (near Ramallah)**   Open daily 24 hours for Israelis, Jerusalem ID holders, foreign passport holders. Palestinians with West Bank IDs not allowed through regardless of any valid permits to enter Israel.

- **Hizma (near Jerusalem)**   Open for Israelis, Palestinians with Jerusalem ID cards and internationals. UN staff have been requested on several occasions to show personal ID/national passports in addition to their UN ID card. Since 3 February 2006 West Bank Palestinians with valid permits are not allowed to cross through this checkpoint unless they belong to one of the new 'facilitated' categories; Palestinians working in international organisations, medical staff, chronic patients, teachers and prominent businessmen (BMC Card holders). The head of the East Jerusalem Hospital Network reported that medical staff have not been permitted to use Hizma, and that in fact the Commander-in-Chief of the checkpoint claimed that [the decision] allowing the medical staff to use it had been reversed.

- **Al Ram (near Jerusalem)**   Open for internationals, diplomats, Palestinians working with international organisations and residents of the southern part of Dahiyat al Bareed (soon to be within the Barrier) with their names and ID numbers registered on a list held at the checkpoint. As this is not one of the four terminals into Jerusalem, West Bank Palestinians with valid permits are not allowed to cross. Delays were reported during morning rush hour. Problems of access were reported by Americans carrying passports with valid entry visas.

- **Al 'Auja (near Jericho)**   Open 24 hours for Palestinians living in Jericho Governorate. Palestinian non-residents of Jericho who hold West Bank IDs going north towards al 'Auja and the Jordan Valley area are prohibited though unless they hold Israeli permits to allow them access to the area. No permit required for those travelling to

Ramallah. Long delays up to 40 minutes were reported by people travelling to Ramallah and Al 'Auja.

- **Beit Iba (near Nablus)** Open from 5 A.M to 7.30 P.M. for humanitarian organisations and Palestinians. Israeli citizens, Palestinian holders of Jerusalem IDs and holders of international passports can pass only following prior liaison with the IDF. Long delays and queues were reported. Public transportation, commercial trucks carrying aggregates and private vehicles need permits to pass the checkpoint. Since 10 March, 120 commercial trucks using special permits to use Taybeh back to back CP were diverted to Beit Iba after closing Qusin CP. Delays and long queues reported this week. Since 10 March, 120 commercial trucks using special permits to use Taybeh back to back CP were diverted to Beit Iba after closing Qusin CP. Closed on 28, 29 March, and 1 April. Delays and long queues reported this week.

- **Gilo (near Bethlehem)** Open 24 hours for humanitarian organisations, diplomats, Jerusalem ID holders and Palestinians with valid permits. West Bank Palestinians (including those working for the UN and other international agencies) have to walk through the terminal to undergo search procedures. Jerusalem ID holders passing into Bethlehem are being asked to prove that they reside in areas falling within Jerusalem boundaries. Yellow-plated tourist buses are allowed to enter Bethlehem only if driven by an Arab Israeli. Palestinians holding valid work permits can access East Jerusalem and Israel through this checkpoint. UN national staff can pass through the checkpoint without having to be physically checked. The checkpoint is currently manned by the Israeli Border Police. On 29 March, the checkpoint was closed off for three hours due to the presence of a suspicious object. In the period between 1–3 April Palestinian workers holding valid working permits were prevented from accessing Israel through the checkpoint. Christians holding permits were allowed entry.

- **Al Kasaba (Hebron)** Permanent checkpoint which filters Palestinian movement from the Kasaba area directed to the Tomb of the Patriarchs. Movement is segregated for incoming and outgoing movement. Palestinians exiting Kasaba are processed through a combination of turnstiles, allowing one person at a time to pass, and a metal detector. The process is slow and problematic during Friday prayers. During the reporting period long queues of Palestinians wanting to access the Ibrahimi Mosque for prayers were reported as IDF soldiers checked their IDs.

- **Tel Rumeida (Hebron)**   Open only to Palestinians travelling on foot living between the checkpoint and the settlement. A military order was issued on 17 July 2006 that declared the area beyond the checkpoint as a "Closed Area" barring the entry of anyone beyond the checkpoint except Israeli citizens, IDF and Israeli Police or those who have an IDF-issued permit.

6

By late 2006, Israel had effectively broken up the West Bank into three or four large pieces, plus East Jerusalem. At the beginning of 2005, Israel banned Palestinians from entering the Jordan Valley (which amounts to almost a third of the whole West Bank), unless they are one of the 27,000 Palestinians who are registered as living there. The ban, to which B'Tselem refers as "the de facto annexation of the Jordan Valley," affected thousands of farmers who own land in the valley but live outside it. They now needed to obtain a permit to enter it, similar to the permit that Mohammad Jalud needs to enter the "seam zone" at the other end of the West Bank. (In April 2007, the Israeli army claimed to have eased the Jordan Valley ban, allowing access to Palestinians entering the desert on foot, but Israeli journalists and researchers for B'Tselem, as well as the staff of the UN-OCHA, found that, as of June 2007, soldiers manning the checkpoints controlling access to the valley "were entirely unaware of the directive and the change to permit pedestrian traffic," so the virtual annexation of the Jordan Valley remains in effect).

Similarly, the Israelis have constructed an elaborate ditch system around Jericho, surrounding it on three sides. Residents of the northern governorates of Tulkarm and Jenin are cut off from access south of Nablus. Nablus itself, a city of over 130,000 people, used to provide specialized health care and higher-education facilities to a further 350,000 residents of the northern West Bank. If they have the right permits, they can now enter the city only in one of the handful of buses and taxis that are allowed through the local checkpoints. Otherwise, access to Nablus is on foot—and Nablus, the largest city in the West Bank, has been under this siege for years. All entrances and exits are regulated by Israeli army checkpoints, where identity papers and permits are checked. And if the army declares a total closure, all permits are invalidated. There was a day of total closure for every three of "normal" movement in 2006; and one day of closure for every two "normal" days in 2005. On such days, some 3 million Palestinians go nowhere.

7

According to the World Bank's assessment of the Palestinian economy in 2004, "the 'back-to-back' system for the transit of [non]humanitarian goods became routine in 2003." Back-to-back transit refers to a system imposed by the Israeli army at various key checkpoints in the West Bank, where vehicles are not allowed to drive through. Goods being transported through such checkpoints have to be completely unloaded from one vehicle, carried through the checkpoint, searched, then loaded on to another vehicle on the other side. In the case of a back-to-back roadblock, the same procedure applies, only without a search of the goods. So, even assuming that a Palestinian farmer can actually work his land (which in many cases is becoming increasingly difficult), he would still face the many hurdles in getting his crop to market. This is especially difficult for a farmer like Mohammad Jalud whose land is in the "seam zone." He would have to work his way through the wall, which involves obtaining all the necessary permits; finding an open gate actually allowing him access to his land; and carrying his crop through the gate, in all likelihood on his own back, one load at a time. Once through the wall, he would have to circumnavigate Israeli army roadblocks; obtain further transportation permits; wait at the various checkpoints between his land and his market; and, finally, find some way to deal with the necessity of organizing serial "back-to-back" transport to get the goods from checkpoint to checkpoint without actually driving through each one—which requires not only unloading and reloading the produce at each checkpoint as it is moved from one conveyance to another, but managing all the logistical complications to make sure that the trucks transporting his goods actually get to the same checkpoint at the same time (which is complicated because each truck could be held up at any number of Israeli army obstacles along its own independent path of travel).

The World Bank says that Israel's closure system has had a devastating effect on the agricultural, and indeed general, economy throughout the occupied territories. "In the West Bank there is evidence of sharp local variations in food prices between localities, due to transport problems," the Bank notes. "In food-producing areas, prices have been severely depressed because goods cannot reach the market, while in non-agricultural areas, especially in larger cities, food prices have risen steeply because of the relative scarcity of these same goods." An investigation by the United Nations Relief and Works Agency (UNRWA) offers further detail to illustrate the World Bank's assessment. It explains, for example, that the city of Hebron and its surrounding towns and villages in the southern West Bank have always been dependent for supplies of fresh fruit and vegetables on deliveries from Gaza, the northern West Bank, and Israel. Checkpoints and closure have led to a large decline in the availability, and a sharp increase in price, of fruits and vegetables reaching the southern West Bank. One Jericho vegetable vendor who sells in Hebron told UNRWA that the trip "that usually took just over an hour will now take between 5 and 6 hours. Time is consumed by driving over long by-pass roads, waiting to cross checkpoints and on-and-off loading of lorries back-to-back at checkpoints, sometimes several times for the same load." The cost of transporting goods to Hebron has tripled; since the city is particularly dependent on Gaza, on days when Gaza is closed (which is now more often than not), the price of a box of tomatoes can jump from 12 NIS to 40 or 50 NIS ($3 to $9 or $12) in a single day. In addition, because of the very long time it takes to get goods to market, fresh fruit and vegetables often rot just awaiting transport, or arrive in a state unfit for human consumption.

The Arroub Refugee Camp, home to about 9,000 refugees, is 9 miles north of Hebron, and its vegetable vendors buy their goods in the city wholesale market and return to the camp to retail it. According to the UNRWA study, before the closure system was imposed, fruit and veg-

Back-to-back cargo transfer at roadblock, West Bank. Courtesy UN-OCHA.

etables were shuttled all day long between the wholesale market and the refugee camp. "Today, vendors and wholesale merchants need to obtain a permit from the Hebron Civil Administration to cross the Dhahi-yyeh checkpoint, something which requires a lot of time and is rarely granted," the study points out. "Consequently, vendors are forced to take alternate routes which increase the daily trip of 15 kilometers [9 miles] to up to 50 kilometers [31 miles]." This again adds to the price of the goods. Delivery trucks are not allowed to enter the camp and are stopped by the Israeli army at the checkpoint at the main entrance to the camp. There the goods are loaded onto one of two donkey-carts available in the camp for the final leg of transport. The donkey-shuttle adds another layer of cost to the goods (and the cost of donkeys has doubled in recent years because of the high demand for their services). The Israeli army requires that the donkey-shuttle operators obtain a permit for the donkeys, valid for a month at a time, allowing two trips a day. In November 2002, a refugee camp vegetable vendor told the U.N., a third donkey cart was stopped by the army at the entrance to the camp. Because it didn't have a permit, the donkey was shot, and the goods it was hauling were destroyed.

One of the vegetable vendors in the Arroub Camp told the UNRWA research team that he used to buy 10,000 NIS (around $2,300) worth of vegetables every day to stock his store. Now he buys 1,000 NIS (around $230) worth of vegetables every other day, and he says that the prices are so high that the refugees can barely afford them. "I swear on the *Qur'an* that I frequently give large families whole boxes of potatoes for free because I know they can no longer afford to buy them and the family would go hungry without them," one vendor said. "Families used to buy whole cases of onions, tomatoes, cucumbers and potatoes for about NIS 50 [$12] altogether, but who can afford to spend NIS 50 now? Who has that much money?" On the day that the UNRWA team visited Arroub, the camp had received its first delivery of fresh fruit and vegetables in two weeks because of a total closure imposed by the Israeli army. "The 'fresh' vegetables were not appetizing and many of them, particularly the eggplant (at a cost of NIS 25/box! [$6]) and tomatoes, were starting to rot," they write. "The vendor explained that the camp residents would not be able to afford the truly fresh vegetables, so he bought these."

The World Bank's 2004 overview of the Palestinian economy revealed that since the intensification of the occupation in 2000 "average Palestinian incomes have declined by more than one third and one quarter of the workforce is unemployed. Nearly one half of all Palestinians live below the poverty line [$2 a day]. More than 600,000 people (16 percent of the population) cannot afford even the basic necessities for subsistence." The Bank's assessment of the primary cause of this dramatic deterioration in living standards is unequivocal: "The precipitator of this economic crisis has been 'closure,' a multi-faceted system of restrictions on the movement of Palestinian people and goods, which the Government of Israel argues is essential to protect Israelis in Israel and in the settlements. Closures, including the Separation Barrier, prevent the free flow of Palestinian economic transactions; they raise the cost of doing business and disrupt the predictability needed for orderly economic life."

The World Bank published another report in May 2007, with an even more dire assessment of the circumstances of day-to-day life and their impact on the overall Palestinian economy. "Together, military orders and ad hoc measures create a system of movement restrictions which is non-transparent and highly unpredictable," the Bank notes. "The combined effect of physical and administrative obstacles is the division of the West Bank into three [trisections] (north, central, south) and additionally ten segments or enclaves, with Palestinians channeled through manned checkpoints in order to move between the trisections and in and out of the enclaves. . . . In economic terms," the Bank concludes, "the restrictions have created a level of uncertainty and inefficiency which has made the normal conduct of business extremely difficult and therefore has stymied the growth and investment which is necessary to fuel economic revival." The results, predictably, have been catastrophic. By mid-2006, two-thirds of the Palestinians living under occupation had been reduced to absolute poverty, and hundreds of thousands are now utterly dependent for their day-to-day survival on food or aid handouts from international agencies.

Occupation by the Numbers

- Number of roadblocks and checkpoints in West Bank as of January 2007: 528
- Number Israel pledged to remove that month as a humanitarian gesture: 44
- Number of those 44 that actually existed, according to Israeli army source: 0
- Number of fixed roadblocks and checkpoints in West Bank as of April 2007: 537
- Number of fixed roadblocks and checkpoints in West Bank as of October 2007: 561
- Number of roadblocks Israel offered to remove in November 2007 as a humanitarian gesture: 22
- Number of those that did not exist, according to Israeli human rights group Machsom Watch: 17
- Number of those physically removed but where Palestinian traffic is still banned: 2
- Number of those genuinely removed, allowing Palestinians to circulate: 2
- Number remaining: 559
- Number of flying checkpoints in West Bank, October 2007: 69

- Number of Israeli search/arrest raids in West Bank, first six months of 2007: 3,144
- Number of Palestinians captured and detained, same period: 3,101
- Number of Palestinians on secret Israeli travel ban list: 180,000
- Number who have been officially informed of this fact: 0
- Number of licensed private cars in West Bank: 46,166
- Number permitted to circulate in the territory as of July 2004: 3,412
- Annual cost of such a permit: $454
- Projected per capita gross national disposable income in occupied territories: $1,200
- Number of Palestinian villages "severely affected" by movement restrictions: 112
- Population of those villages: 180,000

8

Nowhere is the nature of the Israeli project to assert total territorial control of the external spaces in the West Bank more evident than in and around Jerusalem. "Jerusalem," like "Israel" itself, is not a stable concept—it is not one place fixed in space and time. Where Jerusalem is, where it begins and ends, how much land it encompasses, who is counted as a resident, and who is excluded: these have all proved unstable and shifting variables. This is one reason why hardly any country, including the United States, recognizes Jerusalem as Israel's capital: almost all nations, again including the United States, maintain their Israeli embassies not in Jerusalem, but rather in Tel Aviv (though the U.S. Congress has recently passed legislation urging the president to move the U.S. embassy to Jerusalem).

Jerusalem was divided during and after the war in 1948 during which Israel was created. When the fighting ended, the western part of the city had fallen under Israeli control. The eastern part, along with the rest of the West Bank, had ended up under Jordanian control. At that time, what was called East Jerusalem amounted to the area of the Old City and a few outlying neighborhoods, totaling a little over 2 square miles.

After the 1967 War, during which Israel captured East Jerusalem and the West Bank (as well as the Gaza Strip), the Israelis expanded the territorial dimensions of what they called Jerusalem by adding almost 27 square miles of West Bank land to the city's municipal borders. In 1980, they also claimed to annex this additional land to Israel.

In fact, over 90 percent of the eastern part of what the official Israeli slogan refers to as "the eternal and undivided capital of the Jewish people" actually consists of land thus added to Jerusalem after 1967. According to international law, this land is—like the original 2 square miles of post-1948 East Jerusalem itself—part of the West Bank, or, in other words, militarily occupied territory, not subject to unilateral annexation. "East Jerusalem is not part of Israel," the U.N.'s John Dugard has repeatedly said. "On the contrary, it is occupied territory, subject to the Fourth Geneva Convention. Unfortunately, Israel's illegal attempt at annexation of East Jerusalem has obscured this truth. As a consequence, world public opinion tends, incorrectly, to treat Israel's occupation of East Jerusalem as different from that of the West Bank and Gaza." Having claimed to annex it, Israel not only refuses to acknowledge that East Jerusalem is occupied territory, it treats it as though it were its sovereign territory, which legally it is not. For example, immediately following the Annapolis summit in November 2007, which was supposed to have relaunched the peace process, Israel announced plans to construct hundreds of new housing units in one of its East Jerusalem settlements (Har Homa, on Jabal Abu Ghneim), thereby expanding it. Israel's housing minister, Ze'ev Boim, flatly dismissed U.S. Secretary of State Condoleezza Rice's warning that such moves don't help build confidence in the peace process. "The Har Homa neighborhood [sic] is situated within Jerusalem's municipal borders where Israeli law applies," he said. "Therefore, there is nothing preventing construction there, just as there is nothing preventing construction anywhere else in Israel."

The land that Israel illegally added to Jerusalem it took from twenty-eight Palestinian villages in the West Bank, and was in most cases the property of the people of those villages rather than of (Palestinian) Jerusalemites. In some cases, whole villages and their populations were annexed to Jerusalem. In most cases, however—and certainly wherever geographically possible—the Israeli planners drew the new, expanded municipal boundaries of Jerusalem up to the houses of outlying Palestinian towns and villages in such a way that the towns' orchards, olive groves, and pastures were placed on one side of the boundary (inside Jerusalem), while the houses and people were on the other side (outside Jerusalem). For example, land from the towns of Beit Iksa and al-Bireh to the north, and Bethlehem and Beit Sahour to the south, was included within the new municipal borders; but the Palestinian inhabitants of Beit Iksa, al-Bireh, Bethlehem, and Beit Sahour were not given Jerusalem residency. What might look like hairsplitting, however, was actually a matter of deliberate policy. According to Meron Benvenisti, Israel's former deputy mayor of Jerusalem, the delineation of the city's municipal borders after 1967 was explicitly designed to incorporate "a maximum of vacant space with a minimum of Arabs."

The Israeli attempt to incorporate Arab land without Arabs often produced anomalous results. The town of Nu'man, for example, was annexed to municipal Jerusalem when the borders were redrawn in 1967, but its inhabitants were classified as West Bankers. Over the years, the residents of Nu'man filed numerous appeals to the Israeli Ministry of the Interior to change their status to residents of Jerusalem, since their town had been absorbed within the expanded municipal borders. Israel consistently rejected these appeals. As a result, the residents of the village, who are technically West Bankers, are considered by Israeli law to be "persons staying illegally in Jerusalem," because that is where their houses were after the Israelis redrew the municipal borders. They have spent forty years living under constant threat of expulsion. They are also cut off from the infrastructure and services of Jerusalem. Access to educational, medical, and infrastructural services such as water tie the village to the West Bank—but, because the town itself is "inside" Jerusalem, all these arrangements are illegal, and subject to interdiction.

ONE WEEK OF OCCUPATION:
UN-OCHA WEEKLY BRIEFING, 13–19 SEPTEMBER 2006

- 13 September: The IDF issued military order No. T/78/06 requisitioning 16.5 dunums of Palestinian land belonging to Sanniriya (Qalqiliya) to build a temporary wall and a gate south of Azun Atma.

- 13 September: A chicken farm and three water wells were demolished and three Palestinian houses partially damaged by IDF bulldozers in Abu El Ajeen area east of Deir El Balah.
- 13 September: Four IDF tanks and two bulldozers moved from the border fence approximately 400 metres [1,312 feet] into the Khuza' village east of Khan Younis. The bulldozers levelled an unknown amount of agricultural land.
- 13 September: 50 dunums of olive, citrus, palm and almond trees were destroyed by IDF bulldozers in Abu El Ajeen area east of Deir El Balah.
- 13 September: At midnight the IDF imposed a curfew in Fasayel village and carried out a house search campaign. The IDF reported that the curfew was imposed after Palestinians from the village threw stones at Israeli vehicles on Road 90. The curfew was lifted at 2 p.m. after 14 hours.
- 13 September: The IDF closed the checkpoints at Huwwara, Beit Iba, Zaatara, Asira ash Shamaliya, as well as Yitzhar partial checkpoint all day and denied Palestinians from other governorates to enter the city of Nablus. In addition, all Palestinians from the northern West Bank were prevented from heading south.
- 13 September: The IDF closed Kafriat tunnel and Anata checkpoints and prevented Palestinian movement heading to Nablus and south bound.
- 13 September: The IDF closed the Barrier gates of Khirbet Jbara and Kafr Sur (gates T15 and T16) and denied access of farmers to their land at Kafr Sur gate and residents of Khirbet Jbara out of the Khirbet.
- 14 September: The IDF closed Za'atara and Yitzhar partial checkpoint preventing the movement of Palestinians from the northern West bank heading south.
- 14 September: Three dunums of olive trees were destroyed by IDF bulldozers south of Sufa crossing in Rafah.
- 14 September: Land levelling took place in the vicinity of the Israeli settlement of Karmel, south of Yata.
- 15 September: The IDF closed Huwwara checkpoint for one hour.

- 15 September: A four-storey Palestinian house was demolished when an IAF aircraft fired two missiles towards it in Al Brazil Quarter of Rafah. The family living in the house was warned by the IDF to evacuate 30 minutes prior to the air strike. Several near-by houses were partially damaged.
- 16 September: IDF tanks and bulldozers entered the former Erez Industrial Zone and demolished several abandoned factories along the boundary wall near Salah Ed-Din road.
- 16 September: A group of settlers from the settlement of Susiya, south of Yata (Hebron), erected tents south of the settlement on Palestinian land. Similar tents were erected in the same place in the past by the Israeli settlers, and later removed by the IDF.
- 17 September: At 4 p.m., the IDF imposed a partial checkpoint at An Nabi. The IDF soldiers requested all Palestinian males to get out of the vehicles and take off their top clothes. The checkpoint was lifted at 9 p.m. Long delays were reported.
- 17 September: At 5 p.m., hundreds of Palestinians were stranded at Atara checkpoint as the Israeli Border Police stopped all movement going out of Bir Zeit through the checkpoint. Delays of up to two hours were experienced.
- 17 September: The IDF closed the eastern entrance of Qalqiliya city (DCOt) with a flying checkpoint for 11 hours, and denied access for all Palestinians except for residents of Qalqiliya.
- 17 September: The IDF started levelling land and installing a road fence north of Road 505, east of Za'atara checkpoint.
- 17 September: Approximately 100 olive trees were burnt north of Huwwara village (Nablus) when a fire was set in unclear circumstances. The Palestinian and Yitzhar settlement fire brigades worked together to put out the fire.
- 17 September: A group of Israeli settlers from Qedumim settlement entered a Palestinian house in Kafr Qaddum village (Qalqiliya) and prevented the only residents at the time (a group of children) from leaving for 20 minutes.
- 18 September: A three-storey Palestinian house was demolished when it was hit by an IAF F-16 missile in Rafah. The family was

warned by the IDF to evacuate prior to the strike. Four nearby houses were damaged.

9

In 1967, the Israeli expansion of Jerusalem was more often than not a matter of lines drawn on paper. Not only could Palestinian residents cross these imaginary lines until the beginning of the so-called peace process in the mid-1990s, but Palestinian farmers from "outside" Jerusalem could still physically access their land "inside" Jerusalem (unless the land was expropriated and used for settlement). Now that the wall has gone up on what had been merely an imaginary line, "outside" and "inside" have a whole new meaning, and, for example, Palestinian farmers from outside the city's municipal boundaries now no longer have access to their land on the other side of what is today not merely a line on a map, but rather a concrete wall.

Not only do they not have access to their land: the Israeli government began the process of stripping Palestinians who lived outside Jerusalem of their land "inside" Jerusalem by using Israel's notorious Absentee Property Law—the law used originally to take over the land and personal property of Palestinians who were no longer present in newly created Israel after 1948 because they had either been expelled or forced into flight from the country. According to the law, absentees can be stripped of their land even if they are "absent" only because a wall has been built between them and their land. Some estimates suggest that the Israeli government intended to claim half the land "inside" Jerusalem through this mechanism. Once the first expropriation orders had been issued, however, a major international outcry intervened. In the meantime, the wall will ensure that possession remains nine-tenths of the law.

There are today only twelve gates allowing access through the 168 kilometers (104 miles) of the wall that Israel has built in and around East Jerusalem, cutting it off from the West Bank. Of these gates, only four are even theoretically available to West Bank residents, who must go through an exhaustive process to obtain a permit from the Israelis in order to enter Jerusalem—much more difficult to obtain than the kind of permit that enables travel within the rest of the West Bank itself. Even so, some 60,000 Palestinians (mostly those with Jerusalem residency) pass through those gates every day. But a whole generation of West Bank Palestinians has never even seen Jerusalem, and the sites holy to their religions (including the Church of the Holy Sepulchre and the Dome of the Rock). Israel's denying Palestinians access to their sites of worship is a violation of international law, as is denying them freedom of movement within the occupied territories in general. For the lucky few who do obtain permits, crossing the wall into Jerusalem can easily take a couple of hours in either direction. "A Palestinian pedestrian crossing the checkpoint to Jerusalem [at Qalandia] must first follow a passageway bordered by metal fences," a recent U.N. report points out. "Upon entering the checkpoint, five turnstiles or revolving gates have to be crossed by each person before an identification check is made. Only one person can go through these electric gates at a time. From a hidden post, a soldier surveying the area from a television screen can stop the movement of the turnstiles at any time. When the ID check is made, a security scan of any belongings that are being carried is completed." There is, the report

Wall under construction near Jerusalem. Photo by author.

The wall near Jerusalem. Photo by author.

adds, no human contact between Palestinians and Israeli soldiers. "The soldiers are seated in booths, surrounded by reinforced glass. Communication between the soldiers and people crossing is carried out primarily by a speaker system or people are addressed in certain cases through the glass."

Arab Jerusalem has until relatively recently—until the advent of the "peace process" in the mid-1990s—existed in a continuum with the Palestinian communities around it, in the way in which urban centers are tied to surrounding towns and the wider countryside everywhere. Not only do tens of thousands of Palestinians with Jerusalem residency papers work in Jerusalem but live in areas that will soon fall (or have already fallen) on the other side of the wall; many Jerusalem Palestinians also work in places in the West Bank, particularly Ramallah. According to a U.N. report published in July 2007, the wall has cut off a quarter of Jerusalem's Palestinian population from the city. The wall's route "runs deep into the West Bank to encircle the large [Jewish] settlements of Givat Ze'ev (pop. 11,000) and Ma'ale Adumim (pop. 28,000), which are currently outside the municipal boundary," the report notes. "By contrast, densely populated Palestinian areas—Shu'fat Camp, Kafr

Aqab, and Samiramees, with a total population of over 30,000, which are currently inside the municipal boundary, are separated from Jerusalem by the Barrier. Other villages to the north and east of the city, with populations of more than 84,000, are also excluded. In addition, the Barrier runs through the middle of Palestinian communities, separating neighbors and families from one another—this happens in Abu Dis, for example." To the north of the city, but still inside the redrawn municipal limits, the wall and a bypass road completely encircle the 15,000 Palestinians living in four villages near Bir Nabala. Their only point of access to the outside world is a tunnel.

Many Palestinian businesses in Jerusalem rely for their supplies, or their commercial survival, on open linkages with the West Bank hinterland. The wall has greatly worsened the economic prospects facing Palestinians in East Jerusalem, which used to be the commercial heart of Palestinian life. It prevents the normal movement of people and goods and has forced Palestinians to completely alter their economic habits. Bringing goods to market from the West Bank to East Jerusalem now involves in effect importing them across an international frontier into Israel—even though the actual international frontier is miles to the west of the wall. Crossing the new "frontier" requires using the back-to-back system and paying various import taxes. Most small shopkeepers can't afford such expenses. Even if they could, many of their customers can no longer reach them. According to the July 2007 U.N. report, for example, Palestinians in Abu Dis used to shop for fruits and vegetables in the markets of East Jerusalem (a stone's throw away); they now have to go all the way to Bethlehem. Similarly, Palestinians in al-Ram now have to shop in Ramallah rather than Jerusalem. Almost three hundred shops have been forced to close in recent years. The East Jerusalem unemployment rate is approaching 20 percent, compared to around 8 percent in Israel.

The result has been just as bad, or worse, for Palestinian communities around Jerusalem now cut off by the wall, which used to depend on the custom of Palestinians from Jerusalem. Over half the shops in the formerly prosperous al-Ram closed after the wall went up. Sobhi, one of the few remaining vegetable vendors in al-Ram, used to make between $65 and $90 a day in profits from his sales; he is now often unable even to cover his costs. Almost two-thirds of his customers used to come from Jerusalem or neighboring communities. They are now all cut off by the wall. Sobhi is one of three vendors whose shops remain open. Eleven others have had to close. Jaber, who sells poultry and eggs in al-Ram, tells a similar story. He used to sell up to two hundred cages of birds a day before the wall went up; now he counts himself lucky if he can sell forty. He has had to lay off over half his staff. Over two-thirds of his customers also used to come from Jerusalem.

Meanwhile, hundreds of thousands of Palestinians in the Jerusalem suburbs and beyond, in the rest of the West Bank, depend on medical services offered by the six Palestinian hospitals in East Jerusalem, such as al-Makassed and Augusta Victoria, which have no equivalent in the West Bank. On average, over 3,000 West Bank patients are referred to East Jerusalem hospitals every year. Many more seek elective treatment in East Jerusalem hospitals as well. It is theoretically possible for a West Bank Palestinian to obtain a three-month permit to enter Jerusalem for medical care, but obtaining such a permit from the Israeli authorities is a complex and time-consuming process with no guarantee of success; and even if such a permit is granted, there is no guarantee of ease of passage through the various gates allowing entry to Jerusalem. A West Banker facing a medical emergency would not have time to wait for an Israeli permit to enter East Jerusalem.

Ahmad al-Mahahareh, for example, lives in Sheikh Saad, the same village as Laila Shqeirat, at the very edge of East Jerusalem. He is in his mid-60s and facing a range of medical problems, most notably arterial and heart problems. Late one afternoon, he felt pain in his chest and had difficulty breathing. He went to a nearby clinic, where the staff took an EKG and told him to proceed immediately to the Al-Makassed Hospital in East Jerusalem, which was better equipped to deal with heart cases than the clinic. Israeli Border Police refused to allow him through the checkpoint at the village entrance. He had to use a circuitous alternative route, walking uphill most of the way. By the time he was treated, discharged, and had returned home, also on foot, in the middle of the night, the pain was worse than when he had set out.

Because of the proximity of Sheikh Saad to East Jerusalem, Ahmad had at least been able to make it to the hospital. The trip is more complex when it involves getting through checkpoints on the way. Ahlam Nasser, a twenty-seven-year-old paramedic, recalls trying to get Mujahid al-Shati, a nine-year-old cancer patient from Ramallah, a Jerusalem suburb, to the Augusta Victoria Hospital in East Jerusalem, for a blood transfusion (he suffers from a cancer of the blood). Ahlam, a twenty-two-year-old volunteer called Wafa, and the ambulance driver Bassam met Mujahid and his mother at the hospital in Ramallah to take them in to East Jerusalem; luckily, his mother has been able to receive a permit to accompany him. The first Israeli checkpoint they came to was at Beit El. The soldiers there checked papers, took a look at the child on the stretcher, and waved them through. The next Israeli checkpoint was at Hizma. The soldiers asked who the patient was. Bassam, the driver, who had the best Hebrew, explained that they were taking a child who has cancer to Jerusalem for treatment. The soldiers said that this didn't constitute an emergency and asked for their permits to enter Jerusalem. Bassam said that it was an emergency because the child would die without the treatment. He gave the soldiers everyone's papers as well as the child's and mother's permits to enter Jerusalem. The soldiers glanced at the papers and said that the ambulance crew—all employees of the Palestinian Red Crescent, the Muslim equivalent of the Red Cross—didn't have the permits necessary to enter Jerusalem. They could drop the child and his mother at the checkpoint and call an Israeli ambulance to carry them to the hospital from there. Bassam explained that an Israeli ambulance would charge between 300 and 400 shekels ($80–$95), which Mujahid's mother simply doesn't have, whereas the Red Crescent ambulance was free. "All right," the soldier said; "if she doesn't have money to pay, there is no need for her to receive treatment in Israel." And he ordered them to turn around.

Bassam turned around and decided to try a different checkpoint, the one at Anata. Here they were stopped and questioned by an Israeli border policewoman. She had just told Bassam to open the ambulance doors so she could search it; apparently, she was about to let them through. But another Border Police officer called her over, and Ahlam could hear him telling her that Palestinian ambulances are not allowed to enter Israel (although East Jerusalem is not Israel; it is occupied territory with exactly the same status in international law as the rest of the West Bank) and that she should call an Israeli ambulance to take the mother and child on

The wall near Jerusalem. Photo by author.

Palestinians scramble through gap in wall, Jerusalem. Photo by author.

from there. At this point, Ahlam called to them from the ambulance and told them to take a look at the child before deciding to turn them back. The officer told them to call an Israeli ambulance. Bassam repeated his previous explanation. Things deteriorated quickly from there. The Israeli officer started shouting and cursing at them. With a sick child on their hands, the Palestinian ambulance crew got upset in turn. More Israeli officers were called and they began to beat Ahlam and then Bassam (both still in the ambulance). The child started screaming and crying. A few minutes later the Israelis backed off and told the mother and child to get out of the ambulance, walk through the checkpoint, and catch a taxi to Jerusalem. Ahlam doesn't know what happened to them after that. She was beaten further, arrested, interrogated, and ultimately released.

According to the U.N., the number of West Bank and Gaza patients able to access medical facilities in East Jerusalem fell by half between 2002 and 2003, and has continued to decline since then. Al-Makassed Hospital reported a 50 percent drop in emergency room treatments after the wall went up around Jerusalem, from 33,000 in 2002 to 17,000 in 2005. The St. John Eye Hospital also reported a dramatic fall in treatments. Augusta Victoria Hospital, too, registered a one-third drop in its patient load once tightened Israeli controls over Palestinian access to East Jerusalem went into effect. More than two-thirds of the hospital's staff are West Bank residents; they must now apply for permits from the Israelis in order to get to work, and since the number of permits that Israel issues varies randomly from month to month, key staff are sometimes unable to get to the hospital at all.

Meanwhile, thousands of Palestinian college students living in East Jerusalem attend classes at the main campus of al-Quds University, which now lies on the other side of the wall in the suburb of Abu Dis. Every morning, these Palestinians (and countless others like them) face an unpleasant choice: they can try to find ways over, under, or around the as-yet-incomplete wall separating Abu Dis from Jerusalem—or they can risk the traffic jams, roadblocks, and checkpoints studding the long roundabout route that would take them all the way around Jerusalem and halfway to Jericho before snaking its way back to Abu Dis, a stone's throw from where they live in East Jerusalem. The wall has also shattered the normal pursuit of family life, separating cousins, nephews, uncles, aunts, grandparents, and—in one family out of five living east of the wall—one parent or another from the rest of the family. All in all, according to the U.N., a quarter of Jerusalem's Palestinians will find themselves on the east side of the wall when it is finally completed.

Not only are residents of the West Bank unable to enter Jerusalem: Palestinians from Jerusalem are unable to enter the West Bank without a whole new plethora of permits, including having to prove that their presence in Ramallah or Nablus or Hebron or Bethlehem is "essential." The Qalandia checkpoint, which used merely to mark the northern edge of Jerusalem and the entry to Ramallah, has become the equivalent of a border terminal, even though it is miles away from the 1967 border. Jerusalem Palestinians who want to visit Ramallah (which is as far from Jerusalem as Santa Monica is from Los Angeles, or Brooklyn from Manhattan, or Bethesda from Washington) will have to ask for a permit to do so. "Experience shows that 'asking for an entry permit' is not as simple as it sounds," the Israeli journalist Amira Hass points out. "Asking means the Shin Bet [Israel's domestic security service] will try to enlist collaborators in exchange for a permit, asking means waiting days and weeks for an answer, wasting days in lines and on the telephone, and then hearing that you don't have the right to go to Ramallah because you did not prove that your presence there is vital." This, she adds, is not to mention "the humiliation involved in the very need to ask for an Israeli permit in order to do the most natural things in the world: visiting a sister and friends, going to work or the doctor, buying cheaper produce in the market, finding a book in the bookstore, or hearing poet Mahmoud Darwish give a poetry reading in the theater."

10

Israel's policies regarding Jerusalem were incorporated in the set of agreements entered into during the Oslo peace process beginning in 1993, which was, in turn, based on the formula originally established by Israel to maintain its control over the occupied territories in 1967. That formula was first articulated in the weeks immediately following Israel's capture of the West Bank, Gaza, and East Jerusalem. In July of that year, Israel's deputy prime minister, Yigal Allon, proposed to the government that the country should retain permanent control over the Jordan Valley and grant limited autonomy to isolated Palestinian enclaves in the West Bank. The result, he argued, would be "the Whole Land [of Israel] strategically, and a Jewish state demographically." In other words, Allon aimed to permanently safeguard Israel's physical control over all of the occupied territories, while also preserving Israel's claim to Jewishness. This requires the continuous denial or restriction of Palestinian political and human rights, for the simple reason that granting citizenship to all Palestinians who live in the area under Israeli control—and who are politically subject to Israel—would result in the state having a population that is, at most, half Jewish (as it is, one in five citizens of Israel within its pre-1967 borders is a Palestinian Muslim or Christian). Allon resolved the conundrum facing Israel: it wanted the land, but it did not want the people. The Allon Plan would allow Israel to accomplish both ends: controlling, and ultimately settling, Palestinian land without granting citizenship to Palestinians living under Israeli control after 1967.

Allon's territorial vision complemented Israel's longstanding claim that the Palestinians do not constitute a single people—"it was not as though there was a Palestinian people in Palestine considering itself as a Palestinian people and we came and threw them out and took their country from them," former Prime Minister Golda Meir told the London *Times* in 1969; "they did not exist." Instead, the Palestinian population can be broken into separate segments, mirroring the breakup of their homeland: some to be granted second-class citizenship inside Israel; some to remain in foreign refugee camps of permanent exile; and some to live under a military occupation in the territories militarily occupied in 1967.

Although Israeli policy in the occupied territories has gone through various major shifts, the underlying emphasis has always been the same since 1967, with the Allon Plan's basic premises—however reformulated or repackaged—consistently serving as the inspiration. From shortly after the war until the late 1980s, the Israeli approach to the conundrum of territorial inclusion and demographic exclusion posited by Allon was to take advantage of the occupied territories: to colonize them and to integrate them into the Israeli economy, largely as a reserve of cheap labor, while at the same time stifling the political aspirations of the population. By the early 1970s, Jewish settlements were being founded in the occupied territories, against the strong opposition of indigenous Palestinians, who lost land to the new settlements (of which the first was Kiryat Arba, founded in 1968). But, on the other hand, Palestinians from Gaza and the West Bank were also moving freely between the two territories, East Jerusalem, and Israel itself. Friends and relatives could visit each other. Students from one part of the country could attend universities in another. For the first time since 1948, Palestinian families separated by the war could freely see each other. People from Gaza could visit their relations in Jaffa or Nazareth. People from Qalqilya or Nablus could swim in the Mediterranean (something quite unthinkable today). And people from Jaffa or Haifa could visit Gaza and Bethlehem.

Most importantly, Palestinians could work wherever the labor market provided an opportunity. Palestinians worked inside Israel as builders, waiters, busboys, drivers, factory hands, and farm laborers. All told, well over half of Gaza's workforce was employed inside Israel. At the same time, the souks and markets of Ramallah, Gaza, Nablus, and Hebron were captive markets for Israeli goods and products. By the 1980s, in short, the economies of the West Bank and especially Gaza were completely integrated into, and dependent on, the much larger economy of Israel.

Severe political repression accompanied this economic integration, however. Israeli military and police forces kept very strict control over the Palestinian population. Political surveillance was systematic and methodical, and any sign of Palestinian nationalism was swiftly punished. Even the tokens of nationalism were suppressed: one could be imprisoned merely for displaying a Palestinian flag. Any form of Palestinian political organization or agitation was immediately suppressed: towns and villages exhibiting signs of unrest would be isolated and placed under curfew. Meetings were banned. Writing and publishing were strictly controlled. Spies, informants, and collaborators were quietly cultivated, and activists routinely arrested and imprisoned. Arrest and detention without trial was the standard Israeli protocol. Torture was not only routine, but officially approved by Israel's highest legal authorities, who continued to endorse the use of "moderate physical pressure" (including violent shaking, simulated suffocation, and binding in painful positions) during the interrogation of Palestinian prisoners. Only in 1999 did the Israeli High Court rule that some of these methods were illegal, though there is considerable evidence that torture has continued to be used since then. During regular Israeli army raids on towns, villages, and refugee camps, young men and boys would often be rounded up by the hundred and held captive for indefinite periods under appalling conditions, and almost always in prisons inside Israel (a violation of the Geneva Convention, which prohibits the transfer of prisoners across international borders). According to the Palestinian human rights organization Addameer, a cumulative total of 650,000 Palestinians have been held prisoner by Israel since 1967: about 40 percent of today's entire male population.

It was this combination of economic exploitation and political repression that led to the outbreak of the first intifada, or popular uprising, which began in the Jabalia Refugee Camp on the outskirts of Gaza City, in December 1987. The first intifada began with a combination of nonviolent protests and demonstrations, along with civil disobedience and grassroots networking among Palestinian communities seeking to develop independent alternatives to Israeli-controlled markets and institutions, and rejecting the whole apparatus of the occupation. Hundreds of thousands of men, women, and children mobilized themselves to participate in the protests, which—other than episodes of stone-throwing directed against armored vehicles, heavily armed Israeli soldiers, and equally heavily armed Jewish settlers crossing Palestinian land—were generally peaceful events. Israel's response to the first intifada was heavy-handed. Shootings, raids, mass arrests, home demolitions, curfews, and closures—as well as sweeping disruptions of classes at schools and universities—were common. "The first priority of the security forces is to prevent violent demonstrations with force, power and blows," declared the Israeli defense minister at the time, Yitzhak Rabin; "We will make it clear who is running the territories." Rabin allegedly ordered his men to "break the bones" of Palestinian demonstrators, a charge the Israeli parliament decided not to investigate. Israeli forces killed over 700 Palestinians in the first three years of the intifada alone (and some 1,400 by 2000); 20 percent of them were children. In turn, Palestinian factions resorted to violence themselves, in particular from 1994 onward, when militant groups unleashed a bombing campaign inside Israel that would kill almost 200 Israeli civilians by 2000.

The first intifada shifted the focus of the Palestinian struggle away from the official PLO leadership in exile (in Tunis at the time) and to the occupied territories. It also, for the first time, pushed the Palestinians to propose what has since then come to be called the two-state solution to the conflict, which envisaged an independent Palestinian state arising in the territories occupied by Israel in 1967 (that is, what remained of Palestine after 1948; see "Inside Out"). In November 1988, a meeting of the Palestine National Council (PNC), the Palestinian parliament in exile, officially renounced terrorism, offered to recognize Israel, and proposed to enter into negotiations in order to create a Palestinian state peacefully coexisting alongside Israel, in the West Bank, Gaza Strip, and East Jerusalem, on the basis of the demands of international law and various U.N. Security Council resolutions. The PNC also declared the independence of that Palestinian state.

Israel rejected the PNC's offer and reiterated its refusal to negotiate with the PLO. The prime minister at the time, Yitzhak Shamir, dismissed the Palestinian declaration and subsequent speeches by Yasser Arafat as "a monumental act of deception." But the intifada and the 1988 declaration of independence of a Palestinian state in the West Bank, Gaza, and East Jerusalem made it clear that Israel could not continue with its policy of simply repressing Palestinian aspirations in the occupied territories. It would have to devise an alternative—a way to redirect Palestinian political aspirations without either granting citizenship to Palestinians from the occupied territories (which would further compromise the state's claim to Jewishness) or allowing them genuine independence (which would necessitate relinquishing territorial control over the territories that Israel wanted to keep and had been settling with its own civilians); in other words, a way to reformulate the territorial and demographic principles first outlined by Yigal Allon in the summer of 1967.

The result took the form of the Olso Accords, a series of initially secret negotiations entered into in the Norwegian capital between 1993 and 1995 that bypassed the Palestinian parliament-in-exile, circumvented the official multilateral Arab-Israeli negotiations entered into at Madrid in 1991, and aimed to come to a personal arrangement directly with Yasser Arafat and his senior advisors, particularly Mahmoud Abbas, who, because of all the secrecy, were unable (or perhaps unwilling) to consult with their own people. A small army of Israelis was involved in the Oslo negotiations: planners, geographers, demographers, translators, hydrologists, lawyers, mapmakers. Arafat and Abbas and their assistants at Oslo had no intimate or specialist knowledge of cartography, water aquifers, international law, or the Geneva Conventions; and, at best, a very unsteady command of the English language, in which they were negotiating and signing documents. It had been thirty years since either of them had seen the West Bank, which had been transformed by Israeli settlement, and yet they were discussing in minute detail the status of particular towns and villages with a team of Israelis who possessed not only cartographic and topographical knowledge but also personal awareness of the realities on the ground.

For Israel, the Oslo negotiations offered a mechanism to repackage the principles of the Allon Plan in a way that, geographically speaking, looked remarkably like the original. They were premised on four key principles: first, the continuing insistence that the Palestinians do not constitute a single people, and that an arrangement can be concluded with those living under occupation (or those who claim to represent them), while counting on the acquiescence of those inside Israel and the invis-ibility or irrelevance of the refugees in exile; second, the fragmentation of occupied Palestinian territory into discrete units separated from each other by areas of Israeli control; third, the transfer of the day-to-day administration and policing of the population to a severely limited form of Palestinian government; and fourth, the maintenance of Israeli control over all external borders, airspace, and territorial waters, so that all Pales-tinian contact with the outside world would be mediated by Israel.

The initiation of the Oslo negotiations in 1993 overlapped with Israel's announcement of a general closure that permanently barred Palestinians from the West Bank and Gaza from entering Jerusalem: an order that remains in effect up to the present day. Not only were the Gaza Strip and West Bank separated from East Jerusalem; they were also split from each other and from Israel, a key source of jobs for Palestinians. With the start of peace negotiations, then, Palestinians found themselves facing more and more restrictions—and receiving little in return, increasingly cut off from jobs, markets, each other, and the rest of the world. Israel's constant refrain for this restriction was security against Palestinian suicide bombings, but these started inside Israel in 1994, following the suicide-massacre of 29 unarmed Palestinians in Hebron by the American Jewish zealot Baruch Goldstein, and long after the general closure was imposed. After those bombings took place, Israel in effect held the entire Palestinian popula-tion responsible for the acts of a tiny few; collective punishments and the dramatic intensification of the occupation were the result.

All through the period of Oslo, the most crucial issues of the conflict —the uprooting of three-quarters of a million Palestinians during the creation of Israel in 1948, the internationally recognized legal and human right of those refugees and their descendents to return to their homeland, the formation of a genuine Palestinian state, water rights, and the sta-tus of Jerusalem—were studiously ignored, repeatedly deferred to some future occasion. Fewer than half of the Palestinian people live in the West Bank, Gaza, and East Jerusalem—and yet all of Oslo's energies were focused on them, at the expense of the majority of the people, who lived either in exile or inside Israel, and whose interests and rights the accords entirely ignored.

According to Oslo, then, the Palestinians were not a nation or a uni-

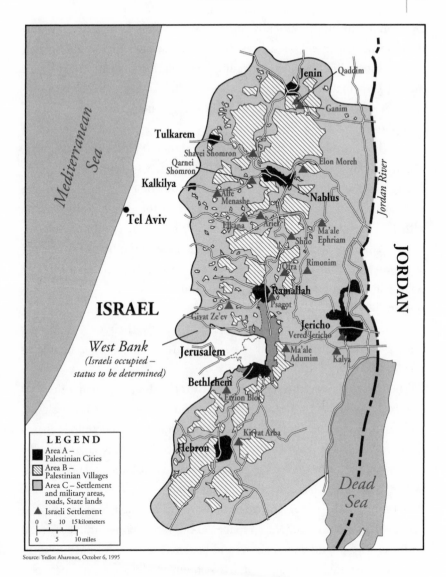

Oslo II, 1995. Courtesy Foundation for Middle East Peace and Jan de Jong.

fied people with one set of collective and inalienable rights, but merely an occupied population to be administered. What the agreement offered to those living under occupation—in exchange for its dismissal of all other Palestinians—was precisely the kind of limited autonomy first proposed by Yigal Allon in July 1967. In this sense (although the 2004 Advisory

Opinion of the International Court of Justice would, despite Oslo and subsequent agreements, reaffirm Israel's status as occupying power with all the responsibilities for the occupied population that are specified in the key documents of international humanitarian law), the Oslo agreements were designed in part to relieve Israel of many of the burdens of occupation—as well as the need to police a restive population on a daily basis. That burden, too, was shifted to the new Palestinian Authority, which quickly developed police and security forces tens of thousands strong, and a repressive apparatus no better, or more just, than the Israeli one it was nominally replacing. "I prefer the Palestinians to cope with the problems of enforcing order," Prime Minister Rabin told an Israeli Labor party meeting shortly before signing the first Oslo accord in 1993. "The Palestinians will be better at it than we are because they [will] allow no appeals to the Supreme Court and will prevent the Association for Civil Rights from criticizing the conditions there by denying them access to the area. They will rule there by their own methods, freeing—and this is important—the Israeli army soldiers from having to do what they will do."

The Palestinian Authority thus took over the duty of policing the Palestinian population on behalf of the continuing, and indeed revitalized, Israeli occupation. As before, the Jewish settlers in the occupied territories were subject neither to PA rule nor to Israeli military law—the ultimate source of authority for Palestinians in the West Bank and Gaza—but rather to domestic Israeli civil law, even though they were living outside the borders of the state. And after Oslo, Israel retained control over the occupied territories' borders, airspace, labor, water and natural resources, and even the population registry: the power to grant residency to individuals and families, or alter or move their residency status (between Gaza and the West Bank, for example), and to authorize the issuance of identity cards, which are so vital to the conduct of everyday life. Moreover, Israel retained control over tax collection: a feature that it would use to devastating effect when, in contravention of the agreements, it suspended the transfer of hundreds of millions of dollars of tax revenues to the Palestinian Authority after the Hamas election victory in 2006, thereby starving the PA of funds. Oslo also granted to Israel the power to veto any Palestinian legislation of which it did not approve.

Nor did Oslo actually return all of the occupied territories even to this nominal Palestinian government. At the very peak of the process, the Palestinians had limited control over dozens of separate bits and pieces of land in the West Bank that, all together, added up to less than 18 percent of the whole territory, designated as Area A (see map, p. 83). The Palestinian Authority was also charged with the administration of the Palestinian population living in Area B, a further 22 percent of the territory, again in bits and pieces, which remained, however, physically under Israeli army control. Everywhere else, in Area C—about 60 percent of the West Bank—Israeli rule continued precisely as though nothing had happened, or as though the future status of the land supposedly under negotiation had long since been determined.

Area C is the land that Israel most desired all along. Here, it continued to maintain its checkpoints and roadblocks, to establish new military installations, to develop the network of bypass roads for Jewish settlers, and to expand the array of settlements whose very existence was a violation of international law. By the time the peace process broke down, not only were borders, roads, airspace, power, and taxation all still firmly under Israeli control—and 80 percent of the West Bank's water still being devoted to Israeli use—but the Israeli settler population in the occupied territories had actually doubled from what it had been when the negotiations began in 1993.

As far as the Israelis were concerned, then, the limited implementation of the Oslo Accords amounted, essentially, to little more than a new form of occupation, enabling the perpetual deferral of the core issues of the conflict. For most Palestinians, however, the institutionalized system of checkpoints, curfews, roadblocks, and closures introduced by Oslo led to ever-greater immobilization and paralysis, political infighting, soaring unemployment, and economic collapse.

The Oslo arrangement did, however, benefit the small Palestinian elite centered on Yasser Arafat and his associates in the Fateh party. Members of this elite gained financially from the monopolies granted by the PA to various loyalists and from the general corruption, cronyism, and mismanagement that was endemic in the Authority. Nearly half of the PA's 1997 budget, for example, was lost to corruption and financial mismanagement, according to an auditor's report. Another audit, by the Inter-

national Monetary Fund in 2003, discovered that Arafat had diverted
$900 million in supposedly public funds to an account under his per-
sonal control, which he could disburse without any accountability. From
the very beginning of the PA, government ministers were regularly being
accused of fraud and corruption, most shockingly when Ahmed Qurie,
the prime minister appointed (at Israel's behest) as a counterweight to
Arafat, was publicly charged with involvement in a company that was
supplying cement for the construction of Israel's West Bank wall.

As long as they were making personal gains of their own—not just
financial gains in the crude sense, but in the sense of proximity to power,
however attenuated, or perhaps simply, as Régis Debray puts it, "a living,
status, dignity and a raison d'être"—the Fateh and PA elite were willing
to go along with the "peace process" narrative made available by Israel
and the United States. This involved more than merely acquiescing to
Israel's demands. For in forfeiting control over language and discourse,
they also abandoned altogether the traditional Palestinian narratives of
self-determination and national liberation. They were so caught up in
an empty Israeli and American negotiating language ("peace process,"
"interim arrangement," "final status," and eventually "Road Map") that
they lacked the means to formulate alternatives, let alone a convincing
counternarrative. Thus, at moments of crisis in the negotiations, Palestinian leaders found themselves literally bereft of language. They were incapable of generating counterproposals when they came up against what
they considered to be an unacceptable Israeli demand: they could only
accept Israel's terms, or reject them.

Part of what would enable Hamas to rise to prominence as a viable
alternative to Fateh in 2006 was its lack of involvement in PA corruption,
its lack of complicity in all the deliberately misleading and often counter-
factual discourses of Oslo, and, perhaps above all, its canny rehabilitation
of a genuinely Palestinian language of self-determination and national
liberation that, ironically, had originally been expressed by the secular
Palestinian parties—above all others Fateh—in the 1960s and 1970s, but
that the secular leadership had progressively abandoned (see "Coda").

From an Israeli standpoint, however, the weak point of the Oslo formula was that it fundamentally required finding a Palestinian partner
willing to go along with Israel's requirements, to buy into its language

and discourse, and to accept that what the accords designated as provisional (including the Palestinian Authority itself) would become permanent with the perpetual deferral of "final status" negotiations, and to be satisfied with the personal trappings of power rather than his people's actual independence and genuine statehood. Yasser Arafat fulfilled that role until he could no longer restrain his people's outrage at finding themselves more impoverished, and their movements more restricted, while the Israeli dismemberment and colonization of their land continued unabated. Mahmoud Abbas would take over in the same capacity after Arafat's death in 2005.

In the summer of 2000, at the invitation of President Clinton, Israeli Prime Minister Ehud Barak met Palestinian leader Yasser Arafat at Camp David. The claim is often repeated that Barak generously offered 90 percent of the West Bank, and a capital in East Jerusalem, to Arafat, and Arafat rejected the offer. In fact, as we know from the published accounts of Israeli, American, and Palestinian negotiators, insofar as there can be said to have been an offer at Camp David (no such offer was formally presented in writing), it would have amounted to this: Palestinians would indeed be given *nominal* sovereignty over most of the West Bank. But within this supposedly "sovereign" space, dozens of Israeli settlements would remain exactly as before, as would a formidable Israeli military presence. The Jordan River valley and the eastern third of the West Bank would remain firmly under Israeli military control. So would borders, airspace, and water. So would the road network—still off-limits to Palestinians—connecting the settlements to each other, to army installations, and to Israel. The proposed Palestinian "capital" would have been in Abu Dis, a Jerusalem suburb, rather than in Jerusalem proper. Moreover, 10 percent of the West Bank's most fertile land would be annexed to Israel, and tens of thousands of Palestinians living on that land would have been left in a stateless limbo, or forced to move. In reality, then, other than a purely nominal sovereignty over their own territory, what the Palestinians were "offered" at Camp David was actual, physical access to somewhat over half of the West Bank: an area to be dotted with Israeli settlements and army posts and crisscrossed with bypass roads to which Palestinians would continue to be denied access. This was more or less what had been proposed years previously at Oslo as an "interim solution."

At Camp David, though, the solution was meant to be permanent and irreversible. "There was no possibility that any Palestinian leader could accept such terms and survive," writes Jimmy Carter in *Palestine: Peace Not Apartheid*; "but official statements from Washington and Jerusalem were successful in placing the onus for the failure on Yasir Arafat." The Palestinian leadership failed disastrously by not coming up with an alternative to the U.S.-Israeli position at Camp David and subsequent negotiations through the end of the Clinton presidency. It also failed by not explaining what was wrong with the terms being negotiated at Camp David, and how the whole peace process, from Oslo on, represented the subordination of international law to Israeli demands.

As the international legal scholar Richard Falk has pointed out, Israel has refused to accept the demands of international law and the repeatedly expressed will of the institutions of the international community; legally speaking, Falk says, this justifies the Palestinian right of resistance (though not illegitimate forms of violence directed against civilians). The international legal requirement is simple: it is that Israel withdraw from the occupied territories, end its abrogation of Palestinian human and political rights, and cease and dismantle its illegal settlement enterprise. Both Oslo and Camp David, on the other hand, embodied the U.S. and Israeli position (often reiterated by pro-Israeli Americans such as Dennis Ross, who served as an advisor to President Clinton at Camp David) that the unambiguous requirements of international law should be, at best, secondary to Israel's demands and security needs, if not altogether irrelevant.

The general consensus among Palestinians is that the outcome of negotiations with the Israelis should be determined by both people's legitimate needs and in keeping with the demands of international law. But, especially since Oslo, the Palestinian political leadership has done an abysmal job—in fact, it has given up altogether—explaining how Palestinian demands are entirely in keeping with the requirements of international law, the Universal Declaration of Human Rights, various United Nations Security Council and General Assembly resolutions, and so on. So the Palestinians far too often look like they are the ones who are being unreasonable, uncompromising, and unjust. Partly this is due to unfair and often distorted media representation, especially in the United States (as the aftermath of Camp David made clear). But mostly it is due to the Palestinians' longstanding inability (certain exceptions notwithstanding) to express their intentions and aims—and above all their conformity to the demands of international law—to a global media market, in that market's primary language of communication, English. Especially since Palestinians lack other means (economic leverage, military power, diplomatic clout), language is virtually the only device left to them. This has made the official Fateh and PA leadership's disavowal of an autonomous Palestinian discourse all the more debilitating. Only now is this situation beginning to change, partly because of the success of Hamas in rehabilitating what had been the secularist language of national liberation from the 1960s and 1970s, and partly because the momentum of the Palestinian struggle is once again shifting away from both Hamas and Fateh—and the occupied territories in general—to those Palestinians living in Israel and in the global diaspora (see "Coda").

It was when the terms discussed at Camp David became clear, and when it seemed obvious to the Palestinians that years of negotiation had only resulted in greater restriction, as well as the immiseration produced by the collapse of the Palestinian economy (first made dependent on the Israeli economy, then suddenly separated from it during the Oslo years), that the second intifada erupted in the summer and fall of 2000. Although the uprising was sparked by Ariel Sharon's provocative stroll—accompanied by hundreds of heavily armed soldiers—across Jerusalem's Haram al-Sharif, the sanctuary enclosing the Al-Aqsa Mosque and the Dome of the Rock, it was as much a revolt against the incompetence of the Palestinian leadership for having squandered seven years in fruitless negotiations as it was against the never-ending occupation itself. Publicly, the Israeli government accused the Palestinian leadership of launching and directing the intifada. Privately, however, various Israeli officials acknowledged that the uprising, with all of its attendant violence, was the inevitable outcome not only of the lopsided nature of the conflict, but also of the stifling of Palestinian aspirations that was essential to the Oslo process. "Under conditions of an asymmetric confrontation, one in which Israel is many times stronger than the Palestinians, we have decisive influence on the course of events," warned Mati Steinberg of the Shin Bet. The Israeli approach, he argued, "dictates just one choice to the Palestinians: either they surrender to Israel's dictates, or they rise up against the dictates at all costs."

Since then, things have only worsened. In addition to the thousands of Palestinians—most of them civilians—killed or injured by Israeli forces, the violence of the second intifada, in particular the Palestinian bombings of civilian targets inside Israel, exacted a toll of hundreds of innocent Israeli lives. For its part, the Israeli army and air force smashed the political, security, and administrative institutions of the Palestinian Authority and formally reoccupied large portions of the West Bank, subjecting them, and Gaza, to much tighter controls, routinely shutting down all movement of people and goods in the occupied territories, and often keeping men, women, and children confined to their homes for days and even weeks on end. Entire communities, notably in Nablus and Jenin in the West Bank, and Rafah in Gaza, were flattened by the Israeli army's Caterpillar D9 armored bulldozers, leaving tens of thousands of Palestinians homeless once again. And the Israelis initiated a program of extrajudicial executions (the only one of its kind to be formally approved by a country's high court although it, too, constitutes a violation of international law) that has left hundreds of Palestinians, a large proportion of them simply innocent bystanders, dead or wounded. The Israeli government publicly claims that this extraordinary violence—its army fired over a million bullets in the first few days of the intifada alone—was directed against what it called "the terrorist infrastructure." But, again, various Israeli officials privately acknowledged what was really at stake in dealing with the intifada, and that Israel's response to the uprising was directed not against armed groups but rather against the entire population. "The Palestinians must be made to understand in the deepest recesses of their consciousness," said General Moshe Ya'alon, who was in charge of the Israeli military response to the uprising, "that they are a defeated people." The Oslo process ended as it had begun, with Israel asserting its control over the occupied territories.

It was against this backdrop, in 2003, that President Bush and the so-called Quartet (the United States, the U.N., the European Union, and Russia) published the Road Map to Peace. The premise of this plan, as the Palestinian historians Samih Farsoun and Naseer Aruri point out, "is that the nearly forty-year-old impasse is not caused by an abnormal and illegal occupation but by the Palestinian resistance to that occupation. Progress was thus linked to ending the intifada and all acts of resistance rather than ending the occupation or reversing decades of colonial impoverishment of land, resources, and institutions." Indeed, the Road Map, which was partly drafted by the Israelis themselves (though in the end, they, unlike the Palestinians, actually refused to accept all of its terms), essentially shifted the burden of responsibility for ending the occupation from the occupiers to the occupied. While imposing a whole series of demands on the Palestinians, the document asked little of Israel other than a few token gestures. It was very specific as to what the Palestinians had to do to prove themselves eligible "partners for peace," but deferred the more substantive questions of ending the occupation and creating a Palestinian state "with attributes of sovereignty" to a series of vague generalizations with no concrete timeline.

It was around this time, with the Palestinians unable to conform to the letter of the Road Map's demands, that the Israeli prime minister, Ariel Sharon, declared his own explicitly unilateral solution to the conflict. He ordered the construction of the wall of concrete and steel to mark Israel's permanent border, which, uniquely among the world's states, had never been declared, and thus to "disengage" from the Palestinians. He also reached a new agreement with the Bush administration, with the approval of the U.S. Senate and House of Representatives, under which Israel's permanent control over large swathes of the West Bank, and all of Jerusalem, would be ensured, irrespective of the demands and requirements of international law, which, again, neither Israel nor the United States had any intention of heeding. "The understandings between the US President and me protect Israel's most essential interests," Sharon proclaimed in 2004; "first and foremost, not demanding a return to the '67 borders; allowing Israel to permanently keep large settlement blocs which have high Israeli populations; and the total refusal of allowing Palestinian refugees to return to Israel." Sharon's senior advisor, Dov Weisglas, boasted to the Israeli newspaper Ha'aretz that the new Israeli government policy—of which he was one of the architects—supplies "the formaldehyde that's necessary so that there will not be a political process with the Palestinians." When you freeze the process, Weisglas explained, "you prevent the establishment of a Palestinian state and you prevent a discussion about the refugees, the borders, and Jerusalem. Effectively, this whole package that is called the Palestinian state, with all that it entails, has been removed from our agenda indefinitely. And all this," he added, "with authority and permission. All with a presidential blessing and the ratification of both houses of Congress."

Part of Sharon's disengagement plan involved redeploying the Jewish settlers from Gaza in order to concentrate on settling the much more important territory of the West Bank. Twice as many settlers moved to the West Bank in 2005, for example, as were pulled out of Gaza that year—and in December 2006 an entirely new settlement was announced in the Jordan Valley in order to accommodate the former settlers of Gaza (though this announcement was subsequently reversed due to U.S. pressure). Gaza itself would be entirely sealed off from the outside world and left to its own devices, but it was only the largest of many such "islands," in what amounted to a Palestinian archipelago surrounded by an Israeli sea. Remarkably, however, the map of the Sharon disengagement plan did not differ significantly from the maps of Camp David or Oslo. A glance at the three maps reveals that the Israelis have been pursuing the same territorial agenda all along. Each proposal has amounted to a variation on the same theme, whereby Israel would retain about half of the West Bank while handing over the remainder—in discontinuous bits and pieces—to some form of Palestinian self-rule. Not surprisingly, the same proportions, along more or less the same lines of control, had been proposed in the very first Israeli formula for the disposition of the West Bank, namely, the Allon Plan of 1967.

"The Middle East peace process may well be the most spectacular deception in modern diplomatic history," writes Henry Siegman, the former head of the American Jewish Congress. "Since the failed Camp David summit of 2000, and actually well before it, Israel's interest in a peace process—other than for the purpose of obtaining Palestinian and international acceptance of the status quo—has been a fiction that has served primarily to provide cover for its systematic confiscation of Palestinian land."

When the U.N. published a new map of the West Bank in May 2007, showing the extent of the territorial fragmentation of the Palestinian population, the *Financial Times* published the map and an article explaining it (see maps, pp. 340 and 341). "The UN mapmakers focused on land set aside for Jewish settlements, roads reserved for settler access, the West Bank separation barrier, closed military areas and nature reserves," the article reads. "What remains is an area of habitation remarkably close to territory set aside for the Palestinian population in Israeli security proposals dating back to postwar 1967." For all the talk of peace, war, and crisis, in other words, the Israeli occupation has slowly and methodically accomplished precisely what it set out to do forty-one years ago.

Insides

1

Samira Aliyan, a Palestinian born and raised in Jerusalem, finally had her turn at one of the booths at the East Jerusalem office of the Israeli Ministry of the Interior.

The East Jerusalem office—the one that caters to the quarter of a million Palestinians who have Jerusalem residency—is the most overcrowded and underserved branch of the entire ministry. It is housed in a dilapidated building on the Nablus Road, about a hundred yards from the Old City's Damascus Gate. Access to the building is provided through a filthy doorway—really little more than a cage door—constructed of thick round steel bars.

The line to gain entry to the ministry on any given day forms in the hours between midnight and sunrise. By dawn, there is usually a queue of a couple of hundred people. There is no shelter for those waiting in line. In the summer's pounding sun—once it rises—or the winter's sleet and rain, men, women, and children have to wait outside. Even babies have to wait: they must be physically present in order for their parents to obtain their birth certificates or other vital documents. There is barely any room to stand other than in the line itself, which runs down the sidewalk and spills into the street. Under the eye of Israeli soldiers standing in their sheltered posts nearby, the line of Palestinians polices itself. Or, rather, it is policed by Palestinian thugs armed with razors and switchblades who harass and intimidate those in line, sometimes offering them a favorable position in the queue in return for cash, sometimes barring them entry unless they pay the "appropriate" fee.

Once the Palestinian writer Daoud Kuttab found himself in this queue in order to help his teenage daughter obtain her identity card. The day before he intended to queue up, he stopped by to evaluate the scene for himself. He had been expecting the usual disaster but was pleasantly surprised to find that since his last time here everything had actually been reformed. A bearded young man was sitting across the street from the ministry office with paper and pen, taking people's names in order of arrival. When he made inquiries, Daoud was told by the young man that he and a few other faithful Muslims had taken it upon themselves to organize things. Applicants were to register with him, return at 10 P.M. for a roll call, and return the following day at 5 A.M. to assume their appropriate position in the queue. Relieved, Daoud gladly signed up and was granted number 16—not bad at all. But he returned for the roll call at 10 P.M. to find that the bearded man had gone and had been replaced by a muscular fellow who was rewriting the list (which had apparently been torn in a fight). Daoud reregistered as number 46: not so good, but not so bad either. He returned with his daughter at 5 A.M. the next day only to find that the muscular man had also disappeared and the line was already long and backed up. What about the list? There was no longer a list.

"Everyone for himself, we were told," Daoud recounts. "We took our place at the end of the line and waited until the Ministry opened at 8 A.M. Shortly before they opened, two police cars arrived and arrested one of the young thugs in line. I later discovered that he had slashed the arm of a person pushing him. I took a deep breath and kept calm. No sooner had the gate opened than a spate of fights started." It was all to no avail, in any case. By 11 A.M., more than eight separate fights for places in line had taken place. Then the queue stalled. By 3 P.M., the official closing time, with the line still stalled, as it had been for hours, Daoud and his daughter gave up and went home. They had been waiting outdoors for ten hours. They were told that the ministry had stopped admitting people early that day because the following day was a Jewish holiday and the Israeli staff didn't want to be late getting home.

The Israeli guards open the gates to the ministry two or three times during the morning, allowing a few dozen people through each time. Once inside, people have to wait all over again, often hours more, before being called to a booth. They must have the appropriate forms and documents scrupulously completed. The forms and documents are only printed in Hebrew; most Palestinians read and write only Arabic. Consequently, as the Israeli human rights organization B'Tselem points out, "the many applicants who do not read Hebrew depend on the goodwill of the clerks to explain what documents have to be brought, or they have to leave the office and pay for a translation of the document, and then wait again in line." Goodwill toward Palestinians is in short supply in the Israeli Ministry of the Interior. The Israeli clerks implement their highly complex rules to the letter. Applicants for virtually any document have to furnish a whole range of irrelevant records, sometimes going back in an uninterrupted series for several years: school certificates for children, electricity and water bills, proof of payment for municipal taxes, proof of title or a property rental agreement, marriage certificates, inoculation documents, and so on. Any gap in the series or other irregularity will result in the application—whatever it may be for—being rejected out of hand. Those whose paperwork does not match the high standards demanded by the Ministry of the Interior risk not merely rejection, but having their papers and even their identity cards confiscated, or worse.

The West Jerusalem branch of the Ministry of the Interior stands not far from the East Jerusalem branch. It caters to the city's Jewish residents. There are no queues outside the West Jerusalem branch. There are no thugs and turn-traders. Applicants are immediately admitted to the building, where they can wait in the lobby or the waiting areas. They can use the building's cafeteria and drink from its water fountains. And they have nothing to fear from the clerks, who are there to serve them.

Back at the East Jerusalem branch, Samira Aliyan's hours of waiting were now past: she was past the thugs and turn-traders and finally called up to a booth. She was here to renew her husband's permit to stay with her in Jerusalem. Her husband—also a Palestinian, but with Jordanian citizenship—had been living in Jerusalem with Samira and their children for four years. During this time, their application to the Israeli authorities for family unification—the state's official permission for her husband to live with his wife and children—was being considered: a process that generally takes years to complete. In the meantime, Samira had been able to apply for a renewable permit in order to allow her husband to stay on until their family unification request could finally be approved, as they hoped it would be. She was here merely to renew the permit one more time.

Good news, she was told: there was no need to renew the permit, as, in fifteen days, Samira and her husband would finally be granted family unification. All she had to do now was return to the ministry with documents showing where she has been and when, in order to establish a record of having lived in Jerusalem: municipal tax records, a rental contract, water bills, electricity bills, and the children's birth certificates. "You must bring everything," the Israeli clerk told her, "and if you lie, you will lose any chance of obtaining family unification." At once thrilled by the news and deeply apprehensive about her ability to assemble a comprehensive set of records going back so many years, Samira rushed home to start gathering all the necessary pieces of paper. A few days later, she returned to the ministry, and, after several more hours of waiting in line, she finally had her turn again. "I sat with the clerk in booth number 1," Samira recalls. "He asked for my identity card, a request they generally make. I gave him my identity card, of course, together with all the other documents he had requested, and then he gave me a piece of paper and said, 'You shouldn't be here. You should go back to where you were. You have two weeks to sell your furniture and leave.'"

Not quite believing what she had heard, Samira burst into tears. She started to scream. She demanded to see the officer in charge. "All right," the Israeli clerk told her, and he took her toward his supervisor's office, Samira still crying. On the way there, they passed another clerk. "Why are you crying," she asked. "They took my identity card," Samira explained. "Apparently, you shouldn't be here," the other clerk said. Still unable to hold back her tears, Samira finally met the officer in charge. "Why are you crying?" he asked. "If you continue to act in this manner, we'll take all the money you received from the National Insurance Institute for two years.

So you should behave properly, because if you don't, we shall also take your oldest son's identity card. You have two weeks to settle your affairs and go back to where you came from."

But Samira was already where she had come from: Jerusalem, the city of her birth. That is not what the officer meant, however. For Samira, like thousands of other Palestinians at around the same time (the mid-1990s), had fallen foul of a new Israeli regulation designed to strip Jerusalem Palestinians like her of their Jerusalem residency papers if they are unable to prove that Jerusalem is and has always continuously been their "center of life." Since Samira had spent several years in Jordan—and even though she had returned home every year to Jerusalem precisely in order to maintain her residency—Jerusalem had not always and continuously been her "center of life." So she had, according to the State of Israel, permanently forfeited her right to live there. And since only Palestinians with valid Jerusalem residency papers could even enter Jerusalem—West Bankers are denied access unless they hold permits, which are extraordinarily difficult to obtain, and Gazans are only rarely allowed out of Gaza—Samira would not only be unable to live in the city in which she was born: she would be unable to visit it ever again. The same thing would apply to a Palestinian who had gone abroad for a few years to study at a foreign university; to a Palestinian who had found a job in the West Bank suburbs; to a Palestinian who had married a West Banker or a Gazan; or to a Palestinian who had ended up renting or buying an apartment in the West Bank suburbs of Jerusalem because he found it impossible to rent, buy, or build a home in Jerusalem proper.

While one branch of the Israeli Ministry of the Interior was revoking Samira Aliyan's right to live in the city of her birth and ancestry, another branch of the same ministry was granting instant citizenships to individuals from all over the world who could establish a claim to being Jewish (or at least a claim in keeping with the prevailing rabbinical standards, which are hotly debated in Israel from time to time). While Palestinians like Samira Aliyan were being forced to leave Jerusalem, their places were being taken by Jewish immigrants from Moldova and Russia—about a million of whom were granted entry to and citizenship in Israel through the 1990s—who had never set eyes on the city.

The bureaucratic procedure of revoking a Palestinian's Jerusalem resi-

dency is only one component of a complex Israeli strategy to reduce—
even by ones and twos, if necessary—the number of non-Jews in the city,
while slowly and steadily increasing the city's Jewish population: a process
the U.N. Special Rapporteur on Human Rights, John Dugard, refers to
as "de-Palestinization." In fact, after an international outcry and various
legal challenges, some of the Palestinians, like Samira, who had had their
Jerusalem residency revoked in the 1990s, had them quietly restored after
the new policy was suspended in 2000. But the policy was, also quietly,
reintroduced, and made more effective by the even more vigilant Israeli
policing of entry into Jerusalem made possible by the wall. In 2006 alone,
Israel stripped 1,363 Jerusalem Palestinians—"many from generations-
old Jerusalem families," as the Economist points out in an article covering
this issue—of their right to live in the city: a number up six times from the
year before, and the highest annual total ever. Between 1967 and 2006,
Israel stripped a total of 8,269 Jerusalem Palestinians of their residency.
A Jerusalem Palestinian is not necessarily officially informed that she has
lost her residency status: like Samira Aliyan, she finds out when she goes
to carry out some routine bureaucratic procedure. Ahmed Jubran, who
was stripped of his Jerusalem residency in 2005, told the Economist that
he would do anything to get it back. "Hell," he says, "I'll even become
Jewish if they want."

Jubran has a point: never has any Jewish Israeli—hundreds of thousands of whom reside in the West Bank, or have studied, worked, lived in
or immigrated from, or back to, other countries—been asked to establish
where his center of life is, much less been asked to assemble an immacu-
late set of documents concerning rent, taxes, and water bills going back
ten or twelve years. According to Israeli law, a Jew's right to live in Jerusalem (or anywhere else in Israel or the occupied territories) arises from
the simple fact of his being Jewish, even if he comes from Moldova—"this
right is inherent in being a Jew," as Israel's first prime minister, David
Ben-Gurion, expressed it when presenting the Law of Return to the
Israeli parliament in 1950. Non-Jews do not enjoy the same right, even if
they come from a Palestinian family that has lived in Jerusalem for generations, simply because they are not Jewish.

What is at stake here, then, is Israel's desire to consolidate its claim that
Jerusalem is, as the official Israeli government proclamation has it, "the

eternal and undivided capital of the Jewish people." By its very nature, the process of consolidating the Jewish claim to Jerusalem excludes the Palestinian claim to the city (even though the latter is not made in similarly exclusive terms). "The Judaization of Jerusalem is a cynical exercise in social engineering," according to the U.N.'s John Dugard. In pursuit of its claim that Jerusalem is a Jewish city, Israel has revoked Palestinians' rights to residency; it has forcibly ejected them from Jerusalem; it has denied their applications for family unification; it has refused to register the birth of their children; it has devised laws intended to compel their children to leave them and move to the West Bank at the age of eighteen; it has built a wall to force them to choose between jobs in the West Bank and homes in Jerusalem, or the other way around; and it has made it as difficult as possible for them to build homes on land in Jerusalem that their families have owned for countless generations—while at the same time confiscating as much of that land as possible in order to build settlements for the city's new Jewish residents, who are settling in East Jerusalem in violation of international law.

Just as Israeli policy has led to the fragmentation of "outside" territory through the construction of walls and roads and the maintenance of roadblocks and checkpoints intended to restrict the movement of Palestinians while enabling the free movement of Jewish settlers in the West Bank, it has also redefined "inside" life as well. Being classified as belonging to one or another of the external spaces divided up by Israel has a decisive influence on a Palestinian's inner private and family life, and the nature, privacy and security of her home, even its vulnerability to demolition by the state. For a Palestinian living under Israeli rule, there's a huge difference between being classified as a Jerusalem resident and being classified as a West Banker, a Gazan, or a citizen of the state (and, similarly, among West Bankers themselves there are major differences among residents of the so-called seam zone, residents of the Jordan Valley, residents of Nablus: each further subdivided exterior space comes with its own peculiar forms of interior restriction). Jerusalem residency doesn't carry the benefits of Israeli citizenship such as those enjoyed (to a limited extent) by Palestinian citizens of Israel, for example. But his Jerusalem identity card allows a Jerusalem Palestinian a degree of freedom of movement that a West Banker or Gazan could only dream of. So for a Palestinian, a Jerusalem identity card offers a kind of middle ground between the second-class citizenship of the Palestinian-Israeli and the restricted life of the West Banker, or the abject life of the Gazan.

It is, however, the Israelis, not the Palestinians, who decide what identity is conferred on which Palestinian, and they make the decision on the basis of criteria that have nothing to do with the "inside" life of the individual person or family in question, but rather according to the division of "outsides" on the basis of Israel's own political and territorial claims and desires. Under these circumstances, family life, intimately personal spaces, the nature (and the very existence) of the family home, and even personal identity—who one is, where one can go, where one can live and work—have all become politically charged as the result of a state policy founded on the ultimate ideological distinction in Israel, which is, by definition, an intimately personal one: namely, the distinction between someone who happens to be Jewish and someone who does not.

SEGREGATION BY THE NUMBERS

- Percentage of Palestinian population of Israel living in poverty: 48
- Percentage of Jewish population of Israel living in poverty: 15
- Average Palestinian family income in Israel as percentage of average Jewish income: 57
- Percentage of state investment devoted to Jewish areas: 90
- Number of localities inside Israel granted priority development status: 429
- Number of those that are Palestinian: 4
- Number of towns in Israel with unemployment rates higher than 10%: 32
- Number of those that are Palestinian: 25
- Ratio of state funding per capita for Jewish vs. Palestinian towns: 159:100
- Infant mortality rate among Palestinians in Israel: 8.4 per thousand
- Infant mortality rate among Jews in Israel: 3.6 per thousand
- Number of religious sites in Israel granted state protection and funding: 135
- Number of those that are not Jewish: 0

2

When Israel redrew the municipal borders of Jerusalem after the 1967 War and later claimed to annex the eastern part of the city, part of what was at stake was the process of asserting its control over the external spaces in and around the city, as was explored in the previous chapter. But integral to that external process was an internal one, whereby the number of non-Jewish (i.e., Palestinian) residents of the city could be gradually reduced while the number of Jewish residents was gradually increased.

As Samira Aliyan discovered, the process of removing Palestinians to make room for Jewish settlers is often a matter of silent and invisible bureaucratic practices. The bureaucratic procedures, however, are themselves structured by the recurring difference between Jews and non-Jews. According to current or former Israeli officials of the municipality of Jerusalem, the distinction between establishing homes for Jews and denying them to non-Jews has been essential to city planning since 1967. "A cornerstone in the planning of Jerusalem is the demographic question," noted Israel Kimchi, director of planning policy for the Municipality of Jerusalem, in 1977; "the city's growth and the preservation of the demographic balance among its ethnic groups was a matter decided by the Government of Israel. That decision, concerning the city's rate of growth, today serves as one of the criteria for the success of the process of Jerusalem's consolidation as the capital of Israel." Amir Cheshin, former Israeli advisor on Arab affairs to the mayor of Jerusalem, explains: "The planning and building laws in East Jerusalem rest on a policy that calls for placing obstacles in the way of planning in the Arab sector—this is done more to preserve the demographic balance between Jews and Arabs in the city, which is presently in a ratio of 72 percent Jews against 28 percent non-Jews."

As the percentage of Jews to non-Jews (that is, Palestinians) began inevitably sliding away from the desired ratio, Israeli policy-makers struggled to devise ways to reverse the trend, with the 72 to 28 ratio firmly in mind as a desirable outcome. Jerusalem's 1978 Master Plan explicitly proposed various ways to promote the growth of the city's Jewish popula-

tion while squeezing and limiting the growth of the non-Jewish population. According to Teddy Kollek, then the mayor of Jerusalem, the plan
says that "it is necessary to make life difficult for the Arabs, not to allow
them to build," precisely in order to preserve the "ideal" ratio of Jews
to non-Jews in Jerusalem. The point, Kollek says, is that "we are giving
expression to our control throughout the entire city and are affirming
principles for the continuing intensification of the city's unification." In
this context, "unification" means distributing areas of Jewish population
in such a way that it becomes difficult to detach them. It is in this sense
that Jerusalem is a kind of microcosm of the West Bank, where Jewish
settlements have also been widely dispersed precisely in order to make
it as difficult as possible to imagine uprooting them. "Every area of the
city that is not settled by Jews is in danger of being detached from Israel
and transferred to Arab control," Meron Benvenisti explains in his book
on town planning in Jerusalem; "therefore the administrative decision
regarding the area of the city's municipal jurisdiction must be translated
into practice by building in all parts of that area, and, to begin with, in its
remotest sections."

A WEEK OF OCCUPATION:
UN-OCHA WEEKLY BRIEFING, 2–8 MAY 2007

- 25 April to date: The IDF continues to occupy the roof of an uninhabited four-storey Palestinian building in Huwwara village (Nablus) and converted it into an observation post to monitor Road 60.
- 2 May: The IDF issued three eviction orders to Palestinian farmers
  from Beit Furik (Nablus). The area in question is located in Area C
  and is—according to the order—described as closed military area.
  The area is planted with olive and almond trees and one structure
  was built in the area.
- 3 May: The IDF issued 12 demolition orders against the Roman
  Orthodox Housing Complex in the town of Beit Sahur (Bethlehem) for reportedly being built in Area C without proper permits.
- 4 May: The IDF issued one demolition order to the owner of a
  house under construction in Jinsafut village (Qalqiliya) for reportedly being built without a permit in Area C.

- 5 May: A group of Israeli settlers from Eli settlement occupied a house in Al Lubban ash-Sharqiya village (Nablus) for five hours. The settlers left only after the IDF arrived (and the IDF remained in the house for a further two hours).
- 5 May: The IDF ordered the remaining 30 residents of Al Hadidiya community to leave the area following an Israeli High Court decision that ruled that they were the threat to the safety of nearby Roi settlement. The IDF warned the families remaining in the location that their tents and animal shacks will be demolished.
- 6 May: A group of Israeli settlers from the settlements of Kiryat Arba and Karmi Tzur, both located in the vicinity of Hebron city (Hebron), occupied a hilltop overlooking Road 60 near the Halhul-Sa'ir Junction in attempt to establish a new outpost. They placed a number of tents and raised the flag before leaving the location.
- 8 May: The IDF issued six demolition orders to the owners of six houses in Al 'Aqaba village (Tubas). The orders describe the area as closed military area. With these orders, the number of structures that have received demolition orders in the village reached 28.

3

A succession of Israeli governments has ordered five major waves of expropriation in and around Jerusalem, involving about a third of the area supposedly annexed to the city in 1967, taking land from its Palestinian owners and giving it over to areas of exclusively Jewish settlement. Palestinians today comprise a third of Jerusalem's population, but they have access to less than 10 percent of the land within the redefined city limits. Ninety percent of the territory annexed to Jerusalem in 1967—all of it Palestinian land—is today off-limits to Palestinian development because the land is either already built on by Jewish settlements or being held in reserve for their future expansion.

In 1974, the municipality of Jerusalem said it would begin developing a regional plan for all the Palestinian areas of the city, on the basis of which the planning for development, zoning, and infrastructure for particular Palestinian neighborhoods, and individual building permits, could be issued. But thirty years later, even as massive construction efforts were contemplated, planned, initiated, and completed for the array of Jewish settlements in and near the city, the municipality still had not published any comprehensive plan for the Palestinian areas of Jerusalem. Meanwhile, local, smaller-scale plans developed slowly—or not at all. The planning process for the Palestinian neighborhood of Arab el-Swahrah began in 1979; twenty years later it had not been completed. Planning procedures for Beit Safafa began in 1977 and were finally approved only in 1990. And even when such plans were completed, over a period of years, they systematically reduced building and growth possibilities for Palestinians.

The planning scheme for Beit Hanina and Shu'afat, Palestinian neighborhoods in (what was redefined as) northern Jerusalem, is a case in point. Planning for this area was initiated in the early 1980s. A full twenty years after the whole process began, the first detailed plans were completed, and so far in the new century several hundred permits have been issued. It is estimated that the remaining permits will be issued over the coming decades (one of the planners estimates that they will be issued over the next fifty to a hundred years). Ze'ev Baran, an Israeli architect who worked on the detailed plans, points out that less than half of the area's building potential can be realized from the new plans. But while all these details for Palestinian neighborhoods were being anxiously debated, Jewish settlement in adjacent and nearby areas of East Jerusalem proceeded apace. Pisgat Ze'ev was built nearby, for example, and Road 1 alongside it, with the area on the other side of the road reserved for future (Jewish) development.

One inevitable result of all the official bureaucratic limitations and controls on Palestinian growth and development in East Jerusalem is a turn to illegal construction. Thousands of housing units have been built without official permits by Palestinians since 1967. But this is done at considerable risk. For one thing, whereas much Israeli construction in the occupied territories is state-funded, Palestinians must fund their own construction out of their own pockets. The owners of an illegally built property can be punished and fined; their structures can be demolished.

Daoud Abu Kaf, for example, wanted to move out of his parents' crowded apartment (where ten people were sharing two rooms) in Ras al-

Amud, in East Jerusalem. Over a period of several years, beginning in 1982, he applied for building permits to build a house next door to his parents, on family property. All his applications were denied. In 1987, he started to build without a permit. He built two apartments. As he was completing construction, inspectors from the Ministry of the Interior showed up and ordered that the entire structure be demolished within twenty-four hours. Daoud appealed, and reached an agreement whereby he would be fined and only half the construction would be demolished. Before this agreement could take effect, however, the membership of the Planning and Building Committee, with which he had been negotiating, changed, and the new members—all Jewish Israelis—disapproved of the plan. A few months later the building (on which Daoud had spent over $100,000 of his own money) was demolished; he was fined several thousand dollars as well.

Yusuf Abu Hamad tells a similar story. He had been living with his wife and two children in one room of his brother's house in East Jerusalem. He owns five plots of land within the city but has been denied permits to build on any of them. In desperation, he started building without a permit in July 1994. As construction was nearing completion, in September, police vehicles and a bulldozer showed up at the site. Yusuf, who was there, demanded to see a demolition permit; the police said it wasn't necessary, and the house was destroyed the same day.

In 2004 alone, over 150 Palestinian homes in Jerusalem were demolished by Israeli authorities. There are today around 9,000 Palestinian homes that have been built illegally in Jerusalem, all of them subject to demolition.

The pace of home demolition in East Jerusalem is, however, less than that of home demolitions in the rest of the occupied territories. One of the measures that got much worse after the intensification of the occupation in response to the second intifada of 2000 was the Israeli policy of deliberate home demolition. Such demolition took a particularly heavy toll in Gaza. Half of the 5,000 Palestinian homes demolished by the Israeli army between 2000 and 2004 were in Gaza, leaving tens of thousands of Palestinians—already refugees—homeless all over again. Such demolitions would frequently take place at night, with the Israeli army suddenly descending on a neighborhood of sleeping families, and starting to bulldoze while men, women, and children, suddenly jolted out of their sleep, fled for their lives.

Mithqal Abu Taha, then a thirty-seven-year-old father of two young children, describes an Israeli army action in the Rafah refugee camp that took place in the middle of one July night in 2001:

> Around 12:40 A.M., I woke up to the sound of gunfire and shelling and the noise of bulldozers and tanks that we hear on a daily basis. We did not expect them to demolish houses in our area. Neither the Palestinian nor the Israeli side gave us any warning to vacate our houses. We thought that the bulldozers were on their way to some other place. We are used to leaving the houses when the gunfire and shelling intensifies. We would flee to safer areas in the camp and stay there until the situation calms down.
>
> Suddenly, one of the children screamed, "Get out, the Jews are demolishing the houses," and began to throw stones at the neighbors' doors to wake them up. He was sobbing and shouting. I was startled and went outside to see what [was happening]. I saw elderly people and women and men carrying their children, leaving their homes and going toward the northern part of the camp. I saw our neighbor Anwar Kalub, whose house is about two meters from the border, removing his children and his flock. Then I understood that they [the Israeli army] were demolishing the houses in our area.
>
> I rushed to wake up my three brothers and their wives and children, and we went outside without taking anything with us. About a half an hour later, one of my sisters-in-law yelled that she couldn't find her son, Hussein Abu Taha, 13. She began to scream: "My son is in the house." We couldn't get to the house because the gunfire was so intense. After a while, we saw him running toward us. I asked where he had been, and he said, "I was sleeping and when I awoke I saw that they were demolishing my uncle's house. I saw the tin roof fall." When the child fled from the house, a fragment struck him in the neck.

Jalal Abu Luz describes the aftermath of a similar round of demolitions, carried out in the spring of 2001, in which he and his family of eight lost their home:

> I was shocked at the destruction and devastation. I was hysterical, and began to cry and scream. I ran all around, but nobody was in the area. I went to where my wife and children were to make sure

they were all right, but nobody was in the house. I returned to the ruins of my house and sat on a pile of stones and dirt and started to cry again. People came to comfort me. My neighbors were also in shock. The women screamed and tried in vain to remove possessions from under the piles of stone. The sun was coming up. Thousands of residents, and also journalists, came to the site. My wife and children came home and saw that the house had turned into a pile of stones. My wife fainted, and the neighbors took her to the hospital. The children started to cry. I was still in shock and couldn't do anything, not even go to the hospital to be with my wife. My wife was treated and returned to the site about three hours later. My children, who had been wandering around among the thousands of people, came to sit with us on the pile of stones, and we all cried until one o'clock in the afternoon. Some neighbors felt bad about what had happened to us and brought us food. We ate while sitting on the pile of stones. We slept at a relative's house. We all stayed in one room and spent the whole night there. The next day, we returned to the ruins of our house and stayed there all day. For two days, the children did not go to school because all their books and notebooks were buried among the ruins. On Thursday afternoon [12 April], the Red Cross began to distribute tents and blankets to the residents. We received a tent and ten blankets. We put the tent on the stone pile. We sat in the tent throughout the day and at night went to sleep with my relative because we were afraid that the army would fire at the tent to prevent us from returning to live on the site. The next day, some good people came and gave every schoolchild a small bag with notebooks, colored pens, and a game. On Sunday, the Palestinian Ministry of Education gave all the children whose houses had been destroyed a bag and fifty dollars. My children went to school, but their behavior changed. They wet the beds at the relative's house, and screamed in their sleep because of their nightmares.

In an extensive 2004 report, Amnesty International points out that although the deliberate demolition of Palestinian homes is a long-standing Israeli policy, the scale of destruction reached an unprecedented level during the second intifada. "Tens of thousands of men, women and children have been made homeless or have lost their livelihood. Thousands of other houses have been damaged, and tens of thousands of others

are under threat of demolition, their occupants living in fear of homelessness," the Amnesty report notes. "The victims are often amongst the
poorest and most disadvantaged. In most cases the justification given by
the Israeli authorities for the destruction is 'military/security needs,' while
in other cases it is the lack of building permits. The result is the same:
families are left homeless and destitute, forced to rely on relatives, friends
and humanitarian organizations for shelter and subsistence." Israel's standard claim of military necessity does not stand up to scrutiny. "In the past
three and half years the Israeli army has carried out extensive destruction
of homes and properties throughout the West Bank and Gaza which is
not justified by military necessity," the report concludes. "Some of these
acts of destruction amount to grave breaches of the Fourth Geneva Convention and are war crimes."

Such demolitions are not restricted to Palestinian homes in Gaza. As is
the case in the West Bank as well, demolitions frequently target agricultural
land, razing trees, orchards, and whole crops to the ground. The Palestinian
Centre for Human Rights in Gaza has documented the deliberate destruction by the Israeli army of 20 percent of the agricultural land in the Gaza
Strip: uprooting of trees, bulldozing of crops, demolition of greenhouses.

Even if it has not been as extensive in East Jerusalem as in Gaza, the
Israeli policy of home demolition has had a significant impact on the
city's Palestinians. The occupation of East Jerusalem in 1967 was inaugu-
rated with the systematic demolition of some 150 Palestinian homes in
the area adjacent to the Western Wall of the Jewish temple, carried out in
order to clear space for Jewish pilgrims and tourists. And in early 2005,
the Jerusalem Municipality announced plans to demolish the houses of
up to a thousand Palestinians in the Silwan neighborhood. According to
Uri Shetrit, the city engineer, the houses were all built illegally. But he
wants them destroyed not merely because they are illegal (he concedes
that many other Palestinian homes were built illegally in East Jerusalem),
but rather because he wants to restore what Jews call the King's Valley to
its original state. "Kidron Stream and Hinnom Valley are of tremendous
historic and landscape importance," Shetrit argues; "I remember walking there 20 years ago and there were gardens and running water. I want
to return to that state." The first eviction orders have already been sent
out to the Palestinians of Silwan. If the demolition goes ahead, it will be
among the largest in Jerusalem since 1967.

OCCUPATION BY THE NUMBERS

- Number of Palestinian homes demolished by Israel in East Jerusalem, 2004–7: 305
- Number of Palestinians made homeless as a result: 958
- Number of West Bank homes demolished for being built without permit, 2006: 44
- Number of Palestinians made homeless as a result: 409
- Number of homes in occupied territories demolished for being built without permit, to 2007: 2,200
- Number of Palestinian homes demolished by Israel as punishment, 2000–2005: 668
- Percentage in which punished person was dead or in prison at time of punishment: 79
- Average number of innocent persons made homeless in each such case: 6
- Number of Gaza homes demolished by Israel, 2000-2004: 2,540
- Number of Palestinians made homeless as a result: 23,900
- Number of Palestinian homes demolished by Israel since 1967: 18,000
- Number of Palestinians stripped of Jerusalem residency, 1967–2006: 8,269
- Number in 2006 alone: 1,363

4

The combination of massive support for Jewish settlement in Jerusalem and severe restriction on Palestinian development has helped enable the Israeli government to maintain more or less its official desired ratio of Jews to non-Jews in Jerusalem ("more or less" because the officially sanctioned ratio has been shifting in favor of the non-Jews). Since 1967, 100,000 housing units have been built for Jewish settlers in East Jerusalem, with active Israeli government sponsorship. Over the same period, the Israeli government has sponsored just 500 units for Palestinians in the city. It has granted a further 9,000 permits for housing units for Jerusalem Palestinians. In other words, a third of the city's population has received 9 percent of the official housing permits.

In July 1993, the Israeli government was able to announce that it had at long last established a Jewish majority in East Jerusalem. By then there were 160,000 Jews and 155,000 Palestinians living in the eastern part of the city. The former mayor of Jerusalem, Teddy Kollek, became forthright in his assessment of Israeli planning principles in Jerusalem only after he left office. According to Kollek, Palestinians remain second- and third-class citizens in Jerusalem. In response to a questioner who said he thought Kollek had done a great deal for the Palestinians of Jerusalem, he replied, "Nonsense! Fairy tales! The mayor nurtured nothing and built nothing. For Jewish Jerusalem I did something in the past twenty-five years. For East Jerusalem? Nothing! What did I do? Nothing. Sidewalks? Nothing. Cultural institutions? Not one. Yes, we installed a sewerage system for them and improved the water supply. Do you know why? Do you think it was for their good, for their welfare? Forget it! There were some cases of cholera there, and the Jews were afraid they would catch it, so we installed sewerage and a water system [to protect] against cholera." To this day, the infrastructure of East Jerusalem is systematically underdeveloped relative to that of West Jerusalem. "The main problem in East Jerusalem is the vast gap in infrastructure between the East and West," admits Ehud Olmert, former mayor of Jerusalem (and currently prime minister of Israel); "the condition of infrastructure in most neighborhoods of [E]ast Jerusalem is terrible, and for the past thirty years, Israeli governments have done too little about it." Today the Jerusalem Municipality spends less than 10 percent of its total budget on East Jerusalem. In other words, it spends about six times as much on a Jewish resident of Jerusalem as it does on a Palestinian one.

A Week of Occupation: UN-OCHA Weekly Briefing, 29 November–5 December 2006

- 29 November: The IDF demolished three pit latrine units in Wadi Al Khalil region in Adh Dhahiriya (Hebron) for reportedly being built without permits.
- 29 November: The IDF demolished a Palestinian home in Al Baqa' village (Hebron) for reportedly being built without a permit.
- 29 November: The IDF demolished an uninhabited Palestinian

home in Wadi Al Samen region, (Hebron) for reportedly being built without a permit.

- 29 November: The IDF demolished two offices belonging to the Palestinian Petrol Authority located close to the Tarqumiya checkpoint (Hebron) for reportedly being built without permits.
- 30 November: The IDF demolished one Palestinian home under construction, two agricultural storage rooms and one scrap-metal shop in Qalqiliya city (Qalqiliya), for reportedly being built without permits.
- 30 November: The IDF demolished a Palestinian home (shelter for a family of six) in Wadi ar Rasha (Qalqiliya), for reportedly being built without a permit.
- 30 November: The IDF demolished two animal sheds in Wadi Qana (Qalqiliya), for reportedly being built without permits.
- 30 November: The IDF demolished two houses and a 100-m³ water cistern in Khallet Sakariya (Bethlehem) for reportedly being built without permits. The first house was home to a family of seven including five children. The second house was home to a family of eight, six of which are children.
- 2 December: The IDF demolished a 75-m³ water cistern in Wadi Abu Al Hasan neighbourhood in Al Khadr (Bethlehem) for reportedly being built without a permit.

5

Israel's quest to maintain a certain proportion of Jews to non-Jews in Jerusalem—and to separate East Jerusalem from the rest of the West Bank, to which it has historically been tied—begins at birth. For example, a Jewish baby born in Jerusalem (or for that matter in Israel or in Israeli settlements in the occupied territories) is automatically granted a birth certificate and a state identity number, which, like a U.S. Social Security number, is one of the keys to life in Israel. A Palestinian baby born in Jerusalem to a family in which only one of the parents is a Jerusalem resident, and the other a resident of the West Bank, is not automatically granted the same privilege. And Palestinian babies in the occupied territories are never granted the same rights as Jewish babies born in settlements on or next to their land (a Jewish child born in the West Bank, but in a Jewish settlement, is classified as an Israeli citizen by virtue of being Jewish, is entered on Israel's population registry, and is ultimately issued an Israeli, not a West Bank, identity card). If one of the Palestinian child's parents is a resident of Jerusalem rather than the West Bank, and the child is born in East Jerusalem, the parents will be given a "Notification of Live Birth," but neither an official birth certificate (a different document) nor an identity number. The parents can use the Notification of Live Birth to complete a secondary application for the child's birth certificate, but they will still not be granted an identity number. "Parents going to the Ministry to obtain a birth certificate and record the child's name in their identity cards are not always aware that the child does not have an identity number," a joint B'Tselem and HaMoked report points out. "[Interior] Ministry clerks do not inform them that they must initiate the process of registering the child, but rather issue a birth certificate without an identity number for the child. Only parents who themselves note that the child does not have an identity number submit a request to register the child." If they notice that the number is missing—and parents in the early sleep-deprived stages of family life are hardly the most astute readers of legal texts and official documents—they can apply for a number as a tertiary procedure. Any of these subsequent applications may require evidence that the family resides in Jerusalem and that Jerusalem is their "center of life," which, again, no Jewish family is ever asked to substantiate. If not all the documents are available or exactly up to the high Israeli standard of proof, not only will the child not be granted an identity number; the entire family could be expelled from Jerusalem.

Lacking an identity number has its consequences for babies just as much as for adults. The story of Hala Odeh is a case in point. In 1996 Hala, a Palestinian resident of Jerusalem, married Ahmad Odeh, a Palestinian with Jordanian citizenship. She submitted a request for family unification—an application for her family to live together as a family— but shortly after their wedding Ahmad was caught in Jerusalem without a permit (not always granted by the Israelis when a family unification case is pending, which can take years) and expelled to Jordan. Hala stayed behind in order to retain her ties to Jerusalem and to be able to give birth there. When her baby daughter was born, the Israeli Ministry of the Interior, following standard protocol, did not give her an identity number. A few weeks after the child's birth, Hala obtained an exit permit from the Israelis in order to visit her husband in Jordan so that he could see his baby for the first time. At the Allenby Bridge, the Israeli soldiers recorded Hala's daughter in her exit permit. When Hala and the baby attempted to return to Jerusalem a few days later, the Israeli soldiers at the bridge were willing to admit the mother but refused to admit the child. They said that since she lacks an Israeli identity number, the baby can only enter on a Jordanian passport. Hala returned to Amman to apply for a passport for her child. Her application was denied on the grounds that she is a resident of Jerusalem, not of Jordan. She tried once more to cross the bridge but was again denied permission by the Israeli soldiers to bring her baby with her. Three more months of applications and appeals went by, after which the Israelis finally let Hala and her daughter return to the city where they were both born.

In general, according to the Israeli human rights organization B'Tselem, requests for family unification submitted by Palestinian residents of East Jerusalem are either not processed by the Israeli authorities or they are processed very slowly. Until 1994, applications from Palestinian women resident in Jerusalem who married men from the West Bank or Gaza were summarily denied family unification papers. The Israelis claimed that this was out of respect for Arab tradition, in which, they said, women follow their husbands (which is not actually the case: according to Arab tradition, a woman's primary ties are always to the family in which she was born, which is why Arab women do not traditionally take their husbands' names—that is a peculiarly modern innovation). That particular restriction was eventually loosened, but others took its place. Until the blanket "closure" imposed on the occupied territories since 1993, Palestinian residents of the West Bank or Gaza married to residents of Jerusalem were allowed to stay in Jerusalem on temporary permits while their family unification appeals were considered. Such permits would be revoked automatically upon the imposition of any of the forms of closure routinely imposed on the occupied territories, and the families concerned would have to reapply for unification permits all over again after each such revocation. By the end of 1997, the Israeli Ministry of the Interior had a backlog of over 7,000 such applications. There are now over 100,000 (including family unification applications for the West Bank). Until 1997, if a couple won its appeal for family unification, the Ministry of the Interior would automatically grant permanent resident status to the spouse from the occupied territories. In early 1997, that changed, and the ministry announced that permanent residency status would be granted only after a further five-year waiting period—on top of the years already spent waiting for the application to be processed in the first place.

Things took a turn for the worse in 2003, when the Israeli parliament enacted a law which, on a renewable temporary basis, prohibits Palestinian residents of the occupied territories who are married to Israeli citizens or Jerusalem residents from acquiring Israeli citizenship or residency status; thus it denies them the right to live with their spouses and their children in Israel or Jerusalem. The law does not affect Jewish residents of the occupied territories (i.e., settlers), or immigrant Jewish spouses of Israeli citizens, who are eligible for instant citizenship under the Law of Return. It is only directed at Palestinian citizens of Israel or residents of Jerusalem. Up to 24,000 Palestinian families are affected by the new law, which has threatened marriages and destroyed families by forcing them apart.

The new law was prompted by the Israeli Population Administration's exaggerated claim that 140,000 Palestinians had entered Israel through family unification since 1993, which the state referred to as a "creeping right of return" that needed to be stopped at any cost. "All the data show that this phenomenon is not some innocent thing, but an attempt to realize the so-called right of return through the back door," said Eli Yishai, the minister of the interior in 2002; "clearly, there is a desire to significantly change the character of the state in many ways." The State of Israel, he added, "is a democratic Jewish state, which believes in humanitarian values of equality and human rights, but it is also a state that clearly has the elemental right to protect itself and preserve its character as a Jewish state, as the state of the Jewish people, against the desire and attempt to misuse its values and its democratic principles."

A similar law had been passed in South Africa at the peak of apartheid in 1980 and had been summarily rejected by that country's (white) supreme court, as an inappropriate and illegal interference with black people's right to marry and establish families. The Israeli law was extended in 2004, 2005, 2006, and 2007, and formally endorsed by Israel's High Court in May 2006.

Under the terms of the law, Palestinian residents of East Jerusalem, or citizens of Israel, married to residents of the occupied territories (or vice versa) must now live apart from their spouses. If the family tries to live in Israel or Jerusalem, it would be breaking the law because Palestinian residents of the occupied territories are not allowed inside Israel. If the family lives in any of the heavily populated parts of the West Bank or Gaza (Oslo's Area A), the Israeli spouse would be breaking the law because of Israeli military orders that prohibit Israeli citizens or residents from living in Area A. The law covers children as well as spouses: at the age of fourteen, the children of Jerusalem Palestinians whose birth was—for whatever reason, including the extreme difficulty of registering in East Jerusalem—registered in the West Bank have to apply for special military permits to go on living with their parents in Jerusalem. When they reach the age of eighteen, the children will have to leave their parents—or the parents will have to leave Jerusalem with their children.

At the age of sixteen, for example, Amal Abu Jawila was already counting the months remaining to her before the new law would force her away from her parents. Amal was born to Mirfat Abu Jawila, a native of Jerusalem who married a resident of Ramallah in 1988—a time when Ramallah was still an ordinary suburb. Four of their children, including Amal, were born, and registered, in Ramallah; another three girls were born in Jerusalem, where the family lives now. Such comings and goings are hardly unusual in most countries—it's normal for children to be born where their parents happen to be living or working. For Palestinians, however, they have enormous and lasting significance. Amal does not dare leave Jerusalem to visit family in the West Bank because she may not be able to return home. Soon, she will be living with her parents illegally; so will three of her siblings, now in their early teens. When they turn eighteen, the kids are supposed to move to the West Bank.

Yasser Abu Marir and his family tell a similar story. In June 1996, Yasser, a Palestinian resident of Jerusalem, married a resident of Yata, from the West Bank. They have three children. When they got married, Yasser submitted an application for family unification to the Israeli authorities so that his wife would be able to live with him. Every six months—for six years—he would check on the status of his application. Eventually, he found out that it had been denied. Since 2002, his wife has been living with him illegally. She used to visit her parents in the West Bank once a month or so. Since she doesn't have the appropriate ID card or a permit to reenter Jerusalem, she was taking a massive risk every time she did so. In July 2002, on one of those trips, she was arrested. Yasser had to plead with the Israeli border police to let her go home with him rather than deporting her. In the end, an Israeli officer let them off, but advised Yasser never to let his wife leave their house in Beit Safafa (East Jerusalem). Yasser recounts:

> Our situation is very bad. Since that day when my wife was stopped, which was about a year ago, she almost never leaves home. We do not leave the neighborhood. I take the kids out, while she stays imprisoned in Beit Safafa. Sometimes, she wants to join us, but the older children do not allow her to come along. They tell her, "Don't come because the army will take you again." Since the incident in Sur Baher, the children have been very frightened. Sometimes, a jeep comes by when they are playing outside the house, and they rush into the house and tell my wife to hide so that the army doesn't take her. Now I am waiting, and I hope that the situation improves and that our request for family unification is approved. My wife cannot return to Yata, because the children and I have Israeli ID cards, and we are not allowed to live with her. I want us to live like a normal family. I know other families that are living in the same horrible situation.

Yasser's story is not unique. When I was visiting Ramallah in the fall of 2004, I met a young Palestinian family. The husband is from Gaza. The wife is a Palestinian from Nazareth, inside what is today Israel, and is hence an Israeli citizen. Their son was born in Ramallah, in the West Bank. The husband and wife met when they were both studying at Birzeit University, near Ramallah, during the first intifada in the 1980s. Because of the endless closures and lockdowns imposed by the Israeli army on Palestinian universities (and on Palestinian life in general), it took them many years to complete their degrees. By that time, they had settled in Ramallah and started a family. Now, according to the dispensations of the Oslo Accords and various Israeli military orders, the only one of the three of them who can legally live in Ramallah is their son. The husband, who is from Gaza, is not supposed to be in the West Bank at all. The wife, who is an Israeli citizen, is not supposed to be in Ramallah because it is part of Area A. If the wife is ever stopped and asked for her ID by an Israeli soldier, she will be sent back to Nazareth. Because she has Israeli papers, she could for a while get back into the West Bank, though that changed in the summer of 2005: now getting in and out of Ramallah requires extensive documentation, like crossing an international frontier. In the meantime, if her husband is ever stopped at an Israeli checkpoint—he has not left Ramallah in years—his papers will be checked and he will be deported to Gaza, from which he will not be allowed to leave again. His wife and child will not be allowed into Gaza either; she because she is a resident of Israel; their child because he is a resident of the West Bank, not on the Gaza population registry. She could move to Israel, but neither her husband nor her son could move with her, because of the 2003 nationality law.

Under such circumstances, all the normal markers of inside, home life—the relationships of family members to each other, the legality of their existence as a family, the security of their most intimate domestic spaces—are undone.

6

If the immediate purpose of redrawing the Jerusalem city limits was to appropriate "a maximum of vacant space with a minimum of Arabs," as former Deputy Mayor Benvenisti says, the longer-term objective was ultimately to fill in those "vacant" spaces with new Jewish residents. For the Israelis did not just add land to East Jerusalem; they added people, covering much of the occupied territory with heavily subsidized housing for Jewish settlers whose residence here, as elsewhere in the West Bank, is forbidden by international law (as the International Court of Justice pointed out in its 2004 Advisory Opinion). Today there are dozens of Jewish settlements in the West Bank and East Jerusalem, with a combined total population of almost half a million; since they were geographically distributed in order to maximize Israel's territorial claims—in order to make it as difficult as possible to ever withdraw them—they now blanket the entire territory.

The settlement movement in the West Bank and East Jerusalem began slowly, but it accelerated quickly as it gained official government support. According to the Israeli architects and planners Eyal Weizman and Rafi Segal, the earliest phase of the settlement program, which was initiated during the Labor governments of 1967 to 1977, concentrated on the Jordan Valley and followed the principles of the 1967 Allon Plan (see "Outsides"). The colonization of the Jordan Valley was an integral part of Allon's vision. "We have never held territory," Allon insisted, "without settling it." The strategy here, according to the Israeli architect Thomas Leitersdorf, who planned the settlement of Ma'ale Adumim to the east of Jerusalem in the mid-1970s, "was to 'capture ground': you capture as much area as possible by placing few people on numerous hills," he explains. "The underlying political idea was that the further inside the Occupied Territories we placed settlers, the more territory Israel would have when the time came to set the permanent international borders [Israel has still not declared its borders]—because we were already there."

The second phase of settlement began in the mid-1970s and was spearheaded by the religious-nationalist settlers' movement Gush Emunim (Bloc of the Faithful); it accelerated after the right-wing Likud leader Menachem Begin came to power in 1977. Its emphasis was on the mountain ridge bisecting the West Bank, in and around the Palestinian cities there, and its guiding principles were outlined in the Drobles Plan of 1978, which would revise certain aspects of the Allon Plan. Allon had suggested avoiding settling areas of the West Bank densely inhabited by Palestinians, principally the mountain ridge and the fertile westward slopes, but "settlement throughout the whole Land of Israel is for security and by right," wrote Mattiyahu Drobles, the author of the new plan, which would guide Israeli government settlement policies through the 1980s and into the 1990s. "A belt of settlements in strategic locations increases both internal and external security," he added; "therefore, the

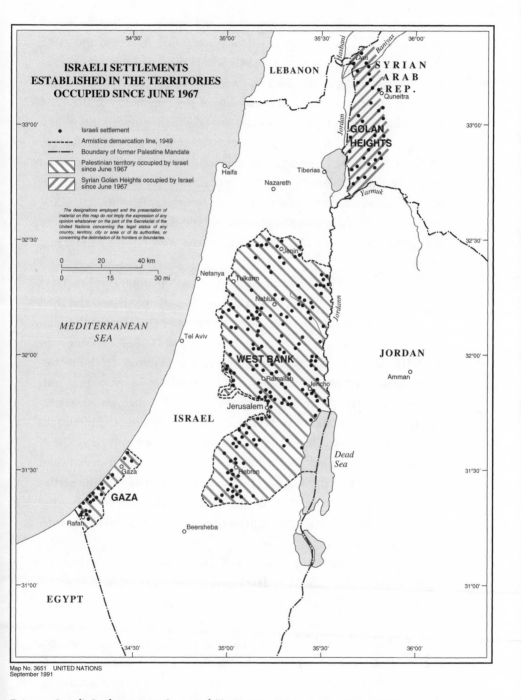

Primary Israeli Settlements in Occupied Territories, 1991. Courtesy United Nations
Cartographic Section.

proposed settlement blocs are spread out as a belt surrounding the mountains, starting along the western slopes from north to south, and along
the eastern slopes from south to north, within the minority population as
well as surrounding it." Drobles refers to the Palestinians as a "minority,"
even though they compose the majority of the population of the West
Bank. This suggests their new status—literally their minoritization—as a
disenfranchised group within a greater Israel that would surround them
on all sides. "Being bisected by Jewish settlements," Drobles explained
on a different occasion, "the minority population will find it hard to create unification and territorial contiguity." Jewish settlements, according
to Drobles, should thus be implanted in order to maximize damage to
the preexisting Palestinian communities of the West Bank, by squeezing
them ever inward.

Incorporating Drobles's suggestions, Israeli planning in the West
Bank has determined the location of Jewish settlements and the road
network linking them partly in order to maximize the damage they can
do to the development of Palestinian areas. Israel's 1980s Master Plan
for settlements in the West Bank points, for example, to the settlements installed along Road 60 as a way to contain "most of the Arab
population in the urban and rural communities," since Jewish settlement here "will create a psychological wedge regarding the mountain
ridge, and will also likely reduce the uncontrolled spread of Arab
settlement." Jewish settlements are often tightly wedged in between
Palestinian towns, confiscating land for the construction of the settlement, and land beyond that for future expansion or what the army
calls "security purposes," hence placing a physical limit on the growth
of the Palestinian areas.

Such physical limits are reinforced by the administrative and bureaucratic methods that Israel has developed to restrict the development of
Palestinian areas. In many cases, the lack of administrative and bureaucratic measures actually serves the same purpose as measures that
actively seek to restrict development. "Over the years, the main tool
used by Israel to restrict building by the Palestinian population outside
the borders of the municipalities was simply to refrain from planning,"
the Israeli human rights organization B'Tselem points out. Development in most of the West Bank (i.e., the entire territory other than

major Palestinian towns and cities and the various Jewish settlements) is still subject to the last regional planning and zoning documents— which were developed by the British in the 1940s. A recent B'Tselem report argues that those documents, which were already unreasonable and unresponsive to the needs of the Palestinian population in the 1940s, are even more so today. Most of the area of the West Bank, it notes, continues to be zoned as "agricultural areas" or "nature reserves," where development is prohibited. In the early 1990s, the Israelis developed localized plans for several hundred villages in the West Bank, but, by drawing demarcation lines along the already developed areas, they prohibited development in the villages' own outlying lands. Palestinian villages were supposed to develop inward rather than outward. Israeli military orders do specifically empower the army commander to appoint "special planning committees" with authority to develop planning on a local scale that could supersede the (dormant) regional plans. But, as B'Tselem points out, "not a single Palestinian village council has ever been defined as a special planning committee for the purpose of this law." Every Jewish settlement, on the other hand, has a special planning committee enabling it to develop and grow.

From the time of the Drobles Plan on, then, the Jewish settlements in the West Bank were conceived of not only in strategic terms (as Allon himself had already envisaged), but also as integral elements in Israel's tactical military control and surveillance of the Palestinian landscape. The settlements' private and domestic spaces were not simply oriented inward to meet Jewish families' needs; they were also oriented outward, and incorporated into Israeli military planning—in effect, turned inside out. "With respect to pure military considerations, there is no doubt that the presence of settlements, even if 'civilian,' of the occupying power in the occupied territory, substantially contributes to the security in that area and facilitates the execution of the duties of the military," noted Israeli High Court justice Alfred Vitkon, while arguing in favor of the legality of the settlement enterprise against the repeated indictments of international law. "One does not have to be an expert in military and security affairs to understand that terrorist elements operate more easily in an area populated only by an indifferent population or one that supports the enemy, as opposed to an area in which there are persons who are likely to observe them and inform the authorities about any suspicious movement. Among them no refuge, assistance or equipment will be provided to terrorists. The matter is simple, and details are unnecessary."

Jewish homes in the West Bank voluntarily sacrifice their "inside" innocence as elements in the "outside" strategic and tactical control of occupied territory: as the Israeli architects Eyal Weizman and Rafi Segal point out, that sacrifice is literally built into their design from the inside out. The Israeli Ministry of Construction and Housing's 1984 guideline for settlement construction, for example, recommends building homes along the West Bank's mountain ridge in order to maximize the outward view of the surrounding landscape, while orienting inward views toward the settlement's inner core, with concentric rings surrounding each mountain peak. "With respect to the interior of each building, the guideline recommends the orientation of the bedrooms towards the inner public spaces, and that of the living rooms towards the distant view," Weizman and Segal explain. "Vision dictated the discipline of design and its methodologies on all scales. Regionally, a strategic function was integrated into the distribution of settlements around the entire territory, creating a 'network of observation' that overlooks the main traffic arteries of the West Bank; topographically, it was integrated into the siting of the settlements on [mountain] summits; urbanistically it was integrated into their very layout, as rings around the summit, and in the positioning of homes perpendicular to the slope; architecturally, it was integrated into the arrangements and orientation of rooms, and finally into the precise positioning of windows."

For Drobles and Vitkon, then, a Jewish home in the West Bank serves not merely as a family's inner and domestic space, but as a key unit of police surveillance and state control. "What becomes evident is that by placing settlers across the landscape, the Israeli government is not merely utilizing the agencies of state power and control, namely, the police and army, for the administration of power, but that it 'drafts' the civilian population to inspect, control and subdue the Palestinian population," argue Weizman and Segal. "The desire for a single family home is being mobilized to serve the quest for military domination, while an act of domesticity, shrouded in the cosmetic façade of red tiles and green lawns, provides visual territorial control." Ordinary houses and homes have lost their banality in serving what is according to international law an illegitimate political and territorial project.

In return, Jewish families moving into the network of settlements in and around East Jerusalem and the West Bank are offered more than merely views over pastoral landscapes. Most of the West Bank settlements are classified as priority development areas by the Israeli government, and, depending on the class of priority they are assigned to, residents are eligible for a generous package of benefits and tax breaks provided by six government ministries. Per capita financial support by the central government to local authorities in the Jewish settlements is much higher than the support it offers to towns inside Israel itself; general government grants averaged NIS 2,224 ($528) per resident of the settlements in 2000, for example, compared to an average of NIS 1,336 ($317) per resident for local councils inside Israel.

The main incentive for residents of the East Jerusalem settlements is probably the ability to live within easy distance of the city, and at the heavily defended inner core of the entire settlement program. There are

Jewish settlement of Gilo, near Bethlehem and Jerusalem. Photo by author.

now twelve settlements inside the expanded municipal borders of Jerusalem, with a combined population approaching a quarter of a million: Neve Yaqov, Pisgat Ze'ev, French Hill, Ramat Eshkol, Ma'alot Dafna, Ramot Alon, Ramat Shlomo, the Jewish settlement in the Old City, East Talpiot, Givat Hamatos, Har Homa, and Gilo. Three or four of these settlements abut Israel; all the others are wedged into, or in between, existing Palestinian neighborhoods, or in between Arab Jerusalem and Palestinian towns and cities with ancient commercial, cultural, and familial ties to Jerusalem.

The settlement of Har Homa, for example, was initiated in 1991, close to the time of the beginning of the peace process launched at the Madrid conference that year. It was established on land the Palestinians call Jabal Abu Ghneim, or Mount Abu Ghneim, which lies just north of Bethlehem. It is from here that the Three Wise Men are supposed to have seen the star over Bethlehem signaling the birth of Jesus. Although the land here belongs to Palestinian families from Bethlehem and neighboring Beit Sahour, and once served as an obvious land reserve to accommodate future growth of those immediately adjacent towns, it was precisely the sort of area—Arab land without Arabs—that Israeli planners were look-

Har Homa, on Jabal Abu Ghneim. Photo by author.

ing for as they expanded the municipal borders of Jerusalem after 1967. For more than two decades following its incorporation into Jerusalem, Jabal Abu Ghneim was left alone as what the Israelis classified as a Green Area (that is, Palestinians were not allowed to use it, and Israelis had not yet established plans for it).

In 1991, the Israeli minister of finance ordered the expropriation of Jabal Abu Ghneim under one of the provisions of a British land law of 1943, which allows for the expropriation of private property for "public use." Since neither Israeli Palestinians nor Palestinians from the occupied territories—including the original owners of the land—are counted as part of the "public" to be thus served, "public use" in such instances actually means Jewish settlement. The Israeli planning scheme for Har Homa calls for the establishment of thousands of housing units as well as schools, shops, hotels, tourist attractions, and the infrastructure associated with them. These housing units are off-limits to Palestinians, but they will eventually house up to 30,000 Jewish residents.

7

In their own references to themselves, some of the inhabitants of the Jewish settlements in the occupied territories, as well as the organizations supporting them, go out of their way to emphasize their banal, domestic, inside-oriented ordinariness. "Har Homa is Jerusalem's fastest growing community since 'opening' in January 2002," proclaims Tehilla, an Israeli organization that helps new Jewish immigrants to find a home in Israel (and the occupied territories, though that's not how it refers to them):

> All the staples you need: health services, supermarket (with many American foods), pizza, and falafel stores plus regular bus service throughout the day are easily available. Residents are friendly and eager to welcome newcomers. Sitting atop a mountain overlooking Ramat Rachel and Bethlehem, we enjoy breathtaking views and breathe fresh mountain air daily. There are playgrounds and

greenery scattered throughout and many more on the way. All the homes are new and more are planned to meet the growing demand. Being in Jerusalem means you have top schools at your doorstep, as well as outstanding shopping. Youth activities are overwhelming: at least once a week there is either an event from the school or the community. There are tons of *chesed* [welfare based on Jewish religious principles] committees with new *gmachim* [charities, also based on Jewish religious principles] forming all the time. The bottom line—Har Homa is a warm, affordable community right at Jerusalem's doorstep.

There is no way to gather from this that Har Homa is a colony established in violation of international law on land violently expropriated from its rightful owners in a militarily occupied territory. Nor would one glean the same reality from reading, in May 2007, the RE/MAX Real Estate Web site listing homes for sale in French Hill ("a quiet tree-lined neighborhood") or Ramat Eshkol ("a bustling microcosm of Jerusalem as a whole"), other settlements built in East Jerusalem; nor from the sales brochure distributed in Brooklyn to attract interest in the settlement of Emanuel (which, according to the brochure, "has a magnificent view of the coastal plain and the Judean Mountains," over a "hilly landscape" that is "dotted by green olive orchards and enjoys a pastoral calm"); nor from perusing an advertisement that was circulated in various American Jewish communities in early 2007 inviting American Jews to "come learn how you can own a house and provide growth of the Zionist dream in Jewish communities." One of the settlements included in that real estate promotion is Eli, which, according to the Web site of the settlers' organization Amana (which sponsored the sale), "is located at the center of Israel, 40 minutes from Gush Dan and 30 minutes away from Jerusalem." Eli is not in the center of Israel—in fact, it's not in Israel at all: it is a colony in the northern West Bank. "Quality of life is not a vague concept at Eli," the Web site continues:

The cultivated gardens, the breath-taking mountain views, life in the shade of olive trees, the well-kept regional sports center, which includes multi-purpose playing fields, a tennis court, a work-out facility and swimming pool, place Eli at the front rank of residential areas in the Shomron [northern West Bank] from the aspect of the quality of life it offers its residents. Eli provides full community services, including health services, Ministry of the Interior, National Insurance, "Lev Eli" shopping center, including shopping mall, post office, clinic and other business enterprises. Synagogues and ritual baths are scattered around the neighborhoods. This is the time to come and visit Eli, inhale the mountain air and enjoy the beauty of the countryside. This is the time to join in and build a new city in Israel. Suddenly you will discover that you, too, can realize a dream—in an expedited process and on the best purchasing terms in the country!! Call the Housing Department to coordinate a tour.

The glib commercialism of such statements makes it difficult to appreciate their enormous political significance, or that of the Jewish settlement program in general. But the mundanities of the settlers' everyday lives—their grocery shopping, their eating patterns, their commutes to and from jobs in Tel Aviv, their gardening preferences, their leisure activities, even their toilet habits—have all been mobilized as parts of the occupation policy.

This mobilization is also conveyed in the accounts of the Jewish settlers themselves, who, particularly in their appeals for reinforcements directed to Jewish communities outside of Israel and the occupied territories, tend to mix the intimately personal and the violently political without seeming to be aware of the collapse of these two ordinarily distinct categories. "Let me indroduce [sic] ourselves," writes one British Jewish settler from the West Bank colony of Eli:

My name is Tovah and my husband's name is Bram. We have 7 children and 15 Grandchildren. We made Aliyah [i.e., immigrated to Israel under the Law of Return] 21 years ago from England and after 1 year in the Merkaz Klita [absorption center] we moved to Moshav Mattityahu as part of a "Garin" (founder members) of the very remote and unfinished Moshav [agricultural settlement]. We now live in Eli and our married children are in the main living in the yeshuvim [settlements]. We have two married daughters who live in Bet El, where it was also our home for ten years. Our oldest daughter lives in Dolev, a beautifull [sic] yishuv situated between Ramallah and Modiin. Our oldest son lives in Petach Tichva [a city

inside Israel]. Altho' he is very much a "Yeshuvnic," he married a
city girl, so he's stuck with the exhaust fumes and shopping malls!!
We have 3 children all Sabras [i.e., born in Israel or the occupied
territories], still "at home." Our son of 21 is in the army, serving
in an elite unit. Which does most of it's [sic] work in and around
the Arab towns and villages in the Shomron seeking out the terrorists! Our youngest son is 17 and learns in an excellent Yeshiva
[religious school] in Meron. He has to travel many kilometers back
and forth most weeks, but reckons its [sic] worth it. Our youngest is
16 and she is "sorting herself out" in a school in Kedumim. Which
was, by the way, the first yeshuv to be established in the Shomron.
You may think that we're a couple of old "fuddy duddies" having so
many Grandchildren, but I can assure you that we are not. We still
work very hard in our own computer business, which is situated in
Eli, our offices are "at home" and we travel "thru'out" the Shomrom
[sic] selling and servicing computers to private individuals, offices,
yeshivas and schools within the Yeshuvim [settlements]. Last week
Bram was offered a "bullet proof" vehicle by Yeshuv Ganin to go
and deliver a computer that they had ordered. He did accept the
offer as Ganin is very close to Jenin, notorious for housing terrorists.
We believe our task in life is to continue as near as normal so that
Arafat and his cronies don't succeed in their mission. We normally
travel with anti-stone windows!! We moved to Eli about 18 months
ago from Bet El. We loved the open spaces of Eli, which is spread
out over seven hills!! From our salon windows we look out over Kfar
Tapuach, the home of Rav Binyamin and Talyah Kahana, who were
murdered by terrorists just over 12 months ago. We look out over to
Male [sic] Lavonah, where our friend Eric and his family live. (We
met Eric and his scotch cap, a long time ago!!) We look out to Ariel,
Yitzar, Male [sic] Ephraim, Shilo and Shvut Rachel and last but not
least Rachalim, a small Yeshuv named after a lady who was also killed
by terrorist gunfire several years ago. There are many activities in
the Yeshuv of Eli, as well as a gorgeous swimming pool, a very well
equipped gym, a well stocked general store, post office, health clinics
etc. We are about 45–50 minutes from Jerusalem. Even closer to the
big shopping malls of Petach Tikvah. There is a Yeshiva (Mechina)
which prepares it's [sic] Talmidim for the Army. Many Betei Knesset
[synagogues] to serve all different kinds in the community. Eli is one

of the most beautiful places that I've ever been to. Where all the neat houses are perched on top of hills, with panoramic views. One feels like they are living on top of the world! Anyone who may be interested in coming to Eli to visit, or chat are more than welcome to mail or phone.

The Jewish experience of the West Bank is premised on the ease of connection and communication not only within the territory, but to the outside world as well, both of which are denied to Palestinians. What constitutes the essence of home—and even the very language of domestic space and homeliness—is recognizably different for Jewish settlers like Tovah than for Palestinians like Samira Aliyan.

When one of the earliest convoys of would-be settlers set out, on 5 June 1974 ("in a mood of extraordinary elation," according to Benny Katzover, one of the participants), for the hills overlooking Nablus in the Northern West Bank, aiming to establish the settlement of Elon Moreh, they carried with them tents, tools, and a library of religious books—but also kitchen equipment, a seesaw, and a playground slide for the children that accompanied them. The Elon Moreh colonists, who were Jewish fundamentalists acting in the name of their God, had the active support of secular politicians like Ariel Sharon, but they lacked the official support of the Labor government at the time, which even made a halfhearted effort to stop them. The defense minister at the time, Shimon Peres, said that he "identified with goals of the group's members," but felt unable to officially bless their plan. "This is a government of settlement," Peres explained, "but it has an earlier and a later."

The government did not oppose settlement, then; rather, it wanted to determine the pace and scale of the enterprise. But, although the Labor government, too, would quickly become a major participant in the enterprise (it was, for example, during the first Rabin premiership in the early 1970s that Yitzhak Rabin and Shimon Peres played an active role in developing, among others, the colony of Ma'ale Adumim, which today serves to sever the northern from the southern West Bank). But in terms of timing, its hand was forced by activists like those of Elon Moreh and their supporters inside the Labor party and outside it. "Our visa to Judea and Samaria [i.e., the West Bank] is that they are Judea and Samaria and we are the people of Israel," declared General Moshe

Dayan from firmly within the Israeli mainstream, shortly after the 1967 war. "The mountains of Samaria are ours and we will no longer leave them in the hands of any other nation," the settler activists pledged; "the government has no right to prevent individuals and groups from living in any place on the soil of the homeland." Thus, as the Israeli author Gershom Gorenberg points out in his history of the settlement movement, the assertion of one people's claim to a home was premised on the negation of another's: "their demand for liberated [i.e., conquered] land meant erasing the rights of another group, which was not unusual, except that they could see the people they hoped to disinherit," Gorenberg writes. "It was the small difference between a city meat-eater and a farm one who has seen the blood."

Although the language of commercialism, tourism, or homeliness is often used to convey the ideals of the settlement enterprise to its supporters and potential new recruits, it is not the only form of expression available to convey the new sense of home that was made available by the colonization of the occupied territories. And although some Israeli government officials (namely, Rabin and Peres) officially sought to distance themselves from the language of the Whole Land of Israel Movement (WLIM)—or similar, more explicitly religious movements, such as Gush Emunim—the urge to settle the occupied territories grew straight out of the mainstream Labor party. The WLIM's founding statement in 1967 was, for example, strongly supported by prominent members of the Labor party establishment. Like the call to arms of the Gush Emunim, the WLIM's manifesto explicitly based the Jewish right to call the occupied territories home on the negation of the same right for Palestinians.

For its part, the Gush Emunim regards the very idea of Arab residence in Palestine as a form of theft. As the Palestinian historian Nur Masalha points out, the expulsion of the Palestinians follows logically. One of the spiritual leaders of the Gush Emunim, Rabbi Yisrael Ariel, conveys this point in an article that appeared in Hebrew in 1980. "Every young student understands that [the Talmudic imperatives of] 'inheritance and residence' means conquering and settling the land," he writes. "The Torah repeats the commandment 'You shall dispossess all the inhabitants of the land tens of times,' and Rashi [an eleventh-century Talmudic scholar] explains that 'You shall dispossess—You shall expel.' " The substance of the commandment "is to expel the inhabitants of the land whoever they may be," Ariel concludes. "Thus according to Rashi the commandment to settle aims at the expulsion of the non-Jew from Eretz-Yisrael and that it be settled with Jews."

In expressing the ideal of settlement in such stridently religious terms, Ariel speaks for a minority of Israelis. But the general principle he evokes has never been very far from the mainstream of secular Israeli politics. "Hundreds of thousands of Arabs are living in the liberated territory," wrote Tzvi Shiloah, a veteran of the dominant Mapai party (one of the precursors of today's Labor party) and chairman of the WLIM, in the daily newspaper *Davar* shortly after the 1967 War. "The inclusion of this hostile population within the boundaries of the State of Israel is considered as a time bomb in the heart of the state," he added; "leaving them in these territories endangers the state and its national Jewish character," he concluded. "The only solution is to organize their emigration and settlement in Arab countries abundant in land and water such as Syria and Iraq." His sentiments were echoed by Eliezer Livneh, another Mapai party activist, writing in the mass circulation Israeli daily *Ma'ariv*. "They will choose, willingly, resettlement in whatever Arab country, or emigration to countries overseas," Livneh wrote confidently; "the Prime Minister of Australia has already suggested cooperation." Dr. Dov Yosefi, a self-styled demographic expert, agreed. "If we want to prevent mutual and continuous bloodshed, there is only one solution—the transfer of the Arab population of the Land of Israel to Arab states," he wrote. "True, this is a little painful (who knows this like us the Jews), but it is inevitable and preferable than cumulative poisoning which undermines the whole body."

Such sentiments were first expressed, with reference to the West Bank, Gaza, and East Jerusalem, shortly after the territories were captured in 1967, but they have been consistently reiterated ever since by politicians both within and without the Israeli mainstream. Deputy Foreign Minister Benjamin Netanyahu, for example, expressed his regrets to an audience at Bar-Ilan University in 1989 that the Israeli government had failed to exploit moments of international crisis and distraction (such as that year's Tiananmen Square massacre) to carry out "large scale" expulsions at a time when "the danger would have been relatively small." And policies of expulsion or transfer are the publicly declared objectives of leading Israeli political parties to this day, most notably the party of Deputy Prime Minister Avigdor Lieberman, Yisrael Beiteinu, or "Israel Is Our Home."

Today the antagonistic relationship between Jewish and Palestinian "insides," or in other words the double process of Jewish settlement and Palestinian unsettlement, is played out on an intimately small scale, and on a daily basis, throughout the West Bank. Palestinian communities such as Jinba and Twaneh, for example, which are home to thousands of herders and farmers in the hills south of Hebron, have been facing the threat of total expulsion for years. There are several Jewish settlements in the immediate vicinity, and the settlers want the local Palestinians removed. The Palestinians, who subsist on small-scale agriculture and herding and live in tents and in the region's warren of natural caves, have been subjected to a campaign of intimidation and harassment by both the settlers and the Israeli army. In 1999 and 2000, Israeli army bulldozers were sent in to destroy their tents and to block cave entrances with earth and boulders, as well as to fill in the Palestinians' water wells; only an emergency appeal stopped them from destroying the entire community. Since then, a series of court cases has suspended the army's actions.

Irrespective of the state's own official position, however, the settlers themselves have kept up the pressure on the local Palestinian population. Jewish settlers in the West Bank are heavily armed, and can act on their own volition, knowing that Israeli police generally turn a blind eye to their actions, and that the Israeli army will not step in to defend Palestinian civilians from settler vigilantism. Palestinian civilians are essentially defenseless against settler attack when it happens, and they have virtually no legal recourse after the fact. "Israeli security forces [make] few attempts to prevent settler violence or arrest offenders," notes B'Tselem. "Many acts of violence [are] not investigated, and in other cases, the investigations [are] prolonged and [have] resulted in no action being taken against anyone. In cases where settlers [are] tried and convicted, they [are] generally given extremely light sentences." This is partly because of the dual system of laws in the occupied territories: the Jewish population enjoys the benefits and protections of Israeli civil law, but the Palestinian population is governed by the much harsher system of Israeli military regulations; settlers are subject to the police (who rarely intervene), Palestinians to the army.

Denied the protection and care of the state which, as the territory's occupying power, bears responsibility for their well-being under international law, beleaguered Palestinian communities are given aid and support by a number of local and international organizations, including Ta'ayush, a peace and solidarity movement bringing together Israelis and Palestinians against the occupation. Ta'ayush (which means "coexistence" in Arabic) has organized protests and demonstrations, and has persistently brought aid and vital supplies to besieged Palestinian populations, braving Israeli police and army barricades, and the bullets, clubs, stones, and fists of the settlers who get especially enraged at the sight of fellow Jews coming to the aid of the Arabs. One of the missions of Ta'ayush, in fact, is to remind the settlers and the rest of the world that there is another side to Judaism than that presented by the settlers.

In his recent book *Dark Hope: Working for Peace in Israel and Palestine*, the Israeli academic and author David Shulman, a member of Ta'ayush, recounts his participation in efforts to bring blankets and other supplies to the families of herders south of Hebron, in the face of often brutal opposition by Jewish settlers. On one occasion, while the volunteers are helping sow barley, they come under attack from a nearby settlement. "These are young men who have found a way, and a reason, to unleash their hatred without check or restraint. They come pouring down the hillside, screaming furiously, some of them shooting short bursts in our direction," Shulman writes:

> Ezra [one of the Israeli Ta'ayush volunteers], who seems almost to relish this moment, cries out to us: "Don't be afraid. Stand your ground." But already the Palestinians are giving way, retreating before the onslaught of shots and stones. By now the settlers are upon us, all in their twenties or so, with long embroidered skullcaps and tzitzit fringes and guns: "You should be ashamed," they scream at us. "What kind of Jews are you?" Helpless, angry, I yell back: "I am a Jew. That's why I am here." And so on, pitting my useless, wishful words against their stones. They seem to hear me and to become yet more enraged, and now one of them hits out at me suddenly,

hard, hurls me to the ground. Brown soggy soil covers my fingers, my knees, my right eyebrow; my right hand is badly scraped and bleeding. He punches me a few more times before moving on to his next target, before I can respond. I feel pain, surprise, fear, rage. What is worse, I have seen their faces up close, and it is perhaps the most unsettling vision I have ever taken in, one I will later try to blot out, for these are not the faces of the usual human mix of good and evil, of confusion and clarity, of love and hate; the eyes are mad, killers' eyes—it is like looking at something utterly demonic, something from the world of myth.

Recovering at home in Jerusalem after a similar incident on a different occasion, Shulman reflects on what it is that he and his Israeli and Palestinian friends in Ta'ayush are confronting in such moments. "What we are fighting in the South Hebron Hills is pure, rarefied, unadulterated, unreasoning, uncontainable human evil," he writes. "Nothing but malice drives this campaign to uproot the few thousand cave dwellers with their babies and their lambs. They have hurt nobody. They were never a security threat. They led peaceful, if somewhat impoverished lives, until the settlers came. Since then, there has been no peace. They are tormented, terrified, incredulous. As am I," he adds. "What black greed, what unwitting hatred, has turned Israeli Jews into torturers of the innocent? The settlers come first, violent and cruel—but above them is a vast, ramified system, official Israel, that sustains them and protects them, that corrupts our minds and our language, God's language, with vile rationalizations."

On 29 October 2007, the Israeli army finally succeeded in eliminating one of the communities of Palestinian cave- and tent-dwellers (refugees who had been expelled from their homes in the village of Beit Jibrin in 1948) near Hebron. According to B'Tselem, soldiers in jeeps and bulldozers began to demolish the tents and caves without giving the residents leave to remove their possessions or even their flocks. "The army loaded the water containers and feeding troughs onto a truck and deposited them beyond the Barrier. Much of the residents' property was crushed and buried among the ruins. After the army's action, the officer told the residents that they had to leave the site by noon the next day, and that they would be arrested and their livestock confiscated if they did not obey. The following afternoon, patrols of the Nature Reserves and Parks Authority came and forced the residents to leave. Most of the residents are now homeless and have had to find temporary housing in the nearby town of Idhna."

8

Nowhere is the vulnerability of Palestinian inner spaces more visible than in the city of Hebron, the largest city in the southern West Bank, and, other than East Jerusalem, the only one with an active Jewish settler presence inside city limits. The Jewish settlers of Hebron have made life virtually impossible for the city's Palestinian population; again, the settlers are heavily defended by a formidable Israeli army and police presence (10 soldiers for every settler), whereas the city's Palestinians have no defenses and no real legal protection from settler intrusions.

This reality was vividly captured on a widely circulated amateur video (available on YouTube), which was entirely shot in the doorway of a Palestinian home that opens onto a street leading to the Jewish settlement of Tel Rumeida, inside Hebron. No Palestinian can drive here: only Jewish traffic is permitted. The Palestinian family was obliged to build a wire cage to protect the home's doors and windows. The video shows a Palestinian mother anxiously waiting for the return of her kids from school. She is standing outside her doorway, but inside the protective cage. The settler boys playing in the street start pelting her with stones, but the cage protects her; the stones bounce and ricochet off the wire. Israeli soldiers stationed here call out to the boys to stop. They don't. One soldier reaches out to one of the boys, pulls him back. The other boys move to either side of the soldier, continuing the stoning. The soldier reaches out to another boy. Again, the other kids move apart, and continue lazily chucking stones. There's no way for one man to control all these kids. A settler woman approaches the cage door and pushes it open. The Palestinian woman starts screaming at her, telling her to back away. The soldier looks on helplessly. The Jewish woman withdraws, but puts her face up to the wire of the cage and, cupping her hands, moans out softly, with her Hebrew-accented Arabic, "*Shaghmouta . . . Shaghmouta.*" (*Sharmouta:* "whore" in Arabic). The Palestinian woman has to face this kind of abuse every time she steps outside the door of her home.

Another scene, in the same neighborhood, on a different day. This, too, was captured on film, but this time by professionals rather than amateurs: a British film crew is visiting to record what life is like for the Palestinians of Hebron. As the crew enters the property of a Palestinian family, they are accosted by two settlers, who, approaching them, start heaping verbal abuse at the British cameramen, who tell them that they can't come in, that it's not their house. "We killed Jesus, and we're proud of it," one of the settlers retorts in English, albeit while backing away; "this is our land, you get the fuck out of here . . . this is my land, you fuck!" Whether out of bravery or folly, the British cameraman shouts back, "This is not your land, it belongs to these families." Still backing away into the Palestinians' olive grove, the settler continues: "We're going to kill you and the Palestinians, you . . . you Nazi! You son of a shit! This is my house, this is my land, God gave it to me—and fuck you!"

The Israeli journalist Gideon Levy says that a visit to Tel Rumeida ought to be made mandatory for every Israeli schoolchild. "Here is where Israeli schoolchildren should be shown the dark side of their country, their state's violent and law-flouting backyard," he writes. "A military barracks under whose cover exists the purest evil that the settlers inflict on their neighbors. There is no other neighborhood like this one. Not a day passes without violence, not an hour passes without the throwing of stones, garbage and feces at the frightened neighbors cowering in their barricaded houses, afraid even to peek out the window. Neighbors whose way home is always a path of torment and anxiety. All this is happening right under the noses of the soldiers and police, representatives of the legal authorities, who merely stand by."

The most remarkable thing, perhaps, is that Hebron is a city with a population of 130,000 indigenous Palestinians—and only around 500 Jewish settlers. A third of a percent of the population of the city effectively dominates the whole.

Much of the abuse directed at the Palestinians of Hebron is intended to loosen their grip on their own land and homes, and ultimately to force them to go away. Najah D'ana, for example, lives in a small house in

Hebron on a four-acre lot some 65 feet from the settlement of Kiryat Arba (which is on the outskirts of the city). Part of the family's farmland was expropriated in 1979 and given to the settlers, who built a parking lot on it. The remaining land is taken up by a century-old olive grove as well as an orchard of fig and peach trees. During the tightening of the occupation in 2002, Israeli soldiers entered the land and cut down a hundred large olive trees, the source of the family's livelihood. They then erected a watchtower on the adjacent land. The newly created open space has given an opportunity for the settlers of Kiryat Arba to increase their harassment of neighboring Palestinian families. "They throw stones at the houses, shatter windows, chase after children, beat them with clubs and strike them with stones, aim their rifles at the children, and damage land and trees," says Najah. "In mid-June [2002], a group of settlers from Kiryat Arba cut the fence separating our land from Kiryat Arba and took control of three to four dunums [about an acre] of our land," he adds. "They put up a fence between us, erected tents and huts, furnished them with things like cabinets, chairs and tables, and put up Israeli flags. They settled permanently on the land, and a number of them keep guard over the area. About fifty settlers, among them women and children, go there daily. On the Sabbath, dozens of settlers come to worship there."

The violent harassment of Palestinians intrudes directly into their homes. Maryam al-Natsheh, a mother of six children, recalls an incident when Israelis from a nearby settlement crept into her house in Hebron:

> I was at home, cooking, when I heard a noise and the sound of the door being pushed open. I went out of the room to see who pushed the door open. My sons, nine-year-old Falah and eight-year-old Ahmad, went ahead of me. As soon as I was out of the room, I saw an old settler with a gray beard. He was tall and fat. He was armed and held a knife in one hand and a large stone in the other. The settler ran up the stairs, and more than ten other settlers, also older, ran after him. When the first settler saw me, he threw the stone he'd been holding in his hand at me. The distance between us was about one meter. I ran back into the room, shouting "Settlers! Settlers!" hoping that the neighbors would hear me and come to help. I thought that all my children were inside the room. When I

discovered that my sons Ahmad and Falah were not there, I thought that they might have been with my sister in the kitchen. I opened a crack in the door, looked, and saw two settlers beating my son Falah. One was lifting him by the ears and the other was punching him. I couldn't take it. I thought that the settlers would kill my son. I decided to defend him myself and pushed my four younger children to the back of the room. I then took a pair of scissors and decided to go out and attack the settlers who had already walked down the stairs toward the door. It seemed that the last settler saw me come out of the room and fired a bullet from his gun. I later found the shell near the door. My husband, who had been sleeping in a room on a higher floor, woke up and saw the settlers beating his son Falah. He retreated, went to the roof and began shouting, "Settlers are attacking us!" When I went back to the room, Falah was still lying on the ground unconscious. I looked for my other son, Ahmad, and found him standing inside the room, with his back bleeding. I thought he must have been shot by the settlers, but as I held him, looked and cleaned the blood from his shirt, I realized that he had been stabbed, not shot. He was still bleeding and I brought his father's clothing and wrapped him with it. The clothing was covered in blood. I thought that my son was about to die. I couldn't move. I just cried.

Maryam's sons survived the attack, though Ahmad had to be hospitalized for a few days. Such house intrusions are all too common among the Palestinian homes near the Jewish settlements in Hebron, which can grow only by intimidating Palestinians into leaving. Fadel al-Samuh lives with his wife and four children in a small house at the edge of the settlement in Beit Hadassah, near the old city. He recalls one time when settlers broke into his house in the middle of the night, during a curfew:

I was woken by loud shouts around my house between 2:30 and 3:00 A.M. My wife and children were also woken up. My children (the eldest is eleven years old) began to cry and asked me to hurry out of the house. I tried to calm them down saying that we didn't have anywhere to go and there was curfew. I took them to an inner room and looked out through the window of the living room. The lights inside were off. From where I was sitting, I could see more than 150 young settlers (both men and women between the ages of twenty and thirty). I also saw about twenty soldiers. They had already jumped onto the balconies of my house and the roof. The settlers came to the window of the room where I was sitting and smashed the glass with iron bars. At the same time, they threw stones [through] the other window. I heard the water tanks falling into the street. There was a loud noise from below. I thought the settlers on the roof had destroyed the tanks and dropped them into the street. I asked my wife, who was watching the children in the next room, to keep quiet and make sure the children don't make a sound so the settlers wouldn't know that they were here. They did keep quiet but they were scared and sat close to the wall. The attack lasted about an hour. Some of the settlers tried to force open the metal door with their iron bars, but they failed. When I went out in the morning, I saw seven water tanks and a satellite dish lying in the street. On the roof, there were five or six more water tanks and another satellite dish, all of them broken and destroyed. They belonged to my neighbors and me. We have had no water since the attack.

It is not unusual for such attacks to end in the appropriation of another house, the displacement of another Palestinian family. Tareq al-Shartabi describes the time he was sitting at home with his brother Muhammad when members of the nearby Avraham Avinu settlement (in the old city of Hebron) began an attack on their house:

My brother, Muhammad, ran away, but I insisted on staying inside and protecting the house from the settlers. The settlers made an opening in the fence. Fifty or sixty of them besieged the house and banged on the doors. I looked through a crack in the door and saw that there were about ten or fifteen soldiers with them. The settlers broke in with iron bars and other tools. I went into one of the rooms in the house, locked the iron door and hid. The settlers knew I was inside. I heard them say that I was a terrorist and should be killed. They tried to break into the room, but didn't succeed. The settlers kept trying to break in until around 11:30 A.M. on Saturday. They were inside the house the whole time.

At around noon, I called my friend Jalal Jibrin. I told him I was trapped inside my house and asked him to notify my family so that they would call the Red Cross and TIPH [Temporary International Presence in Hebron]. My two sisters, three brothers and neighbor, Marzuk Muhtaseb, arrived with some soldiers shortly after. Only then did I open the door and come out. There were still about ten settlers inside. Police and Civil Administration officers came and took pictures of the damage done to my house. An officer told me that I had to leave the house according to a military order. I demanded that he show me an official order. He said he would, but I haven't seen him since. The settlers destroyed everything: chairs, other furniture, three television sets, two tape recorders, a washing machine, kitchenware, a stove, closets, clothes, books, windows, pictures. Everything was broken or destroyed.

The Israeli settlers returned the following day and broke all the windows and doors in the house, when the family was not at home. Tareq and his family have since been unable to return—and the settlers are there to this day.

Occupation by the Numbers

- Number of Israeli army raids conducted inside the occupied territories, 2005: 1,878
- Number in 2006: 5,666
- Number of Palestinians taken prisoner during those raids in 2005: 2,293
- Number taken prisoner in 2006: 5,244
- Days a Jewish settler in West Bank can be detained without charge: 15
- Days a Palestinian resident of the West Bank can be detained without charge: 180
- Number of Palestinians being held prisoner by Israel, mid-2007: 10,000
- Cumulative total number of Palestinian prisoners held by Israel, 1967–2005: 650,000

- Age one is no longer a child, according to civil law applied to Jewish settlers in West Bank: 18
- Age one is no longer a child, according to military law applied to Palestinians in West Bank: 12
- Number of Palestinian children (under 18) arrested by Israeli army in occupied territories, 2000–2005: 3,500
- Number of Palestinian children being held prisoner by Israel, late 2006: 400
- Days a Palestinian child can be detained without seeing a lawyer: 90

9

There are two different administrative and legal structures in place in the occupied territories: Jewish settlers are subject to Israeli civil law, whereas the native Palestinians are subject to Israeli military law. Such forms of legalized discrimination are not restricted to the occupied territories; they are built directly into the political and institutional frameworks of Israel itself. Palestinian citizens of the State of Israel enjoy rights and privileges that are denied to their fellow Palestinians living under occupation, but their home, domestic, and family lives—their "inside" lives—are nevertheless subject to a wide array of legal and institutional controls directed against them as non-Jewish residents of a state that defines itself as Jewish. A line on a map—the 1949–67 border separating Israel from the West Bank—does not prevent Israel from projecting its laws outside its own sovereign space, along with its own citizens, whom it has allowed or encouraged to settle outside the borders of the state. What happens in the occupied territories is the extension of what happens inside Israel itself, and the same play of outsides and insides that structures life in the West Bank structures it inside Israel as well.

American support for Israel is often explained on cultural grounds, in terms of a set of values held in common between Israel and the United States. "Many people in this country support Israel precisely because they admire it as a brave, dynamic and democratic society," writes Tim Rutten in the Los Angeles Times, in an attempt to dispute the claim, made in a recent book by Stephen Walt and John Mearsheimer, that a powerful Israeli lobby determines the nature of relations between the two countries. Americans' support for Israel is explained by shared values, argues Victor Davis Hanson in the *National Review*. "Israel is a democracy. Its opponents are not," he writes; Israel is secular, liberal, pluralistic, tolerant, he adds. Americans can detect in it "free speech and liberality of custom and religion" that they do not see elsewhere in the region, as well as an innovative economy that reflects, according to Hanson, an underlying "culture of freedom," with which Americans can, he says, readily identify.

However, there are great differences between the political systems of Israel and the United States. To begin with, the greatest of all American ideals is that all human beings are equal. Thomas Jefferson wrote that concept into the Declaration of Independence, and it would go on to provide one of the fundamental tenets of the Constitution of the United States. There are today no gradations among citizens of the United States: immigrant, naturalized, native-born, black, white, or brown, an American citizen is an American citizen—they are all equal, and all guaranteed equal treatment before the law. Their individual liberties, and their equality as citizens, are protected by the Constitution, and the laws founded on it, which strictly forbid any kind of discrimination on the basis of race, color, gender, or religion. Americans' freedom of conscience is upheld by the vigorous separation of church and state: they can adhere to whatever religion they want, or no religion at all, without interference from the state, and without it making any difference to the way in which they are treated by the state, or to their rights, duties, and privileges as citizens of the state. Marriage and divorce (and in certain cases same-sex domestic partnerships) are recognized and adjudicated by the state and the civil courts, not just religious institutions. Land can be bought and sold as private property, for real estate (like all other sectors of the economy) is open to all without discrimination; it is a genuinely free market.

In defining itself as the Jewish state, on the other hand, Israel establishes a major juridical distinction between what it calls "nationality" and what it calls "citizenship"; and it is the only state that explicitly identifies itself not as the state of its actual citizens, but rather as the state of a people, most of whom have no connection to it, let alone any intention of ever living there. Because Israel is the state of the Jewish people rather than of its actual citizens, Jewish noncitizens (i.e., the Jewish citizens of other countries) enjoy rights and benefits that Israel denies to its own non-Jewish citizens. Jewish noncitizens, in other words, are potentially entitled to greater rights in Israel than Palestinian citizens of the state. In classifying its citizens, Israel recognizes 140 different "nationalities," including Russian, Polish, French, and so forth, as well as "Arab," the official phrase Israel uses to designate its Palestinian population, who regard themselves not simply as "Arabs," but as members of the Palestinian people, whose political status was changed against their will in 1948 (see "Coda"). According to the State of Israel, however, there is no such thing as *Israeli* nationality. Jewish citizens of the state are recognized as having "Jewish nationality." When a group of Israelis demanded the legal right to have their official identity documents recognize them as Israeli nationals, they had to petition all the way to the High Court, which ruled, in 1972, that "there is no such thing as an Israeli nation separate from the Jewish people."

This places non-Jewish citizens of the state in, at best, a highly ambiguous situation. They may benefit from the rights of citizenship; but they are denied the rights of nationality. The distinction between "citizenship" and "nationality" has proved rhetorically useful to Israel; it can declare that it treats all its citizens equally, for example, because most forms of discrimination in the state are not established on the basis of citizenship as such, but rather on the basis of nationality.

The distinction between nationality and citizenship concerns more than merely rhetorical hairsplitting, however. Israeli law recognizes and grants official status to various "national" organizations, notably the Jewish Agency and the Jewish National Fund (JNF), that are mandated to provide benefits and services exclusively to "Jewish nationals." Whether they are the citizens of Israel or of any other state does not matter, because in Israel "nationality" overrides citizenship. "Jewish National Fund is the caretaker of the land of Israel," reads the banner across the home page of the JNF Web site, "on behalf of its owners—Jewish people everywhere." The JNF has been criticized by international bodies because of its policies. The U.N. Committee on Economic, Social, and Cultural Rights said in 1998 that JNF policies "constitute an institutionalized form of discrimination" in violation of the U.N.'s International Covenant on Economic, Social, and Cultural Rights. In 2007, the U.N. Committee on the Elimination of Racial Discrimination voiced its own concerns about the JNF's policies, which also constitute a violation of the International Convention on the Elimination of All Forms of Racial Discrimination. The JNF's application for official consultative status within the U.N.'s Economic and Social Council was rejected because of the inherently discriminatory nature of its policies.

Israel lacks a written constitution that guarantees the right to equality and prohibits discrimination among citizens. The kinds of covenants that used to forbid home ownership in many American cities to "non-Caucasians," including blacks, Latinos, Asians, and in many cases Jews—which were curtailed by a United States Supreme Court ruling in 1948 and abolished altogether in 1968—remain in force in Israel to this day. Palestinian citizens of the state are barred from living on land held by "national institutions" such as the JNF or the Jewish Agency. They are legally excluded from residing in officially designated "Jewish community settlements" or "Jewish rural settlements" organized into rural councils that, between them, control some 80 percent of the land in Israel. (A High Court ruling in 2000 in favor of the Palestinian Qa'adan family's application to live in the Jewish Agency community of Katzir, which had been blocked for five years, was specifically limited to that one case, and carefully avoided establishing a general precedent, as well as any specific remedy to the family in question; it took another four years before the Qa'adans were actually given permission to access a plot of land). Palestinians are even prevented from living on lands to which their families hold legal title, if they were forced from their lands during the 1948 war. Such lands were given over to Jewish ownership; Jews legally owned only about 7 percent of Palestine before 1948—the rest was taken by force and is today represented in the 93 percent of Israel that is considered state land.

The JNF owns about 13 percent of Israel's state lands. Most of its holdings are the confiscated property of Palestinian refugees and displaced persons, which were transferred to the JNF by the state between 1949 and 1953. Laws passed in the early 1960s created the Israel Land Administration (ILA), which took over the management of all State Lands, including JNF land. However, under the agreement entered into by the state and the JNF, the ILA has to administer JNF lands according to the JNF's own discriminatory criteria. Moreover, the JNF was allotted half the seats on the ILA Council, which allows it to determine the steps taken in the administration of all state lands, not just its own. In response to a 2004 legal challenge to its discrimination against non-Jews, the JNF said that it "is not a public body which acts on behalf of all the citizens of the state. Its loyalty is to the Jewish people and its responsibility is to it [i.e., the Jewish people] alone. As the owner of JNF land, the JNF does not have to act with equality towards all citizens of the state." Moreover, the JNF points out, "Israel's Knesset [i.e., parliament] and Israeli society have expressed their view that the distinction between Jews and non-Jews that is the basis for the Zionist vision is a distinction that is permitted," and that its allocation of land to Jews alone "is in complete accord with the founding principles of the state of Israel as a Jewish state and that the value of equality, even if it applies to JNF lands, would retreat before this principle." In other words, the principle of Jewishness has priority over the principle of equality in Israel.

Such attitudes—and the forms of legalized discrimination attendant upon them—are not merely archaic holdovers from a previous era, nor are they the views of the JNF alone. Woven into the fabric of "national institutions" such as the JNF, they are receiving increasing, rather than decreasing, state recognition and support. In July 2007, for example, the Israeli parliament passed, by a margin of 64 to 16, the first reading of a new bill that would essentially reaffirm the discriminatory nature of the JNF. The bill, introduced by Uri Ariel of the National Union bloc (which includes the explicitly "transferist" Moledet party mentioned in the Introduction), stipulates that land owned by the JNF will be leased only to Jews. That had always been the case, but now the state will be making official and explicit its already tacit and implicit support for JNF policy, protecting it from future attempts to undo its discriminatory logic. "Despite whatever is stated in any law, leasing of [the] Jewish National Fund's lands for the purpose of the settlement of Jews on these lands will not be seen as improper discrimination," the bill states. "For the purpose of every law, the association documents of the Jewish National Fund will be interpreted according to the judgment of the Jewish National Fund's founders and from a nationalist-Zionist standpoint."

What is true of the JNF is true of Israeli law in general. More than twenty separate Basic Laws (the closest documents Israel has to a written constitution) and other forms of legislation explicitly discriminate between Jews and non-Jews. The Law of Return, for example, is a nationality law that is designed exclusively for Jews, who acquire citizenship in Israel on the basis of their already existing "Jewish nationality," which they have simply by virtue of being Jewish. By definition, non-Jews, including Palestinians who were born in, say, Haifa, Jaffa, Nazareth, or Jerusalem, are ineligible for return under the Law of Return, even though the right of return to one's country is enshrined in the Universal Declaration of Human Rights.

Quite apart from the 1948 refugees who remain in exile, a quarter of Israel's Palestinian citizens continue to suffer the consequences of their internal displacement in 1948; they have never been allowed to return to their land and homes, and have never received compensation for their loss. Tens of thousands of them—all told, about 10 percent of Palestinian Israelis—now inhabit dozens of Palestinian towns and villages inside Israel whose very existence the state does not officially recognize, even though they physically preexist it. Their homes are not connected to the national power grid or water supply; they do not have state schools or post offices; and because they do not officially exist, they do not have building permits—and are all subject to demolition (see "Inside Out").

As I mentioned earlier, Israeli citizens who marry foreign spouses can acquire residency and ultimately citizenship status for their partners—unless they are Palestinians from the occupied territories. Such forms of discrimination are woven into the very fabric of the Jewish state, and they have been from the very beginning. And they affect every aspect of personal, professional, domestic, and family life for non-Jewish citizens of the state, literally from birth to death.

However, the forms of discrimination that are part of Israeli law are not only premised on the distinction between Jews and non-Jews. There are political and legal differentiations and inequalities among Jews themselves. There is, for example, no institution of civil marriage in Israel: marriage and divorce (and indeed other personal status issues, including burial) are handled not by the state, but by religious courts empowered by the state. The only Jewish courts in Israel empowered to handle marriage and divorce are those of the Orthodox rabbinate. The Reform and Conservative branches of Judaism in Israel have to hand over their followers to the Orthodox rabbinate for marriage; secular Jews must also turn not to the state and civil institutions (as they can in secular countries), but to the Orthodox rabbinate. "Non-Orthodox Jewish couples are forced to submit to an Orthodox marriage ceremony with an Orthodox rabbi and are compelled to attend classes on family purity," explains Steven Mazie in *Jewish Week*; "no Israeli may marry outside her faith community." Moreover, according to Orthodox religious law, a woman cannot divorce her husband: only he is empowered to end the marriage and release her by providing her a document of permission, or *get*. Some men refuse to do so, leaving their wives unable to remarry religiously (for which there is no alternative in Israel). "The situation of *agunot*, as the trapped women are known, has received increased attention in recent years," writes Nathaniel Popper in the American Jewish weekly *The Forward*. "Such women are at a disadvantage, because while a man can receive a rabbinic allowance to remarry without providing a *get*, a Jewish woman requires one if she is to remarry." If an *agunah* woman enters into another relationship anyway and has children, they will be considered the outcome of an adulterous affair and classified by the rabbinate as *mamzerim*. "They and their offspring, stigmatized with an irrevocable brand of illegitimacy, may marry only other *mamzerim*," notes Mazie. Forming in effect a class of virtual untouchables, they have no recourse in Israel because the Orthodox rabbinate determines all personal status issues for Jews, and because neither secularism nor atheism are recognized by the state.

Nor does the Orthodox rabbinate's authority in Israel affect only marriage and divorce. As a July 2003 editorial in *The Forward* points out, it was only in that month that Israel's Ministry of the Interior broke the Orthodox rabbinate's monopoly on conversion to Judaism, which has implications for the acquisition of citizenship and the wider, recurring debate over who is recognized as Jewish in Israel. "The 'Who is a Jew?' debate has been a political and legal minefield in Israel for five decades," writes *The Forward*, noting that Israel continues to grant monopolies to the Orthodox rabbinate. This debate has often strained relations between Israel and American Jews, 90 percent of whom are not Orthodox, and hence to a certain extent legally stigmatized in Israel. Even Orthodox American Jews sometimes fall short of the standard demanded by the rabbinate in Israel. In May 2006, for example, the rabbinate in Israel refused to accept conversions performed by several leading Orthodox rabbis in the United States, causing a scandal. And in November that year, Israel's chief rabbi proposed draft legislation amending Israel's Law of Return so that not all converts to Judaism would be recognized as eligible for automatic citizenship. If his proposal is taken up as a bill and adopted by Israel's parliament, only Jews born to a Jewish mother or other Jewish relatives currently covered by the Law of Return would be granted automatic citizenship, according to the *Jerusalem Post*.

Israel, then, is not a secular state. Its citizens are afforded none of the guarantees to equality and rights—and the freedom from religious interference in their personal lives—protected by the United States Constitution and also taken for granted in modern European societies.

The ultimate distinction in Israel, however, is not the one among the various streams of Judaism, but rather the legally and politically structuring differentiation between Jews and non-Jews. The rigid distinction between persons who are Jewish and persons who are not defines the limits and possibilities of an individual's personal and family life; it also provides the basic logic defining spaces and places in Israel and the occupied territories, articulating insides and outsides, how outsides can turn in, and insides out.

Segregation by the Numbers

- Proportion of Israeli population that is Palestinian: 20
- Number of child-care centers in Israel for children aged 0–3: 1,600
- Number of those in Palestinian towns: 25
- Number of Israeli children age 0–3 who attend state-subsidized day care: 80,000
- Number of whom are Palestinian: 4,200
- Percentage of Jewish Israeli children age 3 with access to state-subsidized kindergarten: 100
- Percentage of Palestinian Israeli children age 3 with access: 66
- Israel's annual investment per Jewish student age 5–15: $428

- Israel's annual investment per non-Jewish (i.e., Palestinian) student age 5–15: $128
- Number of Israeli communities granted the highest-priority status for education in 2007: 553
- Number of those that were Palestinian: 4
- Number of art schools for Jewish students in Israel: 25
- Number for non-Jewish (i.e., Palestinian) students: 0
- Percentage of Jewish students in Israel who make it to high school: 85
- Percentage of non-Jewish (i.e., Palestinian) students who make it to high school: 61
- Percentage of Jewish applicants to university in Israel who are rejected: 16
- Percentage of non-Jewish (i.e., Palestinian) students who are rejected: 45
- Percentage of undergraduates in Israel who are Palestinian: 10
- Percentage of doctoral students in Israel who are Palestinian: 3
- Percentage of university lecturers in Israel who are Palestinian: 1
- Number of university lecturers in Israel who are Palestinian women: 1

Outside In

1

It was Sunday, the 24th of February 2007, and Dr. Mona el-Farra was happy: she and her daughter were on their way out of Gaza, bound for Ireland, where she was due to present a series of lectures on the situation of women back home.

The month before, she had been supposed to fly to London for a different engagement, but had never been able to get out of Gaza: several trips to the Rafah crossing on the border with Egypt had ended in failure, as the Israelis—who are said to be no longer occupying Gaza, although they still control all of its borders, airspace, and territorial waters—had imposed one of their regular closures. (Rafah had been especially hard hit by such closures, having been shut continually since June 2006.) The border was supposed to have been opened for one continuous week when Mona made her attempt to cross in January. In her repeated attempts to get through Rafah during that week, Mona saw crowds of people—including some two hundred patients trying to leave Gaza to seek urgent medical care in Egypt—waiting in abysmal circumstances in the cold and rain at the border crossing. But the Israelis, citing security concerns, never allowed the crossing to open. Having rearranged her entire schedule to allow for the trip, Mona helplessly watched the days slip by until the event in London at which she was supposed to speak came and went.

This time, Mona hoped, it would be different: she was armed not only with a letter of invitation from the Irish charity and development organization Trócaire, which was sponsoring her visit to Ireland, but with an offer of assistance in leaving Gaza from the Israeli human rights organization HaMoked. She had been promised a permit to leave Gaza at Erez, which is the main crossing point for the few Palestinians still allowed to work inside Israel, and is also used by diplomats, journalists, and patients seeking medical care in Israel. At Erez, she would be permitted to enter and cross through Israel, enter the West Bank, and cross into Jordan over the Allenby Bridge, to fly to Ireland from Amman. (It would have been simpler to fly to Ireland directly from Tel Aviv, but Gazans are not allowed to use the Tel Aviv airport—and Israel, having destroyed Gaza's own airport in 2001, will not allow it to reopen; despite having committed, in a 2005 agreement brokered by the United States, to discussing that possibility.)

By 10 A.M., however, Mona and her daughter were back home. The Israelis had not approved their permits to leave Gaza.

On Monday the 25th, Mona, having unpacked, sent her daughter back to school, as the whole trip didn't seem likely to take place. But later that morning, she received a phone call from the Irish embassy, telling her to prepare to leave, as the embassy would facilitate the granting of her exit permit. Mona packed her bags, but decided not to pick up her daughter from school until the embassy called again to give her the green light: there was no point in raising her daughter's hopes for nothing. At 2 P.M., her daughter returned from school; there had been no news from the embassy. Then, at 4 P.M., the Irish called again and told Mona to rush straightaway to the Erez crossing, where the way had been cleared.

Shortly afterward, Mona and her daughter were at Erez, but were stalled again, held up for several hours. The Israeli soldiers and border guards told her—through the Palestinian border officials, with whom they communicate—to give up and go home. "You cannot cross today, come back tomorrow," Mona was told. At the same time, she received several calls on her mobile phone from HaMoked and the Irish embassy, telling her not to give up, that it would work out and she'd be able to cross. Finally, at 7:30, the Israelis called their Palestinian counterparts and told them to wave Mona through after all. She was past the Palestinian border guards and now halfway through Erez, but the hard part was still to come.

"On my way to the Israeli checkpoint [at the other end of Erez] I walked with my daughter and ten sick people, who were in desperate need for further treatment in Israel," Mona recalls. "We walked through a long cement tube, with cameras looking down on top of our heads and sound from hidden [speakers] giving us instructions." Dazed by the scene's surreality, Mona continued. "I kept walking and before reaching the end of that tube I met tens of Palestinian people of all sorts of ages (children, babies, old women and men) tired, exhausted, and very sad. I stopped one very old woman limping with her walking sticks and asked her who she was. She said that they had been visiting their sons and daughters in the Israeli jails. I burst loudly into tears. I felt speechless and helpless." Still, she was almost through now. "Arriving at the end of this tunnel, one door after another kept opening with red then green lights and we kept receiving instructions from unseen voices. Sondos [her daughter] explained later on to her sister that it is like a riddle or a maze. On arriving at the desk the officer checked our papers and said 'you cannot cross—[this] is an expired permit.' " More frantic phone calls to HaMoked and the Irish embassy followed. Finally, a breakthrough in all the behind-the-scenes negotiations: Mona and her daughter were allowed through, into Israel.

Her daughter was fifteen years old. This was the first time she had seen anything of her native land other than sealed-off Gaza. A native-born Palestinian, she had never set eyes on Jerusalem. She cried with joy and disbelief.

A couple of hours later, they were in Jericho. But by now it was late, and the border at the Jordan River had closed. They would have to spend the night in a hotel. Early the next morning, Mona and her daughter were at the Israeli side of the Allenby Bridge border crossing, over the Jordan River. The Israeli border guards told her that her permit, which was only good for one day (i.e., the day she'd spent trying to get through Erez), had expired. She would have to return to Gaza and reapply for a new permit. Finally, after more frantic phone calls to and from the Irish embassy, more behind-the-scenes negotiations between the Irish and the Israelis—the Israeli border guards stamped Mona's papers and let her go. Seeing the VIP car the embassy had arranged to take her to Amman, where she would fly on to Ireland, she had a flashback. "I remembered Mr. Steig Collin from Sweden who stayed with us and worked voluntarily for three weeks at Al Awda Hospital [in Gaza]. While I was showing him around in Gaza in 1999, we were stopped by the soldiers at one of the Israeli military checkpoints. The soldiers asked if we were VIPs. Mr. Collin replied, 'Every human being is a VIP.' "

Not every human being has an embassy intervening on her behalf, however. For most Gazans, Mona's experience—minus the extraordinary diplomatic intervention—is the norm. Contrary to Palestinian expectations, conditions have actually deteriorated following the Israeli redeployment from Gaza in 2005. Since then, Israel has continued to control land, sea, and air access to Gaza. Israel's tight regulation of Gaza's borders, imports and exports, fishing and agriculture, fuel and electricity, have eliminated any prospect of economic and social recovery. Its refusal to allow road or rail links between Gaza and the West Bank (despite having nominally accepted the terms of a U.S.-brokered agreement on movement and access between the territories in November 2005, which was never implemented) means that Israel has physically separated the two Palestinian territories from one another. Following the Palestinian political crisis of June 2007, Israel has acted to further separate the West Bank from Gaza and to further isolate Gaza from the outside world. Its refusal to relinquish control over the population registry means that Israel alone determines who is a Gazan and who is not—and hence that Israel alone determines who can come and who can go from Gaza: for entry is permitted, when it is permitted at all, only to Palestinians registered in Gaza (and individuals who obtain Israeli permits to enter). According to Meron Benvenisti, the Israeli former deputy mayor of Jerusalem, the Israeli redeployment from Gaza amounted to "the confinement of one and a half million persons in a huge holding pen."

Gaza is, in short, a world turned outside in. It is not unique in this respect: rather, Gaza is the prototype for a form of enclosure and isolation that is now being applied to Palestinian communities in the West Bank as well. "Anyone familiar with Israel's relentless confiscations of Palestinian territory—based on a plan devised, overseen and implemented by Ariel Sharon—knows that the objective of its settlement enterprise in the West Bank has been largely achieved," writes Henry Siegman, the former head of the American Jewish Congress, in a recent article. "Gaza, the evacuation of whose settlements was so naively hailed by the international community as the heroic achievement of a man newly committed to an honourable peace with the Palestinians, was intended to serve as the first in a series of Palestinian bantustans. Gaza's situation shows us what these bantustans will look like if their residents do not behave as Israel wants." Being cut off from the outside world except through points of access under Israeli control; being utterly dependent on Israel for vital communications and supplies; being subject to frequent, even daily, Israeli raids and bombardments; and having to grow used to the idea that one is living under confinement so severe that the tiny territory one inhabits seems to have become a world unto itself: these have become the major features of Palestinian life in the twenty-first century. "The Palestinian economy is becoming an 'island' economy," the World Food Programme's Kirstie Campbell put it in March 2007: "small areas where residents trade among themselves."

OCCUPATION BY THE NUMBERS

- Number of Palestinians from occupied territories working in Israel or settlements, 1987: 180,000
- Number in 2000: 110,000
- Number in 2007: 68,000
- Unemployment rate in West Bank, 1999: 9.6
- Unemployment rate in West Bank, 2006: 18.6
- Unemployment rate in Gaza, 1999: 17
- Unemployment rate in Gaza, 2006: 34.8
- Private sector unemployment rate in Gaza, 2007: 85
- Percentage of people in Gaza living in poverty, 2006: 80
- Proportion of people in Gaza dependent for food aid for day-to-day survival, 2007: 80
- Percent increase in rates of chronic disease in occupied territories, 2005–7: 30

2

Just two or three months earlier, Laila el-Haddad had been facing exactly the same problem as the one Mona had just overcome, only in reverse. She was trying to cross into Gaza from Egypt, with her parents and her two-year-old son Yousuf.

The Rafah crossing was closed, as it would be still when Mona tried to pass through it in January. But there were rumors that the Israelis would allow it to open soon, and so thousands of people were waiting on the Egyptian side of the border: Palestinian patients who had been seen in Egypt and who were trying to get back home to Gaza; businessmen who had crossed the border to find suppliers or markets; students who had been studying abroad and were returning to visit their parents; laborers who worked abroad to send money back to their families.

"One hour turned into two, then three, then five, as we stood shielding our eyes from the piercing midday sun on Wednesday, when we were told the crossing would be opening for a few hours," Laila recalls. "We stood, thousands of us, packed together elbow to elbow like cattle, penned in between steel barriers on one end, and riot-geared Egyptian security guards on the perimeter, who were given orders not to allow anyone through until they hear otherwise from the Israelis—and to respond with force if anyone dared [to cross]."

In July 2006, seven Palestinians waiting to be let into Gaza from Egypt died of exposure and deprivation while waiting to cross the border at Rafah: they had run out of money and had been unable either to leave or to find adequate shelter while continuing to wait. In March 2007, several Palestinians were injured, and a sixty-one-year-old man on his way to Egypt for treatment for his heart condition had a heart attack and died in a surge of the crowd at Rafah when it opened for the first time in days. By then, 5,000 people had piled up at the crossing, and when the Israelis finally relented, there was a stampede as the crowd surged toward the gate.

"There is something you feel as you stand there," says Laila, "for hours at a time, waiting to be let through the Egyptian side of the Rafah crossing. It is something of your humanity slowly drifting away. It is gradual, but unmistakable. And you are never quite the same again." Then the Egyptian border guards told all the Palestinians to withdraw from the crossing terminal, including those who had actually made it to the very front, and even those who had made it to the Gaza side, which was now sealed by Israeli orders. "Everyone out!"

Laila pleaded with an Egyptian officer. "It took us six hours to get inside the terminal, please let us through." Nothing doing: most of the poorly paid Egyptian guards were indifferent to the plight of the Palestinians. One was a little more sympathetic. "What you lot have to understand," he told Laila, "is that no one gives a damn what happens to you—you could sit here and suffocate for all they care. You are simply not human enough for them to care."

Inside the terminal, the scenes were dizzying. "Already disoriented from lack of sleep and little food, I looked around in awe. It was nothing short of an internment camp, and I lost myself somewhere between the silent anguish of old men, aching, teary-eyed women on the verge of collapse, and children, some strewn across the floor in exhaustion, others who were sick, in wheelchairs, wailing." Laila and her family returned to the Egyptian border town of el-Arish to find somewhere to spend the night. Almost every room in the local hostelries had been taken by stranded travelers. The one place they could find lacked hot water, but they didn't care. Besides, a room, with water or without, was luxury compared to the lot of the hundreds of Palestinians who, unable to afford hotel rooms for nights on end—or penniless from having already spent several such nights in succession—simply sleep at the border crossing itself, exposed to the elements and chilled by the nighttime desert air.

The next day, Laila and her family returned to the border crossing. This time they waited only five hours before giving up. "Everyone was looking for answers—some answers, any answers. When would the crossing open? Was there hope it would open today? If so, what time? Should we wait, should we return to Arish? Nobody knew." Every now and then someone would make a call to someone they knew in Gaza or on the border, and rumors would spread like wildfire through the crowd of waiting people. Finally, Laila reports, one man had had enough. He put his bags on a trolley and started out through the crowd of exhausted Gazans.

"Where the hell do you think you're going?" bellowed one of the Egyptian officers. "To Jerusalem! Where do you think?" he replied with bitter irony. It was nearing the end of another long day, and, overcome by exhaustion, Laila didn't know whether to laugh or cry.

3

With a population nearing half a million, Gaza City is today the largest Palestinian city. Established by the Canaanites some five thousand years ago, Gaza is also one of the oldest cities in the world. Its location at the crossroads of Asia and Africa—the place where ancient Egypt met the hinterland of Canaan—contributed to its early growth and development. Gaza was always a city of merchants and traders, commerce always its raison d'être, and open trade routes always its lifeblood.

By 1948, some 80,000 people lived in Gaza and the coastal area around it. The area's population almost tripled in April and May of 1948 with the arrival of waves of refugees expelled or forced into flight from their homes, mostly from Jaffa and the Palestinian villages south of Jaffa. When Israel declared its refusal to allow the Palestinian refugees to return to their homes, they had no choice but to remain in Gaza, which fell under Egyptian control at the end of the 1948 War. They have remained there ever since.

Today, the population of Gaza City and the area around it is overwhelmingly made up of those refugees, their children, and their grandchildren. Because they came here so suddenly and under such traumatic circumstances, rather than as a result of natural growth and development, their numbers are out of all proportion to what the area's economic base can support. Even under ideal circumstances, it would be impossible for the economy of Gaza to sustain such a population.

Almost 1.5 million people now live in the Gaza Strip. Three-quarters of them are the original refugees of 1948 and their descendants. And because the Gaza Strip is so tiny—it is less than 7 miles wide and 35 miles long—it has one of the highest population densities in the world. Almost 80,000 people, for example, are packed into the Beach Refugee Camp near Gaza City. It measures less than 1 square kilometer (247 acres). By contrast, there are "only" about 25,000 people per square kilometer in Manhattan (which is about 3 miles by 13 miles). Gaza also has an extraordinarily young population. Eighty percent of the population is under fifty years old; half are under fifteen. There is little enough work for the current adult workforce in Gaza; when these children grow up, there will be proportionately even less for them to do.

4

By the 1980s, the economies of the West Bank and especially (given its unnatural circumstances) Gaza were completely integrated into, and dependent on, the much larger Israeli economy. Well over half of Gaza's workforce was employed inside Israel. Its people were essentially a low-wage resource for Israeli employers—one of the reasons why the Israelis were so eager to open the borders after 1967. Palestinians soon became so dependent on low-paying Israeli jobs that they readily provided the very labor power that would construct the settlements that would gradually begin to swallow up their own land.

Israel's Gaza settlements never grew as large as those in the West Bank. By the time the Israeli civilian presence inside Gaza was terminated in 2005, there were fewer than 9,000 settlers there, compared with almost 500,000 in the West Bank and East Jerusalem. But those that were there lived in large villas within view of the man-made squalor and desperation of overcrowded refugee camps. They used a hugely disproportionate share of the Strip's resources, particularly its water. They enjoyed swimming pools, while their parched neighbors had to make do in the heat and dust of the Gazan summers. The Israeli settlements occupied about 15 percent of Gaza's surface area, but roads set aside for the exclusive use of the settlers, as well as "security zones" and army checkpoints, further reduced the space available to the already overcrowded Palestinian population of Gaza. By the end, over a third of the entire territory was reserved for the exclusive use of the 1 percent of Gaza's population that was Jewish. The rest of the Strip was broken and truncated, punctuated by roadblocks and checkpoints and frequent curfews and closures.

The Israelis started tightening their control over the West Bank and especially Gaza in the aftermath of the first intifada. The influx of around a million Jewish and quasi-Jewish immigrants from the former Soviet Union, as well as the increasingly efficient market in migrant labor provided by a rapidly globalizing world economy, made Israel's reliance on cheap Palestinian labor less and less necessary. So—other than the Jewish settlers coming and going as they pleased—the occupied territories were gradually sealed off. The closure orders experimented with in 1991 became more regular, and were made permanent by early 1993, and formally institutionalized in the Oslo Accords.

Palestinians would henceforth have to apply for individual permits to leave Gaza. They were no longer allowed to work at night, or to stay overnight, in Israel. And it became more of a hassle for Israeli employers to hire Palestinian labor. They had to fill out more forms, obtain official approval for each worker, and deal with the potentially costly delays caused by waits at checkpoints and border crossings. Some used the closings as an excuse not to pay workers for labor they had already done. Before the institutionalization of Israel's closure policy, 80,000 Gazans used to work in Israel; by the summer of 1993, only some 17,000 Gazans were able to do so. Unemployment became a general condition. Gaza's gross domestic product (GDP) fell by between a third and a half in a few years. Family incomes plummeted. And more and more of the population became utterly dependent for day-to-day survival on food donated by international aid agencies. The U.N. Relief and Works Agency (UNRWA), which had been providing emergency food assistance to fewer than 8,000 Gaza families in the 1980s, was providing for 120,000 families by the mid-1990s, as the Oslo peace process reached its peak.

Not only labor, but also all other forms of economic input, as well as exports from the occupied territories, were severely restricted. Cut off from the Israeli economy, on which it had been made totally dependent, Gaza was, economically speaking, a disaster zone. Circumstances continued to deteriorate in Gaza during the Oslo years and afterward. Between 1993 and 1996—the very peak of the Oslo process—Israel imposed 342 days of total closure on Gaza, during which virtually all movement was shut down. Thus, for a period of three years, there was one day of total paralysis for every two when (restricted) movement was possible.

Two Weeks of Occupation: UN-OCHA Gaza Update, 18 April–1 May 2007

- Rafah crossing was open on 4 days only allowing a total of 3,934 people to cross into the Gaza Strip and 4,293 people out (compared to 7 days during the previous reporting period which allowed 6,420 people to enter and 7,183 people to exit the Gaza Strip).
- Karni crossing was open 11 scheduled operating days enabling a total of 3,140 truckloads of goods into (excluding aggregates/construction materials) and 619 truckloads of goods out of the Gaza Strip. Karni was open for 72% of scheduled hours, a 19% increase compared to the previous period.
- Sufa crossing was open for 4 days during the reporting period (Sufa has been open only 6 days in the last two months).
- Kerem Shalom crossing was open on 1 day (compared to 5 days during the previous month) for the import of humanitarian supplies.
- Erez crossing remains closed for over 13 months (since 12 March 2006) for Palestinian workers and during the reporting period was closed for 2 days for Palestinian traders. An average of 240 traders crossed each day (calculated on the basis of scheduled days open), an increase compared to the previous period (193).

5

Circumstances in Gaza were supposed to improve with the redeployment of Israeli settlers and soldiers from the territory in 2005. The official Israeli plan to "disengage" from Gaza, as originally published in 2004, specifically states that with the redeployment "there will be no basis for the claim that the Gaza Strip is occupied territory." But although so much emphasis was placed on it as a transformative event, the 2005 Israeli redeployment from Gaza did little to change the situation faced by the people of Gaza.

"Gaza is a prison and Israel seems to have thrown away the key," said the U.N.'s John Dugard. "In August 2005, Israel withdrew its settlers and armed forces from Gaza. Statements by the Government of Israel that the withdrawal ended the occupation of Gaza are grossly inaccurate," Dugard pointed out. "Israel retained control of Gaza's air space, sea space and external borders, and the border crossings of Rafah (for persons) and Karni (for goods) were ultimately under Israeli control and remained closed for lengthy periods. In effect, following Israel's withdrawal, Gaza became a sealed off, imprisoned and occupied territory."

There are today six crossings into Gaza, all of them—including Rafah, which is on the Egyptian, not the Israeli, border—ultimately controlled by Israel. Nahal Oz, for example, is used for fuel imports; Sufa for the import of humanitarian aid and construction material; Kerem Shalom for humanitarian aid, though it is mostly closed. Then there are the two major crossings, at Erez and Rafah (see map, p. 342).

Erez—which Mona el-Farra and her daughter faced such difficulties getting through—is used by diplomats, journalists, U.N. officials, workers going to work in Israel, and patients seeking medical treatment in Israel. It is frequently closed; there were 135 days of full or partial closure from September 2005 to April 2006. When open, it operates erratically and very slowly. Under the best of circumstances, no more than 3,000 to 4,000 workers are allowed to cross into Israel (down from 25,000 before 2000). A worker must be over thirty-four years old and married in order to even apply for such work, and he must have a specific employer in Israel. The worker sends his papers to his Israeli employer, who sends the papers to the Israeli Labor Office, which sends the names of approved workers to the Permits Office at Erez, where they are inspected by Shin Bet (the Israeli equivalent of the FBI). If his name is approved, it is sent to the Palestinian Ministry of Labor, which finally issues the permit. He is then forced to queue up at Erez from midnight the day before crossing. This means that workers often sleep in the open near the crossing, after a brutal day of crossing, working, and crossing back. If and when the Israelis open the crossing, only four workers at a time are allowed to enter the search facility. There they are subjected to inhumane and degrading treatment by Israeli soldiers; they are often forced to strip to their underwear; and they are subjected to extortion and blackmail by Israelis trying to recruit informants and collaborators.

Closed for extended periods long before the redeployment of Israeli troops and settlers, Rafah—where Laila el-Haddad and her son Yousuf were held up—was hermetically sealed for sixty-five days from September to November 2005. Thousands of travelers were marooned on the Egyptian side of the border in abysmal conditions, unable to return to their families and homes in Gaza: hundreds of people at a time were forced to sleep in an 8,600-square-foot waiting hall lacking all basic services— the same one that Laila el-Haddad would encounter the following year. People in Gaza also could not get out. In addition to those seeking medical care in Egypt, thousands of Palestinian university students were prevented from attending their programs of study abroad. (This includes students from Gaza studying at West Bank universities, who, barred by Israel from crossing the 20 miles from Gaza to the West Bank, have to cross to Egypt, travel to Jordan and cross into the West Bank from there, assuming they are allowed to enter the West Bank at all: the number of Gaza students in West Bank universities has dropped to virtually zero recently).

In mid-November 2005, an Agreement on Movement and Access (AMA), brokered by the United States, was signed. Lacking any precedent in international frontier law, the AMA called for Egyptians to monitor the Palestinians and Europeans to monitor the Egyptians and the Palestinians, and Israeli surveillance devices to monitor the Europeans, Egyptians, and Palestinians (it also granted Israel the right to block individual passengers to Gaza). All goods other than personal effects, and all non-Gazan people, had to go through Kerem Shalom, which is under direct Israeli control. The AMA, in short, completed the institutionalization of Israeli control over Gaza's borders.

In any event, the AMA made little difference. James Wolfensohn, who helped broker the agreement, told the Israeli newspaper *Ha'aretz* that "powerful forces in the US administration" worked behind his back to undermine the deal. The main official behind these moves, according to Wolfensohn, was Elliot Abrams, who had been convicted for lying to the United States Congress about his role in the 1980s Iran-Contra affair, but was President Bush's deputy national security advisor. "Every aspect of that agreement was abrogated," Wolfensohn complained. "Instead of hope, the Palestinians saw that they were put back in prison. And with 50 percent unemployment, you would [inevitably] have conflict. This is not just a Palestinian issue," he adds; "if you have 50 percent of your people with no work, chances are they will become annoyed."

From summer through fall 2006, according to the U.N., Rafah was opened only intermittently and erratically, which prevented the regular passage of persons between Gaza and Egypt. Gaza's sick and wounded were not allowed to seek medical care in Egypt. Those wanting to leave have to wait patiently, sometimes for weeks, before they are allowed out. In all, Karni was closed 80 percent of the time in January 2006; in April, it was closed for more than half the time. The AMA called, for example, for 400 truckloads of exports per day from Gaza through Karni as of late 2006; according to the U.N., the average number of actual trucks allowed to export goods was 12 per day in 2006. Israel committed to allowing the export of all agricultural products from Gaza; but in fact, only 4 percent of the 2005–6 harvest season was exported: the vast majority of the crops—over 100 tons of strawberries, flowers, tomatoes, cucumbers, peppers—were either given away or destroyed after rotting awaiting shipment.

The same goes for imports; all of Gaza's industries depend on imports of raw materials, which are held up indefinitely at the various border crossings. Even humanitarian imports are restricted; a January 2006 report by the U.N. Office for the Coordination of Humanitarian Affairs records that by the end of that month the U.N. had 90 containers of humanitarian supplies stuck at the Israeli port of Ashdod waiting permission to cross to Gaza via Karni. Closure has also severely limited supplies of essential medical equipment and drugs. Even before the summer assault on Gaza, the main hospital was preparing to close certain departments for lack of supplies; it was lacking dozens of medications, including antibiotics, cancer drugs, intravenous fluids.

Moreover, regular convoys were to be allowed between the West Bank and Gaza as of 15 December 2006; citing security concerns, Israel never let them take place. It is important to note that, according to international law, security concerns do not allow Israel to impose arbitrary restrictions on the freedom of movement of the Palestinian population, or to arbitrarily cut off their access to resources and markets. Such restrictions not only interrupt commercial and economic movement; they damage family life. Gazans studying in the West Bank are cut off from their parents; families in Gaza cannot visit their relatives in the West Bank or East Jerusalem; Palestinian prisoners held in Israeli jails are unable to receive visits from their families (Israel arrested 40,000 Palestinians during the second intifada; it still holds about 10,000, mostly in abysmal circumstances in jails or vast prison camps inside Israel, generally off-limits to their families in the occupied territories).

On top of the damage done by closure, sanctions orchestrated by Israel and the United States after the Palestinian people voted for Hamas and threw the corrupt administration of Fateh out of office in early 2006 only added to the devastation (see the "Coda" for more on the 2006 elections and their aftermath). Palestinian Authority employees—a huge percentage of the workforce—went without pay for months. This placed a particular burden on the health-care system in Gaza. About two-thirds of health care is provided by PA employees whose pay was interrupted because of the sanctions. Both the mental and the physical health of the entire distressed population was placed at risk, especially that of children.

Israel has also severely restricted the flow of medicines and medical equipment into Gaza, with results that are as lethal as any outright military incursion. By November 2007, the health ministry in Gaza was reporting that stocks of 85 essential medications, including chemotherapy drugs, strong antibiotics, and various psychiatric drugs, had been completely depleted, and that there was at most a three-month supply of another 138 medications. A shipment of 3,000 batteries intended for the hearing aids of the children attending the school run by the Atfaluna Society for Deaf Children in Gaza had also been held up at the crossings closed by Israel; many of the school's 300 children have been plunged back into silence. By November 2007, the Nasser Hospital in Gaza had to close half of its intensive care unit because it lacked parts or was unable to replace ventilators needed to keep patients alive. Cut off from many medications, unable to receive the appropriate care in besieged Gaza, and prevented by Israel from leaving, Palestinian patients started dying. In the Nasser Hospital, Dr. Bushra Lubbed watched her patients suffer, knowing that in many cases there was little or nothing she could do to help them. One was a seven-month-old baby girl suffering from kidney failure. She urgently needed dialysis, but there is no pediatric dialysis machine in Gaza; in the past, such cases would have been referred to hospitals in Egypt or Israel for treatment, but the siege on Gaza rules that out. "I sat in front of the patient and I could do nothing for her," Dr. Lubbed reports. "I knew exactly what she needed and we tried giving her all kinds of other treatment, but in the end she needed dialysis and we couldn't give her dialysis."

The baby died. In another case at the same hospital, a ten-year-old boy was suffering from what doctors surmised was a brain tumor, but to determine the exact nature of the affliction they needed to carry out an MRI scan. There is no MRI machine in Gaza. The doctors filed an emergency request to move the boy to the West Bank, but, even after Israel eventually granted permission to move him, delays at the border prevented him from getting out in time. He died too.

In October 2007, another patient, twenty-one-year-old Mahmoud Abu Taha, who had been diagnosed with intestinal cancer two months previously, and who was in desperate need of surgery to open a blockage in his intestines—surgery that no hospital in Gaza was equipped to handle—had to wait weeks to receive a permit from Israel to be treated at an Israeli hospital. On 18 October the permit was finally granted and Mahmoud was taken in a hospital to the crossing at Erez, accompanied by his father. At Erez the ambulance was turned back, and Mahmoud's father was arrested and taken into detention by the Israelis.

Another ten days passed before Mahmoud was finally allowed into Israel. He died a few hours after crossing. The Israelis released his father, who had been imprisoned in the meantime, the following day.

Gaza is a coastal territory. But Gaza's ports, like its airport, remain closed. Israel, citing security concerns, has restricted fishing to three miles from the coast; even then it is frequently interdicted and blockaded by Israeli patrol boats, and it has been prevented altogether since the capture of an Israeli soldier during an unrelated Palestinian raid on a border fort in June 2006. Thirty-five thousand Gazans rely (or relied) on fishing as a source of income. According to a recent B'Tselem report, they are out of work. Some Gaza fishermen, desperate to find some means of supporting their families, have set out to sea despite the Israeli ban, which is a violation of international law. The Israeli human rights organization has documented cases of Israeli warships firing at Palestinian fishermen in their flimsy wooden boats, and, as of winter 2007, even forcing fishermen out of their boats and into the chilly winter waters—after having chased the boats farther out to sea. Fishermen have been ordered, at gunpoint, to strip to their underwear, jump in the sea, and swim dozens of meters to Israeli patrol boats. Those who have said they didn't know how to swim, especially in choppy water, have been told they would be shot unless they complied. Rescue floats have been dangled in the water—and yanked away when the freezing fishermen got close to them. Taken aboard, they have been kept on deck in their soaked underwear for the long ride back to the Israeli port of Ashdod, where they have been held and interrogated for up to forty-eight hours, before finally being dropped back in the bitterly cold waters off Gaza—in their underwear once again.

Ismail Basleh is one of the Gaza fishermen who has experienced this. He set to sea with his brother Samir and a friend, Ayman al-Jabbour. They were stopped by an Israeli patrol boat, which forced them to follow it farther out to sea. The Israeli captain then ordered Ismail to cut his engine and take off his clothes. "I stood there in my underwear. It was very cold and there was a strong wind," Ismail recalls. "The captain ordered me to swim toward the Israeli ship, which was about twenty meters [22 yards] from my boat. I began to swim, and when I got close to the ship, it moved further and further away, until it was about one hundred meters from my boat. . . . I told the captain, 'Have mercy. I am tired,' but he told me to shut up. . . . The sailors threw down a ladder and pulled me up to the deck." In response to B'Tselem's inquiries, the Israeli navy says that its interdiction of Palestinian fishing boats is a security measure, intended to prevent weapons smuggling or attacks on vessels in international waters.

As with fishing, so with other industries in Gaza. Construction workers are out of work because materials are not allowed into Gaza. Farmers are out of work because they can't export their crops (20,000 have lost their jobs since 2005). Factory workers are out of work because they can't import raw materials to work (35,000 textile workers have been affected—and a January 2007 World Bank–financed report showed that 2006 exports of textiles had reached an all-time low of just 15 percent of the sector's capacity). Shopkeepers are out of work because many Gazans have become too poor to shop.

In all, by summer 2007, 85 percent of Gaza's private-sector workforce was out of work or without pay. The great majority of Gazans now eke out an existence below the official poverty line of $2 a day. By March 2007, UNRWA and the World Food Programme (WFP) were providing food to 80 percent of Gaza's population—"and without it they are liable to starve," says the WFP spokesperson. Aid recipients receive flour, rice, sugar, oil, powdered milk, and lentils. Few can afford meat, vegetables, and fruit; fish is virtually unavailable because of the Israeli ban on fishing. Severe food shortages have also been exacerbated by the Israeli closure policy, which severely restricts food imports. Flour, rice, oil, sugar, all come into Gaza from Karni. When Karni is closed, they do not come in at all. Wheat imports, for example, which allow local bakeries to make the local staple, bread, have been sharply reduced and at times cut off altogether. Bakeries have had to close.

As a result of this policy, more than half of the families in Gaza now eat only one meager meal a day; protein intake has dropped dramatically. According to the Palestinian Centre for Human Rights in Gaza, more than 22 percent of children under five suffer from malnutrition, and 16 percent suffer from anemia. This will have long-term consequences for their health—stunted physical and mental development are more or less guaranteed outcomes. John Dugard warns of a humanitarian crisis "carefully managed by Israel, which punishes the people of Gaza without ringing alarm bells in the West. It is a controlled strangulation that apparently falls within the generous limits of international toleration." According to international law, Israel is responsible for the welfare of the people living under its military occupation. But the strangulation of Gaza is explicitly part of Israeli strategy. "The idea," said Dov Weisglas, a senior Israeli government advisor, "is to put the Palestinians on a diet, but not make them die of hunger."

A WEEK OF HUNGER: FROM UN-OCHA HUMANITARIAN UPDATE ON GAZA, 20–27 JUNE 2007

- The official closure of the three main crossing points in and out of the Gaza Strip remains in place—Rafah (17 days), Karni (16 days) and Erez for traders (14 days). The lack of Palestinian-Israeli security coordination is the principal reason for the closures.

- Humanitarian agencies remained concerned about the limited capacity at Kerem Shalom crossing. Since it has been opened, the maximum number of trucks crossing on any one day has been 25. Even assuming that the capacity could be doubled, the total number of trucks entering on any one day would fall short of the 200/ daily average at Karni crossing before the closure. Additionally, all items entering Kerem Shalom have to be broken down and palletized which is time-consuming and logistically more difficult than Karni—where goods entered through large containers.

- The UN estimates that 175 single-trailer trucks of basic foods and essentials are required daily to enter Gaza on a 5 day/week basis to meet minimum needs. During the last week, only 21% of the total daily consumption needs were met by imports.

- Basic food supplies remaining in Gaza as of 25 June: Flour 9 days, Sugar 3 days, Rice 15 days, Oil 14 days, Beans 51 days.

- There must be a continuous flow of basic supplies and commercial stocks and all crossings reopened to avoid shortages. The absence of any open crossing for exports will also have a significant impact on the economy, markets and the purchasing power of the 1.5 million Gazan population that is already deeply impoverished.

- The food items provided by WFP constitute a basic food basket and reach 275,000 persons. UNRWA, which distributes food assistance to 860,000 persons, provides a food package that is supplemental and meets 61% of the recommended calorie intake for two months. In both cases, the food parcel needs to be complemented by additional produce including fruit, vegetables, and meat and dairy items purchased on the market by the individual beneficiary.

- The Palestinian Ministry of Health reports that 81 items on the Essential Drugs List are out of stock while low stock levels are reported for a further 43 items, largely a result of the PA financial crisis and not due to access difficulties. According to WHO, a total of 162 patients left Gaza for Israel between 19 and 27 June.

- On the basis of market surveys conducted by WFP between 18–20 June and 25 June price rises have been recorded for wheat flour (34%), milk powder (30%) and rice (20.5%) sugar (2%) and vegetable oil (6%).

6

An enforced "diet" is only part of the Israeli strategy for controlling Gaza, which is the territory where Israel developed and then perfected its method for isolating Palestinian communities from the outside world—and punishing them when necessary. Alex Fishman, the security correspondent for the Israeli daily *Yediot Aharonot*, reported in early 2001 on Israel's methods for breaking up the occupied territories into a series of "territorial cells." Food, resources, medicines, vital supplies to each of the cells, must all pass through Israel's checkpoints; they can be cut off at will. And each "cell" can be subjected to further "treatment."

Gaza has endured several such "treatments" since the Israeli redeployment in 2005. In June 2006, Israeli forces entered Gaza to retaliate for a guerilla raid on an Israeli border outpost—a strike on a strictly military target—that ended with the capture of an Israeli soldier. Even before that incident, however, Israeli forces had been regularly bombarding Gaza, often in response to the firing of crude homemade Qassam rockets from Gaza (which are militarily ineffective, but do on some occasions inflict damage, and have been responsible for killing several innocent Israeli civilians, including children). Between September 2005 and the raid on the military post in June 2006, Israeli artillery batteries fired more than 6,000 high-explosive shells into northern Gaza. Israeli military regulations permit artillery to fire at targets up to 300 feet from Palestinian homes, although experience has shown that the impact of a heavy artillery shell throws up a shower of metal fragments that can be lethal at twice that distance. As on other occasions, Israeli artillery fire was often reckless and indiscriminate. On 9 June, for example, shell fire targeted a Gaza beach and killed all but one member of a Palestinian family who had been picnicking on the sand; the only survivor was ten-year-old Huda Ghalia, who had been in the water at the time. Pictures of Huda pounding the blood-soaked sand in agony near the dismembered remains of her father and siblings were broadcast around the world and prompted international outrage. "In spite of a growing body of evidence indicating that the victims were killed by Israeli army shelling, the authorities continue to deny all responsibility and have failed to take the necessary measures to adequately investigate the killings," wrote Amnesty International shortly afterward. "The internal inquiries the Israeli army says it has carried out in this and other cases that attracted international media attention fail to meet even the most basic requirements of an independent and impartial investigation. Such procedures, in which the Israeli army effectively investigates itself, have tended to exculpate Israeli soldiers and seem to have been aimed more at fending off international criticism than at establishing the truth."

The Palestinians of Gaza have no protection from Israeli artillery. And they have no protection from another weapon by which they are frequently tormented. With Jewish settlers safely out of the way, the Israeli air force began staging mock air raids over Gaza—sending jet fighters roaring low over densely populated neighborhoods and breaking the sound barrier in the middle of the night. There is nothing like the sound made by a fighter jet flying at low altitude. Coming suddenly in the middle of the night, it is an absolutely terrifying phenomenon; and if the jet also breaks the sound barrier, it is even more overwhelming. "During the last few days, Gaza was awakened from its dreams of liberation with horrible explosions which have shattered our skies, shaken our buildings, broken our windows, and thrown the place into panic," wrote Dr. Eyad el-Sarraj of the Gaza Community Mental Health Programme in September 2005. "We have been bombed [i.e., subjected to mock air raids and sonic booms] since Friday 23 September, day and night. Usually between 2:00–4:00 A.M., between 6:30–8:00 in the morning during the time children go to school, and in the afternoon or early evening."

Soon after the Israelis began using this tactic, the Mental Health Programme started seeing the extent of its psychological impact on Palestinian civilians. "Gaza is in a state of panic, children are restless, crying, frightened and many are wetting their beds. Some children are afraid to leave home and refuse to go to school. Many are dazed, pale, insomniac and have a poor appetite," El-Sarraj reported. "Israel is inducing learned helplessness to the Palestinians in Gaza with the aim of making the whole population captive to fear and paralysis." Children are especially vulnerable to the tactic. "Loud sounds are associated with danger in the minds of children," the Programme reports, "who are unable to comprehend the distinction between real shelling and mock air raids." Parents were coming to Gaza mental health clinics not sure what to do about the trauma being inflicted on their children: increased levels of anxiety, nightmares, bed-wetting, insomnia, depression, and feelings of helplessness. Because Palestinians have no air defenses, Israeli aircraft can fly as low as they like with total impunity.

Despite the protests of a number of human rights organizations, the Israeli air force continued to use the tactic through the fall of 2005—three sonic booms a night were being reported in November, often only an hour apart—and started using it again frequently in the summer of 2006. By July 2006, the Israeli human rights group B'Tselem was reporting that the air force was causing three or four sonic booms over Gaza a night. No one in Gaza was sleeping. "The sole purpose of these sorties is to prevent the residents from sleeping and to create an ongoing sense of fear and anxiety," B'Tselem stated. Pointing out that the terrifying tactic takes a disproportionate toll on children, the organization also conveyed alarming reports from Palestinian medical sources documenting psychosomatic damage to adults as well, notably headaches, shortness of breath, increased numbers of cardiac cases, and a 30-to-40 percent increase in the number of miscarriages. "The use of sonic booms flagrantly breaches a number of provisions of international humanitarian law," it points out, as well as "the principle of distinction, a central pillar of humanitarian law, which forbids the warring sides to direct their attacks against civilians."

Sonic booms were only the beginning, however. The Israeli military operations Summer Rains and Autumn Clouds that followed the raid on the army post represented a major escalation in the postredeployment bombardment of Gaza. Over 400 Palestinians were killed by Israeli army fire, of whom half were civilians—and one in four a child (during the same period, 3 Israeli soldiers and 2 Israeli civilians were killed by Palestinian fire). Palestinian doctors started reporting an unprecedented increase in the number of amputations, as well as witnessing badly burned people bursting into flames again even after having been extinguished. They also reported seeing bodies that seemed to have "melted," and bodies that had no visible exterior wounds but with internal organs completely crushed, burnt, or crumbled in ways that do not correspond to conventional explosives. Reports soon surfaced, following an Italian investigation into the mystery injuries, that the Israelis were experimenting on the population of Gaza with a new weapon, the dense inert metal explosive, or DIME, which uses a projectile comprising a carbon-fiber casing filled with tungsten powder and explosives. Upon detonation, the tungsten powder focuses an enormous blast of heat and energy in a very tight radius, consistent with the kinds of burns and injuries encountered by Palestinian doctors: the powder, rather than larger metal fragments associated with conventional weapons, causes the injuries.

One of the first features of Summer Rains was the deliberate destruction, by the Israeli air force, of Gaza's only power plant, on 28 June. Almost half of Gaza's electricity was generated by the plant (the rest comes from Israel). Since electricity is vital for refrigeration, the water supply, sewage treatment, and medical services, all were in effect the targets of the bombing of the power plant, and indeed all were severely disrupted in the middle of the heat of summer. "This is an urban society," one U.N. official told the Israeli human rights organization B'Tselem, "and like any urban society in the world, it is highly dependent on electricity."

An extensive B'Tselem investigation of the power plant bombing provides extensive documentation on the bombing's enormous impact on hundreds of thousands of Palestinians in Gaza: families that could no longer refrigerate food, had to spend their evenings in darkness, had to suffer in the heat without fans; butchers who could no longer stock reasonable supplies of meat (already a scarcity in poverty-stricken Gaza); bakers who could no longer provide fresh bread because all their machines rely on electricity; hospitals and clinics that could no longer provide essential services, or could do so only on a severely restricted basis, because they lacked power and fuel for emergency generators (also cut off by the state of siege).

"Clearly, the State of Israel has the right to protect the lives of its civilians, including, of course, against Qassam rockets fired from the Gaza Strip," the B'Tselem report concludes. "But not all means of response and attack are acceptable. Aiming attacks at civilians who are not participating in the hostilities, or at civilian objects, is forbidden under international humanitarian law and is considered a war crime. The power plant bombed by Israel was a purely civilian object. The attack did not impede the ability of Palestinian organizations to fire rockets into Israeli territory. Presumably, it was also not intended to achieve that purpose. Possibly," the report adds, "the objective was to collectively punish the entire Palestinian population by transmitting a 'message of deterrence' to those responsible for making and launching the rockets. It may also simply be that the primary motive was revenge for the abduction of the [Israeli army] soldier. Whatever the case, it was forbidden and was a war crime."

Through the rest of the summer and into the fall of 2006, half of Gaza went without electricity. "Following the attack [on the plant], the lack of power for pumps is causing a serious water shortage, and affecting sewage disposal, for tens of thousands of households throughout the Gaza Strip," noted the U.N. Human Rights Council Special Rapporteur. "There are reports of sewage leakage, as well as a reduction in municipal waste collection and disposal. Reported cases of diarrhoea have increased by 163% compared to the same period last year. It is possible that communicable diseases, like cholera and poliomyelitis, will re-emerge. Reduced hospital services are dependent upon generators that are unsuitable for constant, long-term use." Ultimately, the transformers were replaced by the Arab League and Sweden.

The bombing of the power plant only set the stage for the months of violence that followed. Operation Autumn Clouds culminated in the Israeli army's incursion into Beit Hanoun in northern Gaza, in November. During that operation, hundreds of boys and men were lined up and taken away for questioning and detention by the Israeli army. Forty thousand people were confined to their homes as Israeli tanks roamed their streets and armored Caterpillar bulldozers ravaged their neighborhoods, destroying some 300 homes, an almost thousand-year-old mosque, public buildings, electricity and water and sewage networks, as well as schools and hospitals.

In the six days of the Beit Hanoun assault, 82 Palestinians—half of them civilians, and 21 of them children—were killed. More than 260 were injured, including another 60 children. The incursion came to a climax with the Israeli artillery bombardment of the al-Athamah family home, in a densely packed neighborhood, that left 19 civilians dead, including 16 from one family. Israel claimed that a "technical failure" had led to the disaster. But it was not the result of one single incident:

up to fifteen high-explosive artillery shells were fired at the house over the space of half an hour. Israel categorically refused to allow an international investigation into the incident; it refused to allow a Human Rights Council mission led by Archbishop Desmond Tutu of South Africa to enter the country; it refused to respond to a U.N. General Assembly vote that required the secretary-general to send a fact-finding team—and the United States vetoed a Security Council resolution backing up the General Assembly's demand.

Even granting Israel's claim that the raids were in response to the capture of one of its soldiers, and to the firing of Qassam rockets that had killed 2 Israeli civilians, the Israeli attack on Beit Hanoun was, according to the U.N.'s Special Rapporteur on Human Rights John Dugard, "grossly disproportionate and indiscriminate and resulted in the commission of multiple war crimes." Israel's "refusal to allow an international investigation into the killing of 19 persons in Beit Hanoun, or to undertake an impartial investigation of its own," he added, "is regrettable as it seems clear that the indiscriminate firing of shells into a civilian neighborhood with no apparent military objective constituted a war crime, for which both the commanding officer and those who launched the 30-minute artillery attack should be held criminally responsible. The failure to hold anyone accountable for this atrocity illustrates the culture of impunity that prevails in the [Israeli army]."

7

The Israeli incursions into Gaza in 2006 recalled Israel's offensive in the West Bank in 2002. One of the focal points of that offensive was the city of Nablus, in the northern West Bank, which remains under siege to this day. Like Gaza, Nablus is seen as a major site of resistance to the Israeli occupation, and has frequently been subjected to bombardment by Israeli aircraft and artillery, and raids and incursions by Israeli forces. "Every night, until now," a medic named Lutfi told me when I was there in 2004, "they come into the city. I live in the Balata refugee camp, on the eastern side of Nablus, and we haven't had a peaceful night in more than two years. The soldiers usually come in under cover of darkness.

Sometimes they break down people's front doors, but they also often enter a 'suspect's' house from a neighboring house, by blowing holes through the walls, and moving from house to house rather than entering by the front door, or exposing themselves to danger in the streets or alleys between houses."

Such raids have little to do with what the Israelis call "security"—for militarily effective resistance in Nablus, as in the rest of the West Bank, has long since been crushed—and everything to do with asserting their military presence. "On one occasion," an Israeli soldier on occupation duty said, "we were told: peace and quiet is not necessarily good, and if there isn't mayhem, we'll create it. To demonstrate power, to demonstrate that we are everywhere." Much of what the Israelis do in the West Bank and Gaza has to do with the projection of power: to remind people every day not only that their smallest actions are subject to Israeli control, but that at any given moment—even in the middle of the night—the Israeli army can break down the doors to their homes and come in looking for suspects or suspicious possessions. Rather than being a time of repose, the hours of darkness are in Palestine instead a time of heightened dread.

Such Israeli incursions are in this sense really directed not at this or that individual "suspect," but rather at whole neighborhoods. An Israeli soldier in the Golani Brigade recalls one raid into Nablus in order to capture a Palestinian suspect, in January 2002. After weeks of conducting such raids on an almost daily—or rather nightly—basis, his unit had become very familiar with the area. On this occasion, the suspect was staying in a building of around seven stories, with two or three apartments per floor:

> It was an especially cold winter night. When we arrived at the scene, we quite quickly went through procedure, evacuating all the residents from their flats, and moving them outside their building [under supervision]. The suspect we came to arrest would not come out, and when all the other residents were evacuated, a situation of escalation was created in order to force him to come out. In the process, the building was fired at using different sorts of weapons—many of which were imprecise and caused a lot of damage to other

houses. It should also be noted that we were not fired at, at any point. After a few hours of effort, the suspect finally gave up and came out without a fight. Meanwhile, all that time, all the other families—including many women and children—stood in the street without proper clothing, for we did not let them get organized when we evacuated them. For about eight hours all these residents stood outside, not being able to bring blankets, go to the toilet, or anything else as basic as that. When all the first floors were scrutinized for people and weapons and the suspect was already arrested, we asked our unit commander, who commanded the mission, to let the residents into one of the ground floor flats so they will not have to continue freezing up, and got a negative answer. It was a point in which the incident was over [for all operational purposes], and there [was] no reason not to [let them] enter the building. Even in the morning, when two women begged and cried to [be allowed to] go to the toilet—having stood outside all night—they were refused, and couldn't enter the ground floor and use the toilets.

Sometimes Israeli raids evolve into long lasting house occupations. One survivor of the 2002 Israeli assault on Nablus recounts how the apartment block his family lived in was stormed and taken over by Israeli troops:

> On April 5, Israeli tanks stopped in front of our building. Israeli soldiers stepped out, shouting, and pointed their guns at our faces. We were shocked. All residents of the building had to stay in one room. We were with seventeen persons, not allowed to talk or move. The Israeli soldiers started searching the building, moving every object in every room. While we were waiting, the Israeli soldiers were pointing their guns at us. My pregnant sister was afraid and wanted to use the bathroom, however, the soldier refused to let her go, unless he would accompany her. While the Israeli soldiers were occupying the entire five-floor building, we sat in two rooms. We asked the soldiers whether we were allowed to bring some basic needs. My father, who had a stroke two nights ago, could not get his medication. We only had the clothes we were wearing.

In this case, the building continued to be used for the duration of the Israeli assault, during the course of which it was used as a fire base and also as a makeshift detention and interrogation center. The Israeli army forced many of the building's residents to serve as "human shields" during patrols or assaults on other buildings. This tactic was used frequently in Nablus, especially in the Old City, with its narrow alleys and closely packed houses. "Before searching a house, we go to a neighbor, take him out of his house, and tell him to call for the person we want," an Israeli soldier explains. "If it works, great. If not, we blow down the door or hammer it open. The neighbor goes in first. If somebody is planning something, he is the one who gets it. Our instructions are to send him inside and have him go up to all the floors and get everyone out of the house. The neighbor can't refuse; he doesn't have that option."

Sergeant Nati Aharoni describes one case in which his unit was worried that a building they were about to enter was booby-trapped. "We acted as we usually do in such a case," he says; "we took one of the Palestinian neighbors and had him inspect the place. He opened every door and cabinet, and didn't find anything. We shook his hand and thanked him. Then we went in." Anan Abu Dahar, a resident of the Old City of Nablus, recalls one time when he was pressed into service. After being forced to search a couple of what turned out to be empty houses, he categorically refused to venture farther into a third building, because he heard people upstairs speaking Arabic, and he was sure they were fighters who would engage the Israeli patrol he was with. "I sat down on the step and grabbed the water pipe," he says. "The soldiers ordered me to continue, and not to say a word. They tried to loosen my grip on the pipe, but I held on with all my strength. They hit me in the back, head and legs with their rifle butts. They slammed my head into the wall and ordered me to keep quiet so that the Palestinians wouldn't know that soldiers were in the building. One of the soldiers tried to strangle me. I thought I was about to die. Then I screamed. One of the soldiers sat me down by the window with my head sticking out. He rested his rifle on my head and started to shoot. Every time he fired, I felt as if the bullet penetrated my head." Only in May of 2002, under pressure from human rights groups, did the Israeli army agree to stop using Palestinian civilians as human shields (thus confirming that it had used this tactic previously). According to B'Tselem, however, there is continuing evidence of this practice, in violation of international law.

Terrifying Israeli army intrusions into Palestinian homes occur not only during the course of particular operations, or to find "volunteers" to serve as human shields, but also as a matter of the army's routine, daily projection of power even in times of relative stability. "Every day," another Israeli army soldier recalls, "a six-man unit would cross over roofs and enter a [Palestinian] house. First they'd search the entrances and exits, order the entire family into a single room and get them to talk: ID cards, profession, begin to interrogate them. It also serves one of the army's aims—to make its presence felt." This soldier remembers being struck at his sudden awareness, during one such intrusion, of the surreality of the situation he was in, as his unit was harassing an elderly Palestinian in his house: "Wait a minute, here is this man in his own home, and it made me think of my own family home, surrounded by a garden, and greenery, a kind of fortress surrounded by a hedge of lantana and hibiscus," the soldier mused; "and I thought what if someone were to burst into our house like that, entering through an upstairs window, and force my parents and my younger brother into one of the rooms and start interrogating us, questioning us, searching the entrances and exits, and treating us so patronizingly." And yet of course these home invasions were a matter of routine for the soldier's unit:

> Be it during the day or at night, whenever I feel like it, we choose a house on the map, according to the geographic position of our unit at the time. We feel like it, that's the one we choose, we go on in. "Jaysh, jaysh, iftah al bab" [Army, army, open the door] and they open the door. We move all the men into one room, all the women into another, and place them under guard. The rest of the unit does whatever they please, except destroy equipment—it goes without saying—no helping yourself to anything, and causing as little harm to the people as possible, as little physical damage as possible. If I try to imagine the reverse situation: if they had entered my home—not a police force with a warrant, but a unit of soldiers, if they had burst into my home, shoved my mother and little sister into my bedroom, and forced my father and younger brother and

me into the living room, pointing their guns at us, laughing, smiling, and we didn't always understand what the soldiers were saying while they emptied the drawers and searched through my things. Oops, it fell, broken—all kinds of photos, of my grandmother and grandfather—all kinds of sentimental things that you wouldn't want anyone else to see, wouldn't want them infringing on your privacy, your home is your place. There is no justification for this, it definitely should not be happening. If there is a suspicion that a terrorist has entered a house, okay, so be it. But just to enter a home, any home: here I've chosen one, look what fun, there's a number on it in Arabic numerals that I can't even read. I felt like going in there. We go in, we check it out, we cause a bit of injustice, we've certainly asserted our military presence—and then we move on.

Although such raids continue to be nightly occurrences across the occupied territories (albeit more frequently in the West Bank than in Gaza, which tends to be subjected to much heavier and less discriminating displays of Israeli firepower), the period of Operations Defensive Shield and Determined Path in the spring and summer of 2002 represented a kind of focal moment of this Israeli pattern of behavior, a sort of house intrusion on a massive and collective scale—one in which the entire West Bank was reinvaded and reoccupied.

Between 19 and 28 April 2002, an unknown number of Palestinians in the northern West Bank refugee camp at Jenin—civilians and fighters alike—were killed and much of the camp wiped out not merely during the fighting but in extensive follow-up demolition as well. "During their incursion into the Jenin refugee camp, Israeli forces committed serious violations of international humanitarian law, some amounting *prima facie* to war crimes," write the authors of the Human Rights Watch report on the April 2002 attack; "the damage to Jenin camp by missile and tank fire and bulldozer destruction has shocked many observers. At least 140 buildings—most of them multi-family dwellings—were completely destroyed in the camp, and severe damage caused to more than 200 others has rendered them uninhabitable or unsafe. An estimated 4,000 people, more than a quarter of the population of the camp, were rendered homeless because of this destruction. Serious damage was also done to the water, sewage and electrical infrastructure of the camp."

As they did elsewhere during their spring offensive in the West Bank, the Israelis prevented Red Cross rescue operations in Jenin during the incursion there, even after the fighting had ended. For nearly eleven days, medical relief services had no access to the refugee camp: ambulances and doctors could only wait at the surrounding Israeli checkpoints while injured people, including small children, who could have been saved bled to death in muddy alleyways and under the ruins of their devastated dwellings. The Israeli army's acts in Jenin "amount to grave breaches of the Fourth Geneva Convention and are war crimes," concludes the Amnesty International investigation of the assault on the refugee camp; "these acts include some of the unlawful killings described in this report; the torture and ill-treatment of prisoners; wanton destruction of property after the end of military operations; the blocking of ambulances and denial of humanitarian assistance; and the use of Palestinian civilians to assist in military operations [i.e., as human shields]." The report adds that these and the other routine violations that Amnesty has documented over the years "meet the definition of crimes against humanity under international law." When the United Nations assembled a high-level team to investigate the charges of war crimes in Jenin, the Israelis at first stalled, then they refused to cooperate, then they refused access to the U.N. team altogether; the United States threatened to use its veto; Kofi Annan disbanded the team—and that was the end of that.

Moshe Nissim, an Israeli soldier who operated one of the enormous Caterpillar armored bulldozers that the Israelis used in the camp, recalls: "For three days, I just destroyed and destroyed, the whole area. Any house that they fired from came down. And to knock it down, I tore down some more. They were warned by loudspeaker to get out of the house before I come, but I gave no one a chance. I didn't wait. I didn't give one blow, and wait for them to come out. I would just ram the house with full power, to bring it down as fast as possible. I wanted to get to the other houses. To get as many as possible. Others may have restrained themselves, or so they say. Who are they kidding? Anyone who was there, and saw our soldiers in the houses, would understand they were in a death trap. I thought about saving them [the Israeli soldiers]. I didn't give a damn about the Palestinians, but I didn't just ruin with no reason. It was all under orders." He added: "I got a real kick out of every house that was demolished, because I knew that dying means nothing to them, while the loss of their house means more to them. You destroy a house and you destroy forty or fifty people for generations. If one thing does bother me about all this, it is that we didn't wipe out the whole camp."

One of the Jenin houses the Israelis brought down belonged to Fathiya Suleiman, a seventy-year-old camp resident. The night that the Israeli bulldozer started its attack on their neighborhood, Fathiya and most of her family (husband, daughter, daughter-in-law, and two of her sons) moved to a relative's house, and returned to rescue Jamal, her 38-year-old son who is both deaf and a paraplegic. "When the bulldozer approached our house, which is next to my brother-in-law's, we asked the soldiers to let us get Jamal out," Fathiya recounts. "The soldiers refused. Other women, a male neighbor who spoke Hebrew, and I continued to beg them. At first they told us that their commanding officer was sleeping. Then a soldier agreed that we could get him out. But, he said, only the women were allowed to take him out. We went into the house, but the operator of the bulldozer wouldn't even wait one minute so we could take Jamal out of the house. The soldiers who said we could go into the house called out to the soldier who was operating the bulldozer to stop for a moment, but he refused." In the end, the house was brought down with Jamal still inside.

Although the destruction of Jenin in 2002 received more media attention, Nablus, even more than Jenin, took the brunt of the Israeli assault of 2002. More people (around 600) were killed there than anywhere else in the West Bank. And whole sections of the city were completely obliterated by the Israeli army and air force. I first visited Nablus in 1995, and spent time in the narrow alleyways of the old souk, the city's emotional and commercial center of gravity—in particular, the neighborhood of the ancient olive oil soap factories which for hundreds of years contributed to the fame of Nablus across Palestine and beyond. I returned years later in the company of Firas, an ambulance driver and medic who led one of the rescue teams operating during the 2002 Israeli bombings. We drove straight from the clinic to the old city, where an avenue of total obliteration wound hundreds of meters from one end to the other.

We stood exactly where one of the old soap factories had been, and observed an immense path of devastation winding its way uphill to what had been the heart of an ancient community. It looked as if a tornado had torn through Nablus—the result of a combination of artillery, air strikes, and heavy armor. Firas explained that the Israelis had wanted to open a path wide enough for their tanks to penetrate to the core of the old souks so that the Israeli infantry would not expose themselves to Palestinian fire. Three young boys from the neighborhood approached us in the way that kids approach foreign tourists: "Hello!" "Where are you from?" "Want to take a picture?" When they realized that we were Palestinians, they switched from their broken English into Arabic. I asked them to tell me what they experienced in the days and nights that this immense boulevard of destruction was carved out of the old city. "We were under a curfew when all this happened," one of the boys explained, "so we couldn't get away from the area. Also, there was a huge amount of shooting and bombing going on, so it would have been difficult to get away safely. Our parents gathered us in inner hallways and corridors on the lower floors of the building, where there's less chance of artillery getting through, and we had to wait it out. It was scary. When we were finally able to leave our building, this is what we saw."

While the assault on the old souks (and other neighborhoods) of Nablus was underway, the entire city was gripped by a twenty-four-hour curfew that went on for ten days at a stretch, during which water and electricity supplies were disrupted. Anyone violating the curfew for any reason—to seek food or water or medicine, to summon medical assistance, to help someone calling out in pain—could be fired on, and many were killed this way. After ten days, the army paused its attack long enough to allow residents to emerge and forage for food, but as one survivor pointed out, "there was no food to buy. We started to check with family members, relatives and friends, and found out that people we knew had been killed, wounded or arrested. Every family has a disaster." For several days after Israeli missiles destroyed a house in the Nablus neighborhood of Ras al-Ain, no one in the neighborhood could even attempt to rescue survivors. "We could not reach them," says Ala'a Abu Dheer, who lives just down the street; "nobody dared to leave their home. They would be shot and killed immediately. After a week, when the curfew was lifted, we rushed to the building and started to remove some cement blocks. We found the body of the father. We could hardly recognize him. We continued digging. We found the grandfather and the wife of the dead man, they were still alive. Then we found absolute horror. The bodies of eight children, all were dead."

Firas told me that for the first ten days of the Israeli attack on that city in 2002 it was practically impossible to conduct rescue and evacuation missions. For one whole week, the city's main hospitals didn't receive any wounded, despite the very heavy bombardment of the city. A makeshift clinic was set up in a mosque in the old city, but it was woefully unequipped, and no more emergency assistance was allowed in than casualties were allowed out.

"The IDF completely blocked the movement of ambulances in the West Bank during Operation Defensive Shield," a B'Tselem report concludes. "Wounded people who could not reach hospitals bled to death. Patients could not obtain medical treatment. Hospitals had trouble functioning because they were shelled and the roads leading to them were blocked. Tanks damaged basic hospital infrastructure, such as water and electricity and soldiers fired at ambulances that tried to evacuate the wounded."

"If someone was injured in the middle of the camp, he would not be treated," recalls an Israeli soldier serving in the assault on Jenin in 2002. "Palestinians in the camp were not allowed to move about and ambulances were not allowed to enter. IDF evacuation of the [Palestinian] wounded only began about a week later. We were ordered to fire heavy machine guns at ambulances that ignored the inspection point. The orders came from the deputy battalion commander." It is impossible to know just how many people died under such circumstances.

Other than those wounded in the shelling, Nablus residents who required routine medical treatment, such as kidney dialysis, blood transfusions, chemotherapy, were also unable to receive their treatment, and many died, adding to the casualty toll. When Tahani Fattouh, a pharmacist living in Nablus, went into labor in only her seventh month of pregnancy during the siege of Nablus, her husband, a physician, called an ambulance to take her to the hospital, but the ambulance was turned back and then, on a second attempt, fired upon. Her husband delivered the baby at home with the help of a local obstetrician, but there were complications, as she writes: "A bit after 6:00 P.M., I gave birth to a boy. His condition was normal. They gave him water and sugar to check if he would respond to it, and he did. He was in good condition. I was really happy because I didn't think that he was in danger. About fifteen minutes later, though, his condition started to deteriorate. He started to turn blue, and he stopped crying. My husband gave him first aid, but his condition worsened. My husband was unable to save him, and our baby died. My husband, who saves lives on a daily basis, couldn't save our son, for whom he waited so much. Our baby died because he needed an incubator, but we couldn't get to the hospital, which was only two kilometers from our house."

Israeli forces have been raiding Nablus and the surrounding area on an almost daily basis since the massive incursion in 2002. According to UN-OCHA, there were 436 such raids in the Nablus governorate in the first half of 2007, resulting in the detention of over 600 people. During each such raid, curfews are imposed, houses are broken into, people are snatched from their beds or shot in the street. The Israelis imposed 379 continuous hours of curfew on Nablus in 2005; 342 hours in 2006; and 224 hours in only the first half of 2007.

Even these levels of raids and curfews represent, in relative terms at least, a relief for the people of Nablus. There were 4,808 hours of curfew in Nablus from the summer of 2002 until the fall of 2004, or in other words a total of 200 days of total curfew in just over two years. Most of those days of curfew took place in big blocks of time in 2002 and early 2003. In the two months from mid-June to mid-August 2002, for example—a period of around 1,350 hours—there were 1,300 hours of curfew in Nablus, and only 50 hours in which there was a break in the curfew, allowing civilians time to leave their homes and forage for food and vital supplies.

Long periods of curfew are devastating for the Palestinian population. No statistics can truly express what it means to be stuck at home with young children and nowhere to go. "During the curfew, we spend our time talking with neighbors and napping from time to time," says Jihad Muhalad, a resident of Nablus. "The children are antsy during curfew, and that drives me crazy. They want to go outside and I don't let them, because there is a risk that the soldiers will fire at the children if they throw stones at the tanks. I ask the children to play on the steps or at the neighbor's house." Ghazi Bani Odeh, a freelance journalist who was unable to work for extended periods because of the curfews, says that his family's financial position became precarious after 2002. "When a curfew lasts for a week, I am unable to bring home enough food for such a long period," he says. "Sometimes, the girls ask me to bring ice cream, meat, or fruit. When I tell them that I don't have enough money and that I have not been working as much as in previous years, they don't understand and become even more upset. We are unable to leave the house, even for a few minutes, or to speak with relatives. Our life, which was once easy and based on mutual understanding, has turned into hell. We have no contact with our neighbors. We don't see, hear or speak with anybody. We remain in constant fear of the Israeli tanks that pass along the road and sometimes stand next to the house for hours. The tanks also level the ground, which cuts off the supply of electricity and water. Municipal employees don't get around to repairing the problem for a day or two, which aggravates the situation."

In Nablus and elsewhere in the West Bank, Israeli curfews follow an established pattern. "Army routine during curfew involves standing there and shouting, 'Waqif, ta'al jib al-hawiyya' [Stop, come give me your ID card], there's a curfew, go home,'" says an Israeli soldier; "and saying 'I don't care, I don't care. No, no, no':

The word we used the most with them [the Palestinians] was "No." If in the beginning we used to speak with them and tried to understand, what happened was that they "passed us off." A child arrives, you tell him, "Listen, I'll let you pass now, but do me a favor and go home," and five minutes later he's back. Then you tell him, "Listen here, you said you'd go, now get lost," and two months later, I think it's enough, you don't need a year, a month, a week is enough for you to get fed up with this child and with all these people, you are on eight hour guard duty, and you are so tired, and so bummed, and so burnt out, and you don't give a fuck about any of this shit, and then a person comes, and you don't care if he's old, if he's a man, a woman, an adult, a kid, you don't give a damn what species, race or color he is, he arrives and you tell him "La, ruh al beit" [No, go home]. You tell him, "turn around and go home." I'm not interested in any excuses, I'm not interested in anything. You want to buy vegetables? What do I care about your vegetables? There's a curfew. Period. You don't move. Your house is in the other direction? I don't care, find another way, you can't pass from here.

According to international law, curfews are supposed to be used only for the short-term protection of civilians during military operations, not as forms of collective punishment. And yet, according to a number of human rights organizations, the Israeli army routinely uses curfew as a form of punishment. When Palestinians ask him why a curfew has been imposed on their town, one Israeli soldier recalls musing to himself, "Why? Good question. A very good question. I really don't know. Just because. Because it's shit. That's what it is."

Israel's system of curfews is, theoretically, supposed to be announced to the local Palestinian population so that whenever possible they can at least try to prepare by stocking up on food and other supplies and making sure that everyone is at home when the curfew is imposed. Clear announcements are essential for Palestinians to at least know that a curfew has in fact been imposed, so that they don't unknowingly risk their freedom and even their lives by venturing out into the middle of one. According to the Israeli army's standard operating procedures, Palestinian civilians violating curfew can be, and often are, fired on by Israeli soldiers. At the very least, they can be arrested and have their ID cards confiscated.

It turns out that very often neither the Palestinians nor even the Israeli soldiers know that curfew orders are about to be imposed. "I was on patrol one day, it was the morning shift, and there was no curfew that day, which means we have less work, you don't have to go and close shops and stuff," one Israeli soldier recalls; "and then at some point during our shift they told us that there was a curfew, suddenly, and that means we have to go . . . and shut down all the shops and that's a nightmare." He explains:

We shout "curfew" and "mamnu tajawwul" [there's a curfew] and so on, and the shops start closing slowly. And then we get to the square and we are surrounded by scores of people and lots of commerce, you know, business is booming. So we get there and people start telling us, that's impossible, they told us there's no curfew, and, like, there's nothing I can tell them, I tell them, "There is a curfew. Get lost." And they start shouting at me, and at some point things were [getting out of hand], they weren't really paying too much attention to us and we decided [to] throw a stun [percussion] grenade. So there was mayhem and we started, people started, like, running. The operations commander arrived and he started yelling curfew and stuff, and that's it, we started. We took tons of ID cards from people and we detained them . . . we made a mess there to impose the curfew, and then [another] operations commander came and went on with imposing the curfew, with the turmoil. And then we left, we returned to [our] post, and then about half an hour later they announce that there's no more curfew. I felt like an idiot, you know, scores of people coming to plead with me, ask me, beg me, that they cannot live like this, and they try to talk to you immediately, and you've got nothing to say to them. And half an hour later they tell you there's no curfew. Anyway life there feels as if, you know, there's no life there, every other minute someone comes and pushes them this way and that, whichever way he wants.

According to Majdi Alawna, of the Palestinian District Coordination Office (DCO) in Jenin, "the Israelis do not have a clear policy, and the times for breaks in the curfew are set on a daily basis. Our contact with the Israeli DCO is only verbal. We have never received a written document from them listing the times that the curfew will be lifted. The Israeli side usually informs us that the curfew is lifted right when the break begins." He adds, "In some cases, Israeli security forces suddenly reinstate the curfew during a break in curfew. When they do this, it endangers the lives of the civilians. We have protested the practice." Alam Ghanem (who lives in Jenin) describes, for example, one time he unwittingly found himself endangering his own safety by violating a curfew he thought had been lifted. "It was around 3 P.M. when a friend of mine, Muhammad Nasri, and I were walking around town with no particular destination," he recalls. "Around 4 P.M., we heard people in the street announce that soldiers were entering the city, even though the curfew had been lifted that day. Suddenly, we heard gunfire in the northern edge of the city. People began to run away, the shops closed, and drivers sped quickly away."

Palestinians caught out during a curfew face a variety of hazards. An Israeli soldier with the 450th Battalion says that his unit's standard procedure during curfews is to drive around in an armored personnel carrier and to stop any Palestinian out in the open, confiscate his ID card, and subject him to a full body search. "When we stopped a car," he adds, "we would confiscate the car keys, after going through the rigorous checks. Later, if we remembered, we would give the keys to the border police at checkpoint 300. This was how we punished those who broke the curfew." Another Israeli soldier, in a different unit, describes a similar procedure. His unit would "tour the streets of the city, and stop every vehicle driving, and escort it with the armored [personnel] carrier to the improvised 'parking lot,' which was in fact the back yard of the house we sat in. We would confiscate the car keys, and the driver had to walk back home." That's not the end of the story for the Palestinian, however. For, the soldier points out, another standing order "was to take any person caught walking outside, cuff and blindfold him, get him on the armored [personnel] carrier and take him to the house where we sat, which served as a post. We then had to detain him on the staircase leading to the house," he adds, "for as long as the officer saw fit—between two and seven hours. We would sometimes have 20 detainees and more. The house/post was about 30 minutes' walk from the city."

Palestinians caught violating curfews are subject to worse than detention as well. An Israeli sergeant recalls an encounter with stone-throwing children during a curfew: "We stopped, got [out of] our vehicles, and chased them while firing rubber bullets and throwing stun grenades. In the end, we caught one of the kids, tied his hands with plastic handcuffs, blindfolded him with cloth, and led him all the way through the refugee camp alleys to our armored personnel carrier. The kid was barefooted and was forced to walk through the sewer that flowed in the streets. When we reached the personnel carrier, we threw him onto the ground and the whole squad crowded around him." After subjecting the terrified child to a torrent of verbal abuse, the sergeant reports, they brought him to checkpoint 300, which was manned by the border police, who are not known for their compassionate treatment of Palestinians, "and what happened after that I don't know."

In another incident, during the bloody summer of 2002, a large number of Palestinians, under the impression that the curfew on Jenin had been lifted, flocked to the market in search of food. An Israeli tank stationed nearby fired two high explosive shells at the crowd and also opened fire with its coaxial machine gun; four Palestinians were killed, three of them children, and many others were injured. One of those caught in the fire was Ahmad al-Turki, a father of five. After days of curfew, he had taken his children out for a break. While shopping for vegetables, he heard the shooting. "People began to run in all directions, and I immediately went to my car, put my children, who were next to the car, inside, and drove to Abu Bahar Street, where I saw people and cars." The Israeli fire resumed, and "the kids began to scream. I looked behind me and saw a tank standing at the entrance to Abu Bahar Street, about 120 or 150 meters [400 to 500 feet] from us. I saw that my son Na'il had been injured and was bleeding. I did not stop, and continued driving to get out of gunfire range. When I left the market, I stopped to see how Na'il was. I picked up Sojad to move her away from Na'il. When I lifted her, I was shocked to see her lifeless body. I began to scream and drove immediately to al-Ghazi Hospital. The doctors pronounced Sojad dead on arrival." Na'il, for his part, had been wounded in the knee, abdomen and back; a third child, Shada, had been hit in the knee as well. The Israeli army said that the soldiers had fired in error.

Ahmad Sma'aneh recalls a similar incident. An electrician for the Nablus fire department, he and a colleague, Ahmad al-Qurini, had left their fire station on an emergency maintenance call (which had been cleared, as usual, with the Israelis) during a curfew. Near the Crystal Hotel, in the center of the city, they saw an Israeli patrol that had stopped two ambulances and was searching them. "I saw four Israeli soldiers," Ahmad remembers:

Two of them were searching the [Rafidiyya] hospital ambulance, and the other two were standing on the side of the road. A soldier standing on the left side motioned to us to go back. We backed up about two meters. Then he motioned for us to move forward, and he fired a shot in the air. We proceeded slowly. The Palestinian Medical Services' ambulance was about seven meters in front of us, and the soldiers were around twenty-five meters away. The soldier who was on the left side of the road aimed his weapon at us, motioned with his right hand that we proceed, and then fired two more bullets. One of the bullets pierced the front windshield of our vehicle and hit Ahmad [who was driving] in the head. The second bullet shattered the siren on the roof. It was around 3:50 P.M. At first, I didn't realize what happened. I looked at Ahmad and saw that he was missing the left side of his head; the soldier's bullet had blown his head apart. I was screaming as the truck continued to move. I didn't know how to stop it. The truck hit the back of the Medical Services' ambulance. I called to the medical team to help Ahmad. The medics tried to come to us, but the soldier prevented it. He pushed one of the medics back. I continued to shout. Then an Israeli commander got out of the jeep that was standing there. When the commander saw Ahmad, he ordered the Palestinian medics to evacuate him. I saw the commander reprimand the soldier who had opened fire. I asked the commander in Hebrew if he was the commander. With his head bowed, he said that he was. He seemed startled that his soldier had killed Ahmad for no justifiable reason. Later on, I saw the soldier who had fired at us and killed Ahmad speaking with the commander. The soldier aimed his rifle upwards, and explained that he had only fired in the air.

Ahmad was taken to al-Ittihad Hospital, where he was found dead. His wife had died a year before, and there was now no one to take care of their seven children.

Hundreds of Palestinians have been killed under such circumstances, and thousands more injured, since the tightening of Israel's grip on the West Bank in 2000 (and especially since 2002). The Israeli army's open-fire policy officially permits the use of live ammunition against Palestinians, including civilians, even when soldiers' lives are not in any danger. According to B'Tselem, the army claims that its regulations permit the use of force not as a form of punishment, but rather, in the army's own words, "to enforce the curfew against persons who do not comply with the curfew regulations even though the regulations have been explained to them." As B'Tselem points out, however, it is unclear how soldiers can know whether a Palestinian has had the curfew regulations "explained" to him before firing at him. Yet the use of live ammunition "to enforce the curfew" against civilians is perfectly permissible by the army's own regulations. And as a number of human rights organizations have made clear, such regulations represent flagrant violations of international humanitarian law, which prohibit the disproportionate and excessive use of force against civilians under any circumstances.

8

Both the 2002 incursions into Jenin and Nablus and the summer and fall 2006 attacks on Gaza demonstrated the powerlessness of the Palestinians. While Palestinian factions could—and do—kill and injure Israeli civilians with bombings and rocket attacks, such attacks (however illegitimate) do not pose a mortal threat to the State of Israel. The reverse, however, is not true: Israel could devastate whole Palestinian communities at a time, and it could (and does) completely shut down the Palestinian economy and cut it off from the outside world. Israel could, moreover, unilaterally surround, cut off, isolate, and punish an entire Palestinian community, irrespective of the demands and requirements of international law and international institutions (notably the U.N.)—and it could do so with total impunity. And what was true for Gaza was, and remains, equally true for the increasingly isolated pockets of Palestinians in the West Bank.

Bethlehem, for example, like Gaza and Nablus, has been turned outside in by the Israeli army. The city lies only a few miles outside of Jerusalem. Here the Israeli wall runs across the land, separating the people of Beit Jala, Beit Sahour, and Bethlehem itself from their ancestral olive groves. "Urban Bethlehem," according to a recent U.N. report, "is surrounded by a combination of nine Israeli settlements, a stretch of the Barrier, roads restricted to Israelis and a multitude of checkpoints, earth mounds and roadblocks. Approximately 78 physical obstacles surround

Bethlehem as seen from the north. Photo by author.

Bethlehem today, along with the Barrier, which is nearing completion along the northern and western sides of the city." If, the report points out, "the spiritual, cultural and economic lifeline of Bethlehem has traditionally been tied to Jerusalem, located just a few kilometers away, allowing residents of both cities to freely visit their holy sites," today "this centuries-old link is being undermined." The report adds: "To a visitor wishing to reach the holy sites in Bethlehem, the concrete Barrier erected at the entrance of the city is the most visible manifestation of its physical separation from Jerusalem. For Palestinian residents of Bethlehem, the Barrier is the latest of a series of restrictions—including dirt mounds, road gates, checkpoints and roadblocks, known collectively as 'closure'—implemented over the past decade that has cut the historical road that connects Jerusalem to Bethlehem and Hebron in the south."

As is the case elsewhere in the West Bank, the Israeli wall, and the dozens of other obstacles, run along the very edge of built-up Palestinian communities. Not only are Bethlehem and its sister towns cut off from Jerusalem as well as their agricultural land (whose subsequent lack of development will now provide for even more expansion of the Jewish settlements), they have lost all their open green space, and hence any capacity for future growth. The combination of physical closure and the curfew system (Israel imposed 156 days of 24-hour curfew on Bethlehem in 2002, for example) has devastated the area's social fabric. Hundreds of Palestinians have been forced to leave—10 percent of Bethlehem's Christian population has emigrated in the past few years alone, which has affected the multisectarian social fabric of the city where Christ was born. The once-thriving area immediately around Rachel's Tomb, at the northern edge of Bethlehem, has been particularly hard hit. Of the eighty Palestinian businesses open there in 2002, only 10 percent survive today. Bethlehem's tourist industry has also been devastated: almost 100,000 tourists used to visit the city each month before 2000. Since the tightening of the occupation, that number has plunged to barely 7,000. "Once a bustling cultural and spiritual centre hosting tourists and pilgrims from around the world," the UN report concludes, "Bethlehem has become an isolated town, with boarded-up shops and abandoned development projects."

OCCUPATION BY THE NUMBERS

- Number of Palestinian children killed by Israeli army, 2000–2007: 854
- Percentage of Palestinian children living in fear, according to 2003 USAID study: 93
- Percentage who have personally experienced violence: 48
- Percentage displaced from home due to violence: 21
- Percentage who feel their parents can't protect them: 52
- Percentage who value their education as a means of improvement: 96
- Number of Palestinian schools closed due to Israeli curfews and closures, 2002: 580
- Number of Palestinian schoolchildren affected: 226,000
- Number of Israeli assaults on Palestinian schools, 2003–5: 180
- Number of students and teachers killed as a result: 181
- Schooldays lost due to Israeli closures in West Bank and Gaza, 2003–5: 1,525

- Number of university-age people in Gaza: 400,000
- Capacity of Gaza's university system: 70,000
- Percentage of university-age Gazans denied the right to an education: 75
- Number of Gazan students attending Birzeit University in West Bank, 2000: 350
- Number in 2005: 35
- Number in 2007: 15
- Number of those who are there with permits from Israel: 0
- Number who can visit their families and then return to university: 0
- Number who can freely move around the West Bank: 0
- Number of registered physically disabled people in Gaza: 24,000
- Number of educational courses addressing physical rehabilitation in Gaza: 0
- Percentage of disabled Gazans barred by Israel from studying in West Bank: 100
- Length of closure imposed on Hebron universities by Israeli army, 2002–3: 8 months

The wall, Qalqilya. Photo by author.

9

The greatest symbol of the isolation of Palestinian communities in the occupied territories is the wall, which not only cuts farmers off from their fields (see "Outsides"), but also represents the "Gazafication" of whole cities at a time. Nowhere is this more visible than in the city of Qalqilya, in the northern West Bank, which is surrounded by Israel's wall. Until the period of the Oslo Accords, Qalqilya had been a thriving town, home to about 60,000 people, and, like other Palestinian cities, the commercial and administrative focal point for towns and villages scattered all around it, whose combined population is another 40,000 to 50,000 people. Qalqilya was the place where the people of the surrounding villages brought their goods to market, and where they in turn did much of their own shopping, or met friends and relatives. Because Qalqilya also lies at the edge of the 1949 Armistice Line, which from 1967 to 1993 only nominally separated the West Bank from Israel, it used to be possible for Palestinians from neighboring towns inside Israel itself to come to the Qalqilya market and also to meet with friends and relatives once separated by the Armistice Line. The region was also a natural jumping-off point for Palestinians entering the labor market in the heavily Palestinian north of Israel. Finally, Qalqilya itself was also a major agricultural town, whose fields, orchards, greenhouses, and olive groves lie, of course, outside the city itself.

Israel's wall smashed all of these historic, commercial, agricultural, social, cultural, and familial relationships. Nowhere is this more obvious than in the well-watered and fertile agricultural region around Qalqilya. North of the city, the wall runs deep into the West Bank, absorbing an area of about 6,000 acres of rich farmland between Qalqilya and Tulkarm. A somewhat smaller amount of land is similarly absorbed south of Qalqilya, which is now isolated as the westernmost tip of a virtual peninsula created by the wall. As a result, not only Qalqilya and Tulkarm, but another twenty or so towns and villages in the immediate vicinity now find themselves separated from their agricultural land by the network of concrete slabs, electric fences, and ditches that constitute the separation wall. What's worse, another six or seven Palestinian towns now find themselves wedged in between the separation wall and the Green Line. Similar stories are unfolding all along the route of the separation wall to the north and south in the rest of the West Bank.

Qalqilya, cut off from its lifeblood of commerce and farming, is a dying town. The traditional souk or marketplace, once thriving, is listless, bare. To the north of the city, the road that used to take farmers to their fields is now interrupted by, in this order: a mound of earth and concrete cubes; a metal gate; rolls of razor wire; a wire grate topped by more razor wire; a patrol road; more razor wire; an electric fence; more razor wire; another patrol road; and then on the other side more of the same. All this is protected by an immense fortified tower, bristling with machine guns, with the Israeli flag hanging from it.

On the western edge of the city, the wall is made entirely of concrete. The bulldozed and leveled area on either side of the wall used to be farmland and orchards. On the inside of the wall, the desolation extends a few hundred yards back from the first row of razor wire. Israel has banned all construction within a certain distance of the wall, and, in order for its snipers and machine-gunners to maintain a clear line of sight from the tower, nothing is allowed to grow there. Not only is a swath of permanent

The wall, Qalqilya. Photo by author.

The wall, Qalqilya. Photo by author.

devastation a hundred yards wide by several miles long already more than a poor community can easily sustain—but the *miri* lands' expropriation clock is ticking away on a huge amount of additional land that, if it isn't watered or tended (even if that condition is being imposed by force, as it is here) may be subject to permanent confiscation within a few years.

The sense of desolation is even more striking on the western side of the city, where all the roads that used to link Qalqilya to Israel and to neighboring villages run into—and are cut off by—massive concrete slabs. The slabs are by far the most impressive feature of the separation wall that they have come to symbolize. The parts of the complex composed of razor wire, ditches, and electric fences are just as impenetrable, but somehow they seem less hostile; at least one can more or less see through to the other side. Here the complex is composed of slabs of featureless concrete rising 24 feet from an earthen rampart: twice the height of the Berlin Wall. Every 100 yards or so, there is an armored camera housing, and every few hundred yards there is a guard tower. A sluice allows water from the Palestinian side to seep to the Israeli side. Water is the most valuable resource in this part of the world.

From the rooftops of buildings standing a few dozen yards back from the wall, one can clearly see a line of trees and houses just on the other side of the wall that belonged to Qalqilya until 1948. There are still Palestinians living there, but they are now on their own. Immediately on the other side of the wall is the Trans-Israel Highway. From a vantage point here, one can see the entire arc of the separation wall around Qalqilya: the wall running north-to-south on the city's west side and then, shortly after the bend to the east, the sections where the wire sections take over. I have seen it for myself, and it really does look like an enormous open-air prison. On the western horizon one can easily see the towers of Tel Aviv—another world—only 10 to 15 miles from here.

The red-tiled houses of the formerly Palestinian town of Kafr Saba, inside what is today Israel, can also be seen quite clearly. They stand out from an industrial area that has overtaken them. The Palestinian residents of Kafr Saba were expelled from their homes during an attack of the Alexandroni Brigade of the Haganah (the forerunner of the Israeli army) on 13 May 1948, the day before the State of Israel declared its independence. The Israeli town of Kefar Sava (named after its Arab predecessor) has taken over where Kafr Saba used to be; as is the case throughout Israel, the formerly Palestinian houses are now lived in by Israelis, while their former owners wait in squalor, sometimes within eyesight.

To the southeast, one can see the towns of Habla and Ras Atiya. They used to be contiguous to Qalqilya, but two different sections of the wall, and the Israeli bypass road leading to the Jewish settlement of Alfe Menashe, now separate them. The Israeli army opened a tunnel in order for Palestinians to get under the wall and the bypass road. Meanwhile, on the other side of Ras Atiya, the wall snakes down and separates it and Habla from the villages of Daba'a and Ras Tira; the area from Daba'a to Ras Atiya has been designated for the expansion of the settlement of Alfe Menashe, so that land will be taken as well.

As Palestinians enter the tunnel leading from Qalqilya to Habla and Ras Atiya, they can glimpse yellow-plated Israeli cars rushing by overhead on their way to and from Alfe Menashe and the other Jewish settlements deeper in the West Bank. Down below, the Palestinian road is partly an underpass and partly a deep asphalted trench flanked on either side by earthen walls leading up to the surface some 15 feet above. On top of the trench walls there are the usual razor-wire emplacements

The wall, Qalqilya, as seen from Israeli side. Note the use of landscaping to offset the scale. Photo by author.

running up to an electric fence. Finally, the road curves upward and emerges from the trench.

The walled peninsula imprisoning Qalqilya comes within 200 yards of the opposite peninsula containing Habla and Ras Atiya, like a thumb and forefinger making an "OK" sign, except that the two concrete peninsulas don't touch. To the west, the gap leads to the Green Line; and the hollow created to the east contains the settlement of Alfe Menashe and three or four Palestinian villages, including Ras Tira and Daba'a, now caught in the "closed area" on the other side of the wall. The Israeli bypass road leading through this pocket of territory to Alfe Menashe and beyond was plowed through much of the village of Daba'a, whose mosque and main school were now on the other side not merely of the road, but of the wall as well.

It is difficult to say who has it worse: Palestinians in walled-in prisons like Qalqilya, or those caught on the west side of the wall, trapped in the "seam zone" between the wall and the 1967 border. There are tens of thousands of Palestinians who live in this area. They too have to apply for permission from the Israelis to go on living on the land that their families have lived on for generations. The inhabitants of the villages in the "seam zone" have had to apply for a document that the Israeli army calls a permanent resident permit. As its name suggests, this document is something like a U.S. Green Card, except that in this case the person applying for the permit only wants to stay where he already is, on the land where he has been living all his life. By November 2007, dozens of men, women, and children living in the area had not received permanent resident permits from the Israelis, thereby restricting, or preventing altogether, their freedom of movement outside the "seam zone." Even when granted, of course, the permits are subject to Israeli military regulations and can be withdrawn or canceled at any time. This means that the people in this area can be subjected to summary expulsion from their land and homes whenever it suits the State of Israel. As it is, they are already cut off in many cases from work, schools, and health care. A UN-OCHA survey published in November 2007 showed that almost half of the communities in the "seam zone" reported that households had left because of the way the wall had disrupted their lives; more than half the communities reported that heads of households had left to find work elsewhere. A third of the West Bank's villages will have problems in getting access to vital social services once the wall is completed. It is not yet complete—30 villages have already been cut off from access to medical care, and that number will rise to over 70 once the wall is completed; 22 are already cut off from schools; 8 from primary water sources; and 3 from electricity networks.

According to Colonel Shaul Arieli of the Israeli army reserves, the point of making life so difficult for Palestinians in the gap between the border and the wall is to push them to leave for good. "The objective is for them to not have access to the State of Israel, for demographic reasons," he points out. "Conversely, the Palestinian authorities will have a hard time supplying the residents of this area with health, education, and legal services, not to mention jobs. The village residents," he continues, "will not be able to continue living under these sorts of conditions. They will abandon their homes and go to the big cities, at which point it will be possible to expand the borders of the State of Israel without paying the demographic price. It would be voluntary transfer." There has, he adds, "never been such a horrid, stifling jail as this. A terrible cry will arise here."

10

Even before Israel declared Gaza an "enemy entity" in September 2007 and threatened to cut off the last remaining supplies of fuel and electricity to the impoverished and still-occupied territory, Gaza's 400,000 schoolchildren were facing problems of their own. Israel's refusal to allow imports into the territory meant that Gaza was short not just of raw textiles and other economic inputs, but also of paper, ink, and vital school supplies. Gaza's schoolchildren entered the new year missing one textbook in three.

But the missing textbooks were the least of their problems. John Ging, the Gaza director of the United Nations Relief and Works Agency (UNRWA), whose schools take care of 200,000 refugee children in Gaza, says that children come to school "hungry and unable to concentrate" (because so many Gazan families can only afford to give their children one meager meal a day) and rattled from too many nights of sleep lost to Israeli sonic booms or air or artillery bombardments. UNRWA is now reporting failure rates in its schools of up to 80 percent in some subjects.

An entire generation of Palestinians in Gaza is growing up stunted: physically and nutritionally because they are not getting enough to eat; emotionally because of the pressures of living in a virtual prison and facing the constant threat of displacement, homelessness, and physical destruction; and intellectually and academically because they cannot concentrate—or, even if they can, because they are trying to study and learn in circumstances that no child should have to endure. The irony is that the overwhelming majority of Gaza's schoolchildren say that they value their education as a means of improvement.

When these children grow up, they will, if only because of their sheer numbers (Gaza has one of the youngest populations in the world), face even greater difficulties than those facing their older brothers and sisters today. There were 400,000 people of university age in Gaza in 2007. But the capacity of Gaza's already overcrowded university system is at most 70,000. Three Gazans in four are unable to pursue a university education because there is no room for them in the system—and because they can't get out of Gaza. For a Gazan student to enter a foreign university requires not only winning a scholarship that few university systems give away to foreign students. It also requires finding a means of traveling to the foreign university, which is difficult not only because Gazans, like all Palestinians in the occupied territories, are stateless and therefore lack normal travel documents like a passport, but also because just getting in and out of Gaza is difficult at best, and often impossible. Of course, Gazan students ought to be able to attend universities in the West Bank, because both territories legally constitute a single unit and because Israel, which occupies both, has the legal obligation to allow passage between the two territories. Wantonly disrupting a person's freedom of movement, forbidding his or her education, access to which is recognized as one of our fundamental human rights—these are violations of international law.

And yet the statistics speak for themselves. Before the closures associated with Oslo, the West Bank university system was open to Gazan students. By 2000, there were only 350 Gazan students in West Bank universities; by 2006, there were 35; by 2007, 15. All of them are in the West Bank in violation of Israel's permit and pass system regulating Palestinian movement. If they are caught by Israeli soldiers at a roadblock or random "flying" checkpoint, they could be arrested and sent back to Gaza. They are unable to return home to visit their families.

Even students—including schoolchildren—in the West Bank and East Jerusalem have a hard time coming and going between home and school. Tens of thousands of Palestinian students across the length of the West Bank have to negotiate their way through or around Israeli army checkpoints, barriers, roadblocks, and the wall every single day. Sometimes they face miles of detours because of Israeli closures (see "Outsides"). Ahmed Malhi, who lives in East Jerusalem, has to pass through three separate Israeli checkpoints on his walk to school every morning; any one of them could hold him up long enough to miss class or an important exam. "If it's a tough day getting through checkpoints," he says, "I start feeling bad early in the day, and I stop concentrating." Omar Musallam, an eighteen-year-old who studies in Jenin, in the northern West Bank, is rarely able to return home to visit his parents in Ramallah, which would only be an hour away under normal circumstances. "It makes me feel frustrated and angry because I can't see my family in Ramallah," he explains. "It's only a short distance but it's like they are living in another country."

But, as bad as they are, the problems faced by the West Bank students are nothing compared to those of their compatriots from Gaza. One Gazan, a twenty-year-old unable to pursue a degree in Gaza, spent three years trying to get out just to attend a two-week course. He asks himself why—why he has to "see my best friends leaving Palestine and never come back because there's no way to live here?" And he asks himself "why I prefer to die [than to go] on living this situation any more."

Even in Israel itself, Palestinian students—citizens of the state—face great difficulties, when compared with their Jewish peers. The state provides 1,600 subsidized day-care centers, for example, but only 25 of those are in Palestinian towns. Only 4,200 of the 80,000 Israeli children aged zero to three who attend day care are Palestinian, though had that number been in proportion to the actual population, it would have been closer to 20,000. Israel invests more than three times as much in a Jewish student than it does in a non-Jewish one. The state's list of the 553 towns and villages granted top priority for education excluded all Palestinian towns inside Israel other than four villages. There are 25 special art schools for Jewish children, and none for Palestinians. And at the higher levels of its school system, Israel opens far more curricular tracks to Jewish students than to Palestinian ones. As a result of all these forms of discrimination—and despite the fact that Palestinians traditionally place great emphasis on their children's education, a fact attested to by the disproportionately large numbers of Palestinians among the Arab intelligentsia—a far greater proportion of Jewish students make it through high school, get accepted to university, and graduate. Only 10 percent of Israel's university students are Palestinian, for example, though proportionately speaking it ought to be double that number. Only 3 percent of its Ph.D. students are Palestinian. Only 1 percent of its university lecturers are Palestinian.

Of all the confines and limitations facing any human society, education has always provided a way out. Intellectual nourishment allows us to expand our mental and cultural horizons even if we are physically confined. It teaches us to look outside ourselves; it allows us to take the outside world in; it encourages us to look inside ourselves. Education and learning can move us in ways that can compensate for our inability to move; thought allows us to move others even when we cannot move ourselves (a point made so powerfully in Wordsworth's poem "Old Man Travelling," where we see an old vagrant, standing quite still, who "does not move with pain, but moves / With thought"). An education provides Palestinians virtually the only way to transcend all the limits imposed on their inside and outside lives by Israeli rule. But under the present circumstances, even this last avenue of escape is gradually being blockaded, narrowed, and closed.

Inside Out

1

It is a scene repeated, with minor variations, virtually every day: a group of Palestinian schoolgirls, huddled together with their mothers, their teachers, and a team of international volunteers, is picking its way across a rocky hillside. Behind them is the school from which they have just departed: the Qurtuba Elementary School in the Tel Rumeida neighborhood of Hebron. Before them is the path along the hillside, terminating in a narrow set of stairs leading down to a paved road. In between, there is a group of Jewish settler girls, accompanied by a detachment of heavily armed Israeli soldiers. It is a Jewish holiday: the settler girls have been enjoying a picnic on the sunny hillside. They see the Palestinian schoolchildren approaching and stand up to obstruct the path, heaping verbal abuse at the Palestinian girls and their mothers. Pushing and shoving follows, a minor scuffle. The Israeli soldiers, overburdened with assault rifles, helmets, radios, webbing, and extra clips of ammunition, try to intervene, but they are under strict orders. Their duty is to protect the Jewish girls: they are not allowed to physically restrain them. The girls are emboldened, because they know that there's nothing the soldiers can do to stop them—and that if any Palestinian so much as lifts a hand to them, the soldiers will instantly step forward to protect them. The soldiers plead with the girls to make way for the Palestinians; at the same time, they bark orders at the Palestinian mothers and daughters, "Yalla, imshi!" (Come on, get moving!). Finally, the procession breaks through the crowd of settler girls.

The Palestinian children's ordeal is not over, however. As they approach the top of the steps, Jewish settler boys, who had been playing in the street beneath the hillside, start pelting them with stones. The path narrows and bottlenecks as it reaches the top of the stairs. The stairs themselves are narrow and slippery: they descend along the side of a building, but there is no banister facing the street side, no protection of any kind—and an open drop to the street below. The Palestinian children and their mothers, crowded together and gingerly picking their way down the slippery steps one by one, are exposed to the stones. Some of the Jewish boys pelting them are as young as five or six. There are adults—Jewish settlers—watching them. None intervenes. There is another detachment of Israeli soldiers here as well; but the boys, like their sisters on the hillside above, know that the soldiers are incapable of stopping them. The stoning continues.

The main entrance to the Qurtuba School was sealed with razor wire by the Israeli army in 2002: this dangerous path is the only way for the Palestinian schoolchildren to get to and from their school. Because of the nature of the harassment and intimidation the children face, there are at least three different international organizations providing escorts and observers to accompany them as they come and go from school, including Temporary International Presence in Hebron (TIPH) and the Ecumenical Accompaniment Program in Palestine and Israel (EAPPI), sponsored by the World Council of Churches. The escorts observe and record what happens on a daily basis, and relay their observations, pictures, and videos, but they can't physically protect the Palestinian children or their mothers. On the contrary, they must frequently practice the Christian virtue of turning the other cheek. In June 2006, Duduzile Masango, a young South African Christian volunteer with EAPPI, was assaulted by an elderly settler woman near the Qurtuba School, who attempted to smother her with a towel. In April of that year, a German social worker, a Norwegian sociologist, and a Swiss lawyer, all also with EAPPI, were stoned by settlers near the school while accompanying Palestinian children. The lawyer needed seven stitches for a head wound as a result.

In November 2006, Tove Johansson, a Swedish human rights worker with TIPH, was among a group of international volunteers accompanying Palestinian schoolchildren when the group was surrounded by Jewish settlers—adults this time, not kids. The settlers closed in and started spitting on the Palestinian children and their international escorts—so much spit that one of the observers said it felt like rain. Pushing and kicking followed. Then one of the Jewish men reached forward and broke a glass bottle on Tove's face, shattering her cheekbone. As she fell to the ground, the crowd of settlers surged forward, cheering and chanting. At that point, the Israeli soldiers who had been so far standing by called for the crowd of settlers to back off. They backed off a little, but continued jeering. The Palestinian children were terrified; their young escorts, tending to Tove, were hardly less shaken. Finally, the Israeli police intervened—threatening to arrest the international human rights workers if they did not move off.

The international observers come and go. For the Palestinian children of Hebron, however, these are scenes of everyday life. It doesn't always end in blood, but they face this ordeal twice each day, going to and from school.

In Hebron, the only Palestinian city (other than East Jerusalem) in which there is an active Jewish settler presence, all of the features that define "outside" and "inside" life throughout the West Bank also define life here, but on a smaller and much more intimate scale. Just as the Oslo Accords divided the rest of the occupied territories into Area A, Area B, and Area C, a 1997 agreement divided Hebron itself into H1 and H2 (see map, p. 343). H1, comprising about 7 square miles, is the equivalent of Area A; over 100,000 Palestinians live here. H2, just over 1.5 square miles, is the equivalent of Areas B and C (an arrangement that violates the principles of Oslo, such as they are, which stipulates that Palestinian cities should all be considered parts of Area A, the part of the West Bank under Palestinian control, i.e., about 18 percent of the territory).

The collective life of the 30,000 Palestinians who live—or used to live—in H2 was effectively sacrificed to the interests of the few hundred

Jewish settlers who have nestled here—along with the 4,000 soldiers who protect them—since they started evicting Palestinian residents and taking over their homes in the Old City during the 1980s. One percent of the population of H2 thus completely dominates the 99 percent who "share" it with them; a third of a percent of Hebron's overall population effectively dominates the whole.

Hebron is not merely a microcosm of the entire West Bank, however. It is an ongoing experiment in the science and politics of ethnic separation and systematic dispossession. Even a senior figure in the Israeli military establishment, quoted anonymously in a recent report published by the Israeli human rights organization B'Tselem, describes Israeli policy in the center of the city as "a permanent process of dispossessing Arabs to increase the Jewish territory." The Israeli army itself says that the idea that Palestinians can "live a normal life in the area" is "inconsistent with the principle of separation that underlies the security forces' plan to safeguard the space." According to B'Tselem, ongoing restrictions and prohibitions imposed by the Israeli army on Palestinians living in the center of Hebron have made it "impossible for Palestinians to renovate and rejuvenate the area." What was once the vibrant heart of the city, says its scathing report of May 2007, "has become a ghost town." Hebron is living evidence of what it means for Palestinians to be inexorably forced out of their homes and pushed off their land. It is a slow-motion "portrait" of Palestine being turned inside out.

2

I had the opportunity to visit Hebron when I was last in the West Bank. My guide was Abu Karim, a gentle, generous, and altogether hospitable man of about forty-five, and a lifelong resident of the city. "We will walk all the way to the Old City, through the souk, and to the Ibrahimi Mosque and the settlers' bypass road," Abu Karim announced, "and as we walk along, you will see the nature of the city's life transforming itself before your very eyes, a transformation you have to see with your own eyes in order to believe and understand it." We began by strolling down the crowded open market of Bab al-Zawiyah. I was impressed by the

Jewish settlers go for a stroll while Palestinians are under curfew, Hebron. Photo by
Mamoun Wazwaz, Maanimages.

extent of commercial activity, and the quality of produce on offer here.
"Yes," Abu Karim responded; "but notice how all the stalls are set up in
a makeshift way, on car tops or the sidewalk: none of them really belong
here, and this area was not originally a marketplace—for the real market
was down in the souk area, where we're headed now. As you will soon see,
the old markets have closed down and all the activity has shifted to here,
from H2 to H1."

H2 used to be the very heart of the entire city of Hebron. It used to
house the main fruit and vegetable market, not just for Hebron, but for
all the towns and villages around it. There was once a huge wholesale
market as well, and a once-bustling light industrial zone which, in the old
days before Oslo, used to produce some 40 percent of the whole region's
economic output. As we walked through Bab al-Zawiyah, we reached
a street leading off to the right that had been completely closed off by
concrete blocks and an enormous steel gate. "That's Martyrs Street down
there," said Abu Karim, pointing through the blockade. On the other side
of the blockade, we could see the continuation of the street, which was

Makeshift market, Hebron. Photo by author.

once one of the city's main thoroughfares. The houses and stores on the other side looked exactly like the ones here. But it was a ghost town: all the windows and doors had been welded shut. "That area," Abu Karim explained, "has been completely shut down by military orders. No Palestinians are allowed in it—all the shopkeepers lost their shops, all the residents their homes and belongings." Why? "Because there's a Jewish settlement at the other end of the street, so the whole area is off-limits to Palestinians. 'Closed military area.' " Right up against the permanently closed gate, a Palestinian shopkeeper, evicted from his shop on the other side, had set up his stall here: racks of clothing hung surreally in the open air.

We now proceeded past the Israeli army post that had been set up there (a heavily sandbagged machine-gun emplacement with, as far as I could tell, only one soldier manning it), and on into the heart of the Old City. The farther we walked into the Old City, the quieter it got. Every so often we would see an Israeli observation post on top of a Palestinian house: a tower hung with camouflage netting that made it impossible to tell if anyone was inside looking out at you. As we made our way into the network of ancient streets, we found ourselves walking by a few closed shops in between lots of open ones; but as we went deeper,

Shuttered shops in Old City of Hebron. Photo by author.

fewer and fewer shops were open. Soon we were in streets where all the shops were closed, street after street of closed shops. But there's no closure order right now, no curfew: where are the shopkeepers, I wondered? "Gone, finished, wiped out," said Abu Karim. "How long do you think a small shopkeeper can last with months of not being able to get to his shop, never mind going without new stock, or not having any customers? They're all finished here, there's hardly anyone left. Those who could, have moved to the open-air market at Bab al-Zawiya. The others are just gone."

I noticed that many of the shop doors had been welded shut. "Yes," said Abu Karim, "that's the mark of the army. They were enforcing closure orders at some earlier point. Now there's no one to open the doors anyway, so the welding is just the final touch. Either way the shops are dead." We passed more and more alleys and streets off to the right, leading to dead ends: gates welded shut; steel barricades blocking the path; rolls of razor wire; concrete blocks. Unlike the blockade at the entrance to Martyrs Street, here it was actually impossible to see through to the other side. The streets and alleys had been completely sealed off. "Again, there's a Jewish settlement on the other side of those blockades," Abu

Karim pointed out. "But we'll soon get to a place where you will see the Jewish settlement right over our heads, looking over the main street here." Indeed, a couple of dozen yards farther along, the Jewish settlement could be seen looming overhead, in formerly Palestinian homes.

There was an iron grate, or in certain places a kind of chicken-wire netting, covering the main street of the souk down which we were proceeding. All along the overhead grate or netting—and in several different places weighing so heavily that the netting sagged under the load—there were piles and piles of stinking garbage. I could make out plastic bags and bottles, banana peels, kitchen waste, and soiled baby diapers, dripping onto the street below.

"That's the garbage that the Jews throw from their kitchen windows, down onto the Arabs below. At first it was much worse, because there was no grate or netting, so you could be walking along and suddenly find disgusting garbage cascading down on your head." "Garbage!" said an old man walking down the street with a disgusted look on his face; "I wish garbage were all they threw down. You should see the things they throw: diapers, human and animal feces." The man continued on his way, shaking his head. "Let's get going," said Abu Karim, "you don't want to be standing there when they throw something out."

The garbage, the harassment, the curfews, the closures: all had taken their toll on the Old City of Hebron. It was a dead place now. In the Old City and Bab al-Zawiyah alone, between 2,000 and 2,500 small businesses and shops have been wiped out. Thousands of workers have been laid off (the unemployment rate is some 70 percent), and tens of millions of dollars lost—a major blow to the already shaky Palestinian economy. Of the 500 shops that used to dot al-Casbah Street (the one with the garbage netting), only 15 survive today, their owners adamantly returning to work every day that it is physically possible. Three schools formerly attended by almost 2,000 Palestinian schoolchildren have also been closed and taken over for use by the Israeli army in H2. The children have had to make do with overcrowded makeshift accommodations elsewhere.

B'Tselem's investigation of the part of the Old City where we were walking revealed that almost half of the Palestinian residents had been forced out because of the sustained pressure on them by the settlers and

Iron grate over street, Old City of Hebron. Photo by author.

the army. Nidal al-Awiwi, a resident of the Old City, summed up what life has been like in the district for those who have managed to hang on against all odds:

> The curfew makes it almost impossible for my wife and me to meet with friends and family. We are like prisoners in our house. The last time I visited my parents was during the holiday. Sometimes, more than two months go by before I am able to visit them. Our financial

Garbage hanging in netting, Old City of Hebron. Photo by author.

situation has deteriorated, and I do not earn enough to meet our needs. I had to disconnect the telephone and do not have money to buy furniture and replace items that are worn out. As for food, we eat the minimum necessary. The prolonged curfew and harassment has also affected our neighbors, some of whom have moved to Area H-1. On the two-hundred-meter [650-foot] section of the road between the entrance to the Casbah and my house, only six of the twenty-three families remain. Two hundred and forty shops located in the area between the entrance of the Casbah and the Tomb of the Patriarchs have closed. A large number of shop owners who shut down their businesses opened new businesses or moved to shops in Area H-1. Even the market is closed now. It wasn't enough for the army that the shops were closed for a long time; in the past two weeks, the army has welded shut the doors of more than twenty shops near the Avraham Avinu settlement.

Abu Karim and I had now come to the end of Casbah Street, where the ancient Hebron souk runs up to one of the Old City's gates. Here Hebron's two principal religious sites stand literally on top of each other: the Ibrahimi Mosque, and, beneath it, the Jewish Tomb of the Patriarchs. On 25 February 1994, one of the settlers from Kiryat Arba, Baruch Goldstein (born and raised in Brooklyn, as is the case with a sizable proportion of the settlers in Hebron and elsewhere in the West Bank), stormed into the Ibrahimi Mosque during prayers. He opened fire on the worshipers with his assault rifle, which most settlers carry with them at all times. He was able to kill 29 Palestinians and wound dozens of others before unarmed Palestinians managed to overcome him and beat him to death. Ever since the massacre, Goldstein has been something of a saint to the most extreme of the Jewish settlers in the West Bank (notably the ones of Hebron, who especially revere him). "Here lies the saint, Dr. Baruch Kappel Goldstein," his tombstone in Kiryat Arba reads; "blessed be the memory of this righteous and holy man, may the Lord avenge his blood, who devoted his soul to the Jews, Jewish religion and Jewish land. His hands are innocent and his heart is pure. He was killed as a martyr of God on the 14th of Adar, Purim, in the year 5754."

The main legacy of Goldstein outside the site of the massacre is a large metal detector, through which Palestinians must pass on their way to their mosque. When I was there with Abu Karim, we saw an Israeli soldier slouching against a guard booth while a queue of Palestinians formed to one side to have their papers checked and their bags searched before they could enter the mosque, or the gate of the Old City itself. Even though we were leaving rather than entering the Old City, we were called forward to have our papers checked. I showed the guard in the booth my passport. The soldier, still slouching at her post, started complaining to me in Hebrew. She wanted to know why I was using a U.S. passport and not the normal identity cards issued to the "other Arabs."

Once we had our papers checked, we walked down to the army post and the street below. "Now, be careful on this street," Abu Karim cautioned me; "this is the settlers' bypass road to Kiryat Arba [a nearby Jewish settlement], and only their vehicles are allowed on it. They will come down here at a hundred miles an hour, and if you're in their way, it's just too bad for you, they'll hit you without giving it a second's thought." I didn't have much time to ponder the point: soon enough a yellow-plated white car came screaming down the road toward us, going at least 60 or 70 mph down a very narrow street. Abu Karim quickly pulled me to the side of the road as the car blazed past. "Told you so," he said, shaking his head. "Remember, as far as he's concerned, you're just a dirty Arab, and one fewer of you is one fewer obstacle for him." I could see two or three Palestinian girls, schoolkids, walking on the other side of the road, hugging the wall. "Anyway, it's dangerous for us to go much farther down this road toward their settlement," Abu Karim said, "but I just wanted you to see their access road."

We headed back up Casbah Street into the Old City, underneath the garbage-laden netting, and back to Bab al-Zawiyah. As we went, we experienced the reverse of what we had seen on the way into the souks; the farther we got from the Jewish settlement, the more the street seemed to come back to life; first no shops at all, then one or two in between the closed ones, then more and more, until we got back to the bustle of Bab al-Zawiyah. On the way out, I'd noticed that in each shop's doors, even the closed ones, there was a little white paper. Wondering what it was, we pulled one out and unfolded it. It was an electricity bill. At the last Israeli post marking the beginning of H2, I looked back at the sad Old City and its still mostly shuttered shops. It was a remarkable contrast with the color and life of Bab al-Zawiyah.

The situation in Hebron may be particularly stark, but in general terms the logic at work here is the same as the wider logic of the occupation. The Israeli journalist Amira Hass meditates on the ironies of this logic, and the moral calculus of the wider occupation. "For the sake of 400 or 500 Jews living today in the Old City of Hebron, it is completely sensible and perfectly appropriate that a full curfew should be imposed on the 26,000 Palestinians living there," she writes; "for the sake of the 6,000 Jewish residents of Kiryat Arba, it is completely sensible and perfectly suitable that the 120,000 Palestinians living in Hebron should be encircled. And for the sake of the 200,000 Jews living today in the settlements of the West Bank (except for east Jerusalem) and the Gaza Strip and for the sake of the thousands of IDF [Israeli army] soldiers protecting those settlers, it is correct and just that communities with a total population of 3 million Palestinians should be encircled." But, as Hass points out, "this logic is the bullet-proof vest of a line of thinking that has developed over

a number of decades and which, since 1967, has become the hallmark of
Israeli rule in the West Bank and Gaza Strip."

The process of turning Palestine inside out did not begin in 1967,
however.

3

There is a scene in the Palestinian novelist Emile Habibi's *The Secret Life
of Saeed, the Ill-Fated Pessoptimist*, in which Saeed, having returned from
Lebanon in the aftermath of the 1948 War, has managed to find his way
back to the city of Acca, in northern Palestine. He ends up having to
camp out for a night in the courtyard of the Jazzar Mosque, which he
finds crammed with refugees from across the villages of the Galilee, who,
like hundreds of thousands of other Palestinians, had been driven from
their homes during the creation of Israel. Seeing Saeed, the refugees
immediately gather around to ask who he is and where he has come from.
He explains that he has just returned across the border from Lebanon.
One of them cries out, "Now there's one of our boys for you, folks! And if
he can come back, why, the others certainly can too!" The refugees surge
forward: they want to know just how he was able to cross the border, and,
more importantly, if he happened to have seen any of their relatives who
had taken refuge in Lebanon while he was there:

"We're from Kwaykaat. They demolished it and evicted everyone.
Did you meet anyone from Kwaykaat?"

I was much tickled at the repetition of the *k* in Kwaykaat but
managed to suppress my laughter.

Then a woman's voice rising from behind the sundial over to the
west saved the situation. We heard her say, "The girl isn't sleeping,
Shukriyya; she's dead." There was a stifled scream and everyone
caught their breath until it stopped. Then they continued their questioning.

I answered that I had met no one from Kwaykaat.

"I am from Manshiyya. There's not a stone left standing there
except the tombs. Did you meet anyone from Manshiyya?"

"No."

"We are from Amqa. They plowed all its houses under and spilled its oil onto the ground. Did you meet anyone from Amqa?"

"No."

"We over here are from Berwah. They forced us out and obliterated it. Did you meet anyone from Berwah?"

"I did see one woman from there hiding with her child among the sesame stalks."

I heard many voices trying to guess who this woman was, and they enumerated more than twenty mothers. Finally one old man shouted: "That's enough. She is Mother Berwah. Stop guessing. God is her only refuge and ours."

And they did stop guessing. But soon voices erupted again, persisting in drawing out their relationships to their villages, all of which I understood to have been razed by the [Israeli] army:

"We are from Ruwais." "We are from al-Hadatha." "We are from el-Damun."

"We are from Mazraa." "We are from Shaab." "We are from Miy'ar."

"We are from Waarat el-Sarris." "We are from al-Zeeb." "We are from el-Bassa."

"We are from el-Kabri." "We are from Iqrit." "We are from Kufr Bir'im."

"We are from Dair el-Qasi." "We are from Saasaa." "We are from el-Ghabisiy."

"We are from Suhmata." "We are from al-Safsaf." "We are from Kufr 'Inan."

Kwaykaat, Manshiyya, Berwah, Ruwais, al-Hadatha: these are (or were) real towns and villages; their inhabitants were driven from their homes during the creation of Israel and concomitant destruction of Palestine in 1948. Hundreds of other towns and villages suffered a similar fate. Three-quarters of a million Palestinians were driven from their homes, and have never been allowed to return.

The history of the Israeli-Palestinian conflict has undergone a revolution in recent years. A new generation of academic historians, granted access in the late 1980s and 1990s to Israeli state and military archives, has reconstructed in painstaking detail the circumstances surrounding the creation of Israel (and the dispossession of the Palestinians) in 1948, as well as the series of wars that followed. The effect of the joint Israeli-Palestinian revolution in historiography has been to systematically deconstruct the official and widely propagated myths concerning the creation of Israel, and in so doing to confirm the basic Palestinian account of 1948 as a war of deliberate expulsion.

However, books by academic historians, such as Simha Flapan's *Birth of Israel*, Nur Masalha's *Expulsion of the Palestinians*, Walid Khalidi's *All that Remains*, Ilan Pappé's *The Ethnic Cleansing of Palestine*, Benny Morris's *Birth of the Palestinian Refugee Problem*, Rashid Khalidi's *Palestinian Identity*, Meron Benvenisti's *Sacred Landscape*, Samih Farsoun and Naseer Aruri's *Palestine and the Palestinians*, and Avi Shlaim's *Collusion Across the Jordan* are not, for the most part, intended for a general audience (Shlaim's *The Iron Wall* is one notable exception). Partly as a result of this, the consensus that has developed among both Israeli and Palestinian historians has not yet filtered through to the general literary or media marketplace in the United States, which is still dominated by myths that are no longer taken seriously by most academic scholars of the conflict.

In addition to the scholarship, there are plenty of eyewitness accounts of the events of 1948. A particularly striking pair of narratives was captured in the 2003 documentary *Route 181: Fragments of a Journey in Palestine-Israel*, a joint project by the Palestinian filmmaker Michel Khleifi and the Israeli filmmaker Eyal Sivan that traces the lines of division proposed in the U.N.'s 1947 Partition Plan (U.N. General Assembly Resolution 181, hence the film's title). Khleifi and Sivan followed the path of the partition plan, conducting impromptu interviews in Arabic and Hebrew with Israelis and Palestinians they encountered along the way, people from all walks of life and randomly representing, from the ground up, the entire political spectrum in contemporary Palestine-Israel. The pair of interviews that caught my attention were with a veteran of the Israeli army in 1948 and a Palestinian survivor of that year's trauma.

They interviewed the veteran, Aaron Greenberg, against a backdrop of Israeli flags at an outdoor café in Kibbutz Farod in the Galilee. As he recounts his experience of the 1948 War, a group of children play in the background (the documentary effect is somewhat surreal, but it's not intended that way). Greenberg was born in Tel Aviv; his parents came to Palestine in the early twentieth century from Russia and Lithuania. In 1948, at the age of seventeen, he went to war; he saw service with the Palmach (one of the forerunners of the Israeli army) in the Galilee during Operation Matate, which was a subsidiary action during the larger Operation Yiftach, led in late April and early May 1948 (weeks before Israel's declaration of independence) by Yigal Allon, who would go on to become deputy prime minister of Israel in the 1960s (and author of the Allon Plan; see "Outsides"). Greenberg's account of Operation Matate emerges from his interview with Khleifi and Sivan:

AG: In the Galilee, there were many Arab villages. But not only, also a lot of Bedouin camps. They moved around with tents and camels. We needed a front to stop the Arab armies invading—the Syrian, Jordanian and Lebanese armies. We couldn't leave so many of the enemy [i.e., the villagers and Bedouin] behind us. We had to chase them out. But not kill them.

K/S: How?

AG: We chased them to Jordan.

K/S: But how?

AG: How? You don't have to kill. You fire in the air and they scram. The Bedouins. The Arabs [i.e., the Palestinian villagers] were different.

K/S: Why "Operation Matate?"

AG [making a sweeping gesture with his arm—"matate" is Hebrew for "broom"]: We swept them out. We needed them out of the region, to create Jewish territorial contiguity.

K/S: And the villagers?

AG: We drove them out toward Jordan.

K/S: The villagers?

AG: Them too. Some we expelled, some stayed. But mostly we expelled.

K/S: How?

AG: We'd go in trucks, disperse in an area, and when we went over them, they ran.

K/S: How?

AG: We formed a chain. We were armed, of course. When they saw us coming, they fled.

K/S: Did you see them?

AG: Of course. We were the Yiftach Regiment, a battalion of 1,500 men.

K/S: So you'd storm a village.

AG: It's not complicated. When we approached, they were afraid we'd kill them. They ran. But we didn't come to kill them. They didn't know that. When you see a group of armed men, with guns, arms, coming at you, what do you do? You flee.

K/S: You saw them flee?

AG: Sure. [Making more sweeping gestures with his arms] We gave chase, we advanced. We went up the hills, pushing them toward Jordan. Once in Jordan, they couldn't come back. We stayed in our positions until they disappeared. Most fled. Usually to Lebanon or Syria. It didn't take long, we didn't have a lot of time. It didn't take us long to create an Arab-free zone.

K/S: But they wanted to return?

AG: They couldn't. It was before the Arab invasion.

K/S: Before?

AG: It was in anticipation of an invasion.

K/S: By whom?

AG: The Arab armies.

K/S: Did you attack to intimidate them?

AG: No need, us coming at them would be enough. No more. There was no need for more.

K/S: What did you do with the houses?

AG: Nothing, they stayed. It was the people who were in the way. We needed to block the armies that would invade from Lebanon, Syria, Jordan. That was our aim.

K/S: You saw the families go with your own eyes?

AG [in a softer voice]: Yes.

K/S: Close up?

AG: Close up, sure.

K/S: Were they afraid?

AG: Yes.

K/S: You saw mothers and children?

AG [Looking off to one side, distractedly]: Yes.

K/S: How did they leave?

AG: Usually on foot, with horses—no, donkeys. They didn't have cars.

The border wasn't far, they didn't have far to go. They knew what would happen.

K/S: What were they afraid of?

AG: It didn't take a lot to scare them. Fear in the mind is worse than anything. "They're going to kill us!"

K/S: So you killed some?

AG: We killed many.

K/S: I'm interested in Operation Matate.

AG: Why?

K/S: Who gave the orders?

AG: We had commanders. We were an army.

K/S: You knew the purpose?

AG: We had superiors, commanders, sub-commanders, units, sub-units. It was just like the army.

K/S: When did you hear the name of the operation?

AG: Shortly after it. It had a name, all operations did.

K/S: What was it?

AG: Operation Matate. It was exactly like I tell it. I can see it now.

K/S: Which villages did you conquer?

AG: We didn't think about it, that wasn't the goal. The purpose was expulsion. It wasn't to conquer and control the people. That wasn't the aim. The aim was to get rid of them. That was the goal. Not to have enemies at our backs. To block the coming invasion.

K/S: They didn't try to come back?

AG: No, not then. I don't think so. Later, they set up the refugee camps. That's a different story.

K/S: Were villages razed?

AG: Sure, sure. For Jewish settlements, for kibbutzim. The land went to moshavim and kibbutzim. Some houses are still standing. Empty. In the north.

K/S: Did people try to come back?

AG: They couldn't. You needed a visa to enter the country.

K/S: Even for their own homes?

AG: Their homes? Come on.

The parallel interview was with an elderly Palestinian woman living in the Galilee town of Tur'an. She was born and raised in the village of

Shajara, which was attacked by a unit of the Golani Brigade on 6 May 1948—a week before Israel's declaration of independence—and entirely cleared of its native population, some 900 people. The townspeople dispersed, some to Syria, Lebanon, and Jordan, others to towns elsewhere in the Galilee, or to what would become the West Bank. The woman herself ended up in Tur'an. She recalls the events of May 1948, when she was a teenager, very clearly in her interview with the filmmakers:

EW: The only thing that saved us was our legs. We left the village intact, they didn't bring anything down on our heads. After we left, and they took it over, they did what they wanted with it. They erased it. Erased it. The old people who had been left behind with nobody to carry or help them out, were captured, and thrown out, into the cacti, toward the village walls. I swear to God, it was unbelievable. They rounded them up and drove them down to the walls, to the valley, near the spring, and threw them. They made them suffer, really suffer. Their children went back to look for them at night. Some carried their mothers, others their grandmothers, on their shoulders, on their backs. Some didn't even know who they were carrying—they would just pick someone up, lift them up, and carry them off. Once they were safely away from the town, they would say, "I am so-and-so," "I am your son," "I am your nephew." It was at night; they would go at night to rescue those who hadn't got out on their own, the ones who couldn't run on their own.

K/S: Did you see people running from Loubieh [a nearby town]?

EW: Many. I went to Loubieh to help my uncle pick his crop. He told me to come help him. The first night I was there, in my uncle's house, Loubieh was surrounded and attacked. They shot all night. We were all stuck until the sun came up. People were crying and shouting. Then someone came and told the women, the road to the north is open—those of you who can get away should run, or else surrender. People started running. We ran as far as Nemrin. In Nemrin they took us in. There, people stayed, under the olive trees there. We stayed for a while, then people began to disperse. Some to Lebanon, some to Syria, some to Jordan. They went, all of them. Only a few of us, a few families, stayed behind.

The village of Shajara was completely razed by Zionist forces after its capture. "The ruins of houses and broken steel bars protrude from beds of wild vegetation," writes Walid Khalidi in his description of the town's ruins. "One side of an arched doorway still stands. The western part of the site and the nearby hill are covered with cactus. On the northern edge is a wide, deep well with a spiral stairway inside (used for periodic cleaning and maintenance of the well). Fig, doum-palm, and chinaberry trees grow in the area."

DISPOSSESSION BY THE NUMBERS

- Land captured by Israel in 1948 war: 7,954 sq. miles.
- Amount to which either the state or private Jewish owners held title: 1,081 sq. miles.
- Land further expropriated from Palestinian owners since 1948: 3,142 sq. miles.
- Land remaining in Palestinian hands: 270 sq. miles.
- Percentage of land in Israel under direct state control: 93
- Percentage of state lands held by Jewish National Fund: 13
- Percentage of Jewish National Fund lands formerly owned by Palestinians: 80
- Percentage of Jewish National Fund lands now accessible by non-Jews: 0
- Percentage of towns in Israel classified as Jewish by the state: 89
- Percentage of those towns from which non-Jewish residents are excluded: 78
- Percentage of population of Galilee that is Palestinian: 72
- Percentage of Galilee land under the jurisdiction of Palestinian municipalities: 16
- Number of new towns inside Israel established for Palestinian citizens since 1948: 0

4

One way to get a sense of the trauma of 1948 (to which the Palestinians refer as the *nakba*) is to visit one of the "unrecognized" Palestinian villages scattered throughout Israel today, none of which are on an official map of contemporary Israel. I'm not talking about forcibly depopulated villages like Kwaykaat, Manshiyya, Berwah, Ruwais, al-Hadatha—or Shajara—many of which, after their inhabitants were expelled, were methodically leveled to the ground by Israeli forces in the years after 1948; I'm talking about villages in which Palestinians continue to live to this very day, though their existence is not officially recognized by the State of Israel.

When Israel passed its first systematic building and construction law in 1965, plans were drawn up to identify existing and projected built-up areas within the state. The official plans included cities and Jewish settlements, as well as 123 Palestinian towns and villages. But they did not include Palestinian villages in more rural areas—villages that, in almost all cases, predated the State of Israel. In the state's planning documents, in other words, these villages simply do not exist. Because they don't officially exist, the land on which they are built was retroactively classified by Israel as agricultural, which means that no residences or other buildings are permitted there. This in turn means that any buildings that do exist are illegal, and subject to demolition. These Palestinian villages are not connected to the national road network. They are not connected to the national power grid. They are not connected to water mains. They are not wired into the telecommunications network. They are not served by state clinics. Their children are not officially schooled.

And yet for decades after the *nakba*, the Palestinians in these villages managed to eke out a kind of existence, and so to cling to the land on which they lived. For many years, Israel generally turned a blind eye to their existence. In 1986, however, the Israeli government appointed the Markowitz Commission to investigate what it termed illegal construction in "the Arab Sector." The Markowitz Commission systematically mapped out unlicensed Palestinian dwellings all over Israel: the first time that this had been done. It classified the Palestinian villages that had been neglected in the state's 1965 official planning maps. In effect, the commission recognized the villages' lack of recognition. All the houses, the commission decided, would have to go.

The commission slated tens of thousands of Palestinian homes in the "unrecognized" villages for demolition; pending the actual demolitions— which would take years to carry out—the villages would continue to be denied essential services such as water, power, health care, and schools. The residents of the "unrecognized" villages are all in fact citizens of the state. However, the Markowitz Commission classified the impoverished inhabitants of these villages as "violators," and said that, as their homes are demolished, some of them (particularly in the Naqab Desert) should be relocated to planned townships in what it referred to as "concentration points." Parked for the most part in the middle of the Naqab, severely lacking in infrastructure, and without any economic base, these are the only settlements that the Israeli government has ever built for its non-Jewish citizens.

Because they do not officially exist, there are no official estimates for how many "unrecognized" villages there are. Such a count also depends on what constitutes a village: is it five houses, fifteen, a hundred? It is estimated, in any case, that close to 100,000 Palestinians live in these villages. In other words, some 10 percent of the Palestinians living inside Israel are deliberately denied water, roads, electricity, and other essential services by the state.

The best-known "unrecognized village" is Ayn Hawd al-Jadida, or New Ayn Hawd, in the north of Israel, close to where Saeed the Pessoptimist sought shelter with his fellow refugees. The original Ayn Hawd still exists. It is a seven-hundred-year-old Palestinian village whose residents, like those of Kwaykaat, Manshiyya, Berwah, Ruwais, and al-Hadatha, were expelled from their homes by Zionist forces in 1948. Most of the former residents of Ayn Hawd ended up in dismal refugee camps in the West Bank (notably the one in Jenin, which would be ravaged and largely destroyed by Israeli forces in 2002). Unlike most of the other Palestinian refugees, however, some 150 residents of Ayn Hawd managed to remain inside the borders of what would become the State of Israel. In the early 1950s, the Israeli state planners and engineers engaged in the systematic demolition of the depopulated Palestinian towns and villages decided to leave the picturesque Ayn Hawd intact, turning it, instead, into an artists' colony.

Under the guidance of the Romanian Zionist Marcel Janco (who, with the Frenchman Marcel Duchamp, had been one of the founders of the Dada movement), Ayn Hawd was renamed Ein Hod and repopulated with Israeli painters, potters, and sculptors. To this day, the Israeli artists live and work in the old Palestinian houses, which Janco had found remarkably suitable for the antibourgeois aesthetic of Dada. The village mosque was converted into a restaurant modeled on the famous Dada haunt the Café Voltaire in Zurich. Ein Hod remains one of the focal points of Israeli art, the site of galleries, exhibits, and festivals. It has a Web site where one can find out about the latest shows and read an abbreviated history of the site. "The village has managed to preserve its original, historic nature and the romantic and simple charm of Israel in its first years of independence," the official Ein Hod Web site boasts. "Very few places in Israel have managed to retain the authentic quality of the Mediterranean. One can still discern in the old structures the many textures and architectural forms of earlier occupants—from the Christian Crusades to the Turkish Empire."

The Arab presence in Palestine is studiously ignored, and not a word is mentioned of the Palestinians whose village this is, many of whom settled on what had been their pastures and orchards just outside the town, and remain refugees on their own land, within earshot of the music coming from the festivals taking place in their former homes and their former town square. Physically prevented by the Israeli army from returning to their then still empty homes a few hundred yards away, they had set up tents and lean-tos, and gradually began to build makeshift houses, in what they would eventually come to call the New Ayn Hawd, or Ayn Hawd al-Jadida.

And there they have remained ever since. Ayn Hawd al-Jadida is today one of the "unrecognized" villages, albeit one that, unlike most of the others, was actually constructed after rather than before 1948. Its residents are classified under Israeli law as "present absentees," a term invented by Israeli state planners and applied to Palestinians who had been displaced from their homes in 1948 but who had remained within the borders of what would become the State of Israel. Thus they were "present," unlike the hundreds of thousands of their compatriots who had been driven out altogether. But because they had been displaced from their homes, they were, like the Palestinian refugees now in Lebanon or Jordan, also "absentees," and their family property was confiscated by the state, to be given over to national—that is, Jewish—institutions.

For years after 1948, Ayn Hawd lay empty, deserted. The townsfolk, camped out in their orchards, made various attempts to return to their

homes. "Mostly there were unofficial attempts to talk to this or that Jewish official to get permission to return, but they all failed," recalls Muhammad Abu al-Hayja, who lives in Ayn Hawd al-Jadida. "Before the 'present
absentee' law, there were also a few failed attempts by villagers to move
back into their vacant houses without permission. Even after 1951, there
was one attempt, by a cousin of my grandfather who now lives in Tam-
rah. He tried to enter his home in Ayn Hawd but the police came and
threw him in jail. After that, no one tried." Muhammad, a civil engineer,
is the founder and director of the Association of Forty, an organization
campaigning on behalf of the Palestinian "unrecognized villages" inside
Israel. It is so named not because there are forty such villages—there are
far more—but because the association was founded in the fortieth year
after the *nakba*, 1988; the name stems also from the fact that Arabs com-
monly recommemorate a person's death forty days after his passing.

Reflecting on what it means for a village not to be recognized, Muhammad muses: "It means that your village doesn't get any services at all—no
electricity, no running water, no schools, no medical clinics. There are
no planned or paved roads to the area where you live. There are no tele-
phones—though recently some people have cell phones. It means you're
cut off from the rest of the world—not just the larger outside world but
even from Israel and what goes on there. The isolation is total except
for communications with the government, which are conducted through
the courts or via the police," he adds. "When it comes to harassing us,
we exist and are in communication with the various offices of the state
administration. But when it comes to giving us anything at all that could
make us feel that we are in some way part of this state, we are forgotten."
Asked if the villagers have any contact with the Israeli artists who live
in their homes less than a mile away, Muhammad reflects. "About ten
years ago, I said in a newspaper interview that even though our present
struggle is about our new village and being given rights, this does not prevent us from dreaming about our old homes. The [Jewish] inhabitants of
Ein Hod were up in arms about this, and said that they would not help us
any more. But when had they ever helped us? In fact," he continues, "the
people who live in our homes and on our lands in the original Ayn Hawd
do not like to hear about us because they do not want to be reminded of
what happened. A person who is living in your house against your will,

and who knows whose house he's living in—what kind of feelings must this person have, especially if he is an artist?"

In the case of Ayn Hawd al-Jadida, the Israeli government has tried in another way to blot the town out from the landscape. The Israel Land Administration and Jewish National Fund, which administer the land on behalf of the Jewish people, planted cypress trees around the new village to cover it up. The cypresses were planted among the village's much older olive and fruit trees; since they grow very quickly, they soon overshadowed and suffocated the shorter olive trees. Eventually, the olive trees stopped producing olives and died. The same thing happened with the village's fig, apple, and plum trees. "To this day I hate cypress trees, because they killed our fruit trees and were planted right in front of our houses to close us in, to shut out the air, to block the view of the sea," says Muhammad.

The state's unrelenting pressure on the villagers of Ayn Hawd has not, however, been enough to weaken Muhammad's sense of attachment to his village. "After I began to understand what was going on in this country, I began to feel like I know who I am," he says. "I am a native of this land, and this is actually my country—the stranger is the one who came from outside and refuses to recognize me. I live in my own country. My people and my ancestors are buried here. I belong to this land. I do feel like a stranger among the Jews, and they feel like I am not of their world. But I am not a stranger to this soil."

DISPOSSESSION BY THE NUMBERS

- Number of Palestinian towns and villages destroyed or depopulated in 1948: 531
- Percentage of those deliberately razed to the ground by the Israeli army: 70
- New Jewish towns established inside Israel between 1948 and 1953: 370
- Number of those built on land confiscated from "absentee" Palestinians: 350
- New Palestinian towns established inside Israel since 1948: 0
- Number of Palestinians inside Israel who are internally displaced: 276,000

- Number of Palestinian communities recognized by Israel's 1965 Building Law: 123
- Approximate number of existing Palestinian communities not recognized: 176
- Number of those since supplied with water and electricity by the state: 0
- Number of Palestinians living in those communities: 115,000
- Percentage of homes therein vulnerable to retroactive demolition orders: 95

5

All of Israel is marked by the signs of the incomplete erasure of the Palestinian presence; this absence that stubbornly remains present. Nowhere is this more obvious than in old Jaffa, once Palestine's ancient port town, and now merely a part of greater Tel Aviv. Walking down a street in central Jaffa, one could easily be mistaken for walking down a street in practically any Arab-Levantine city on the Mediterranean, from Beirut to Alexandria. The architecture of old Jaffa is exactly like the architecture of contemporary Beirut neighborhoods such as Achrafieh or Gemmayze: late-nineteenth and early-twentieth-century buildings, red terracotta roofs, classic arabesque double and triple arches, wooden shutters, decorative circular windows over the arches. A simple, compact, unadorned minaret rises up over one neighborhood in Jaffa. But its doorways are sealed with concrete and cinder blocks, the Arabic engravings chiseled off its face. An overfilled garbage dumpster stands nearby, its contents overflowing onto the street near the entrance. Much of Jaffa has the same neglected feel.

Jaffa looks and feels the way it does today because 95 percent of its native Palestinian inhabitants had either fled or been expelled by 13 May 1948, when Jaffa fell to Zionist forces: the day before the State of Israel declared its independence, and two days before the first Arab armies entered Palestine. Three months of random sniping and shelling from the neighboring Jewish settlements in the area around Tel Aviv culminated in a full-scale attack on Jaffa on that day, by one of the forerunners of the Israeli army, the Haganah.

Jaffa. Photo by author.

By the end of that day, between 2,000 and 5,000 of Jaffa's original 70,000 inhabitants remained in their homes. All the others were gone. They would never be allowed to return. As had happened at Haifa a month previously, the city's Palestinian population was forced down to the port by the Zionist forces; there they were crammed onto boats, skiffs, and trawlers—and driven out to sea, to make their way to Gaza, el-Arish, even as far away as Beirut, leaving behind everything: homes, furniture, clothing, family papers, heirlooms, photographs, libraries. Much of the city was systematically demolished after the fighting. Its souks and commercial districts were entirely flattened. The famous orange groves surrounding the city were cleared away. All that remained of Jaffa after 1948 was the central district, whose homes were parceled out to new Jewish residents: European Jewish immigrants got the pick of the choicest residences in Jaffa; Sephardim and Mizrahim—Arab Jews—got the rest.

"Jaffa will become a Jewish city," declared David Ben-Gurion, Israel's first prime minister, a month after the city had been cleared of its Arab inhabitants; "to allow the return of the Arabs to Jaffa would be," he added, "foolish." Ben-Gurion had had it out for Jaffa long before 1948. "Jaffa's destruction, the town and the port, will happen, and it is good that it will happen," he had noted in his diary a dozen years previously; "if Jaffa goes to hell I will not participate in its grief."

DISPOSSESSION BY THE NUMBERS

- Number of Bedouin Palestinians living in Naqab (Negev) Desert: 140,000
- Percentage living in "unrecognized" villages: 50
- Area of land available to Bedouin in Naqab in 1948: 3.2 million acres
- Area available to them today: 59,000 acres
- Area sprayed with toxic chemicals by Israel Land Administration: 5,930 acres
- Percentage of Bedouin population of Naqab: 14
- Percentage of Naqab land area available to Bedouin: 0.8
- Number of Bedouin in the Naqab Desert criminalized as "trespassers" by new law: 70,000
- Number of new single-family farms authorized in Bedouin area of Naqab: 30
- Number of those intended for Jewish families: 29
- Annual per capita water consumption in Omer (Jewish town in Naqab): 5,332 cubic feet
- Annual per capita water consumption in Rahat (Bedouin town in Naqab): 1,236 cubic feet

6

When the 1948 War began—after four decades of intensive Jewish immigration—two-thirds of Palestine's population was still Palestinian. When the war ended, half of that population—three-quarters of a million people—had either fled or been driven from their homes, never to be allowed back. The origins of the war go back, however, to the closing years of the nineteenth century, and the opening decades of the twentieth. The Viennese journalist Theodor Herzl is widely acknowledged as the founder of modern Zionism. His 1896 book *The Jewish State* pro-

Formerly Palestinian homes, Jaffa. Photo by author.

vided all the details of the founding of just such a state other than its actual location: Palestine was one possibility; an uninhabited patch of land in Argentina another. This geographical uncertainty was settled by the time of the First Zionist Congress of 1897, held in Basel. The declared aim of the congress was to establish a "home" for the Jewish people in Palestine. "At Basel I founded the Jewish State," wrote Herzl. "If I said this out loud today, I would be answered by universal laughter. Perhaps in five years, and certainly in fifty, everyone will know it." The declared intention of the Zionist movement provoked various reactions among the European Jewish community. Some thought it commendable; others found it outrageous, even blasphemous; still others feared that it would provide food for thought to European anti-Semites (which it did). Viennese rabbis organized a deputation to Palestine to survey the actual circumstances there (about which Herzl had only the vaguest ideas). "The bride is beautiful," they wrote in a cable sent back from Palestine; "but she is married to another man."

This was the conundrum that Zionism faced from the beginning, and that it continues to face to this day. Another people also had claim to the land of Palestine, on which they had been living for generations.

According to the Israeli historian Avi Shlaim, the received view that the Zionist movement was generally unaware of the Arab Palestinian presence in Palestine, or tended conveniently to ignore the Palestinians while planning for the creation of a Jewish state in an obviously Arab land, is fatally flawed. It is not true, Shlaim points out, "to say that the Zionists were unaware of the existence of an Arab population in Palestine or of the possibility that this population would be antagonistic to the Zionist enterprise." Zionist planning went ahead, along with various proposed remedies for what was identified early on as the Arab "problem." Herzl himself suggested that the Zionists could try to "spirit the penniless population across the border by procuring employment for it in the transit countries, while denying it employment in our own country." But whole populations, penniless or otherwise, are generally reluctant to leave their ancestral homes, especially when they have employment enough in their own farms and pastures, their own long-established commercial and maritime centers.

This fact made little difference either to European Zionists or to the European empire-builders with whom they quickly developed close ties. British Foreign Secretary Lord Balfour's 1917 declaration, in a letter to Baron Rothschild, that "His Majesty's Government view with favour the establishment in Palestine of a national home for the Jewish people" was only the most obvious of the results of those ties. The Balfour Declaration was bitterly opposed by Edwin Montagu, the only Jewish member of the British cabinet at the time. Montagu registered his profound disagreement with Balfour and with the philosophy of Zionism in general. Reflecting on Balfour's promise, Montagu wrote, "I do not know what this involves, but I assume that it means that Mahommedans [i.e., Muslims] and Christians are to make way for the Jews and that the Jews should be put in all positions of preference and should be peculiarly associated with Palestine in the same way that England is with the English or France with the French, that Turks and other Mahommedans in Palestine will be regarded as foreigners, just in the same way as Jews will hereafter be treated as foreigners in every country but Palestine. Perhaps also citizenship must be granted only as a result of a religious test." Such a test, he added, "seems to me to be only admitted by those who take a bigoted and narrow view of one particular epoch of the history of Palestine, and claim for the Jews a position to which they are not entitled."

Moreover, Montagu warned, Zionism would almost inevitably strengthen European anti-Semitism and all *its* attendant violence as well. If put into practice, Montagu pointed out, the argument to which Balfour subscribed, that Jews constituted "a nation apart," would mean that the Jewish citizens of European states might be regarded once again (perhaps with calamitous results) as incomplete citizens, homeless wanderers, undesirables deserving expulsion. Zionism would only strengthen the position of those who said that Jews could not assimilate into European society. "I wish to place on record my view that the policy of His Majesty's Government is anti-Semitic in result and will prove a rallying ground for anti-Semites in every country in the world," Montagu warned. "When the Jews are told that Palestine is their national home," he predicted, "every country will immediately desire to get rid of its Jewish citizens, and you will find a population in Palestine driving out its present inhabitants, taking all the best in the country, drawn from all quarters of the globe, speaking every language on the face of the earth, and incapable of communicating with one another except by means of an interpreter." The European Jew, he warns, will face the choice, "whatever country he belongs to, whatever country he loves, whatever country he regards himself as an integral part of, between going to live with people who are foreigners to him, but to whom his Christian fellow-countrymen have told him he shall belong, and of remaining as an unwelcome guest in the country that he thought he belonged to."

Quite apart from Montagu's warning, hardly anyone in London seemed to notice that the vision proclaimed in the Balfour Declaration could not be reconciled either with realities on the ground—the Jewish population of Palestine at the time constituted far less than 10 percent of the total—or with the British undertaking to support the establishment of an independent Arab state in return for Arab support against the Ottoman Empire in the First World War (as agreed to in the 1915–16 correspondence between Sir Henry McMahon, British high commissioner in Egypt, and Sherif Hussein of Mecca). Nor could it be reconciled with the secret Anglo-French negotiation of 1916 known as the Sykes-Picot Agreement, in which the two great empires amicably worked out a way to divide the Middle East between themselves.

These competing claims were all brought to the table at the Paris negotiations following the end of the First World War. As the great powers got down to specifics about how to draw the various borders separating one power's area of control from the other's—and how to sort out the mutually contradictory promises made to each other as well as to the Arabs and the European Zionists—President Wilson suggested that it might be a good idea to send a commission to the region to survey the conditions on the ground and consult with the local inhabitants. The French adamantly refused to participate in the commission. The British initially appointed commissioners but, upon further reflection, agreed with the French and disbanded them. Only the American commissioners, appointed by President Wilson, went ahead with the mission to see what the local inhabitants thought of the plans that were being drawn up for them in Paris.

Henry King and Charles Crane arrived in Jaffa in June 1919 and traveled extensively through the region to survey conditions and talk to local people. Upon its completion, the King-Crane Commission recommended that the plans being drawn up in Paris take the form not of old colonialism—i.e., a crude division of the spoils of war—but be premised instead on the creation of a mandatory power (a kind of temporary caretaker administration), appointed by the League of Nations, whose job would be to serve the "well-being and development" of the local population, whose interests should be held in a "sacred trust," and whose ultimate objective should be the creation of an independent Arab state in all of geographical Syria (that is, present-day Syria, Lebanon, Jordan, and Palestine/Israel).

One of the King-Crane Commission's most specific recommendations was the "serious modification" of the Zionist program in Palestine. King and Crane had, they explained, landed in Palestine predisposed in favor of Zionism. "The Commission was abundantly supplied with literature on the Zionist program by the Zionist Commission to Palestine; heard in conferences much concerning the Zionist colonies and their claims; and personally saw something of what had been accomplished," the Commissioners noted. "They found much to approve in the aspirations and plans of the Zionists, and had warm appreciation for the devotion of many of the colonists, and for their success, by modern methods, in overcoming great natural obstacles." But when they actually had a chance to see circumstances on the ground, they realized that the Zionist program could not possibly succeed without extreme violence. "No British officer, consulted by the Commissioners, believed that the Zionist program could be carried out except by force of arms," King and Crane warned. "The officers generally thought a force of not less than fifty thousand soldiers would be required even to initiate the program. That of itself is evidence of a strong sense of the injustice of the Zionist program, on the part of the non-Jewish populations of Palestine and Syria. Decisions, requiring armies to carry out, are sometimes necessary, but they are surely not gratuitously to be taken in the interests of a serious injustice. For the initial claim, often submitted by Zionist representatives, that they have a 'right' to Palestine, based on an occupation of two thousand years ago, can hardly be seriously considered."

The warnings of the King-Crane Commission were entirely ignored as the great powers continued their negotiations in Paris. The British and French had their own ideas of what was best for the region. "For in Palestine we do not propose even to go through the form of consulting the wishes of the present inhabitants of the country, though the American [King-Crane] Commission has been going through the forms of asking what they are," wrote Lord Balfour. "The four great powers are committed to Zionism, and Zionism, be it right or wrong, good or bad, is rooted in age-long tradition, in present needs, in future hopes, of far profounder import than the desire and prejudices of the 700,000 Arabs who now inhabit that ancient land."

Edward Said, in *The Question of Palestine*, points out that Balfour's logic was the product of decades of European imperial thought: emerging from a sense of entitlement and empowerment in which the European alone possessed wisdom and the scales of justice. It was essential, Said argues, for the Zionist movement to align itself with imperialists like Balfour, thus defining itself as a modern European phenomenon rather than as a primitive tribalism or as merely a resurgence of ancient Judaism; and for Israel, then as now, to be seen as an ally to the great powers, an outpost of Western civilization in an otherwise barren desert of Eastern despotism (or "a democracy in a rough neighborhood," as one of the current formulations has it).

The earliest Zionists were consistent in deploying this strategy, much of which hinged on an emphasis of the Arab's essential otherness. "The

Arabs, who are superficially clever and quick-witted, worship one thing, and one thing only—power and success," claimed Chaim Weizmann, who had assumed the leadership of the European Zionist movement by the time of the First World War, in a letter to Balfour. In establishing the postwar settlement after 1918, Weizmann therefore urged the British authorities to take into account "the treacherous nature of the Arab," and to be careful "that nothing should happen which might give the Arabs the slightest grievance or ground of complaint. In other words, the Arabs have to be 'nursed' lest they should stab the [British] Army in the back," Weizmann explained. "The Arab, quick as he is to gauge a situation, tries to make the most of it. He screams as often as he can and blackmails as often as he can." The fairer the British are, then, and the more that democratic principles are taken into account, "the more arrogant the Arab becomes. It must also be taken into consideration that the Arab official knows the language, habits and ways of the country, is a *roué* and therefore has a great advantage over the fair and clean-minded English official, who is not conversant with the subtleties of the Oriental mind."

Said sees Weizmann's candor as instructive. "His principal rhetorical device is to identify himself with Balfour as a European who knows the difference between the Oriental and the Occidental mind," he explains. "From this distinction all sorts of conclusions follow. Arabs are Oriental, therefore less human and valuable than Europeans and Zionists; they are treacherous, unregenerate, etc. Most of all, they do not deserve to own a country, even if their numerical advantage seems otherwise to entitle them to it." Zionists and Europeans, on the other hand, can properly appreciate the ideals of fair play and progress.

It was often in the name of progress that Zionists conceived of their mission in Palestine; progress, and the establishment of a Western beachhead in the Middle East. Vladimir Jabotinsky, the founder of what came to be identified as Revisionist Zionism—the ideological basis of today's Likud party in Israel—had many disagreements with Weizmann, but on the matter of seeing the conflict between Zionism and the Palestinians in civilizational terms, they were in full accord. Jabotinsky was somewhat blunter than the careful Weizmann. Weizmann was very good at talking in general terms of the project to—as he put it—"make Palestine as Jewish as England is English," but he left it to people like Jabotinsky to fill in the details and describe what that would look like in real life. Jabotinsky's solution (see Introduction) was the creation of an "iron wall" behind which what he referred to as "Zionist colonization" can continue "in defiance of the will of the native population."

Jabotinsky's assessment of the situation was more forthright than Weizmann's, but it had difficulties of its own. One problem with the concept of the iron wall, for example, is that such a wall—even if it is metaphorical rather than material—is of little use if too many natives are left standing on the wrong side. It was precisely this difficulty that led to the consolidation of the Zionist concept that would come to be known as "transfer." In practical terms, as the Israeli historian Benny Morris and others have pointed out, there could have been several different ways to achieve a state with a Jewish majority in all or part of Palestine. The first involves mass immigration. The problem here is that Jewish immigration never produced enough numbers to overwhelm the native Arab Palestinian majority. Another solution lay in the creation of a state with minority rule, which ran counter to the logic of a purely or largely Jewish state. A third possibility lay in the way of partition. But no matter how the partition would have been arranged, there still would have been a substantial Palestinian minority in the Jewish state. "The last and, let me say obvious and most logical, solution to the Zionists' demographic problem lay the way of transfer," Morris explains; "you could create a homogeneous Jewish majority by moving or transferring all or most of the Arabs out of the prospective territory. And this, in fact, is what happened in 1948." He adds that "thinking about the transfer of all or part of Palestine's Arabs out of the prospective Jewish state was pervasive among Zionist leadership circles long before 1937, when Lord Peel recommended transfer alongside partition as the only possible solution to the conflict, and continued to exercise the Zionist imagination during the following decade."

The Peel Plan of 1937 recommended partitioning Palestine into a Jewish state in the north (from Galilee to the coast and down to the edge of Jaffa), an Arab state in what is today the West Bank, Gaza and the Naqab Desert, and a Mandatory Territory around Jerusalem with a corridor leading to the coast. The plan also called for the compulsory transfer—removal—of a quarter of a million Palestinians from what would be the Jewish state. David Ben-Gurion was struck at the beauty and simplicity of the concept of transfer as formulated by Peel. For all the drawbacks of the plan from the Zionist standpoint (principally that it did not offer enough territory to the Jews), "the compulsory transfer of the Arabs from the valleys proposed for the Jewish state" offered something new, Ben-Gurion wrote. "With the evacuation of the Arab community from the valleys we achieve, for the first time in our history, a real Jewish state—an agricultural body of one or more million people, continuous, heavily populated, at one with its land which is completely its own." He added a final flourish: "As with a magic wand, all the difficulties and defects that preoccupied us until now in our settlement enterprise [will vanish]." But as though acknowledging to himself the terrible reality of what it meant to speak of the possibility of uprooting tens of thousands of families from lands they had lived on for generations, Ben-Gurion steeled himself: "We must first of all cast off the weakness of thought and will and prejudice—that [says that] this transfer is impracticable," he noted. "What is inconceivable in normal times is possible in revolutionary times; and if at this time the opportunity is missed and what is possible only in such great hours is not carried out—a whole world is lost." Therefore, "any doubt on our part about the necessity of this transfer, any doubt we cast about the possibility of its implementation, any hesitancy on our part about its justice may lose [us] an historic opportunity that may not recur." In a letter to his teenage son Amos, Ben-Gurion was even more frank. "We must expel Arabs and take their places," he wrote, "when we have force at our disposal."

Ben-Gurion and others were very careful to be circumspect in discussing plans for transfer. They recognized that the less there was said about it the better. Morris points out that it was common practice among the Zionist leadership in the 1930s and 1940s to order stenographers to "take a break" when the topic came up in formal discussions, so as to keep the transfer question out of the public record for as long as possible. "The transfer can be the archstone, the final stage in the political development, but on no account the starting point," wrote Moshe Shertok (who would later change his last name to Sharett and become prime minister of Israel). By talking prematurely about transfer, however, "we are mobilizing enormous forces against the idea and subverting [its implementation] in advance," he warned. "What will happen once the Jewish state is established—it is very possible that the result will be transfer of Arabs." Others were more frank. Eliahu Dobkin, director of the Jewish Agency's immigration department, said, "There will be in this country a large minority and it must be ejected. There is no room for our internal inhibitions [in this matter]." Eliezer Kaplan, who would become Israel's first finance minister, said, "Regarding the matter of transfer I have only one request: Let us not start arguing among ourselves," as "this will cause us the most damage externally." Dov Joseph, who would become Israel's first justice minister, agreed. Werner David Senator added, "I do not regard the question of transfer as a moral or immoral problem." Shlomo Lavi, one of the kibbutz movement's early leaders, went further. The "transfer of Arabs out of the country in my eyes is one of the most just, moral and correct things that can be done." Avraham Katznelson of the dominant Mapai party could conceive of nothing "more moral, from the viewpoint of universal human ethics, than the emptying of the Jewish State of the Arabs and their transfer elsewhere," which, he acknowledged, "requires the use of force." In a discussion of transfer at the Zionist world labor movement conference in 1937, Eliahu Lulu declared that "this transfer, even if it were carried out through compulsion—all moral enterprises are carried out through compulsion—will be justified in all senses." It is, he added, "a just, logical, moral, and humane programme in all senses." In a frank moment, Weizmann himself pointed out to the Soviet ambassador to London in 1941 that "if half a million Arabs could be transferred, two million Jews could be put in their place. That, of course, would be a first installment; what might happen afterwards was a matter for history."

Zionist discussions and formulations of "transfer" went on through the 1930s and early 1940s, as Jewish immigration into the country—and Arab resistance to it—ebbed and flowed. According to the Palestinian historian Nur Masalha, transfer committees were set up by the Jewish Agency between 1937 and 1942 in order to formulate the plans for removing the Palestinians from their land.

The Zionist concept of transfer reached the decisive tipping point with the outbreak of actual fighting in late 1947 and early 1948, following the issuance of the United Nations Partition Plan of 29 November. The Partition Plan (see map, p. 247) recommended giving over more than half of

Palestine to the one-third of its inhabitants who were by then (thanks to the immigration campaign) Jewish, and who owned less than 7 percent of the total land area. Even in the 5,500 square miles proposed for the Jewish state, Jews legally owned only about 600 square miles. The proposed Jewish state would have had almost equal Jewish and Arab populations. The Palestinian historian Walid Khalidi observes that nearly all of Palestine's citrus groves, 80 percent of its cereal land, and 40 percent of Palestinian industrial capacity would fall within the borders of the proposed Jewish state. Jaffa would be cut off from its hinterland, facing the Mediterranean sea in one direction—and surrounded by the Jewish state in the other. Hundreds of Palestinian villages would be separated from their fields and pastures.

The Palestinians, Khalidi notes, "failed to see why it was *not* fair for the Jews to be a minority in a unitary Palestinian state, while it *was* fair for almost half of the Palestinian population—the indigenous majority on its own native soil—to be converted overnight into a minority under alien rule in the envisaged Jewish state according to partition." The Arab Higher Committee, speaking for the Palestinians, rejected the plan as unfair, inequitable, and inherently absurd.

The heirs of Jabotinsky also rejected the plan. "The partition of Palestine is illegal. It will never be recognized," declared Menachem Begin, another future prime minister of Israel. "Jerusalem was and will forever be our capital. Eretz Israel will be restored to the people of Israel. All of it. And forever." The dominant wing of the Zionist movement, under Ben-Gurion's leadership, however, took the same pragmatic attitude to the 1947 Partition Plan as it had toward the 1937 Peel Plan, which Ben-Gurion had accepted, noting quietly that "we will be able to settle in all the other parts of the country, whether through agreement and mutual understanding with our Arab neighbors or in another way." Better, Ben-Gurion said in 1937, to "erect a Jewish State at once, even if it is not in the whole land. The rest will come in the course of time. It must come." His attitude in 1947 was much the same. "Every school child knows that there is no such thing in history as a final arrangement," he noted; "not with regard to borders, and not with regard to international agreements. History, like nature, is full of alterations and change." The official acceptance of the partition resolution was, according to the Israeli historian

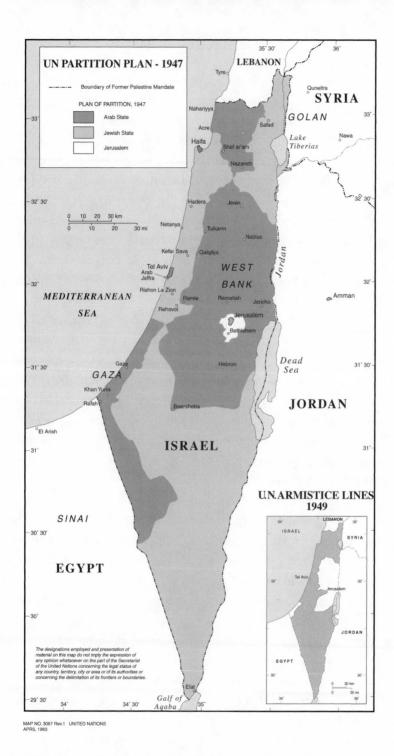

U.N. Plan to Partition Palestine, 1947. Courtesy United Nations Cartographic Section.

Simha Flapan, "an example of Zionist pragmatism par excellence. It was a tactical acceptance, a vital step in the right direction—a springboard for expansion when circumstances proved more judicious."

It was in the wake of the Partition Plan that fighting broke out in earnest. The 1948 War has often been portrayed as a mortal struggle between a Jewish David and an enormous Arab Goliath. ("Having rejected Jewish self-determination in 1937," writes Alan Dershowitz in *The Case for Israel*, for example, "the Arab world rejected it once again in 1948 and attacked Israel in an effort to destroy the new Jewish state, exterminate its Jewish population, and drive the Jews into the sea.") In fact, as we now know from the work of a new generation of Israeli, Palestinian, and American academic historians, the Arab states attacked Israel only after it was far too late, and even then their intervention was little more than useless.

Palestinian forces entered the 1948 War already severely weakened from their fight against the British during uprisings in the 1930s, which the British army had severely repressed, leaving the Palestinians in disarray and much of their leadership dead, imprisoned, or scattered. They were able to field no more than 7,000 poorly trained and badly equipped militiamen. These were supplemented by some 3,000 Arab volunteers, equally poorly trained and badly equipped. They confronted a Jewish fighting force of 50,000, mostly members of the Haganah, the precursor to the Israeli army. Arab militiamen generally had between 20 and 50 rounds of ammunition each: that's about the equivalent of a single clip of ammunition for a modern assault rifle, though a Palestinian militiaman could count himself lucky if he had a 1915 Lee Enfield at his disposal. The Zionists, on the other hand, had a massive arms procurement program in Europe—and by September 1947 had already stockpiled 10,489 rifles, 702 light machine guns, 2,666 submachine guns, 186 medium machine guns, 672 two-inch medium mortars, and 92 three-inch heavy mortars—as well as an impressive local arms production apparatus, which produced over 3 million 9-mm bullets, 150,000 grenades, 16,000 submachine guns, and 210 three-inch heavy mortars between October 1947 and July 1948.

The fighting began months before Israel's declaration of independence, but it was only after that declaration, in mid-May, that the armies of the surrounding Arab states came to the defense of Palestine. By then, the total number of Arab troops in the Palestine theater, including the Arab armies, was under 25,000. The Israeli army would grow to 65,000 by July, and 96,000 in December: rates of increase that the Arabs (whose combined strength peaked at less than 50,000) did not match. They were also far better equipped than the Arab armies, and included many battle-hardened Jewish veterans from frontline units of the European armies in the Second World War. "Thus, at each stage of the war, the IDF [Israel Defense Forces, or army] significantly outnumbered all the Arab forces arrayed against it, and by the final stage of the war its superiority ratio was nearly two to one," writes Avi Shlaim. "The final outcome of the war was therefore not a miracle but a reflection of the underlying Arab-Israeli military balance." The Israeli historian Simha Flapan concurs: "The [military] superiority of the Jews over both the Palestinian Arabs and the invading Arab armies was never in dispute." Flapan argues that the 4,500 men of Jordan's Arab Legion constituted the most effective Arab unit engaged in Palestine. But they were trained by the British and dependent on its 45 British officers and its British commander, Sir John Bagot Glubb; the British also financed the legion and controlled its ammunition supply. Glubb was following strict British orders during the entire conflict. And as we now know from the work of the Israeli historians Avi Shlaim and Benny Morris, Jordan's King Abdullah had reached an agreement with the Zionist leadership before the fighting actually started that his forces would not enter the areas of Palestine which the U.N. Partition Plan had proposed allotting to the Jewish state; in return, the Zionists would not object to his annexation of what would later come to be called the West Bank.

With the outbreak and spread of fighting—especially given the massive military superiority of the Zionist forces—came the time to put into practice all the long-discussed theories of clearing Palestine as much as possible of its indigenous Arab population. The process of depopulating Palestinian towns and villages proceeded with Zionist and Israeli attacks. "The [Palestinian] refugee problem was caused by attacks by Jewish forces on Arab villages and towns and by the inhabitants' fear of such attacks, compounded by expulsions, atrocities and rumors of atrocities—and by the crucial Israeli Cabinet decision in June 1948 to bar a refugee return," writes Benny Morris. "On the basis of the revelations, documentation, and factual finding brought to light by Morris (and other 'new' historians), the traditional Palestinian contention that there was a Zionist consensus on the question of finding a 'solution' to the 'Arab demographic problem,' " Nur Masalha writes, "through transfer of Arabs to areas outside the prospective Jewish state and barring their return to their villages and towns, is corroborated." The clearances began taking place long before Israel's actual declaration of independence, and hence long before the Arab world mounted its own halfhearted effort to save Palestine and the Palestinians from destruction. As early as 11 January 1948, Joseph Weitz, the Jewish National Fund executive and a tireless advocate of transfer, asked, "is not now the time to be rid of them? Why continue to keep in our midst these thorns at a time when they pose a danger to us?" The next month he said, "It is possible that now is the time to implement our original plan: to transfer them."

Clearing away the Palestinian population was one of the central objectives of Plan Dalet, or Plan D, initiated in March 1948. "The aim of Plan D was to secure all the areas allocated to the Jewish state under the UN partition resolution as well as Jewish settlements outside these areas and corridors leading to them, so as to provide a solid and continuous basis for Jewish sovereignty," notes Avi Shlaim. "By implementing Plan D in April and May, the Haganah thus directly and decisively contributed to the birth of the Palestinian refugee problem." Plan D was executed in April and May, but the final details for it were worked out on the afternoon of 10 March 1948, when, as the Israeli historian Ilan Pappé explains, a group of eleven veteran Zionist leaders, together with young Jewish military cadres, met in the so-called Red House of Tel Aviv—more than two months before Israel's declaration of independence and the halfhearted intervention of the surrounding Arab states. "That same evening, military orders were dispatched to the units on the ground to prepare for the systematic expulsion of the Palestinians from vast areas of the country," writes Pappé. "The orders came with a detailed description of the methods to be employed to forcibly evict the people: large-scale intimidation; laying siege to and bombarding villages and population centres; setting fire to homes, properties and goods; expulsion; demolition; and, finally, planting mines among the rubble to prevent any of the expelled inhabitants from returning." Each military unit carrying out Plan D "was issued with its own list of villages and neighborhoods as the targets of this master plan," the unambiguous aim of which was "the destruction of both the rural and urban areas of Palestine." It was called Plan D, in fact, because it was the fourth and final in a series of such plans (A, B, and C) articulating how to deal with the non-Jewish population of Palestine. Once the decision was taken, Pappé adds, it took six months to complete the mission. "The plan decided upon on 10 March 1948, and above all its systematic implementation in the following months," he writes, "was a clear-cut case of an ethnic cleansing operation, regarded under international law today as a crime against humanity."

Palestinian towns were consistently emptied of their populations during and after Zionist attacks in the spring of 1948. Those Palestinians who were physically capable fled, often with little or no warning. Those who could not flee were often left behind. "It was standard Haganah and IDF policy," explains Benny Morris, "to round up and expel the remaining villagers (usually old people, widows, cripples) from sites already evacuated by most of their inhabitants."

One of the biggest clearances of Palestinians took place in the coastal city of Haifa, which culminated on 21 April, little less than a month before Israel's declaration of independence. The Jewish mayor of Haifa, Shabtai Levi, appealed to the city's Palestinians not to flee and promised that no harm would befall them. But, as Ilan Pappé points out, "it was Mordechai Maklef, the operation officer of the Carmeli Brigade, not Levi, who called the shots. Maklef orchestrated the cleansing campaign [in Haifa], and the orders he issued to his troops were plain and simple: 'Kill any Arab you encounter; torch all inflammable objects and force doors open with explosives.'" According to an officer in the Haganah, the attack on Haifa involved psychological operations, such as the broadcast of "shrieks, wails, and anguished moans of Arab women, the wail of sirens and the clang of fire-alarm bells, interrupted by a sepulchral voice calling out in Arabic: Save your souls, all ye faithful! Flee for your lives!" Despite all this, according to the Israeli military historian Uri Milstein, "the commander of the Carmeli Brigade, Moshe Carmel, feared that many Arabs would remain in the city. Hence, he ordered that three-inch mortars [i.e., medium artillery] be used to shell the Arab crowds on the market square. The crowd broke into the port, pushing aside the policemen who guarded the gate, stormed the boats and fled the city. The whole day mortars continued to shell the city, even though the Arabs did not fight." Watching the Arabs flee, Ben-Gurion is reported by a Jewish eyewitness to have said, "What a beautiful sight!" When he actually entered Haifa afterward, however, Ben-Gurion was shocked at the sight of what he called "a dead city, a corpse city." But "what happened in Haifa can happen in other parts of the country if we will hold out," he noted in his journal; "it may be that in the next six or eight months of the campaign, there will be great changes in the country, and not all to our detriment. Certainly, there will be great changes in the composition of the population of the country."

Much the same was going on elsewhere in the country. Operation Yiftach—encompassing Operation Matate—led by Yigal Allon, aimed to "clear" the eastern Galilee completely of all Arab forces and inhabitants. Operation Ben-Ami, led by Moshe Carmel, aimed at the conquest and evacuation of the Palestinians of western Galilee. Carmel's operational order on 19 May 1948 read as follows: "To attack in order to conquer, to kill among the men, to destroy and burn the villages of Al Kabri, Umm al Faraj and An Nahr." Ultimately, "it makes no difference whether people were forcibly expelled, fled in fear, or were evicted by order of Arab commanders [the official Israeli explanation for why the Palestinians left their homes, which has been proven false]. The moment they left their homes—even if they took refuge in the immediate vicinity of their villages—they lost their whole world and became refugees with nothing, not even the right to receive monetary compensation for the loss of their property," writes the Israeli historian (and former deputy mayor of Jerusalem) Meron Benvenisti.

By the time Israel declared its independence in mid-May, the job of clearing away the indigenous population of Palestine was already more than half done. Two hundred villages had been cleared of their inhabitants. Meanwhile, the clearing of Israel's interior continued. The biggest operation after the declaration of independence was the clearing of Lydda and Ramleh, in mid-July. "In Lydda, the exodus took place on foot," writes Simha Flapan; "In Ramleh, the IDF provided buses and trucks. Originally, all males had been rounded up and enclosed in a compound, but after some shooting was heard, and construed by Ben-Gurion to be the beginning of an Arab League counteroffensive, he stopped the arrests and ordered the speedy eviction of all the Arabs, including women, children and the elderly." As many Palestinians (some three hundred) died in the forced march from Lydda as had been killed in the clearing of the town itself. Some 57,000 Palestinians were driven out of the area of Ramleh and Lydda by force. By now, some in the Zionist leadership, particularly in the Mapam party, were questioning the justice and morality of forced expulsions, but such questions were not enough to overturn the consensus in favor of transfer.

The first question faced by the leaders of the new state of Israel was what to do about the hundreds of thousands of Palestinian refugees who had fled or been driven from their homes. Would they be allowed back home? Golda Myerson (who would later change her last name to Meir and become prime minister of Israel) visited the desolated Arab city of Haifa shortly after its conquest. "It is a dreadful thing to see the dead city," she reported. "Next to the port I found children, women, the old, waiting for a way to leave. I entered the houses, there were houses where the coffee and pita bread were left on the table, and I could not avoid [thinking] that this, indeed, had been the picture in many Jewish towns [i.e., in Europe, during the Second World War]." Still, Myerson was more concerned by practical matters, such as what should be done with all the abandoned Palestinian towns and villages. "Are we prepared to preserve these villages in order that their inhabitants might return," she asked, "or do we want to wipe out every trace that there had been a village on the site?" The new state's answer to that question was very quickly formulated.

Expelling the Palestinian population in time of war was one thing; not letting them return in time of peace quite another, especially since United Nations General Assembly Resolution 194 demanded, in December 1948, that "the refugees wishing to return to their homes and live at peace with their neighbors should be permitted to do so at the earliest practicable date, and that compensation should be paid for the property of those choosing not to return and for loss of or damage to property." When it admitted Israel to membership in the United Nations, the world body explicitly recalled Resolutions 181 (the Partition Plan of 1947) and 194 as among the bases for Israel's admission. Neither resolution has been implemented.

"It was not the brutality and horrors of war that haunted the departing refugees and nurtured their hatred," writes Benvenisti, "but an abiding sense of the injustice of their being barred from returning home." It was quite early on—barely a month into its existence—that Israel took the momentous decision to bar the return of the refugees. "This is our policy: they are not coming back," declared Foreign Minister Moshe Shertok. "The most spectacular event in the contemporary history of Palestine—more spectacular in a sense than the creation of the Jewish State—is the wholesale evacuation of its Arab population," Shertok wrote to Nahum Goldmann, the chairman of the World Jewish Congress. "The reversion to the status quo ante is unthinkable. The opportunities which the present position open up for a lasting and radical solution of the most vexing problem of the Jewish State [that is, the Arab minority] are so far-reaching as to take one's breath away. Even if a certain backwash is unavoidable, we must make the most of the momentous chance with which history has presented us so swiftly and so unexpectedly." For Weizmann, the "miraculous cleaning of the land" amounted to "the miraculous simplification of Israel's task."

Although the policy to bar the return of the Palestinian refugees was declared in June, an unofficial Transfer Committee, led by the indefatigable Joseph Weitz of the Jewish National Fund, was established in May to formulate ways to ensure that the refugees never returned home. "Let us not waste the fact that a large Arab population has moved from its home, and achieving such a thing would be very difficult in normal times," wrote Weitz's colleague and fellow committee member Ezra Danin. The committee worked swiftly and had by early June 1948 prepared a document, *Retroactive Transfer: A Scheme for the Solution of the Arab Question in the State of Israel.* "The uprooting of the Arabs should be seen as a solution to the Arab question," the document stated; "and, in line with this, it must from now on be directed according to a calculated plan geared toward the goal of 'retroactive transfer.'" The committee called for a policy preventing Palestinians from returning to their homes; destroying as many villages as possible during military operations; prevention of Palestinian cultivation of land; and settlement of Jews in Arab towns and villages to fill in any "vacuum" resulting from depopulation.

By the middle of the summer of 1948, the new Israeli government met to discuss the available options. Ben-Gurion insisted that Palestinians should be prevented from returning to their homes. Orders went out to the Israeli army to bar refugees from returning. Moshe Shertok was clear about the new government's policy. "With regard to the refugees, we are determined to be adamant while the war lasts," he explained to Chaim Weizmann, Israel's first president; "once the return tide starts, it will be impossible to stem it, and it will prove our undoing. As for the future, we are equally determined," he added, "to explore all possibilities of getting rid, once and for all, of the huge Arab minority which originally threatened us. What can be achieved in this period of storm and stress will be quite unattainable once conditions are stabilized."

The Israelis quickly set in motion a number of processes in order to prevent the Palestinians' return to their country. Palestinian villages were systematically pulverized; Palestinian fields and crops were either destroyed or taken over by Jewish farmers; Palestinian land was redistributed to new Jewish settlements; Jews now pouring in from Europe were resettled in vacated Palestinian houses. "Taken together," writes Benny Morris, these steps "assured that the refugees would have nowhere, and nothing, to return to." After the fighting was over, the Israelis methodically demolished over 400 Palestinian villages. Under the tireless leadership of Weitz, the Transfer Committee pursued its work. "I was surprised that nothing moved in me at the sight," Weitz noted as he watched his bulldozers complete the demolition of one depopulated Palestinian village; "not regret and not hatred, as [if] this is the way of the world." All through the summer and fall of 1948, through 1949, and into the early 1950s, Israel's destruction of abandoned Palestinian homes and villages continued unabated. "By then," according to Morris, "the threat of a [Palestinian] return had disappeared and the destruction was part of the process of clearing areas and renovating houses for Jewish cultivation or habitation rather than directed against would-be returnees."

The U.N. Mediator in Palestine, Count Folke Bernadotte, pleaded with the Israeli government to allow even some of the refugees, already suffering terrible conditions in makeshift camps, to return to their empty homes. "It would be an offence against the principles of elemental justice if these innocent victims of the conflict were denied the right to return to their homes while Jewish immigrants flow into Palestine and, indeed, at least offer the threat of permanent replacement of the Arab refugees," Bernadotte wrote. He was shortly afterward assassinated by the Stern Gang under the leadership of future Israeli Prime Minister Yitzhak Shamir, and discussion of the fate of the refugees was deferred indefinitely.

It was not just farmland but whole cities that had been emptied of their populations. "Commercial centers, residential quarters, schools, banks, hospitals, clinics, mosques, churches, and other public buildings, parks and utilities, all passed en bloc into the possession of the citizens of the nascent State of Israel," notes Walid Khalidi. "Also appropriated intact by Israelis were the personal moveable assets: furniture, silver, pictures, carpets, libraries, and heirlooms." One-third of the immigrants entering Israel in the late 1940s and early 1950s took over formerly Palestinian homes. At first, these takeovers were arranged in a more or less haphazard, ad hoc fashion. The situation in Haifa following the mass exodus of the city's Palestinians was a little more organized. There someone called Naftali Lifshits divided Palestinian property into different categories. Household goods, for example, were sold, destroyed, or used to furnish formerly Arab homes for their new Jewish tenants. Lifshits scrupulously recorded all information. Palestinian residents who resurfaced in Haifa were given a receipt noting how much money the state owed them, which, according to the American historian Michael Fishbach, they were told they could collect "later."

In July 1948, the Israelis created a new office, the custodian of abandoned property, who would be in charge of the process of recording and redistributing captured Palestinian property. The newly appointed custodian could draw upon a law passed in June 1948 that extended Israeli jurisdiction to all "abandoned areas," which the law defined as "any area or place conquered by or surrendered to armed forces or deserted by all or part of its inhabitants, and which has been declared by order to be an abandoned area." Fishbach points out that such a definition meant that almost all Arab land that came under Israeli control could be labeled "abandoned," and hence taken over by the state, and, moreover, that the law applied not just to land but to "animals, crops, fruits, vegetables and any other agricultural produce, factories, workshops, machinery, goods and commodities of all kinds, and also a right to moveable or immoveable property and any other right." A new law, passed in December 1948, shifted legal definitions away from the property and to its former owner. "Instead of declaring land to be 'abandoned,' " Fishbach points out, "people were now declared 'absentees' whose property could now be seized by the state." A person could be declared an absentee if, on or after 29 November 1947, he or she was a citizen of an Arab state; was in any Arab state for any length of time; was in any part of Palestine not under Jewish control; or was "in any place other than his habitual residence, even if such place as well as his habitual abode were within Israeli-occupied territory."

According to this new law, almost all Palestinians could be declared "absentees," even if they were physically present. This led to the creation of that strange Israeli juridical entity, the "present absentee." With the passage of the first ("Emergency") version of this law, the custodian of abandoned property became the custodian of absentee property. After the war, a new, more permanent law was drafted to replace this emergency regulation, Israel's notorious Absentee Property Law of 1950. This new law allowed the custodian not only to seize property, but also to transfer it to a Development Authority. All these laws were superseded by Israel's Basic Land Law of 1960, according to which virtually all of Israel's land (93 percent) was in effect to be held in perpetuity for the Jewish people.

Meanwhile, of the 250 villages in the north of Palestine, some 190 had been emptied. About 220,000 Palestinians from these towns were now refugees, in addition to the 100,000 residents of cities like Haifa who had suffered the same fate. But "the emptying of the north of three-quarters of its Arab inhabitants was nothing compared with the total emptying of central and southern Israel, where approximately 330,000 souls, from 180 villages and four towns, became refugees," writes Benvenisti. "All that remained in the central and southern regions were a few thousand Arabs living in half a dozen villages (and three towns) and approximately 12,000 Bedouin in the Negev." Twenty-four of the 29 villages in the district of Tiberias had been destroyed, as well as 78 of the 83 villages in the vicinity of Safad—both in the Galilee. By contrast, all of the 56 villages near Ramleh had been wiped out; so had all of the 26 villages of the Jaffa district, all 46 of Gaza, all 26 of Beersheba. Joseph Weitz, one of the men who pushed hardest for Israel to get rid of the

Arabs and take possession of their land, wrote the following account in his diary toward the end of 1948:

> And the road continues eastward between mountains and over mountains, and the Galilee is revealed to me in its splendor, its hidden places and folds, its crimson smile and its green softness and its desolation. I have never seen it like this. It was always bustling with man and beast. And the latter predominated. Herds and more herds used to descend from the heights to the valleys of the streambeds, their bells ringing with a sort of discontinuous sound, which vanished in the ravines and hid among the crevices, as if they would go on chiming forever. And the shepherds striding after them like figures from ancient times, whistling merrily and driving the goats toward the trees and bushes—to gnaw at them hungrily; and now the picture has disappeared and is no more. A strange stillness lies over all the mountains and is drawn by hidden threads from within the empty village. An empty village; what a terrible thing! Fossilized lives! Lives turned to fossilized whispers in extinguished ovens; a shattered mirror; moldy blocks of dried figs and a scrawny dog, thin-tailed and floppy-eared and dark-eyed. At the same time—at the very same moment—a different feeling throbs and rises from the primordial depths, a feeling of victory, of taking control, of revenge, and of casting off suffering. And suddenly the whispers vanish and you see empty houses, good for the settlement of our Jewish brethren who have wandered for generation upon generation, refugees of your people, steeped in suffering and sorrow, as they, at last, find a roof over their heads. And you knew: War! This was our war. But has it ended? For a full day we galloped over the roads of the Galilee and saw the deep-rooted agricultural heritage that the fleeing villagers had left behind them. With this, my heart became heavy beneath the weight of our circumstances: have we among us the human resources to carry on this heritage, to deepen it, and to broaden it? And will we be able to bring thousands of Jews here to banish the desolation, the human desolation, so that the Galilee will continue to blossom?

Of the 900,000 Palestinians who had been living in what became the State of Israel, only 150,000 remained by the end of the war. Some three-quarters of a million Palestinians, about half the total prewar Palestinian population, had either fled or been driven from their homes. In the process, as Michael Fishbach points out, "they left behind farmland, tools and animals, homes, factories, bank accounts, and personal property." It would be meaningless "to give a detailed account of the physical destruction of the Arab landscape: of whether the houses were destroyed by looters, blown up by the army, or demolished by bulldozers," Benvenisti argues. "In the absence of the human beings who had molded that landscape to suit their needs, their culture, and their way of life, the destruction of their handiwork was unavoidable, and would have been even had the damage not been caused intentionally. How much more so, then, when the destruction was accomplished with the express intent of preventing the return of those who had left, of obscuring all traces of the civilization that had been annihilated, and of fashioning in its place a different human and physical landscape?"

The slow, methodical work of the destruction of the Palestinian landscape began in 1947 and carried on through the 1950s and 1960s. "As we went through Israel, the former Arab villages were a broken, distorted mass of mud bricks and falling walls," wrote an American traveler in 1951. "They were slowly going back into the earth where they came. In the cities, the Arab quarters were being demolished for new streets and modern shops." The Israeli General Moshe Dayan said frankly in 1969 that "we came to this country which was already populated by Arabs, and we are establishing a Hebrew, that is a Jewish state here. In considerable areas of the country we bought the lands from the Arabs. You do not even know the names of these Arab villages," he added, "and I do not blame you, because these geography books no longer exist; not only do the books not exist, the Arab villages aren't there either. Nahalal arose in the place of Mahalul, Gevat—in the place of Jibta, Sarid—in the place of Haneifs and Kefar Yehoshua—in the place of Tel Shaman. There is not one place in this country that did not have a former Arab population." Between 1987 and 1991 Palestinian geographer Ghazi Falah carried out a survey of the Arab landscape inside Israel. He found that two-thirds of the Palestinian villages had been completely wiped out, including 80 that are completely unidentifiable because the very land had been plowed up. "Other villages were totally demolished, but their outlines have been preserved thanks to prickly pear cactus hedges, stone terraces, or fruit trees gone wild," notes Benvenisti. As the Israeli scholar Israel Shahak observes, houses, gardens, cemeteries, and tombstones were all wiped from the earth, "so that literally a stone does not remain standing, and visitors are passing and being told that 'it was all desert.' "

On the coastal plain, between Jaffa and Gaza, not one single Palestinian village remains. It is, in the words of the Israeli journalist Gideon Levy, "the most Arab-free area in Israel. It was the scene of total ethnic cleansing, which left not a vestige apart from the heaps of ruins and the sabra [prickly pear] bushes." Levy points out the irony that the settlers from the Gush Katif bloc in the Gaza Strip, who would be pulled out of Gaza according to Sharon's so-called disengagement plan of 2005, will be resettled precisely here, to live on the ruins of the homes of the people who were their invisible neighbors in the Gaza refugee camps. "Again they will see nothing. From Gush Katif they saw nothing of the devastation that was wrought in Khan Yunis and in its refugee camp [in Gaza]; and in the Nitzanim region they will see nothing of the rich fabric of life that existed here and was destroyed," writes Levy in *Ha'aretz*. "It was all erased from the surface of the earth," he adds; "only the skeletons of a few beautiful homes, which somehow still stand, and the piles of stones, the orchards and the natural fences made of sabra bushes remain as mute testimony among the eucalyptus groves, the new settlements and the orchards that were planted on the sites of the destruction. From the Ashdod-Ashkelon road it is possible to see a few of the ruins, but who pays attention? Who asks himself what these houses are, what used to be here and where the former residents are as he shoots past on the highway?" Levy describes a trip across the rolling hills: "We drove like detectives across the dunes, between the natural brush, the fruit groves, the garbage dumps, and the local communities, hunting for any sign of earlier life. In one orchard we found an old faucet, in another the remnants of a millstone." He encounters a local school director, the Israeli Yair Farjun, who is very knowledgeable about what happened in 1948: "In terms of the Zionist ethos, the best work [of 1948] was done in the south," Farjun tells Levy. "If not for that work, Ahmed and Mustafa would now be holding a discussion about us, and I prefer me holding a discussion about Ahmed and Mustafa." He continues: "Anyone who tells you that there was no ethnic cleansing here will be lying, and anyone who tells you that without the ethnic cleansing Israel would have been established will also be lying."

Palestine was turned inside out in 1948. Because of what happened that year, the Palestinians have been scattered across many different countries and around the world.

There are today almost 5 million officially registered Palestinian refugees, including almost 2 million in Jordan, and about half a million each in Lebanon and Syria. Palestinian refugees do not necessarily enjoy the rights or privileges of citizenship in the countries in which they live. Many do not have passports. Their civil, political, and human rights are often severely circumscribed (those in Jordan are the notable exceptions to this rule) or entirely abused. They live in squalid camps that were established on a temporary basis after 1948 but have since morphed into permanent towns and cities, lacking proper facilities, often even basic sewage systems. They are constantly exposed to violence, as the large-scale violence and displacements from the Palestinian refugee camp at Nahr el-Bared in northern Lebanon in the spring and summer of 2007 reminded us. They have no one to protect them. Treated as a "problem," an inconvenience, a logistical burden, rather than as human beings with rights and interests, they were left out of the political equation established at Oslo in the mid-1990s.

Not all Palestinians in exile are stateless, however. Many have acquired citizenship in other countries and have permanently settled into the middle and upper classes of Lebanon, Jordan, and the Gulf countries. Palestinians have prominent places in businesses, government offices, hospitals, and universities around the world. Many would not consider themselves at home anywhere other than where they live now.

Irrespective of their individual successes or failures or the scattered nature of their present existence, however, Palestinians consider themselves to be a single people. The peace process of the 1990s, which focused on the portion of the Palestinian people living under Israeli occupation while excluding the majority of the people, was doomed to failure in large part because of that very exclusion. No genuine and lasting peace can be accomplished unless the needs, interests, and rights of the entire Palestinian people are taken seriously.

Not all Palestinians would choose to return to their native land, but their right to do so—as well as their right to be compensated for their personal or family losses in 1948, irrespective of whether they choose to return or not—has an unequivocal foundation in U.N. resolutions (particularly Resolution 194, which the General Assembly has reiterated countless times since 1948) and in the Universal Declaration of Human Rights. A peaceful and genuine resolution to the Israeli-Palestinian conflict must be founded on the principles of justice and international law, not at their expense, which was the approach taken by the so-called peace process of the mid-1990s.

"Few things are more important to a social group than its sense of belonging, not only to each other but to a place," declared Britain's Lord Justice Smedley in May 2007. "What has sustained peoples in exile, from Babylon onwards, has been the possibility of one day returning home." Smedley was referring not to the Palestinians, but to hundreds of Chagos Islanders who, following their eviction from their homeland in order to make room for the establishment of the American bomber base on the Indian Ocean island of Diego Garcia, finally won their right to return home after forty years of enforced exile at the hands of Britain and the United States. The rights of the Palestinian people are no less important than those of the Chagos Islanders. Nor, it should be added, is the Palestinian right of return more important than that of Arab Jews who left or were forced out of their own countries following the foundation of Israel.

The rights of the Palestinians do not depend on or imply the negation of the rights of Israeli Jews. Rather, the rights of Palestinians are inseparable from the rights of Israelis; the security and prosperity of one people are inseparable from those of the other. The only way to establish a just and lasting peace is to ensure that both peoples' fundamental rights are protected.

Coda

- Number of Israel's Basic Laws that guarantee equality of citizenship: 0
- Number of Israeli High Court rulings upholding equality as a right: 0
- Approximate ratio of Jews to Arabs in Israel plus occupied territories: 1:1

1

In June 2007—exactly forty years after the West Bank and Gaza fell to Israel—the occupied territories were gripped by the most intense interfactional fighting in Palestinian history. Almost 200 people, including many civilians, were killed. When it was over, Hamas was in control of the Gaza Strip, and a new Israeli- and U.S.-backed Palestinian Authority government—appointed by Fateh leader Mahmoud Abbas—was installed in the West Bank.

The fighting, and the subsequent apparent split between the West Bank and Gaza, marked the culmination of a political crisis set in motion by the Palestinian Legislative Council elections won by Hamas in January 2006. Palestinians rejected the long-dominant Fateh in those elections because the party was perceived as corrupt and generally inept—and as having become far too close to Israel, and comfortable with the occupation (see "Outsides"). It seemed obvious to an increasing number of Palestinians that the so-called peace process championed by Fateh would never lead to the end of the by then thirty-nine-year-old occupation, let alone to the creation of an independent Palestinian state. On the contrary, since the beginnings of the Oslo negotiations over a decade previously, Israel had effectively broken the occupied territories into several separately besieged cantons, each turned outside in; doubled its settler presence in the West Bank and a systematically de-Arabized East Jerusalem; turned Gaza into what the U.N.'s John Dugard, former World Bank president and Middle East envoy James Wolfensohn, and others bluntly referred to as a "prison"; and imposed a system of closures and curfews that had led directly to an economic and humanitarian catastrophe that was reducing more and more Palestinians to penury. With Fateh's connivance, the Palestinian Authority had been transformed from a transitional structure (it was to have been dissolved by 1999) into a permanently circumscribed assistant to Israel, assigned the task of administering and policing the Palestinian population on behalf of the occupation, while indefinitely ceding all the most important aspects of sovereignty—from control over borders and territory to taxes and the population registry—to Israel. The Road Map to Peace specifically called for the "final and comprehensive settlement of the Israeli-Palestinian conflict," including the creation of a "Palestinian state with provisional borders and attributes of sovereignty" by 2005. And yet by 2006, the PA was a "government" in name only; a government without a state to govern, and without even the prospect of such a state.

Palestinian skepticism concerning the prospects for a genuine resolution of the conflict under these circumstances was reinforced by the unilateral approach undertaken by the Israeli government under Ariel Sharon, and after him by Ehud Olmert, as well as by the statements of Israeli government officials who made it clear that Israel was uninterested in the establishment of a real Palestinian state, which, as senior government advisor Dov Weisglas boasted to the Israeli newspaper *Ha'aretz* in 2004, had been "removed from our agenda indefinitely."

The leader of Fateh is Palestinian Authority President Mahmoud Abbas. One of the lead Palestinian negotiators at Oslo, his popularity is so depleted that opinion polls regularly show that twice as many Palestinians trust no one as trust him (a March 2007 poll conducted by the Jerusalem Media and Communications Center, for example, found that 12 percent of Palestinians trust Abbas, compared to 27 percent who trust none of their leaders). Especially under the leadership of Abbas, who is more popular with Americans and Israelis than with his own people, it was clear to most Palestinians that Fateh had nothing new to offer in January 2006. A considerable number of secular Palestinian politicians— including the co-founder of the Palestine Liberation Organization, Haidar Abdel-Shafi—had been expressing strong and principled criticisms of the leadership of first Yasser Arafat and then Mahmoud Abbas, and they had been doing so since they first learned of the secret deal made at Oslo in 1993 (which Arafat and his closest associates, including Abbas, had undertaken on their own and without consulting many of the most experienced and dedicated advocates of the Palestinian cause). Many of these secular figures devoted themselves to a new organization, the Palestinian National Initiative, that, under the leadership of Mustafa Barghouti, was intended to challenge what they perceived as the corruption and arrogance of the PA leadership, and to offer a genuinely democratic and secular alternative both to Fateh and to Hamas. Others struck out on their own. But ultimately none of them was able to gain the political traction necessary to win an election (and they were not helped by constant Israeli interference and harassment during the campaigning season). And to many Palestinians encouraged by international calls for democratization and reform to express their beliefs in the ballot box, Hamas seemed to offer a genuine alternative.

2

In the United States, Hamas is identified with attacks on Israeli civilians, and especially with its notorious campaign of suicide bombing during the second intifada. There can be no excuse for indiscriminate attacks on innocent civilians, whether in the form of suicide bombings or Qassam rocket attacks on Israeli towns.

However, there also should not be a double standard when it comes to indiscriminate attacks on civilian targets. Such attacks are either right, or they are wrong; either one approves of them, or one does not—and, having experienced war myself, I do not. More importantly, however, one of the founding principles of international humanitarian law is that such attacks are wrong, no matter who engages in them.

Many reports published by human rights organizations, journalists, the International Red Cross, and various U.N. offices have illustrated that Israel, too, is guilty of what international law considers the disproportionate and indiscriminate use of force, and on a much larger scale than Hamas. When the Israeli air force killed the Hamas leader Salah Shehadeh in his Gaza home in July 2002, for example, it did so with a one-ton aerial bomb that killed 14 innocent people, including 8 sleeping children, along with Shehadeh himself. The bombing (which, as an extrajudicial execution, would have constituted a breach of international law even if no civilians had been killed) destroyed an entire apartment building in a densely packed residential neighborhood in the middle of the night. Ariel Sharon referred to the attack as "a great success," but governments around the world condemned it. "This was a deliberate attack on the site, knowing that innocents would be lost," said President Bush's spokesman. The Israeli air force commander Dan Halutz admitted that "the aerial assassination was decided upon with knowledge that there were women and children near the wanted man."

Nor is the Israeli killing of Palestinian civilians merely a matter of indiscriminate carelessness, as was the case in the Shehadeh killing or in dozens of other illegal extrajudicial executions (which invariably kill innocent bystanders)—or the Gaza beach shelling that killed Huda Ghalia's family in June 2006, or the shelling of the al-Athamah family home in Beit Hanoun in November that year, which the U.N.'s John Dugard condemned as a war crime (see "Outside In"). There are countless reports of Israeli soldiers, in both the first intifada and the second, deliberately shooting to kill unarmed Palestinian demonstrators who posed no threat to them. On assignment in Khan Younis (Gaza) in 2001, the *New York*

Times reporter Chris Hedges witnessed Israeli soldiers not just firing at Palestinian demonstrators, but actually taunting Palestinian children— then killing them as they got within firing range:

> It is still. The camp waits, as if holding its breath. And then, out of the dry furnace air, a disembodied voice crackles over a loud-speaker.
>
> "Come on, dogs," the voice booms in Arabic. "Where are all the dogs of Khan Younis? Come! Come!"
>
> I stand up. I walk outside the hut. The invective continues to spew: "Son of a bitch!" "Son of a whore!" "Your mother's cunt!"
>
> The boys dart in small packs up the sloping dunes to the electric fence that separates the camp from the Jewish settlement. They lob rocks toward two armored jeeps parked on top of the dune and mounted with loudspeakers. Three ambulances line the road below the dunes in anticipation of what is to come.
>
> A percussion grenade explodes. The boys, most no more than ten or eleven years old, scatter, running clumsily across the heavy sand. They descend out of sight behind a sandbank in front of me. There are no sounds of gunfire. The soldiers shoot with silencers. The bullets from the M-16 rifles tumble end over end through the children's slight bodies. Later, in the hospital, I will see the destruction: the stomachs ripped out, the gaping holes in limbs and torsos.
>
> Yesterday at this spot the Israelis shot eight young men, six of whom were under the age of eighteen. One was twelve. This afternoon they kill an eleven-year-old boy, Ali Murad, and seriously wound four more, three of whom are under eighteen.
>
> Children have been shot in other conflicts I have covered— death squads gunned them down in El Salvador and Guatemala, mothers with infants were lined up and massacred in Algeria, and Serb snipers put children in their sights and watched them crumple onto the pavement in Sarajevo—but I have never before watched soldiers entice children like mice into a trap and murder them for sport.

Deliberate Israeli attacks on unarmed civilians are not restricted to episodes like this, in which individual soldiers take advantage of what

John Dugard and others refer to as the culture of impunity within the Israeli army, which encourages (or at least does not discourage) the callous disregard for human life. A long litany of killings of unarmed civilians spots the Israeli army's history, of which the most notorious was the massacre at the Sabra and Shatila refugee camps in Beirut in 1982, though there are many other examples as well (including the still-ongoing killing of farmers, shepherds, and children as a result of Israel's massive cluster-bombing campaign in southern Lebanon in 2006, which left the countryside littered with a million unexploded bomblets).

However, these events are introduced into discussions of the conflict in the United States with all the sense of immediacy of ancient history: it is as though with each new conversation they need to be consciously remembered and exhumed and reintroduced, only to be quickly forgotten again. By contrast, Hamas's track record of violence against Israeli civilians is so well established in the United States—and so deeply ingrained—that it almost automatically structures the way in which Western commentators approach and frame their discussion of the conflict. In part, this has to do with the phenomenon of suicide bombing, which, however appalling it is, tends to become an object of almost obsessive interest in itself, perhaps because members of a Western audience can more readily identify with the victims of suicide bombing than with the victims of aerial or artillery bombardment, fuel-air explosives, flechette rounds, cluster bombs, depleted uranium, phosphorous and napalm. In far too much media coverage, especially in the United States, the conflict between Palestinians and Israelis ends up being reduced simply to sheer violence, and in particular to those forms of violence that lend themselves in one way or another to televisual spectacle. This has the effect not only of decontextualizing the violence of both sides, but also overshadowing, even displacing, the much less visible but equally deadly effects of the Israeli apparatus of bureaucracy and control in the occupied territories, which by its nature does not lend itself to televised images (unless you can imagine a five-hour video sequence of a man standing in line).

What we need, if we are opposed to suicide—or any other kind of—bombing, and to home demolitions, and the whole apparatus of closure and control that is slowly suffocating an entire population, is to understand what is going on, in order that we can know how to bring the conflict to a just and lasting resolution. The main problem with the hostility toward Hamas in the United States, in this sense, is that it has become so deeply ingrained that it clouds the possibility of sound analysis, and Hamas is seen as part of a regional conspiracy of unacceptable "extremism," rather than as the almost inevitable product of forty years of military occupation.

In the 30 July 2007 issue of *The New Yorker*, for example, David Remnick writes: "Hezbollah's ideological ally in Palestine, Hamas—the Islamic Resistance Movement—led a violent uprising in the Gaza Strip, overwhelming its secular rival, Fatah. Suddenly, Israel, backed by the United States, found itself propping up the Fatah leadership, in order not to lose the West Bank to Hamas as well." Implicit here is that Hizballah and Hamas, as "ideological allies," share a violent vision of the region in which, as Remnick puts it in the previous paragraph, Israel can be eliminated "from the map of the Middle East." It is important, first, to note that Hizballah—the resistance movement that ended Israel's two-decade-old military occupation of southern Lebanon by forcing the Israeli army from the country—is a Shia organization that emerged among the impoverished agricultural villages of southern Lebanon, whereas Hamas is a Sunni organization based in the urban slums of Gaza and the West Bank. It is also important to note that Hizballah has the strong support of a major segment of the Christian population in Lebanon, as represented, for example, in the widespread backing (demonstrated most recently in a parliamentary by-election in August 2007) among Lebanese Christians for the former army commander, and now (as this book goes to press) presidential contender, Michel Aoun. Aoun offered strong political support for Hizballah during the 2006 Israeli war on Lebanon—on the basis of nationalism rather than religion—and he and other Christian politicians continue to maintain an alliance with it that makes it impossible, or at best hopelessly simplistic, to consider Hizballah simply in Muslim terms, or merely as the actualization of some underlying extremist "ideology."

Such subtleties, altogether absent from Remnick's account, deeply complicate his vision of the relationship between Hizballah and Hamas.

But the most striking absence from Remnick's account is any recognition of the fact that both organizations were born, and gained popularity, in resisting the Israeli invasions and occupations of their respective homelands—invasions and occupations the international community repeatedly condemned, and called on Israel to end. People across Lebanon's complex religious and political spectrum, from Shia Muslim to Maronite Catholic, supported Hizballah's resistance operations against the Israeli army in the years leading up to the Israeli withdrawal in 2000 not because they believed in its Islamism, or its ideology, but simply because they wanted an end to Israel's brutal occupation of Lebanon. It is impossible to understand Hizballah without acknowledging this elementary fact. And the same thing goes for Hamas—though in neither case would this justify indiscriminate attacks on civilian targets. "It is not to sanction the murder of civilians to observe that such violence occurs, sooner or later, in most situations in which a people's drive for national self-determination is frustrated by an occupying power," as the former head of the American Jewish Congress Henry Siegman points out. Insofar as there is any connection at all between Hizballah and Hamas, then, it lies in the coincidence that they both emerged in response to Israel's military occupations of other people's land. What Remnick does in his piece, though, is to invert matters and approach them almost exactly back to front: on his account, Hizballah and Hamas are ideological allies first and foremost—thus their fight against Israel is mystified, lifted out of its historical context and turned into nothing more than the manifestation of an "ideology" that somehow preexisted them.

The right of a people living under military occupation to resist that occupation is enshrined in international law, as is every people's right to self-determination. Nowhere do these rights—nor for that matter the wrongs of Israeli occupation—figure in Remnick's analysis. It is this nearly total lack of a sense of historical and legal context that sets Remnick up for his main claim, that Hamas "led a violent uprising in the Gaza Strip." However, Hamas was at the time in charge of the democratically elected government; it is, by definition, impossible for an elected government to lead an uprising against itself.

3

Here we need to reset the clock to the elections of January 2006, which led to Hamas's victory, to try to think through what happened with a little greater clarity and focus—not least in order to try to assess where things might go from here. The idiosyncrasies of the Palestinian electoral system somewhat distorted the extent of the support for Hamas among Palestinian voters (that is, they won approximately 46 percent of the votes cast, but gained over half the seats in the Legislative Council). Nevertheless, the election was a major setback for Fateh, and a sure sign of the extent to which more and more Palestinians were looking for an alternative to the established leadership, even if they did not necessarily agree with everything that Hamas stood for.

People voted for Hamas not because of its Islamic ideology and sloganeering (only a small minority of Palestinians favor the creation of an Islamic state), but because of the substantive political program it held out; because of its demonstrated record in providing social assistance to underprivileged Palestinians; and because, unlike Fateh, it refused to cooperate with the occupation, and to compromise on the principled demands of the Palestinian people. "In contrast with the decay and the corruption and the fecklessness of the Palestinian Authority under Fateh, which has essentially lost touch with the people," argues the former U.N. envoy Alvaro de Soto, "Hamas was widely seen as attentive to their needs, and largely untainted by corruption. Furthermore, Hamas' undisguised skepticism, if not outright rejection, of the Oslo accords and framework, resonates among many, even though a majority appears still to adhere to a two-state solution."

Some of the support for Hamas demonstrated by the 2006 elections undoubtedly had to do with the party's successful appropriation and rehabilitation of the language of Palestinian national liberation that had originally been devised by the secular parties—notably Fateh—in the 1960s and 1970s, but had been dropped by the Fateh and PA elites as they grew more comfortable with the Israeli and American language of the so-called peace process, and with the managerial role assigned to them by the occupation after Oslo. To a Palestinian population not only embittered by the actual practices of the Israeli occupation, but also sick and tired of the bureaucratic and managerial language of Oslo and the Road Map, Hamas offered a discourse of genuine struggle and of commitment to a principled cause. Many secular Palestinians, who otherwise would have had little in common with Hamas ideologically, found this an irresistibly refreshing alternative to the dry communiqués—which seldom, if ever, feature words like "liberation," "return," or even "occupation"—published by the office of Mahmoud Abbas.

"Our message to the Palestinians is this," wrote Khaled Meshaal, head of the political bureau of Hamas, shortly after the electoral victory in 2006: "Our people are not only those who live under siege in the West Bank and the Gaza Strip but also the millions languishing in refugee camps in Lebanon, Jordan and Syria and the millions spread around the world unable to return home. We promise you that nothing in the world will deter us from pursuing our goal of liberation and return. We shall spare no effort to work with all factions and institutions in order to put our Palestinian house in order. Having won the parliamentary elections, our medium-term objective is to reform the PLO in order to revive its role as a true representative of all the Palestinian people, without exception or discrimination." Hamas, Meshaal added, "is immune to bribery, intimidation and blackmail. While we are keen on having friendly relations with all nations we shall not seek friendships at the expense of our legitimate rights. We have seen how other nations, including the peoples of Vietnam and South Africa, persisted in their struggle until their quest for freedom and justice was accomplished. We are no different, our cause is no less worthy, our determination is no less profound and our patience is no less abundant." Here were sentiments expressed in a clear and straightforward language with which all Palestinians could identify, in a way that they never could with the repeatedly deferred and ultimately hollow promises of Oslo or the Road Map. In voting for Hamas, then, Palestinians were certainly not just voting for Islamism and violence; they were voting for a vision of Palestine, and a vision of the Palestinian cause, which Fateh seemed to have abandoned. And in the final analysis it is an attachment to that cause, rather than to any particular party or its narrow ideology, that motivates most Palestinians. The object of faith that Hamas held out to Palestinian voters, in other words, was not Islam, but Palestine itself.

The Hamas-affiliated candidates who participated in the 2006 elections did so not as representatives of Hamas but rather as members of the "Reform and Change" electoral list. Thus they campaigned not on the basis of the Hamas charter (which calls for the creation of an Islamic state in all of Palestine) but rather on the basis of a much more limited and pragmatic electoral agenda directed specifically against the perceived limitations of Fateh as well as the widely recognized corruption and mismanagement of the Palestinian Authority. Hamas thus came to power on the basis of a drastically scaled-down set of political objectives.

Unlike virtually all political parties across the Arab world, Hamas published its government's political program. The program's main demands included calls for political reform and financial transparency and an end to corruption in government; an end to the occupation; an affirmation of the right of return of the 1948 refugees and their descendants; and negotiations with Israel for the creation of a genuinely independent Palestinian state in the West Bank and Gaza, with a capital in Jerusalem. Far from being controversial, the principal elements of the Hamas political program were entirely in keeping with the demands of international law and the framework provided by decades of U.N. Security Council resolutions.

The election results had been certified by international observers, including the Carter Center, as free and fair. Still, they were rejected both by Israel and by the United States, and then in effect by the so-called Quartet (the United States, the U.N., the EU, and Russia), which had taken over the role of the Great Powers—notably Britain and France—that had helped precipitate and then attempt to "manage" the Palestine crisis since 1917. De Soto, the U.N.'s envoy to the Quartet, pleaded with his colleagues at a meeting immediately after the January elections that the international community should recognize the legitimacy of the elections and try to work with Hamas, to offer some acknowledgment of the efforts the party had made. To wind down its violent struggle against Israel it had generally adhered to a unilateral cease-fire and embarked upon a democratic path. De Soto advocated continuing to draw it away from violence and toward the negotiated settlement that it claimed to want. "Predictably, I was unsuccessful in these endeavors," de Soto comments in a confidential internal U.N. report that was leaked to the press and published in May 2007. And, as he points out, with its refusal to accept Hamas's electoral victory, the Quartet was transformed "into a body that was all-but-imposing sanctions on the freely elected government of a people under occupation as well as setting unattainable preconditions for a dialogue."

The "unattainable preconditions" to which de Soto refers included the United States and Israeli demand that Hamas recognize Israel and renounce violence. Though this sounds mild, unobjectionable, even essential to American ears, to most Palestinians it was unreasonable and unjust to offer any such concessions in advance of real negotiations. Hamas was asked to renounce violence—but no such demand was made of Israel. And Palestinians were asked to recognize Israel in the absence of any Israeli recognition of Palestine. Moreover, as many Palestinians (including myself) pointed out, in the absence of a negotiated framework it was far from obvious what the "recognition" of Israel would mean: since Israel has always refused to declare its borders, which Israel, precisely, were Palestinians being asked to "recognize"? An Israel that ended at the limits proposed by the 1947 U.N. Partition Plan, on the basis of which it declared independence? An Israel that ended at the 1949 Armistice Line? An Israel that includes the illegally annexed East Jerusalem? An Israel that includes territory virtually if not formally annexed by the West Bank wall, which the Israeli government has repeatedly said it intends to be an approximation of its territorial aspirations? Were Palestinians being asked to recognize an Israel that agrees to the demands of international law, adheres to the requirements of dozens of U.N. Security Council resolutions, and accepts the 2004 Advisory Opinion of the International Court of Justice—or an Israel that considers itself above the law? In which case, why should recognition make any difference? Why were no reciprocal demands being made of Israel? And, above all, why was the onus for ending an illegal occupation being placed on its victims rather than on its perpetrators, when the demands of international law made it clear that things ought to proceed the other way around?

All these questions remained academic. In what former President Jimmy Carter would denounce as a "criminal" policy, the U.S. government tried to subvert the outcome of a legitimate election. It and the EU imposed sanctions on the newly elected government. Israel suspended transfers of what would ultimately amount to hundreds of millions of dollars of tax revenues, Palestinian monies that it collected on behalf of the Palestinian Authority and that provided two-thirds of the PA's revenues—the funds it needed to pay doctors, teachers, and policemen. The freeze further deepened the already calamitous economic and humanitarian crisis facing the Palestinians, ultimately to leave over 80 percent of the population in Gaza dependent on food aid for their day-to-day survival. Then Israeli forces stormed the Palestinian territories and kidnapped two dozen Hamas legislators and a third of the cabinet, which to many Palestinians was an indicator of how seriously Israel would take the "sovereignty" of a future Palestinian state.

The effect of the international response to the election of Hamas, as de Soto points out, was to remove what little pressure there had been on Israel to end its settlement enterprise, its construction of the wall, the closure system it had imposed on the Palestinian population, and, in general, its undermining of the possibility of the creation of a genuinely independent Palestinian state. Whether in response to the anticipated pressure, or as a reflection of a genuine political strategy, Hamas tried to reach out to Fateh and other Palestinian factions and form a national unity government immediately after the 2006 elections. The United States worked to block this endeavor, in order to cement the isolation of Hamas. According to President Carter, "the United States and Israel decided to punish all the people in Palestine and did everything they could to deter a compromise between Hamas and Fatah."

In spite of American and Israeli pressure, a short-lived national unity government was ultimately formed during Hamas-Fateh negotiations held in Mecca under Saudi auspices—but those negotiations did not take place until early 2007. In the meantime, the United States continued to push for a confrontation between Fateh and Hamas—and even a Palestinian civil war. The United States channeled funds to Fateh, and Israel allowed huge quantities of weapons and ammunition to get through, despite its often-expressed anxieties concerning "security"—to both official and unofficial Fateh militias, notably the paramilitary organization led by Muhammad Dahlan in Gaza, to destabilize the Hamas government. Dahlan's closest associate in the U.S. government was (and remains) Deputy National Security Advisor Elliot Abrams, who is best known for having been convicted for lying to Congress about his role in a strikingly similar project during the Reagan administration in the 1980s, namely, establishing and arming the Contra militia to topple the legitimate government of Nicaragua. According to James Wolfensohn, the former president of the World Bank, Abrams was also responsible for undermining the 2005 Agreement on Movement and Access that Wolfensohn helped negotiate, thereby turning Gaza back into a "prison" and encouraging the rise of Hamas (see "Outside In").

A week before the Mecca agreement was reached, as Palestinian infighting was escalating in Gaza, de Soto recalls twice hearing the U.S. envoy to the Quartet declare " 'how much I like this violence,' referring to the near civil war that was erupting in Gaza in which civilians were regularly being killed and injured, because 'it means that other Palestinians are resisting Hamas.' " De Soto appealed to his U.N. readers: "Please remember this next time someone argues that the Mecca agreement, to the extent that it showed progress, proved that a year of pressure 'worked,' and we should keep the isolation going. On the contrary, the same result might have been achieved much earlier without the year in between in which so much damage was done to Palestinian institutions, and so much suffering brought to the people of the occupied territory, in pursuit of a policy that didn't work [i.e., isolation]."

Even after the Palestinian national unity government was formed in early 2007, U.S. and Israeli efforts to destabilize it continued, and fighting erupted sporadically in the West Bank and especially in Gaza between security forces loyal to Hamas and militias—notably Dahlan's—supported and armed by the United States and Israel, which aimed to weaken and ultimately to undermine the Hamas-led national unity government. Finally, in June, Hamas cracked down on Dahlan and the extra-governmental Fateh armed presence in Gaza, which quickly collapsed. In response, Mahmoud Abbas announced the dissolution of the Hamas-led national unity government and the appointment instead of a new prime minister, Salam Fayyad, whose electoral list had garnered barely 2 percent of the same vote that had swept Hamas to victory in 2006. Muhammad Dahlan ironically started referring to Gaza as "occupied territory," a reference not to Israel, but to Hamas. With U.S. and Israeli encouragement, and even the overt support of the America Israel Public Affairs Committee (AIPAC), the most formidable of Israel's lobbying organizations in Washington, Abbas refused to enter into negotiations with Hamas, which continued to appeal for Palestinian unity and the respect for legitimate elections, the outcome of which had been bypassed by Abbas and Fateh.

Nor did Abbas merely refuse to negotiate with his fellow Palestinians in Hamas while swiftly restoring ties to Israel. In mid-July 2007, even as the United Nations was escalating its urgent appeals for worldwide assistance to deal with the looming humanitarian catastrophe in Gaza (where the unemployment rate had rocketed to 75 percent, and where the U.N. and other relief agencies were by then feeding 80 percent of Gaza's population just to keep them alive), and was warning of the territory's total economic collapse, the Israeli newspaper *Ha'aretz* reported that Abbas had been asking Israel to keep the Rafah crossing on the border with Egypt closed—and to let Gaza continue to starve, because that would also punish Hamas. *Ha'aretz* also reported that Abbas had asked that his request to Israel not be made public. It was shortly after that story broke that Abbas met with Israeli prime minister Ehud Olmert at the home of one of his (Abbas's) associates, Saeb Erekat, to resume once again Palestinian-Israeli negotiations and the stalled so-called peace process. Press reports seemed to focus more on Olmert's satisfaction with the feast laid out for him by his Palestinian hosts than with any substantive outcome of the negotiations (perhaps because there were none). But the spectacle of Abbas and Erekat treating the prime minister of Israel to a feast when the people of Gaza were unable to feed their children was taken by many Palestinians as a reminder of precisely why Fateh had lost the 2006 elections in the first place.

The meeting between Olmert and Abbas arranged by President Bush at Annapolis in November 2007 revealed more clearly than ever before the gap between words and realities, and the futility of negotiations as they have been conceived so far—as though justice and international law could simply be dispensed with. In the buildup to the meeting, Israel offered to freeze settlement expansion, though it followed this loud declaration with a *sotto voce* series of equivocations seeking to distinguish "expansion" from what it calls "natural growth." In holding out the possibility that it might dismantle a few "illegal outposts," Israel once again shrugged off the reality that all of its settlements are violations of international law. It made much of its "goodwill" release of 429 Palestinian prisoners on the eve of the summit, a move that in U.S. media coverage has overshadowed the fact that, according to recent UN-OCHA data, Israel captured 2,421 Palestinians since June 2007 alone and was still holding over 10,000 in all. Israel preceded the Annapolis meeting by announcing, in September, the expropriation of a fresh 1,100 dunums (272 acres) of

Palestinian land in the West Bank, to facilitate the construction of an additional 3,500 housing units between Jerusalem and Ma'ale Adumim (thereby finally severing the northern West Bank from the southern); and it followed the summit by announcing the expansion of the Har Homa settlement in East Jerusalem by an additional 300 housing units. Those concrete realities matter far more than the announcement, at Annapolis, of a "new beginning" for a political process that has already had far too many beginnings and far too little to show for them.

4

The restoration of Fateh power in the West Bank, and the apparently increased isolation of Hamas in Gaza, seemed to some outside observers to have marked a U.S. and Israeli victory, and a return to business as usual between Israel and a newly pliant Palestinian Authority. But there is reason to think otherwise. Partly by so starkly revealing the real limits of Palestinian power in the occupied territories—and the structural permanence of Israeli control—it is, ironically, more likely that recent events might one day be seen to mark the beginning of the end of the four-decade-old formula established by Israel to maintain its control over the territories it has occupied since 1967.

That formula was first articulated by Yigal Allon's proposal that Israel should retain permanent strategic control over the occupied territories, while denying their residents citizenship, which would further undermine Israel's claim to being a Jewish state (see "Outsides"). Since then, although Israeli policy has changed, the fundamental vision of its occupation has remained the same: to keep control of most of the land, and settle it with Jews; and to maintain ultimate control over Palestinians' lives, to subject them to Israeli rule while denying them any of the benefits of inclusion in the Israeli polity. Allon devised this formula; Oslo reiterated it; so did Camp David; and so does current Israeli policy. Only the details and external packaging of the formula have been changed.

As Régis Debray put it in a report he submitted to the French government at the request of President Jacques Chirac in January 2007, "there is a huge gap between what is said because we want to hear it (local withdrawals, easing of travel restrictions, removal of one checkpoint out of 20, a change of tone) and what is being done on the ground, which we don't want to see (interlinking of settlements, construction of bridges and tunnels, encirclement of Palestinian towns, expropriation of land, destruction of houses)." The reality, as Debray points out, may not be visible from Geneva, Paris, or New York, but it is obvious to anyone visiting the West Bank. "It is a land carved up by military force, where the Israeli settlements are no longer shapes on a Palestinian background—instead the Palestinian areas appear as shapes on a solidly-infrastructured Israeli background: a land where water reserves are confiscated and a temporary travel restriction is very close to a permanent ban." Henry Siegman presents an equally bleak assessment of the situation. The realities on the ground are what matters, and it is precisely these circumstances "that the uninformed and/or cynical blather in Jerusalem, Washington and Brussels—about waiting for Palestinians to reform their institutions, democratize their culture, dismantle the 'infrastructures of terror' and halt all violence and incitement before peace negotiations can begin—seeks to drown out." Only an immediate and dramatic intervention by the international community, he says, including, if necessary, the dispatching of an armed U.N. force to impose the rule of law, can bring about a change in course on Israel's part and salvage the prospect of an independent Palestinian state, as part of a two-state solution. Debray, for his part, is not so sanguine. The two-state solution, he concludes, is already an empty phrase "belonging to the realm of might-have-been."

There is good reason to believe that Debray is right. A massive report on the humanitarian impact of Israeli settlement on the Palestinian population of the West Bank, published in July 2007 by the U.N. Office for the Coordination of Humanitarian Affairs, completely bears out his assessment (see maps, pp. 340 and 341). "More than 38% of the West Bank now consists of [Israeli] settlements, outposts, military bases, closed military areas, Israeli declared nature reserves or other related infrastructure that are off-limits or tightly controlled to Palestinians," the report notes. The remainder of the territory, it says, "has been dissected into dozens of enclaves by the settlements and the related infrastructure." Moreover, the Jewish settler population, now almost half a million, has been growing at a rate of 5.5 percent a year, the equivalent of one and a half busloads of new settlers each and every day—and a rate of increase three times greater than that of Israel itself. Based on the current growth rate, the Jewish settler population will double to almost one million in just twelve years.

The West Bank's resources, especially its land and water, are very limited. As the settler population expands, the indigenous Palestinians of the West Bank and East Jerusalem—today some 2.5 million people—will find themselves under ever-greater pressure. Based on trends established over the previous four decades, the report says, it is inevitable that "the growth of roads, settlements and other infrastructure will come at the expense of Palestinian development and freedom of movement around the West Bank." And because of the way in which Israeli infrastructure has broken the Palestinian areas of the West Bank into dozens of separate enclaves, even if transport contiguity could be established between those enclaves (by bridges and tunnels linking them to each other, which the Israeli government is now building), that kind of contiguity might, the report adds, satisfy short-term humanitarian needs, but "it cannot ultimately lead to a sustainable economy. It also does not provide the basis for a two-state solution." That, by the standards of OCHA, is something of an overstatement: political assessments are not part of its purely humanitarian brief, and it is actually quite remarkable that the report goes as far as it does in making this point.

What we are to conclude from this report, then, is that a genuinely independent Palestinian state in the West Bank, Gaza Strip, and East Jerusalem has become a geophysical impossibility.

The Hamas electoral victory in 2006 brought to a head the period of violent uncertainty and Israeli unilateralism that had begun with the eruption of the second intifada in 2000. Everything that had been deferred since Oslo suddenly had to be reckoned with. Unlike Fateh, Hamas insisted that it would not be willing to go along with the perpetual—indeed, the permanent—deferral of urgent issues, such as the rights of the 1948 refugees, or the reality that the Palestinians are one people, no matter how separated they are by other countries' borders, while the Israelis carried on breaking up the occupied territories, building new settlements and expanding existing ones. Hamas in effect called Israel's bluff: what it demanded was what Oslo promised but would never deliver, namely, a genuinely independent Palestinian state, and an actual Israeli withdrawal to the 1949–67 borders.

The abrupt U.S.-Israeli-engineered removal of the Hamas-led national unity government revealed that such demands are unacceptable according to Israel's post-1967 paradigm of territorial inclusion and demographic exclusion. This paradigm in itself is only a response to the same contradiction the Zionist movement faced in 1948 (and was resolved, in the case of Israel within its pre-1967 borders, only by the forcible removal of half of Palestine's indigenous population)—namely, the Israeli desire to politically exclude the Palestinian people while physically controlling their land.

Covered up or displaced in various ways over the previous forty years of occupation, that contradiction is more obvious than ever as a result of the crisis of June 2007. The restoration of Mahmoud Abbas and his deeply unpopular associates, whose appointment lacks any real legitimacy (it was never validated by the Legislative Council, still dominated by Hamas), is likely to offer the Israelis at best a temporary fix. For the Oslo formula is premised not simply on the cooperation of a few carefully chosen Palestinian leaders—the definition of whose "moderation" is, as Siegman puts it, "acquiescence in the Israeli dismemberment of Palestinian territory"—but also on the willingness of the people as a whole to have faith in those leaders. It is simple enough for Israel to find or hire men like Dahlan, or to reinstall a pliant and cooperative Palestinian government; but it is quite another matter to try to coerce faith from the people as a whole.

Having tried both persuasion and coercion, Israel has run out of options. By the summer of 2007, a new paradigm shift was already underway. Alvaro de Soto's report, filed shortly before the final violent confrontations of June, notes that "the notion of dissolving the PA entirely is often bandied about as a threat to Israel so that it will face up to its [legal and humanitarian] responsibilities as an occupying power." Such a development "no longer seems entirely absurd, if not as a result of deliberate decision, then possibly by an implosion of the PA government," he writes. "Should it happen, the responsibility for the welfare of the population would revert directly to Israel as occupying power, while the major institutional achievement of the Oslo Accords would vanish." Moreover, he adds, "the combination of PA institutional decline and Israeli settlement expansion is creating a growing conviction among

Palestinians and Israeli Arabs [i.e., Palestinian citizens of Israel], as well as some Jews on the far left in Israel, that the two State solution's best days are behind it." Given that a Palestinian state requires both a real government and continuous territory, and that the basis for both is being steadily undermined by Israel's own policies, he writes, "they believe the only long-term way to end the conflict will be to abandon the idea of dividing the land, and, instead, simply insist on the civil, political and national rights of the two peoples, Jews and Arabs, who populate the land, in one State."

De Soto is right. Although it is nowhere on the official agenda, more and more Palestinians—and a small number of Israelis—are abandoning the very concept of the two-state solution, which, at best, offered a palliative only for the segment of the Palestinian people living under occupation, while ignoring the majority of the people, who remain in exile or live as second-class citizens inside Israel. Reaffirming the indivisibility of the people, and recognizing that, in any case, the territory once considered for a Palestinian state has been irreversibly broken up and colonized, Palestinians—two-thirds of them, according to a poll recently conducted by Birzeit University in the West Bank—are calling for an end to the structural distinction between Jews and non-Jews and the foundation of a single democratic and secular state in all of historic Palestine, with equal rights for all citizens, regardless of their religious beliefs.

Palestinians in the occupied territories are being joined in this demand by their fellow Palestinians in exile—many of whom are actively involved in redefining the national agenda from the outside, often in dialogue with like-minded Israelis—and by those who have Israeli citizenship. In late 2006 and early 2007, a coalition of Palestinian civil- and human-rights organizations inside Israel published a series of calls for Israel to become like all other states—the state of its citizens, rather than the state of the Jewish people—and hence a genuine democracy. Those calls were denounced by Zionists from across the Israeli political spectrum as tantamount to a demand for the end of the Jewish state. Yet the aim of these peaceful reformers is not the destruction of the state, let alone its people, but rather the stripping away of forms of privilege and racism that are incompatible with the Universal Declaration of Human Rights and the International Convention on the Elimination of All Forms of Racial

Discrimination. The most important documents produced by the informal coalition include the *Haifa Covenant* drafted by the Arab Center for Applied Social Research; *The Future Vision of the Palestinian Arabs in Israel*, published by the Committee of Arab Mayors in Israel; and, above all, *The Democratic Constitution* published in March 2007 by Adalah, the Legal Center for Arab Minority Rights in Israel. Having lived under military rule for the first two decades of their experience as a minority, Israeli Palestinians had once been quiescent, and reluctant to challenge their classification by the Jewish state as deracinated "Arabs" rather than members of the Palestinian people. Israel could once count on their silence while dealing with the national aspirations of the Palestinians living under its occupation. That is no longer the case.

The *Democratic Constitution* was intended to fill a gap left by contemporary constitutional debates in Israel, which, according to Adalah's Marwan Dwairy, "have been preoccupied with the question of, 'Who is a Jew?' and have neglected the primary constitutional question of, 'Who is a Citizen?' " The document is founded on the principles enshrined in the Universal Declaration of Human Rights, notably the idea that all human beings are equal and that no nation or people possesses rights that can cancel out those of another. It affirms the fact that "the Palestinian Arab citizens of Israel have lived in their homeland for innumerable generations" and are "an inseparable part of the Palestinian people," and that they have "not relinquished their national identity" but had their political status "changed against their will" when they became "a minority in their homeland" in 1948. It insists that the point of departure for peace and reconciliation between Israel and the Palestinian people—and the entire Arab world—must be for Israel to recognize "its responsibility for the injustices of the Nakba and the Occupation; recognize the right of return of the Palestinian refugees based on UN [General Assembly] Resolution 194; recognize the right of the Palestinian people to self-determination; and withdraw from all of the territories occupied in 1967." But the document's principal aim is to propose a constitution for a state "that does not control or occupy another people and that is based on full equality between all of its residents and between all of the different groups within it," a state in which "Jewish and Arab citizens shall respect each other's rights to live in peace, dignity and equality, and will be united in recognizing and respecting the differences between them, as well as the differences that exist between all the groups in a democratic, bilingual and multicultural state."

The publication of Adalah's *Democratic Constitution* happened to coincide with the publication of the report of the U.N.'s Committee on the Elimination of Racial Discrimination (CERD), also in March 2007. That report challenged Israel to explain how its understanding of itself as a Jewish state "does not result in any systematic distinction, exclusion, restriction or preference based on race, colour, descent, or national or ethnic origin in the enjoyment of human rights," which would constitute a violation of the International Convention on the Elimination of all Forms of Racial Discrimination. The CERD report refers specifically to Israel's revised citizenship law (which denies the right of a Palestinian citizen of the state to marry and live with a Palestinian from the occupied territories); to the unequal provision of state services; to structural inequalities between Arab and Jewish "sectors" of the Israeli economy; to the differential accessibility of land; to the "unrecognized villages," and to many other issues. It respectfully recommends that Israel eliminate all forms of discrimination within the state. As it is presently constituted, however, Israel could not possibly do that, because those forms of discrimination are inherent in its claim to be a Jewish state despite its large (and growing) non-Jewish population.

As the Jewish National Fund pointed out in justifying its own discriminatory policies to the Israeli courts (see "Insides"), "Israel's Knesset and Israeli society have expressed their view that the distinction between Jews and non-Jews that is the basis for the Zionist vision" is "in complete accord with the founding principles of Israel as a Jewish state." As the JNF itself admits, in Israel this principle overrides the principle and value of equality. It has to. Israel can either be a Jewish state, or it can be a state of equal citizens, Jewish and non-Jewish. It is literally impossible for it to be both. Israelis therefore face a choice: they can go on insisting that Jews ought to have rights that non-Jews are denied, or they can relinquish the privileges of Jews and allow Israel to become a state of all its citizens. This is the position favored by Adalah.

Although Adalah's proposal is explicitly intended as a constitution for the State of Israel within its pre–1967 borders, if all of its principles of equality and justice were to be applied, Israel would no longer be, or claim to be, a Jewish state. And if that were to happen, there would be no need for two separate states at all. Adalah's *Democratic Constitution* thus serves implicitly as a draft constitution for one democratic and secular state—a bilingual and multicultural state—in all of historic Palestine, a state in which Jews and Palestinian Arabs could live together as equal citizens.

The notion of a genuinely multicultural democracy in both Israel and the occupied territories is gaining the support of Israeli Jews. The Israeli historian Ilan Pappé, the Israeli anthropologist Jeff Halper, and the Israeli former deputy mayor of Jerusalem Meron Benvenisti, among many others, have all published statements supporting a one-state solution. In addition to actual endorsements of the one-state solution, there are many Israeli or Israeli-Palestinian organizations—Ta'ayush, B'Tselem, Machsom Watch, Women in Black, Gush Shalom—and countless Israeli and Jewish individuals who (whatever their sense of the ultimate ideal outcome of the conflict, in one state or two) have courageously worked to transcend the rigid opposition between Jews and Arabs, to develop new modes of cooperative action and mutual affirmation, and to develop new forms of Arab-Jewish coexistence in defiance of existing political structures.

If de Soto is right to argue that "the so-called 'one State solution' is gaining ground," however, that is not to say that it does not face resistance. Ironically, one of the most tenacious sites of resistance to the one-state solution is to be found among the mainstream peace camp in Israel, particularly those who identify themselves with left-wing Zionism. The Israeli novelist Amos Oz is one of the best-known exponents of this tradition, which seeks peace with the Palestinians, but only on the basis that Israel remains a Jewish state. "The Zionist enterprise," according to Oz, "has no other objective justification than the right of a drowning man to grasp the only plank that can save him." But he says that there is "a vast moral difference between the drowning man who grasps a plank and makes room for himself by pushing the others who are sitting on it to one side, even by force, and the drowning man who grabs the whole plank for himself and pushes the others into the sea." This, he argues, "is the difference between making Jaffa and Nazareth [i.e., Israel] Jewish, and making Ramallah and Nablus [i.e., the West Bank] Jewish." The "drowning man" here refers to European Jews fleeing Nazi persecution.

Palestinians do not see it this way, however. For Palestinians, making Israel Jewish in 1948 also involved pushing people into the sea, to use Oz's metaphor; therefore, they see his attempt to carefully separate the events of 1948 from those of 1967 as a false distinction. Most Palestinians, however, do acknowledge that many, if not all, Jewish immigrants came to Palestine in the twentieth century not by choice, but because they were facing destruction at the hands of European anti-Semitism, and ultimately the Holocaust: a point that was powerfully registered as early as 1969 in the novella *Returning to Haifa* by the revolutionary Palestinian writer Ghassan Kanafani (who was assassinated by the Israelis in the 1970s). In the novella, a character named Miriam conveys in her own voice the brutality of the Nazi persecution of the Jews, in parallel with Kanafani's narrative of the Zionist persecution of the Palestinians.

Miriam's father, we learn, was among the millions exterminated at Auschwitz. She witnessed her own brother (a child of ten) being gunned down by Nazi troops as he attempted to run away from them. She came to Palestine a broken refugee who had lost her world. Once in Haifa, she and her husband are allocated the recently vacated home of a Palestinian couple, Said and Safiyya, who had lost *their* world in the terrifying Palestinian exodus from Haifa—forced to leave behind not just their home, but, in their panicked flight, their infant son Khaldun. Khaldun, it turns out, comes with the flat given to Miriam and her husband (the Zionist housing authority doesn't know what else to do with him); they rename him Dov and raise him as a Jewish Israeli. When, after the 1967 War, Said and Safiyya are finally able to return to Haifa, they learn everything, including the fate of Khaldun/Dov, by then an Israeli soldier on active service. There is anger and resentment when Said and Safiyya finally meet Miriam; but she understands their feelings precisely, and they ultimately understand hers, too. Their story of dispossession collides with Miriam's. The anger and resentment fade to a kind of reconciliation: it is not exactly forgiveness, much less an abandonment of their claim to their home, but a sense that there is no point trying to resurrect the past exactly as it used to be: what had been their home is now shared with another family; what had been their beloved child is also the beloved child of another family. The true Palestine, Said discovers, lies not in the past, but in the future: the point is not to try to recreate a lost Palestine just as it was, nor is it to give up and go away, but rather to invent a new one, one that takes into account the new reality expressed by Miriam and the suffering of European Jewry, but also the needs and desires of the Palestinians, who have also suffered. Both peoples—not one—seek justice and peace, and the justice and peace they seek can only come through mutual affirmation, not denial.

What seemed revolutionary in Kanafani's time (the heyday of the nationalist struggle) is increasingly regarded as commonplace today. Most Palestinians understand that Zionism wasn't only a colonial project, but in addition a response to the legacy of European anti-Semitism that culminated in the Holocaust, and an expression of the need that Jews felt for a homeland of their own. Palestinians do not feel that it was right for them to have paid the price for crimes and atrocities committed by Europeans—to atone for German sins—but on the other hand they also understand that Israel's Jews are there to stay. If neither people's former ideal will be realized—if the Palestinians will never recuperate Palestine as it was before the arrival of Zionism, and Israelis will never realize a purely Jewish state—they can at least put their two impossible ideals aside for the sake of a common future.

As Palestinians see it, then, to return to Amos Oz and the "plank" metaphor, the solution is for the "plank" that is now in effect a joint homeland to be shared equally—with no one left in the sea. For Oz and others like him, however, the resolution to the two equal claims to the land is not an equal sharing, but rather a distinctly unequal partition, whereby Israel should retain 78 percent of historic Palestine (i.e., Israel within its pre-1967 borders) as a "Jewish state," while the Palestinians should get 22 percent of their original homeland (i.e., the West Bank and Gaza, assuming the settlements are removed and Palestinians would get that land back) for a state of their own. What matters most for left-leaning Zionists like Oz, however, is not the sheer percentages of land involved; it is the separation of a putatively Jewish from a non-Jewish state—a characteristic they share with the right-wing Zionism of Avigdor Lieberman or Moledet. "I definitely did not agree, and will not agree, to a permanent settlement that will ultimately worsen the demographic balance inside sovereign Israel," insists Yossi Beilin, another exponent of the mainstream peace camp in Israel (and one of the principal architects of the Oslo Accords). "That is my sharpest red line. On that issue I am absolutely tough. I am generous geographically but tough demographically. A Jewish majority within the sovereign state of Israel is the main thing as far as I am concerned. For me it is the most important thing."

Yet the creation of a Jewish majority in any part of an historically multicultural and religiously heterogeneous Palestine has always required—and its maintenance will always require—the use of violence. Left-leaning Zionists like Beilin or Oz may elide or dismiss or argue their way out of this point, but right-wing Zionists have always openly admitted it, and they openly admit it to this day. This was, after all, the point of Vladimir Jabotinsky's prophetic 1923 essay "The Iron Wall," which argues that as long as the Palestinians retain "a spark of hope that they can get rid of us, they will not sell these hopes, not for any kind of sweet words or tasty morsels, because they are not a rabble but a nation, perhaps somewhat tattered, but still living. A living people makes such enormous concessions on such fateful questions only when there is no hope left," he adds, uncannily predicting current Israeli policy. "Only when not a single breach is visible in the iron wall, only then do extreme groups lose their sway, and influence transfers to moderate groups." Thus, for Jabotinsky, agreement with the Palestinians is not impossible, "but the only path to such an agreement is the iron wall, that is to say the strengthening in Palestine of a government without any kind of Arab influence, that is to say one against which the Arabs will fight. In other words, for us the only path to an agreement in the future is an absolute refusal of any attempts at an agreement now."

Jabotinsky's argument, that the establishment and ultimately the maintenance of a Jewish state in Palestine can "continue and develop only under the protection of a force independent of the local population—an iron wall which the native population cannot break through," is reiterated in Israel up to the present day. "The Palestinians must be made to understand in the deepest recesses of their consciousness," said General Moshe Ya'alon, who was in charge of the Israeli military response to the second intifada, "that they are a defeated people." Asked by a *Jerusalem Post* interviewer in 2004 what Gaza would look like after the separation plan goes into effect and the territory is cut off from the outside world, the demographic expert and Israeli government advisor Professor Arnon Sofer of Haifa University—one of the leading proponents of separation as instituted by Sharon and Olmert—replied bluntly. "When 2.5 million people live in a closed-off Gaza, it's going to be a human catastrophe," he said. "Those people will become even bigger animals than they are today, with the aid of an insane fundamentalist Islam. The pressure on the border is going to be awful. It's going to be a terrible war. So, if we want to remain alive, we will have to kill and kill and kill. All day, every day." Sofer admits of only one worry with all the killing which will, he says, be the necessary outcome of a policy that he himself helped to invent. "The only thing that concerns me," he says, "is how to ensure that the boys and men who are going to have to do the killing will be able to return home to their families and be normal human beings." But in the end the point of all this is not just killing for the sake of killing. "Unilateral separation doesn't guarantee 'peace,' " Sofer says; "it guarantees a Zionist-Jewish state with an overwhelming majority of Jews."

A similar point was registered by the Israeli historian Benny Morris, when he said, in a 2004 interview with Ari Shavit of *Ha'aretz*, that "there are circumstances in history that justify ethnic cleansing." A Jewish state, Morris argued, "would not have come into being without the uprooting of 700,000 Palestinians. Therefore it was necessary to uproot them. There was no choice but to expel that population. It was necessary to cleanse the hinterland and cleanse the border areas and cleanse the main roads. It was necessary to cleanse the villages from which our convoys and our settlements were being fired on." If one believes in the goal of establishing a Jewish state in the manner and the place in which that state was founded as a matter of historical fact, Benny Morris is absolutely right. So is Sofer. And so was Jabotinsky. Is imprisoning and starving a whole people really that much better than (or in the long run all that different from) simply expelling them and having done with it? Are religiously ordained expulsion and even genocide really that different from the overwrought scientific and demographic calculations underlying Sofer's dispassionate assessment, in one of Israel's leading newspapers, that the policy *that he himself proposes* will result in what he himself identifies as "a human catastrophe?"

The point that the Zionist program in Palestine fundamentally requires violence is not just evident in hindsight. It was obvious to the King-Crane Commission in 1919 ("decisions, requiring armies to carry out, are sometimes necessary, but they are surely not to be gratuitously taken in the interests of a serious injustice"). It was obvious to Edwin Montagu, the only Jewish member of the British cabinet when Balfour issued his fateful promise to Rothschild, who warned prophetically that having Muslim and Christian Palestinians "make room" for Jewish immigrants would result in their expulsion, so that wherever they go they "will be regarded as foreigners, just in the same way as Jews will hereafter be treated as foreigners in every country but Palestine" (see "Inside Out").

5

There is an alternative to this history—and future—of violence, however. More and more people, on both sides of the conflict, are coming to realize that the age of the two-state solution has drawn to a close, as Alvaro de Soto also admits in his confidential report to the U.N. Committed Zionists from across the political spectrum will resist the move toward the one-state solution in the way that privileged groups have always historically resisted the erosion of their privileges. The resistance, even the violent resistance, of privileged groups did not stop South Africa from abandoning *apartheid*; the United States from abandoning Jim Crow laws or the institution of slavery itself; or, for that matter, the British aristocracy from relinquishing its privileges in the great reform bills of the nineteenth century. And so it is with those who seek to protect the privileges of the Jewish community in Israel/Palestine today.

History shows that—short of an actual genocide—it is utterly futile for one people to try to achieve security at the expense of another. And in fact the Jewish people of Israel have never felt secure; they clearly do not feel secure today; and as long as they insist on maintaining their situation at the expense of the Palestinian people—who will go on resisting their own cantonization and imprisonment—it is most unlikely that they will ever feel secure. They are, on the contrary, far more likely to find the security they have been searching for in the context of a democratic and multicultural state that would protect their rights in affirmative—rather than destructive—ways, and that would allow individuals and communities to express their identities culturally, socially, aesthetically, and religiously, rather than in terms of a discourse of exclusivist political sovereignty that

Israelis and Palestinians alike inherited from Europe: a discourse whose time has passed.

Historically speaking, privileged groups have always felt insecure about relinquishing their privileges. Even after the Civil War and Reconstruction, whites in the American South were convinced that they needed the Jim Crow laws to protect themselves from black encroachment. The privileged classes in Britain in the eighteenth and nineteenth centuries were convinced that opening up the electoral franchise to the mass of the population would lead them to be swamped by those Edmund Burke identified as the "swinish multitude." Whites in South Africa were convinced that if they let go of apartheid they would be swallowed up in a black sea. All these groups eventually gave up (or were stripped of) their privileges, only to discover that they can actually enjoy greater security and prosperity without them.

There is no reason to think that the situation of Israelis and Palestinians is any different. There is, in particular, no reason to think that their conflict may not be resolved along the lines in which the South African conflict was finally resolved (which was not with the eradication of the white South African population, but rather with the removal of the forms of privilege that that population had enjoyed while withholding them from the country's black and colored peoples). Veteran South African antiapartheid campaigners, including Archbishop Desmond Tutu and Ronnie Kasrils, have compared the situation in Israel/Palestine with that of South Africa under apartheid. "Yesterday's South African township dwellers can tell you about today's life in the occupied territories," wrote Tutu in an article he coauthored with Ian Urbina. "To travel only blocks in his own homeland, a grandfather waits on the whim of a teenage soldier. More than an emergency is needed to get to a hospital; less than a crime earns a trip to jail. The lucky ones have a permit to leave their squalor to work in Israel's cities, but their luck runs out when security closes all checkpoints, paralyzing an entire people. The indignities, dependence and anger are all too familiar." Even the term "bantustan" that is frequently applied to Palestinian enclaves like Gaza is, after all, an explicit reference to the little "homelands" with which South Africa experimented at one point in order to artificially reduce its black population.

Yet those in power see the comparison between Israel and apartheid-era South Africa as a dangerous, even fatal, one. "There is no doubt in my mind that very soon the government of Israel is going to have to address the demographic issue with the utmost seriousness and resolve. This issue above all others will dictate the solution that we must adopt," Ehud Olmert was already warning in November 2003. "We don't have unlimited time. More and more Palestinians are uninterested in a nego-tiated, two-state solution, because they want to change the essence of the conflict from an Algerian paradigm to a South African one. From a struggle against 'occupation,' in their parlance, to a struggle for one-man-one-vote. That is, of course, a much cleaner struggle, a much more popular struggle—and ultimately a much more powerful one." Olmert reiterated the same warning following the Annapolis summit in November 2007, making it clearer than ever why Israel is so committed to the discourse, if not the substance, of a separate Palstinian state. "If the day comes when the two-state solution collapses, and we face a South African–style struggle for equal voting rights [also for the Palestinians in the territories]," he told *Ha'aretz*, "then, as soon as that happens, the State of Israel is finished."

"The clock is ticking rapidly on the very viability of the two-state solution," echoes the Israeli analyst Gershon Baskin. "The correct read-ing of the preceding sentence should be that the clock is rapidly run-ning out on the viability and the feasibility of the Zionist enterprise. Without fulfilling the two-state solution, there will be no Jewish State of Israel. The ticking clock is not solely because of the physical realities on the ground in the West Bank and Gaza, which impede the possi-bility of creating a Palestinian state there," he adds. "The main factor accelerating the clock is the rapid movement of Palestinian intellectuals away from the idea of a separate Palestinian state in the West Bank and Gaza. It was the Palestinian intellectuals who led their national move-ment to support this solution from the 1970s onward, and it is today the Palestinian intellectuals who are the driving force toward adoption of the South Africa model for Palestine." Baskin concludes: "Should the Palestinian masses reject the solution of two states in favor of one dem-ocratic state from the [Jordan] river to the [Mediterranean] sea, it is only a matter of time before the entire international community comes to their support, and then the end of the Zionist dream is in sight. If the Palestinian masses adopt the one-state democratic solution, Israel cannot win that battle."

The argument for a single-state solution—that is, a real democracy—is obviously also expressed in positive, not just in fearful and negative, terms, and by both Israelis and Palestinians. "It would be a serious mistake to think that cosmetic changes like the Oslo Accords could bring an end to the Israeli-Palestinian conflict," writes the Israeli peace activist Miko Peled, in his survey of the prospects for a peaceful resolution of the conflict following the crises of summer 2007. "The era of cosmetic changes together with the two-state solution is gone forever. Only full equal rights for both people in their historic homeland will bring an end to this conflict. And while there are those who will claim that this . . . is a naive dream and will never become a reality, we would do well to remember that the success of any struggle depends on the determination of its leaders and the clarity of its purpose, not the doubts of naysayers."

For Peled, the nonviolent and increasingly coordinated and cooperative struggle of both Israelis and Palestinians against the injustice of the occupation is something more than an inspiring model to be followed. Pointing to one especially well-known site of protest in the West Bank (which recently resulted in a change, however minor, in the routing of Israel's West Bank wall), he writes that "we should note the courage, persistence and the determination of the unarmed, joint resistance that has been taking place in the small Palestinian town of Bil'in in the West Bank. For several years now Bil'in residents, together with Israeli peace activists and others have conducted a nonviolent, joint struggle against the confiscation of Bil'in lands and the erection of the separation barrier." For Peled, such a cooperative movement, bringing Israelis and Palestinians together on the ground, is a model not only of nonviolent resistance, but also of a future of cooperation that is already embodied in actions, not just words.

Speaking in an interview in August 2007, the Israeli-American journalist Nir Rosen expressed similar sentiments. "What needs to happen at this point is a one-state solution, where Palestinian refugees are allowed to go back to their homes, where Israel is a state for Jews and non-Jews alike, a state for its citizens," Rosen argues. "And this one-state solution is inevitable." One way or the other, he says, "Israel can't exist as a Jewish state that doesn't give equal rights to its non-Jewish Arab citizens."

The contours of a one-state solution, and the forms of resistance it would face not only from Zionists but also from Palestinian nationalists, have been thoroughly explored in recent books, including Virginia Tilley's *The One-State Solution* and Ali Abunimah's *One Country*. "Israel's insistence on maintaining its exclusivist Jewish character, in spite of the reality that Palestine-Israel is and has always been a multicultural, multireligious country, is a chauvinistic appeal to ethnic tribalism that stands no chance in a contest against democratic and universal principles," writes Abunimah, the cofounder of the Web site Electronic Intifada. Looking at the current disastrous situation in Israel/Palestine, the question he asks is "whether we can conceive of an alternative that leads us out of our current impasse, one that addresses the fears and needs of Israeli Jews, preserves their identity, and allows their community to flourish, while restoring to the Palestinians the rights they have been denied for so long." The answer he, like Tilley, proposes, is one democratic and multicultural state where both peoples can express their identities socially, culturally, and linguistically, rather than in terms of exclusivist political sovereignty designed to exclude or contain the other.

The one-state solution is not, however, something that has to be worked out in advance, with a series of "interim agreements" negotiated by armies of committees and subcommittees over a period of decades. It is the present reality. The one-state solution was put into effect in 1967, when Israel captured what had remained of Palestine after the 1948 War.

Israel has never officially accepted that the West Bank (let alone East Jerusalem, which it claims to have annexed) is occupied territory. It denies that the Geneva Conventions apply there. It has ignored decades of U.N. Security Council Resolutions condemning its activities there. It has shrugged off the 2004 Advisory Opinion of the International Court of Justice. The most it ever conceded to the international community is that the West Bank is "administered" territory—to which Israel has as valid a claim as the Palestinians. When it even talks about relinquishing parts of the West Bank, it employs the language not merely of "wrenching concessions" but also of "generosity," a term Ehud Barak used to such effect at Camp David in 2000. By definition, however, it is impossible to be "generous" in returning something that is not one's own. That, clearly, is not how Israel regards the West Bank. Israel officially refers to the West Bank not as the West Bank but by using the biblical terms Judea and Samaria. Not only has Israel never declared its borders, but textbooks used in Israeli schools show maps of the country from which the Green Line, or 1949–67 border, has been deleted, along with major Palestinian cities (such as Nazareth) inside the state. The maps show what they refer to as Judea and Samaria as integral parts of Israel. So Israeli children are taught that all of historic Palestine (plus Syria's Golan Heights, which Israel also claims to have annexed, in violation of international law) is theirs. And when the Minister of Education aired the suggestion, in late 2006, that perhaps the maps in Israeli school textbooks ought to show the Green Line, she faced an uproar in parliament.

There is today only one state in all of historic Palestine. As the UN-OCHA report from July 2007 makes abundantly clear, the creation of a genuinely independent Palestinian state has become a physical impossibility precisely because of the measures Israel has taken over the previous four decades to ensure its hold over the territory. And Israel's own leaders have made it perfectly clear that the only reason they are now even talking about the creation of a Palestinian state is so that as many Palestinians as possible can be artificially deleted from the Jewish state's demographic account. "We simply don't have enough Jews in the Land of Israel to keep it all to ourselves," laments Uri Dromi of the Israel Democracy Institute.

"The existence of a Jewish majority in the State of Israel cannot be maintained with the continued control over the Palestinian population in Judea, Samaria and the Gaza Strip," Israel's then–deputy prime minister, Ehud Olmert, said in a major speech in January 2006. "Every hill in Samaria and every valley in Judea is part of our historic homeland," he continued. "We do not forget this, not even for one moment. However, the choice between the desire to allow every Jew to live anywhere in the Land of Israel [and] the existence of the State of Israel as a Jewish country obligates relinquishing parts of the Land of Israel. This is not a relinquishing of the Zionist idea, [but] rather the essential realization of the Zionist goal—ensuring the existence of a Jewish and democratic state in the Land of Israel. In order to ensure the existence of a Jewish national homeland, we will not be able to continue ruling over the territories in which the majority of the Palestinian population lives. We must create a clear boundary as soon as possible, one which will reflect the demographic reality on the ground. Israel will maintain control over the security zones, the Jewish settlement blocs, and those places which have supreme national importance to the Jewish people." If the Palestinians "abandon the path of terror," he added, "they can receive national independence in a Palestinian state with temporary borders, even before all the complicated issues connected to a final agreement are resolved. All these issues will be resolved later during negotiations between the two countries, in the accepted manner in which countries resolve their differences."

Since a territorially contiguous Palestinian state has become a physical impossibility, it is clear that what Olmert is referring to as a "state" would actually be exactly the same series of disconnected and impoverished cantons (of which Gaza is the prototype) that Israel has been working so hard to realize in recent years. Even if the label "Palestinian state" were attached to this patchwork of open-air prisons, it is a fiction that is unlikely to last very long—probably not even as long as the fictional states of Transkei, Ciskei, and Bophuthatswana that South Africa created when it, too, was trying to artificially delete as many black people as possible from its demographic accounting books. And just as those fictional "homelands" were finally reincorporated into the new South Africa after the collapse of apartheid—thereby ending the pretense that they were real states—that is likely to be the case with the Palestinian "state," assuming that the fiction goes even that far (which is doubtful).

Mutual and democratic cooperation between Palestinians and Israelis is not only feasible, it offers the only alternative, the real hope for peace in the long run. The idea that people should be forcibly separated from each other according to their religious preferences has no place in the twenty-first century. And if such an approach—separation based on religion—is a guaranteed recipe for future conflict, only its opposite— secular and democratic cooperation between people—offers a chance for genuine peace. No one was more eloquent in making an appeal for such a state than the late Edward Said, who spent the final years of his life articulating ways in which Palestinians and Israelis could find ways of living *with* rather than *against* each other. "Two people in one land.

Or, equality for all. Or, one person one vote. Or a common humanity asserted in a binational state." He adds: "There can be no reconciliation unless both peoples, two communities of suffering, resolve that their existence is a secular fact, and that it has to be dealt with as such."

Attempts to legislate—or to physically impose—homogeneity, exclusion, and intolerance have historically always been accompanied by violence and abuses of what the peoples of the world have universally acknowledged as the rights that we should all enjoy by virtue of being human. "The international community, speaking through the United Nations, has identified three regimes as inimical to human rights—colonialism, apartheid and foreign occupation," observes the U.N.'s John Dugard. "Numerous resolutions of the General Assembly of the United Nations testify to this. Israel's occupation of the West Bank, Gaza and East Jerusalem contains elements of all three of these regimes, which is what makes the Occupied Palestinian Territory [OPT] of special concern to the international community." There are other regimes, Dugard admits, particularly in the developing world, that suppress human rights; "but there is no other case of a Western-affiliated regime that denies self-determination and human rights to a developing people and that has done so for so long. This explains why the OPT has become a test for the West, a test by which its commitment to human rights is to be judged."

The test that Dugard (a South African himself) is speaking of is not only a matter to be decided by politicians and policy-makers. It is a test confronting ordinary citizens in the everyday choices they make. That, clearly, is the appeal being made by the growing movement to boycott and divest from Israel, a movement manifestly modeled on its South African predecessor. "Divestment from apartheid South Africa was fought by ordinary people at the grassroots," write Desmond Tutu and Ian Urbina. "Faith-based leaders informed their followers, union members pressured their companies' stockholders and consumers questioned their store owners. Students played an especially important role by compelling universities to change their portfolios. Eventually, institutions pulled the financial plug, and the South African government thought twice about its policies." The same approach, they argue, can be used to pressure the Israeli government to change its policies. "If apartheid ended, so can the occupation," they write, "but the moral force and international pressure will have to be just as determined."

However, the test of which John Dugard speaks also faces Israelis and Palestinians. They must decide between remaining locked in a deadly struggle that neither side is in a position to win—or taking the path of peace and reconciliation. For Jewish Israelis, that would mean giving up on the dream of a state that was meant to be Jewish but never really was; for Palestinians, it would mean giving up on the dream of a sovereign Palestinian state, for which they have yearned for so long. But there is no longer any other way out.

ACKNOWLEDGMENTS

This book would not have seen the light of day without the help of relatives and friends new and old. I must thank all those who took the time to talk with me, answered my questions, offered suggestions, made criticisms, provided logistical support during the research or writing of the book, introduced me to people, helped clarify the complexities of the Palestinian-Israeli conflict or its history, or simply provided encouragement of one kind or another (though at the end of the day the book represents my point of view, not necessarily anyone else's). They include Sam Bahour, Mustafa Barghouti, Azmi Beshara, George Bisharat, Shermine Boustany, Wissam Boustany, Rita Giacaman, Rachel Giora, Amira Hass, Deborah Karl, Rebecca Karl, Michel Khleifi, David Miller, Gabriel Piterberg, Shira Robinson, Grace Said, Mariam Said, Wadie Said, Tami Sarfatti, Yehuda Shaul, Raja Shehadeh, Yehouda Shenhav, and Muzna Shihabi.

In addition, I could never thank enough all those countless Palestinians I met in Jerusalem and the West Bank who generously took the time to talk to me, to share their points of view, to recount their experiences, and to show me around. They are models of endurance, humanity, and hope in the face of adversity.

I must also thank those Israelis who have had the courage and moral commitment to speak out against their country's occupation policies. Their work for or with organizations such as B'Tselem and Ta'ayush or Machsom Watch shows the world what Israeli-Palestinian solidarity and cooperation look like in practice; it offers a living, tangible alternative to a relationship founded on antagonism and violence.

Ali Behdad, Erin Cooney, Richard Dienst, Karin Dienst, Patrick Wolfe, James Chandler, Karim Ibish, Gabriel Piterberg, Naseer Aruri, Nadia Saba, Bradin Cormack, Robert Blecher, Ali Abunimah, Sherene Seikaly, Richard Falk, and Cesare Casarino read versions of chapters or the whole book, helped with images, and/or offered advice on how to frame the book. I thank them all.

Thanks are also due to Philip Wilcox and Jan de Jong at the Foundation for Middle East Peace in Washington for kindly agreeing to grant me permission to reproduce their maps; to Sarit Michaeli of B'Tselem for kindly agreeing to give me permission to quote from B'Tselem's publications; to Vladimir Bessarabov of the United Nations Cartographic Section for his invaluable assistance with U.N. maps; to the U.N. itself for granting me permission to reproduce those maps here; and to Juliette Touma, Majed Abu Kubi, and Fuad Hudali of the United Nations Office for the Coordination of Humanitarian Affairs in the occupied territories, who also granted me permission to reproduce maps and photographs and to quote from publications.

All of my work depends on the able support of Nora Elias, Janet Bishop, Joan Aberbach, Molly Misuraca, Rick Fagin, Doris Wang, Jeanette Gilkison, Ivonne Nelson, and Elizabeth Krown Spellman of the English Department at UCLA. I thank them all, and also Thomas Wortham and Rafael Pérez-Torres, the previous and current chairs of the department when I wrote this book.

I am grateful for the unwavering support of my agent, Melanie Jackson, and the rigorous criticism (and also encouragement) offered by Alane Mason and Alexander Cuadros at Norton, exemplary editors both.

My family has always both supported and had to endure my work. I thank my children, Samir and Maissa; my parents, Samir and Jean Makdisi; and my wife, Christina (this book really is as much hers as mine: she more than anyone had to tolerate the ups and downs of the writing and publication process, offering support and encouragement all along). I have felt the presence of my uncle Edward all through this adventure: he showed me the way, and I can only hope that he would have liked the result. As for my brothers Ussama and Karim: they *have* always been with me—or there for me to turn to—and it is to them that this book is dedicated.

NOTES ON SOURCES

This book depends on a combination of personal narratives and factual analyses presented in the reports of human rights organizations, United Nations agencies, and major news organizations, as well as secondary and historical research published in books on the Israeli-Palestinian conflict or its history. My two major sources for present-day factual claims and figures are the Israeli human rights organization B'Tselem: The Israeli Center for Human Rights in the Occupied Territories, and the United Nations Office for the Coordination of Humanitarian Affairs, both of which publish reports and statistics (e.g., the number of checkpoints in the West Bank) on a regularly updated basis. The sources for all factual claims and figures are given below. For ease of reference, I have organized them according to particular issues or themes within each chapter. I have often drawn upon the same source (e.g., the World Bank's May 2007 report on the Palestinian economy) with reference to different issues, in which case the source is listed more than once in the following notes. In many cases, I have cited the sources for quotations in the body of the text itself (e.g., "according to the World Bank's May 2007 report on the Palestinian economy . . ."); where I have not, I provide sources for quotations here, in the order in which they appear in each chapter (e.g., Eitam quotation on expulsion: see Jack Khoury, "Leftist MKs Blast Eitam's Statements on Arabs," *Ha'aretz*, 11 September 2006). Some of the testimonies in the book come from accounts given to me in person, in which case I say so in the body of the text (though I have changed the names of Palestinian sources); most come from affidavits documented and published by human rights organizations such as B'Tselem, or United Nations agencies (notably the U.N. Office for the Coordination of Humanitarian Affairs), or the Israeli veterans' organization Shovrimshtika (Breaking the Silence), in which case I cite the source of the story in the following notes, again with sources presented in the order in which they appear in the text.

INTRODUCTION

Story of **Sam Bahour**: based on media accounts (cited below) as well as personal correspondence with Sam Bahour.

On the **denial of visas**: see Sharmila Devi, "Palestinians Hit Out as Israel Tightens Visa Controls" (*Financial Times*, 11 September 2006); Zahi Khoury, "Things Go Better with Rights" (*Wall Street Journal*, 30 September 2006); Amira Hass, "The Slippery Slope of Expulsion" (*Ha'aretz*, 1 October 2006); Amira Hass, "The Silent Expulsion" (*Ha'aretz*, 6 October 2006); Ben Lynfield, "Get-Tough Visa Policy May Mean West Bank Palestinian Exodus" (*The Scotsman*, 8 September 2006); Aluf Benn, "U.S. Protests Restrictions on its Citizens Entering West Bank" (*Ha'aretz*, 18 October 2006). Story of Amal al-Amleh, testimony given to B'Tselem and published in *Perpetual Limbo: Israel's Freeze on Unification of Palestinian Families in the Occupied Territories* (B'Tselem and Hamoked, July 2006). For further details on Israel's family unification policy: see same report.

On **Israeli military regulations** governing Palestinian life: see *Broken Lives—A Year of Intifada* (Amnesty International, 2001).

On **Geneva Conventions** and their applicability to the occupied territories: see sources as listed on p. 306 for international law.

Amnesty International quotation regarding **Israeli violence against civilians**; from *Broken Lives* (Amnesty International, 2001).

On **West Bank road system**: see *Territorial Fragmentation of the West Bank* (U.N. Office for the Coordination of Humanitarian Affairs [UN-OCHA], May 2006); *Forbidden Roads: The Discriminatory West Bank Road Regime* (B'Tselem, August 2004).

On **West Bank checkpoints and roadblocks**: see *Humanitarian Monitor: Occupied Palestinian Territory* (UN-OCHA, May 2007).

On Israel's **West Bank wall** and impact on Palestinian life in West Bank: see *Humanitarian Update: Occupied Palestinian Territory* (UN-OCHA, February 2006); "West Bank Closure Count and Analysis" (UN-OCHA, September 2006, May 2007, available at UN-OCHA Web site: www.ochaopt.org); *The Humanitarian Impact of the West Bank Barrier* (UN-OCHA, January 2006); *West Bank Wall Main Cause of New Displacement Amid Worsening Humanitarian Situation* (Internal Displacement Monitoring Centre, June 2006).

For figures on days of **Israeli closure, economic impact of movement restrictions,** and **international sanctions**: see *Movement and Access Restrictions in the West Bank* (World Bank, May 2007); U.N. Consolidated Appeals Process 2007 (http://domino.un.org/pdfs/CAP2007.Pt.pdf).

On number of **Palestinians applying to leave** West Bank, see Khaled Abu Toameh, "Fatwa Forbids PA Muslims to Emigrate," (*Jerusalem Post*, 10 June 2007); Uriya Shavit and Jamal Bana, "The Secret Exodus" (*Ha'aretz*, 5 October 2001); Samar Assad, *The Demographic and Economic War Against Palestinians* (Palestine Center, December 2006).

Sharon quotation on **disengagement**: speech at press conference, May 2005, quoted in Jonathan Cook, "Israel's Demographic Demon in Court" (*Middle East Report*, 1 June 2006); also see Sharon's speech at Conference of Presidents of Major Jewish Organizations (19 February 2004, on Israeli Prime Minister's Office Web site).

Sofer quotation on **demographics**: see Ruthie Blum, "One on One: It's the Demography, Stupid" (interview with Arnon Sofer, *Jerusalem Post*, 20 May 2004).

On concept of **transfer** in Israel and Zionism: see Benny Morris, *The Birth of the Palestinian Refugee Problem Revisited* (Cambridge: Cambridge University Press, 2004); Nur Masalha, *Expulsion of the Palestinians* (Washington, D.C.: Institute for Palestine Studies, 1992).

Moledet Web site: www.moledet.org.il/english/.

Eitam quotation on **expulsion**: see Jack Khoury, "Leftist MKs Blast Eitam's Statements on Arabs" (*Ha'aretz*, 11 September 2006).

Israeli military orders: see, e.g., Israeli Defense Force, "Declaration Concerning the Closure of Area Number s/2/03 (Seam Area)," available at United Nations Web site (http://domino.un.org/UNISPAL.NSF/d80185e9f0c69a7b85256cbf005afeac/c6114997e0ba34c885256ddc0077146a!OpenDocument).

Avigdor Lieberman quotation: see Azmi Bishara, "Why Israel Is After Me" (*Los Angeles Times*, 3 May 2007).

Israel High Court ruling on Israeli nationality: quoted in, among other sources, Nissim Rejwan, *Israel in Search of Identity: Reading the Formative Years* (Gainesville: University of Florida Press, 1959).

Kimmerling quotation: see Baruch Kimmerling, *Politicide* (London: Verso Books, 2003).

Jabotinsky quotation: see Vladimir Jabotinsky, "The Iron Wall," trans. Lenni Brenner, in Lenni Brenner, *The Iron Wall: Zionist Revisionism from Jabotinsky to Shamir* (London: Zed Books, 1984).

OUTSIDES

Story of **Mohammad Jalud**: from testimony given to UN-OCHA, published in *Crossing the Barrier: Palestinian Access to Agricultural Land* (UN-OCHA, January 2006).

Kaplinsky orders: Israel Defense Force: "Declaration Concerning the Closure of Area Number s/2/03 (Seam Area), 2 October 2003," published at United Nations Web site (http://domino.un.org/UNISPAL.NSF/d80185e9f0c69a7b85256cbf005afeac/c6114997e0ba34c885256ddc0077146a!OpenDocument).

On the impact of Israel's **West Bank wall**, **land laws**, relevant **Israeli military regulations** and their impact on Palestinian life: see *Not All It Seems: Preventing Palestinians Access to their Lands West of the Separation Barrier in the Tulkarm-Qalqilya Area* (B'Tselem, June 2004); *Behind the Barrier: Human Rights Violations as a Result of Israel's Separation Barrier* (B'Tselem, April 2003); *Land Grab: Israel's Settlement Policy in the West Bank* (B'Tselem, May 2002); *The West Bank Wall: Humanitarian Status Report, Northern West Bank Trajectory* (UN-OCHA, July 2003); *Preliminary Analysis of the Humanitarian Implications of the February 2005 Projected West Bank Barrier Route* (UN-OCHA, 22 March 2005); John Dugard, *Report of the*

Special Rapporteur on the Situation of Human Rights in the Palestinian Territories Occupied Since 1967 (U.N. Human Rights Council, 5 September 2006; 17 January 2006; 29 January 2007); *Crossing the Barrier: Palestinian Access to Agricultural Land* (UN-OCHA, January 2006); *West Bank Wall Main Cause of New Displacement Amid Worsening Humanitarian Situation* (Internal Displacement Monitoring Centre, 21 June 2006); *Displaced by the Wall: Pilot Study on Forced Displacement Caused by the Construction of the West Bank Wall and Its Associated Regime in the Occupied Palestinian Territories* (Badil Resource Center for Palestinian Residency and Refugee Rights, Norwegian Refugee Council and Internal Displacement Monitoring Centre, September 2006); *Movement and Access Restrictions in the West Bank: Uncertainty and Inefficiency in the Palestinian Economy* (World Bank, May 2007); *Four Years: Intifada, Closures and Palestinian Economic Crisis: An Assessment* (World Bank, October 2004); Dror Etkes and Hagit Ofran, *Breaking the Law in the West Bank: The Private Land Report* (Peace Now, November 2006); *The Barrier Gate and Permit Regime Four Years On: Humanitarian Impact in the Northern West Bank* (UN-OCHA, November 2007).

On the status of the **wall** and **Israel's occupation regime** in **international law**: see, in addition to the publications cited above, *Geneva Convention Relative to the Protection of Civilian Persons in Time of War* [Fourth Geneva Convention],1949, and other key documents constitutive of international humanitarian law, all available on the Web site of the International Committee of the Red Cross (www.icrc.org); Ardi Imseis, "On the Fourth Geneva Convention and Occupied Palestinian Territory" (*Harvard International Law Journal*, Winter 2003); United Nations Security Council Resolution 465, published on United Nations Web site (http://domino.un.org/UNISPAL.NSF/0a2a053971ccb56885256cef0073 c6d4/5aa254a1c8f8b1cb852560e50075d7d5!OpenDocument); International Court of Justice, *Advisory Opinion on the Legal Consequences of the Construction of the Wall in the Occupied Palestinian Territory*, 9 July 2004, available at UN Web site (http://unispal.un.org/unispal .nsf/0/b59ecb7f4c73bdbc85256eeb004f6d20?OpenDocument); "The Place of the Fence/ Wall in International Law" (Amnesty International, February 2004).

Quotations from **Haggai Alon** regarding the **wall**: from an interview with *Ha'aretz*, in Meron Rappaport, "The Spirit of the Commander Prevails" (*Ha'aretz*, 27 May 2007).

Story of **Eid Ahmad Yassin**: from testimony given to UN-OCHA, published in *Crossing the Barrier: Palestinian Access to Agricultural Land* (UN-OCHA, January 2006).

Figures on **permit applications and rejections**, and details of wall's impact on Al-Ras: see *Crossing the Barrier: Palestinian Access to Agricultural Land* (UN-OCHA, January 2006).

Story of **Mohammad Salim**: testimony given to B'Tselem and published on B'Tselem Web site (http://www.btselem.org/english/Testimonies/20040330_Muhammad_Salim_Bar rier_in_Jayyus_Village.asp).

Story of **Abdel-Latif Odeh**: testimony given to B'Tselem and published on B'Tselem Web site (http://www.btselem.org/english/Testimonies/20050721_Separation_Barrier_in_a_ Daba_witness_Odeh.asp).

On the village of **Jubara**: see *The West Bank Barrier, Profile: Kirbet Jubara* (UNRWA, August 2005).

Story of **Mu'atasem Omar**: testimony given to B'Tselem and published on B'Tselem Web site (http://www.btselem.org/english/Testimonies/20070217_Adel_Omar_died_after_delay_of_medical_treatment_Azzun_Atmah.asp).

On Israel's **road system** in **West Bank**, **closures**, **barriers**, **checkpoints**, **restrictions on movement,** and their impact on Palestinian life: see *Forbidden Roads: The Discriminatory West Bank Road Regime* (B'Tselem, August 2004); *Territorial Fragmentation of the West Bank* (UN-OCHA, May 2006); *Civilians Under Siege: Restrictions on Freedom of Movement as Collective Punishment* (B'Tselem, January 2001); Akiva Eldar, "IDF Extends Seal on Territories as Humanitarian Situation Worsens" (*Ha'aretz*, 19 March 2006); Stephanie Khoury, "West Bank Road vs. Peace" (*Washington Post*, 19 November 2005); Gideon Levy, "Enough Palestinian Cars" (*Ha'aretz*, 23 October 2005); Amira Hass, "New Checkpoint to Sever W. Bank South of Nablus" (*Ha'aretz*, 30 October 2005); "Surviving Under Siege: The Impact of Movement Restrictions on the Right to Work" (Amnesty International, September 2003); John Dugard, *Report of the Special Rapporteur on the Situation of Human Rights in the Palestinian Territories Occupied Since 1967* (U.N. Human Rights Council, 5 September 2006; 17 January 2006; 29 January 2007); "Enduring Occupation: Palestinians Under Siege in the West Bank" (Amnesty International, June 2007); Amira Hass, "The 'Jewish Only' Roads" (*Ha'aretz*, 18 July 2001); Jeff Halper, "The 94 Percent Solution: A Matrix of Control" (*Middle East Report*, Fall 2000); Amira Hass, "Israel's Closure Policy" (*Journal of Palestine Studies*, Spring 2002); Amira Hass, "Harassment as a Military Duty" (*Ha'aretz*, 20 October 2004); Chris McGreal, "Israel Seeks Funds for Separate Arab Roads" (*The Guardian*, 6 September 2004); Emad Mekay, "World Bank May Fund Israeli Checkpoints" (Inter Press Service, 25 February 2005); Associated Press, "Sharon in Drive Towards Palestinian Bridges and Tunnels" (15 January 2001); Amira Hass, "PA: Road System Shows Israel Intends to Keep Settlements" (*Ha'aretz*, 1 December 2004); Samira Shah, *The By-Pass Road Network in the West Bank* (Ramallah: Al Haq, 1997); Uzi Benziman, "The Roads to Perdition" (*Ha'aretz*, 26 October 2002); Sara Roy, *Failing Peace: Gaza and the Israeli-Palestinian Conflict* (London: Pluto Press, 2007); "Restrictions on Movement" (B'Tselem Web site: http://www.btselem.org/English/Freedom%5Fof%5FMovement/); Jeff Halper, "E-1: The End of a Viable Palestinian State" (Occupation Magazine online: http://www.kibush.co.il/show_file.asp?num=1266); *The Humanitarian Impact on Palestinians of Israeli Settlements and Infrastructure in the West Bank* (UN-OCHA, July 2007).

For statistics on **checkpoints** and **roadblocks**, see B'Tselem Web site: (http://www.btselem.org/english/Freedom_of_Movement/Statistics.asp); for further details on checkpoints, roadblocks, earth mounds, flying checkpoints, see weekly briefings and humanitarian updates published by the United Nations Office for the Coordination of Humanitarian Affairs and available on the UN-OCHA Web site (www.ochaopt.org).

On the **geography** of occupation: see Eyal Weizman, "The Politics of Verticality," published on Open Democracy Web site (www.opendemocracy.net); and Eyal Weizman, *Hollow Land: Israel's Architecture of Occupation* (London: Verso Books, 2007).

Story of **Yasser Alian**: testimony given to B'Tselem and published on B'Tselem Web site (http://www.btselem.org/English/Testimonies/20021121_Soldiers_block_kids_way_to_school_in_Aba.asp).

On **Israeli pressures on Palestinians to collaborate** with the Israeli occupation: see "Collaborators in the Occupied Territories: Human Rights Abuses and Violations" (B'Tselem, January 1994); "Human Rights Violations of Palestinians from the Occupied Territories Working in Israel and the Settlements" (B'Tselem, August 1999).

Story of **Palestinian truck driver** pressured to collaborate with occupation: testimony given to B'Tselem and published in *Forbidden Roads: The Discriminatory West Bank Road Regime* (B'Tselem, August 2004).

Story of **Leila Shqeirat**: testimony given to B'Tselem and published on B'Tselem Web site (http://www.btselem.org/english/Testimonies/20060620_Sheikh_Saed_Laila_Shqeirat.asp).

Story of **Farid Subuh**: testimony given to B'Tselem and published on B'Tselem Web site (http://www.btselem.org/English/Testimonies/20030924_Soldiers_at_Hawara_Checkpoint_Delay_Family.asp).

Story of **Abdallah Khamis**: testimony given to B'Tselem and published on B'Tselem Web site (http://www.btselem.org/english/Testimonies/20060812_Beating_of_Abdallah_Khamis_at_Huwwara_Checkping.asp).

On **Palestinian women giving birth at checkpoints**: see *Report of the UN High Commissioner of Human Rights to United Nations General Assembly*, 23 February 2007 (http://domino.un.org/UNISPAL.NSF/99818751a6a4c9c6852560690077ef61/c3f001363757e66 4852572a400774d62!OpenDocument); "U.N. Fears over Checkpoint Births," BBC report, 23 September 2005 (http://news.bbc.co.uk/1/hi/world/middle_east/4274400.stm).

Story of **Mahmoud Yaqoub** and **Mohammed Kheiri**: testimony given to B'Tselem and published on B'Tselem Web site (http://www.btselem.org/english/Testimonies/20011113_Death_of_Mouhammad_Kheiri_Zaban_Witness_Yaqub.asp).

Israeli soldiers' statements about checkpoint duty: testimony given to B'Tselem and published on B'Tselem Web site (http://www.btselem.org/english/Testimonies/20030801_Soldiers_Testimonies_Witness_S_M.asp; and http://www.btselem.org/english/Testimonies/20030701_Soldiers_Testimonies_Witness_Y_K.asp); also see *Breaking the Silence: Israeli Soldiers Speak Out About Their Service in Hebron* (Shovrimskhtika, 2004); and further Israeli officers' and soldiers' testimonies published on the Shovrimskhtika Web site (www.shovrimshtika.org).

On the impact of **closure** on **Palestinian economy**: see *Four Years—Intifada, Closures, and Palestinian Economic Crisis: An Assessment* (World Bank, 2004); *Nutritional Assessment of the West Bank and Gaza Strip* (U.S. Agency for International Development, 2003); *A Psychosocial Assessment of Palestinian Children* (U.S. Agency for International Development, 2003); "Movement and Access Restrictions in the West Bank: Uncertainty and Inefficiency in the Palestinian Economy" (World Bank, May 2007); "West Bank and Gaza Household Economy Assessment" (International Committee of the Red Cross, 21 Nov 2006); "Comprehensive Food Security and Vulnerability Analysis" (joint report published by World Food Programme, Food and Agriculture Organization, and European Union, January 2007);

"Report on Assistance to the Palestinian People" (United Nations Commission on Trade and Development [UNCTAD], 19 July 2006); "Prolonged Crisis in the Occupied Palestinian Territory: Recent Socio-Economic Impacts on Refugees and non-Refugees" (United Nations Relief and Works Agency [UNRWA], November 2006).

On **Israel's Jerusalem policies**: see "The Humanitarian Impact of the West Bank Barrier on Palestinian Communities: East Jerusalem" (UN-OCHA, June 2007); Meron Benvenisti, *City of Stone: The Hidden History of Jerusalem* (Berkeley: University of California Press, 1996); *Forbidden Families: Family Unification and Child Registration in Jerusalem* (B'Tselem, January 2004); *Greater Jerusalem: A Special Report* (Washington, D.C.: Foundation for Middle East Peace, Summer 1997); Danny Rubinstein, "The Battle for the Capital" (*Ha'aretz*, 31 March 2005); Jeff Halper, "The Three Jerusalems and Their Role in the Occupation," (*Jerusalem Quarterly File* 15, 2002); Meir Margalit, "Discrimination in the New Master Plan of Jerusalem" (Israeli Committee Against House Demolition, 4 November 2004); *A Policy of Discrimination: Land Expropriation, Planning and Building in East Jerusalem* (B'Tselem, May 1995); *The Quiet Deportation Continues: Revocation of Residency and Denial of Social Rights of East Jerusalem Residents* (B'Tselem, September 1998); *Nu'man, East Jerusalem: Life Under the Threat of Expulsion* (B'Tselem, September 2003); *Facing the Abyss: The Isolation of Sheikh Sa'ad Village Before and After the Separation Barrier* (B'Tselem, February 2004); John Dugard, *Report of the Special Rapporteur on the Situation of Human Rights in the Palestinian Territories Occupied Since 1967* (UN Human Rights Council, 5 September 2006; 17 January 2006; 29 January 2007).

On November 2007 **expansion of Har Homa settlement**: see Yoav Stern and Barak Ravid, "Housing Minister: There's No Reason to Cease East Jerusalem Construction" (*Ha'aretz*, 12 December 2007).

Stories of **Sobhi** the vegetable vendor and **Jaber** the poultry vendor, as well as status of **East Jerusalem hospitals**: from "The Humanitarian Impact of the West Bank Barrier on Palestinian Communities: East Jerusalem" (United Nations Office for the Coordination of Humanitarian Affairs [UN-OCHA], June 2007).

Story of **Ahmad al-Mahahareh**: testimony given to B'Tselem and available on B'Tselem Web site (http://www.btselem.org/english/Testimonies/20060520_Sheikh_Saed_Ahmad_al_Mashahreh.asp).

Story of **Ahlam Nasser**: testimony given to B'Tselem and available on B'Tselem Web site(http://www.btselem.org/English/Testimonies/20051212_BP_Officers_assault_ambulace_team.asp).

On the impact of the **wall** and Israel's **closure regime** in and around **East Jerusalem**: see Danny Siedmann, "The Separation Barrier and the Abuse of Security" (Washington, D.C.: Foundation for Middle East Peace, 8 December 2004); Amira Hass, "Palestinians Also Sleep in the Day" (*Ha'aretz*, 31 March 2005): Amira Hass, "IDF Said Changing its Checkpoint Policy" (*Ha'aretz*, 29 March 2005); Amira Hass, "Separating 'Jerusalem' from the 'West Bank'" (*Ha'aretz*, 26 January 2005); Amira Hass, "East Jerusalemites Will Need Permits to Visit Ramallah" (*Ha'aretz*, 25 January 2005); Meron Rappaport, "Government Decision Strips Palestinians of their East Jerusalem Property" (*Ha'aretz*, 20 January 2005);

"The Humanitarian Impact of the West Bank Barrier on Palestinian Communities: East Jerusalem" (UN-OCHA, June 2007); "Access to Jerusalem—New Military Order Limits West Bank Palestinian Access" (UN-OCHA, February 2006).

On **Israeli settlement policy** and the **Allon Plan**: see *Land Grab: Israel's Settlement Policy in the West Bank* (B'Tselem, May 2002); Gershom Gorenberg, *The Accidental Empire: Israel and the Birth of the Settlements, 1967–1977* (New York: Times Books 2006); Rafi Segal and Eyal Weizman, eds., *A Civilian Occupation: The Politics of Israeli Architecture* (London: Verso Books, 2003).

Yigal Allon quotation regarding the **Allon Plan**: from Gershom Gorenberg, *The Accidental Empire: Israel and the Birth of the Settlements, 1967–1977* (New York: Times Books, 2006).

Golda Meir quotation regarding **Palestinians**: from interview with Meir conducted by Frank Giles of the (London) *Sunday Times*, 15 June 1969.

On **Palestinian prisoners** held by Israel: see reports and statistics published by the human rights organization Addameer (www.addameer.org); *Parallel Report Jointly Submitted to the U.N. Committee on the Elimination of All Forms of Racial Discrimination, 69th Session, Geneva* (Al Haq and other human rights NGOs in Israel/Palestine, July 2006); "Mass Detention in Cruel, Inhuman, and Degrading Conditions" (Amnesty International, May 2002); "Under Constant Medical Supervision": Torture, Ill-Treatment, and the Health Professionals in Israel and the Occupied Territories (Amnesty International, August 1996); "Administrative Detention: Despair, Uncertainty, and Lack of Due Process" (Amnesty International, April 1997).

On **Israel's use of torture**: see, e.g., B'Tselem Web site (http://www.btselem.org/english/torture).

On the Palestinian-Israeli conflict from the **first intifada** to 1993, **Oslo negotiations**, **Camp David**, and afterward: see Ilan Pappé, "The Geneva Bubble" (*London Review of Books*, 8 January 2004); Tanya Reinhart, *Israel/Palestine: How to End the War of 1948* (New York: Seven Stories, 2002); Norman Finkelstein, *Image and Reality of the Israel-Palestine Conflict* (London: Verso Books, 2003); Amira Hass, *Reporting from Ramallah* (New York: Semiotext(e), 2003); Roane Carey, ed., *The New Intifada* (London: Verso Books, 2001; Edward Said, *The End of the Peace Process: Oslo and After* (New York: Vintage, 2001); Roane Carey and Jonathan Shainin, eds., *The Other Israel* (New York: New Press, 2002); Robert Malley and Hussein Agha, "Camp David: The Tragedy of Errors" (*New York Review of Books*, 9 August 2001); Clayton Swisher, *The Truth About Camp David* (New York: Nation Books, 2004); Tanya Reinhart, *The Road Map to Nowhere: Israel/Palestine Since 2003* (London: Verso Books, 2006); Jimmy Carter, *Palestine Peace Not Apartheid* (New York: Simon & Schuster, 2006); Baruch Kimmerling, *Politicide: The Real Legacy of Ariel Sharon* (London: Verso Books, 2006); Sara Roy, *Failing Peace: Gaza and the Israeli-Palestinian Conflict* (London: Pluto Press, 2006); Shlomo Ben-Ami, *Scars of War, Wounds of Peace* (Oxford: Oxford University Press, 2006); Dennis Ross, *The Missing Peace* (New York: Farrar, Straus & Giroux, 2004); Norman Finkelstein, "The Camp David II Negotiations: How Dennis Ross Proved the Palestinians Aborted the Peace Process" (*Journal of Palestine Studies*, Winter 2007); Nur Masalha, *Imperial Israel and the Palestinians*

(London: Pluto Press, 2000); Samih Farsoun and Naseer Aruri, *Palestine and the Palestinians* (Boulder, Colo: Westview Press, 2006); "The Disengagement Plan of Prime Minister Ariel Sharon," published in *Ha'aretz*, 16 April 2004; Richard Falk, "International Law and the Peace Process" (*Hastings International and Comparative Law Review*, Spring 2005).

Yitzhak Rabin quotations regarding **first intifada**: quoted in, among other places, Penny Johnson et al., "The West Bank Rises Up" (*Middle East Report*, May-June 1988), and "Yitzhak Rabin and Yasser Arafat" (*Time*, 3 November 2005).

On **casualty statistics** from **first intifada**, see figures published by B'Tselem (http://www.btselem.org/english/Statistics/First_Intifada_/Tables.asp).

Yitzhak Rabin quotation regarding Palestinians handling **security matters** in occupied territories: quoted in, among other places, Israel Shahak, "Oslo Agreement Makes PLO Israel's Enforcer," (*Washington Report on Middle East Affairs*, November-December 1993).

On **corruption in the Palestinian Authority**, see, for example, Martin Asser, "The Running of Palestine" (BBC World News, 30 November 2001); Sam Ghattas, "Audit: Arafat Diverted Millions" (AP, 21 September 2003).

Moshe Ya'alon quotation regarding Palestinians as a **defeated people**: quoted in, among other places, Yonatan Mendel, "Diary" (*London Review of Books*, 22 February 2007).

Ariel Sharon quotation regarding 2004 agreement with **U.S.**: from Sharon's keynote address at 2004 Herzliya Conference, published in *Ha'aretz*, 16 December 2004.

Dov Weisglas quotation regarding **formaldehyde**: from interview with Ari Shavit of *Ha'aretz* (Ari Shavit, "The Big Freeze," *Ha'aretz* Magazine, 8 October 2004).

Henry Siegman quotation regarding the **peace process as a deception**: from Henry Siegman, "The Middle East Peace Process Scam" (*London Review of Books*, 16 August 2007).

Financial Times article on new UN-OCHA **map of West Bank**: Sharmila Devi and Harvey Morris, "New U.N. Map Charts West Bank Reality" (*Financial Times*, 11 June 2006).

INSIDES

Story of **Samira Aliyan**: testimony given to B'Tselem and published in *The Quiet Deportation Continues: Revocation of Residency and Denial of Social Rights of East Jerusalem Residents* (B'Tselem and Hamoked, September 1998).

Story of **Daoud Kuttab**: see Daoud Kuttab, "A 16-Year-Old in Palestine: Life Is an ID Card" (*Counterpunch*, 9 August 2003).

For more information on the East Jerusalem branch of the **Israeli Ministry of the Interior**, see B'Tselem's notes on East Jerusalem, published on the B'Tselem Web site: (http://www.btselem.org/English/Jerusalem/Infrastructure_and_Services.asp); Danny Rubinstein, "Moving Toward Full Palestinian Control" (*Ha'aretz*, 18 June 2002); Arab Thought Forum (http://www.multaqa.org/etemplate.php?id=317#).

On **Israel's policies in East Jerusalem**: in addition to materials cited in notes to previous chapter, see *Forbidden Families: Family Unification and Child Registration in Jerusa-*

312

lem (B'Tselem, January 2004); Danny Rubinstein, "The Battle for the Capital" (*Ha'aretz*, 31 March 2005); *The Quiet Deportation Continues: Revocation of Residency and Denial of Social Rights of East Jerusalem Residents* (B'Tselem and Hamoked, September 1998); *A Policy of Discrimination: Land Expropriation, Planning, and Building in East Jerusalem* (B'Tselem, May 1995); *Nu'man, East Jerusalem: Life Under the Threat of Expulsion* (B'Tselem, September 2003); John Dugard, *Report of the Special Rapporteur on the Situation of Human Rights in the Palestinian Territories Occupied Since 1967* (U.N. Human Rights Council, 5 September 2006; 17 January 2006; 29 Jan 2007); "Eviction, Restitution, and Protection of Palestinian Rights in Jerusalem" (Badil Resource Center for Palestinian Residency and Refugee Rights, April 1999); "A Capital Question" (*Economist*, 10 May 2007).

John Dugard quotation regarding **"de-Palestinization"** of Jerusalem: from John Dugard, *Report of the Special Rapporteur* (U.N. Human Rights Council, September 2005).

Ahmed Jubran quotation: from "A Capital Question" (*Economist*, 10 May 2007).

David Ben-Gurion quotation: from *Parallel Report Jointly Submitted to the U.N. Committee on the Elimination of All Forms of Racial Discrimination, 69th Session, Geneva* (Al Haq and other human rights NGOs in Israel/Palestine, July 2006).

John Dugard quotation regarding the **"Judaization"** of Jerusalem: from *Report of the Special Rapporteur* (U.N. Human Rights Council, September 2006).

Israel Kimchi, **Amir Cheshin**, and **Teddy Kollek** quotations regarding **demographic principles** underlying Israeli city planning in Jerusalem: from *A Policy of Discrimination: Land Expropriation, Planning, and Building in East Jerusalem* (B'Tselem, May 1995).

Meron Benvenisti quotation regarding **city planning**: from Meron Benvenisti, *City of Stone: The Hidden History of Jerusalem* (Berkeley: University of California Press, 1996).

Story of **Daoud Abu Kaf**: testimony given to B'Tselem and published in *A Policy of Discrimination: Land Expropriation, Planning, and Building in East Jerusalem* (B'Tselem, May 1995).

Story of **Yusuf Abu Hamad**: testimony given to B'Tselem and published in *A Policy of Discrimination*.

Figures on **home demolitions in Jerusalem**: from data compiled by B'Tselem, and published on its Web site (http://www.btselem.org/english/Planning_and_Building/East_Jerusalem_Statistics.asp); also see Meron Rappaport, "City to Raze Homes of 1,000 Residents in East Jerusalem Neighborhood" (*Ha'aretz*, 31 May 2005).

On **home demolitions**, see *Razing Rafah: Mass Home Demolitions in the Gaza Strip* (Human Rights Watch, October 2004); *Policy of Destruction: House Demolitions and Destruction of Agricultural Land in Gaza Strip* (B'Tselem, February 2002); *Through No Fault of Their Own: Punitive House Demolitions During the al-Aqsa Intifada* (B'Tselem, November 2004); "Demolition and Dispossession: The Destruction of Palestinian Homes" (Amnesty International, December 1999); Amnon Regular, "Court Bars IDF from Demolishing Additional Rafah Homes" (*Ha'aretz*, 15 May 2004); Gideon Levy, "Today Rafah, Tomorrow Jenin" (*Ha'aretz*, 16 May 2004); Amira Hass, "Gazans Pile Up Their Belongings and Flee" (*Ha'aretz*, 17 May 2004); "Alarmed at Planned Demolitions" (UNRWA press release, 16

May 2004); Amira Hass, "Darkness at Noon" (*Ha'aretz*, 21 May 2004); Meir Margalit, "Playing with Fire" (Occupation Magazine [Kibush], 31 May 2005); Gideon Levy, "End of the Rainbow" (*Ha'aretz*, 3 June 2007); "Under the Rubble: House Demolition and Destruction of Land and Property" (Amnesty International, May 2004); "Uprooting Palestinian Trees and Leveling Agricultural Land" (Palestinian Center for Human Rights, 2004); "Cut-Flowers in Gaza: A Special Report on the Impacts of Israeli Rights Violations on Gaza's Cut-Flower Business" (Mezan Center for Human Rights, March 2007).

Story of **Mithqal Abu Taha**: testimony given to B'Tselem and published in *Policy of Destruction* (B'Tselem, February 2002).

Uri Shetrit quotation regarding **home demolition** in Silwan: from Meron Rappaport, "City to Raze Homes of 1,000 Residents in East Jerusalem Neighborhood (*Ha'aretz*, 31 May 2005).

Teddy Kollek quotation regarding provisions for Palestinians of **East Jerusalem**: from *A Policy of Discrimination: Land Expropriation, Planning, and Building in East Jerusalem* (B'Tselem, May 1995).

Ehud Olmert quotation regarding gaps in **infrastructure** between East and West Jerusalem: from *The Quiet Deportation Continues: Revocation of Residency and Denial of Social Rights of East Jerusalem Residents* (B'Tselem and HaMoked, September 1998).

Figures on **discrimination in Jerusalem budget**: from *A Policy of Discrimination: Land Expropriation, Planning, and Building in East Jerusalem* (B'Tselem, May 1995).

On **registration of births** and **family unification**: see *The Quiet Deportation Continues* (B'Tselem and HaMoked, September 1998); *Forbidden Families: Family Unification and Child Registration in Jerusalem* (B'Tselem, January 2004); "Torn Apart: Families Split by Discriminatory Policies" (Amnesty International, July 2004).

Story of **Hala Odeh**: testimony given to B'Tselem and published in *The Quiet Deportation Continues* (B'Tselem and HaMoked, September 1998).

On **Israel's Nationality Law**, as amended in 2003, see *Forbidden Families* (B'Tselem, January 2004); *NGO Report: Suggested Issues for Consideration Regarding Israel's Combined 10th, 11th, 12th, and 13th Periodic Report to the U.N. Committee on the Elimination of Racial Discrimination* (Adalah, 15 December 2005); *Parallel Report Jointly Submitted to the U.N. Committee on the Elimination of All Forms of Racial Discrimination, 69th Session, Geneva* (Al Haq and other human rights NGOs in Israel/Palestine, July 2006); *Concluding Observations of the [U.N.] Committee on the Elimination of Racial Discrimination* (International Convention on the Elimination of all Forms of Racial Discrimination, March 2007); Tom Segev, "I Am a Jerusalemite" (*Ha'aretz*, 10 February 2006); Peter Beaumont, "Israel Fears Invasion of Immigrants" (*Observer*, 16 June 2002); "Israel: Don't Outlaw Family Life" (Human Rights Watch, July 2003, available on HRW Web site http://www.hrw.org/press/2003/07/israel072803.htm); "Right to Family Life Denied: Foreign Spouses of Palestinians Barred" (Amnesty International, March 2007); "Israel/Occupied Territories: High Court Decision Institutionalizes Racial Discrimination" (Amnesty International, 16 May 2006).

Story of **Amal Abu Jawila**: from Tom Segev, "I Am a Jerusalemite" (*Ha'aretz*, 10 February 2006).

Story of **Yasser Abu Marir**: testimony given to B'Tselem and published in *Forbidden Families: Family Unification and Child Registration in Jerusalem* (B'Tselem, January 2004).

Meron Benvenisti quotation regarding planning Jerusalem **city limits**: from Meron Benvenisti, *City of Stone: The Hidden History of Jerusalem* (Berkeley: University of California Press, 1996).

On **Israeli settlement policy** and its history: see Rafi Segal and Eyal Weizman, eds., *A Civilian Occupation: The Politics of Israeli Architecture* (London: Verso Books, 2003); *Land Grab: Israel's Settlement Policy in the West Bank* (B'Tselem, May 2002); Gershom Gorenberg, *The Accidental Empire: Israel and the Birth of the Settlements, 1967–1977* (New York: Times Books, 2006); *Report on Israeli Settlement in the Occupied Territories* (Foundation for Middle East Peace, 1990–2007, published on FMEP Web site: www.fmep.org).

Yigal Allon quotation regarding **settlement**: from Gorenberg, *The Accidental Empire*; "No One Knows Full Cost of Israel's Settlement Ambitions" (*USA Today*, 14 August 2005).

Thomas Leitersdorf and **Matiyahu Drobles** quotations regarding Jewish **settlement** plans: from Segal and Weizman, eds., *A Civilian Occupation*.

Quotation from Israel's **1980 Master Plan** for settlement: from *Land Grab* (B'Tselem, May 2002).

Alfred Vitkon, **Eyal Weizman**, **Rafi Segal** quotations regarding incorporation of **settlements** into military planning: from Segal and Weizman, eds., *A Civilian Occupation*.

Figures on **subsidies for settlements**: from *Land Grab* (B'Tselem, May 2002).

On **Har Homa**: see *A Policy of Discrimination: Land Expropriation, Planning, and Building in East Jerusalem* (B'Tselem, May 1995).

Quotation from **Tehilla** regarding **Har Homa**: published on Tehilla Web site (http://www.tehilla.com/aliya/places.asp?id=86).

Quotations from **RE/MAX ads** for property in **East Jerusalem**: from RE/MAX Web site (http://remax-capital.com/new/html/location.php).

Quotations from **advertising** aimed at American Jewish community regarding property in **occupied territories**: see advertising on Amana Web site (http://www.amana.co.il/Index.asp?CategoryID=108&ArticleID=350); for description of Emanuel, see Segal and Weizman, eds., *A Civilian Occupation*; also see "Settlers to U.S. Jews: Help Us to Stay" (*Jerusalem Post*, 9 February 2007).

Quotation regarding **settlement of Eli**: from Eli Web site (http://www.eli.co.il/site/english.html).

Quotation from **Jewish settler in Eli**: published on JewishGroups Web site (http://www.jewishgroups.org/AliyaBSimcha/Eli.html).

Benny Katzover, **Shimon Peres**, **Moshe Dayan**, and **Gershom Gorenberg** quotations regarding **settlement**: from Gorenberg, *The Accidental Empire*.

On **Gush Emumim** and the **Whole Land of Israel Movement**, see Nur Masalha, *Imperial Israel and the Palestinians* (London: Pluto Press, 2000).

Yisrael Ariel, **Tzvi Shiloah**, **Eliezer Livneh**, **Dov Yosefi**, and **Benjamin**

Netanyahu quotations regarding **expulsion** of Palestinians: from Nur Masalha, *Imperial Israel*.

On situation in hills south of **Hebron**, see Means of Expulsion: Violence, Harassment and Lawlessness Against Palestinians in the Southern Hebron Hills (B'Tselem, July 2005); David Shulman, *Dark Hope: Working for Peace in Israel and Palestine* (Chicago: University of Chicago Press, 2007).

David Shulman quotations regarding South **Hebron** hills: from his *Dark Hope*.

On **expulsion of Palestinian cave- and tent-dwellers**: see B'Tselem Web site (http://www.btselem.org/english/Separation_Barrier/20071125_Forced_Eviction_of_Khirbet_al_Qassa_Residents.asp).

Weizman and **Segal** quotations regarding visual strategy expressed in **settlement architecture**, from Segal and Weizman, eds., *A Civilian Occupation*.

Videos of Jewish **settlers intruding into Palestinian homes** in **Hebron**: available on YouTube Web site (http://www.youtube.com/watch?v=XJxPgQ9Qx8Y); (http://www.youtube.com/watch?v=GSAvaYY-y7Q); (http://www.youtube.com/watch?v=tAKMtig_mP8); (http://www.youtube.com/watch?v=Nhlw7WK8gzo). Also see B'Tselem video on the situation in Hebron, available on YouTube (http://www.youtube.com/watch?v=CPvGZjkMb3A).

Gideon Levy quotation regarding situation in **Tel Rumeida**: from Gideon Levy, "Mean Streets of Tel Rumeida" (*Counterpunch*, 12 September 2005; originally published in *Ha'aretz*).

On situation in **Hebron**: see *Breaking the Silence: Soldiers Speak Out About Their Service in Hebron* (Shovrimskhtika, 2004); *Free Rein: Vigilante Settlers and Israel's Non-Enforcement of the Law* (B'Tselem, October 2001); *Standing Idly By: Non-Enforcement of the Law on Settlers, Hebron, 26–28 July 2002* (B'Tselem, August 2002); *Hebron, Area H-2: Settlements Cause Mass Departure of Palestinians* (B'Tselem, August 2003); Amira Hass, *Reporting from Ramallah: An Israeli Journalist in an Occupied Land* (New York: Semiotext(e), 2003); *Ghost Town: Israel's Separation Policy and Forced Eviction of Palestinians from the Center of Hebron* (B'Tselem, May 2007).

Story of **Najah D'ana**: testimony given to B'Tselem and published in *Hebron, Area H-2*.

Story of **Maryam al-Natsheh**: testimony given to B'Tselem and published in *Standing Idly By*.

Story of **Fadel al-Samuh**: testimony given to B'tselem and published in *Standing Idly By*.

On **discrimination in the legal systems** in the occupied territories, and legalized discrimination inside Israel, see *NGO Report: Suggested Issues for Consideration Regarding Israel's Combined 10th, 11th, 12th, and 13th Periodic Report to the U.N. Committee on the Elimination of Racial Discrimination* (Adalah, 15 December 2005); *Parallel Report Jointly Submitted to the U.N. Committee on the Elimination of All Forms of Racial Discrimination, 69th Session, Geneva* (Al Haq and other human rights NGOs in Israel/Palestine, July 2006); *Concluding Observations of the [U.N.] Committee on the Elimination of Racial Discrimination* (International Convention on the Elimination of All Forms of Racial Discrimination, March 2007); Sheldon Richman, " 'Who is a Jew' Matters in Israel" (*Washington Report on Middle East Affairs*, March 1990); Uri Avnery, "A Nation? What Nation?" (Gush Shalom, 25 September 2004); Jonathan Cook, *Blood and Religion: The Unmasking of the Jewish and Democratic State* (Ann Arbor: University of Michigan Press, 2006); Amira Hass, "Can You Really Not See?" (*Ha'aretz*, 30 August 2006); *Democratic Constitution* (Adalah, 20 March 2007); "Knesset Approves Bill on Preliminary Reading to Restrict Jewish National Fund Lands Exclusively to Jewish Citizens," *Adalah Newsletter*, July 2007, published on Adalah Web site (http:// adalah-english.c.topica.com/maahg5GabAfWKbJCJItc/).

Quotation from **Israeli High Court** regarding **nationality**: from Richman, " 'Who is a Jew' Matters in Israel."

Quotation from **Jewish National Fund** regarding its role as **caretaker of the land**: from JNF Web page (www.jnf.org).

Quotation from **Tim Rutten** regarding **American support for Israel**: from Tim Rutten, "Israel's Lobby as Scapegoat" (*Los Angeles Times*, 12 September 2007); quotation from **Victor Davis Hanson**: from Hanson, "Why Support Israel?" (*National Review* online, 4 February 2002).

Quotations from **JNF** asserting **the right to discriminate**, and from Knesset bill to protect JNF discrimination: see "Knesset Approves Bill on Preliminary Reading to Restrict Jewish National Fund Lands Exclusively to Jewish Citizens," *Adalah Newsletter*, July 2007, published on Adalah Web site: http://adalah-english.c.topica.com/maahg5GabAfWKbJ CJItc/).

On **marriage and conversion in Israel**: see Michele Chabin, "Chief Rabbinate Barring Conversions from Top U.S. Orthodox Rabbis" (*Jewish Week*, 5 May 2006); Amiram Barkat, "Chief Rabbinate Preparing Bill to Change Law of Return" (*Ha'aretz*, 22 November 2006); Matthew Wagner, "Chief Rabbi for Changing Law of Return" (*Jerusalem Post*, 20 November 2006); Steven Mazie, "Changing Israel's Marriage Laws" (*Jewish Week*, 28 April 2006); Nathaniel Popper, "Divorce Bill Leaves Feminists and Ultra-Orthodox in Bed Together" (*The Forward*, 2 February 2007); " 'Who is a Jew' Redux" (editorial in *The Forward*, 4 July 2003).

Outside In

Story of **Mona el-Farra**: From information published on her Web site (http://fromgaza .blogspot.com).

On the **closure of Gaza**: see "The Agreement on Movement and Access One Year On" (UN-OCHA, November 2006); regularly updated reports on Movement and Access published by UN-OCHA and available on the UN-OCHA Web site (http://www.ochaopt .org/?module=displaysection&section_id=119&format=html); "Poverty in the Gaza Strip" (Palestinian Centre for Human Rights, 12 May 2006); Amira Hass, "Who's in Charge Here?" (*Ha'aretz*, 19 January 2005); "Special Report on the Israeli Closure of the Gaza Strip" (Palestinian Centre for Human Rights, 12 June 2006); "Gaza on the Edge" (UN-OCHA, October 2004); "Facilitating Trade Flows Between WBGS and Israel Project" (Palestine Trade Center, 13 February 2007); John Dugard, *Report of the Special Rapporteur on the Situation of Human Rights in the Palestinian Territories Occupied Since 1967* (U.N. Human Rights Council, 5 September 2006; 17 January 2006; 29 January 2007); "The State of Gaza Strip Border Crossings" (Palestinian Centre for Human Rights, 3 December 2006); "Israeli Human Rights Organizations Call for Respect of Human Rights and International Humanitarian Law in the Gaza Strip" (B'Tselem and others, Autumn 2006); "Prolonged Crisis in the Occupied Palestinian Territory: Recent Socio-Economic Impact" (UNRWA, November 2006); *Four Years: Intifada, Closures, and Palestinian Economic Crisis: An Assessment* (World Bank, October 2004); "Gaza Strip: Impact of the International Embargo and the Attacks by the Israeli Army on the Population's Health Status" (Médecins du Monde, 2006); "Israel's Control of the Airspace and the Territorial Waters of the Gaza Strip" (B'Tselem report, available on B'Tselem Web site: http://www.btselem.org/english/Gaza_Strip/Control_on_Air_space_and_territorial_waters.asp); Gideon Levy, "A New Consensus" (*Ha'aretz*, 19 March 2006); *One Big Prison: Freedom of Movement to and from the Gaza Strip on the Eve of the Disengagement Plan* (B'Tselem and Hamoked, March 2005); Avi Issacharoff, "International Aid Agency: 80 Percent of Gazans Now Rely on Food Aid" (*Ha'aretz*, 7 March 2007); "Divide and Rule: Prohibition on Passage Between the Gaza Strip and the West Bank" (B'Tselem, May 1998).

Meron Benvenisti quotation regarding **Gaza** as a holding pen: from Meron Benvenisti, "Founding a Binational State" (*Ha'aretz*, 22 April 2004).

James Wolfensohn quotations regarding Gaza as **"prison"** and **Agreement on Movement and Access**: from interview with *Ha'aretz*, in Shahar Smooha, "All the Dreams We Had Are Now Gone" (*Ha'aretz*, 21 July 2007).

Henry Siegman quotation regarding **Gaza**: from Henry Siegman, "The Middle East Peace Process Scam" (*London Review of Books*, 16 August 2007).

Kirstie Campbell quotation regarding **"island economy"**: from Issacharoff, "International Aid Agency."

Story of **Laila el-Haddad**: from her blog, Raising Yousuf (http://a-mother-from-gaza.blogspot.com).

On stampede at **Rafah crossing**: see Karin Laub, "Palestinians Injured in Crush at Border" (AP, 8 March 2007).

On details of **Gaza's population**: see UNRWA Web site (http://www.un.org/unrwa/refugees/gaza.html); Palestine Central Bureau of Statistics Web site (http://www.pcbs.gov.ps/Default.aspx?tabID=1&lang=en); and the International Database of the U.S. Census Bureau (http://www.census.gov/ipc/www/idb/country/gzportal.html).

On **Gaza settlements** and the **exploitation of Gaza's workforce** by Israeli employers: see Amira Hass, *Drinking the Sea at Gaza* (New York: Owl Books, 1999); Sara Roy, *Failing Peace: Gaza and the Israeli-Palestinian Conflict* (London: Pluto Press, 2007); Tanya Reinhart, *The Road Map to Nowhere: Israel/Palestine Since 2003* (London: Verso Books, 2006); "Human Rights Violations of Palestinians from the Occupied Territories Working in Israel and the Settlements" (B'Tselem, August 1999); "Israeli Settlements in the Occupied Territories as a Violation of Human Rights" (B'Tselem, March 1997).

On **Israel's 2005 redeployment from Gaza**, see Reinhart, *The Road Map to Nowhere*; The Gaza Strip After Disengagement" (UN-OCHA Humanitarian Update, November-December 2005); Jeff Halper, "A Palestinian Prison-State" (*Boston Globe*, 11 April 2005); John Dugard, *Report of the Special Rapporteur on the Situation of Human Rights in the Palestinian Territories Occupied Since 1967* (U.N. Human Rights Council, 5 September 2006; 17 January 2006; 29 January 2007); "The Disengagement Plan of PM Ariel Sharon" (*Ha'aretz*, 16 April 2004); Amira Hass, "The Remaining 99.5 Percent" (*Ha'aretz*, 25 August 2005); Peretz Kidron, "Sharon's Sights on Strategic Objective" (*Ha'aretz*, 14 April 2004); Henry Siegman, "Sharon and the Future of Palestine" (*New York Review of Books*, 2 December 2004); Naseer Aruri, "Wa'ad Balfour al-Jadid," (*Al-Hayat*, 26 April 2004); Ilan Pappé, "Israel Is Heading for a Disaster" (*London Review of Books*, 6 May 2004); Azmi Bishara, "Separation Spells Racism" (*Al-Ahram Weekly*, 1–7 July 2004).

John Dugard quotation regarding **Gaza as a prison**: from "U.N. Human Rights Envoy Says Gaza a Prison for Palestinians" (Reuters, 27 September 2006).

John Dugard quotation regarding situation in **Gaza after Israeli redeployment**: from John Dugard, *Report of the Special Rapporteur on the Situation of Human Rights in the Palestinian Territories Occupied Since 1967* (U.N. Human Rights Council, 29 January 2007).

For figures on **crossing into and out of Gaza** and details of **treatment of workers** at crossings: see sources for closure of Gaza, above. "Agreement on Movement and Access": Full text available at UN-OCHA Web site (http://www.ochaopt.org/documents/ Agreement_on_Movement_and_Access_Final_15_Nov_2005.pdf).

On **Palestinian prisoners in Israeli jails**: see John Dugard, *Report of the Special Rapporteur on the Situation of Human Rights in the Palestinian Territories Occupied Since 1967* (U.N. Human Rights Council, 29 January 2007); *Parallel Report Jointly Submitted to the U.N. Committee on the Elimination of All Forms of Racial Discrimination, 69th Session, Geneva* (Al Haq and other human rights NGOs in Israel/Palestine, July 2006); also see reports and statistics published by the human rights organization Addameer (www .addameer.org).

On impact of **closure** on **Gaza**, see sources for closure of Gaza, above; also see *Gaza Strip: State of Disaster* (Israeli Physicians for Human Rights, September 2006); "Statement on Gaza by United Nations Humanitarian Agencies Working in the Occupied Palestinian Territory" (United Nations, 3 August 2006); "Israeli Human Rights Organizations Call for Respect of Human Rights and International Humanitarian Law in the Gaza Strip" (B'Tselem and others, Autumn 2006); "As Gaza Parents Go Unpaid, Children Go Hungry" (*New York Times*, 13 September 2006); "Palestinians in Gaza Suffer Record Poverty" (Reuters, 25 January 2007); "Gaza Humanitarian Situation Report" (UN-OCHA, June 2007); "Facilitating Trade Flows Between WBGS and Israel Project" (Palestine Trade Center, 13 February 2007); Rory McCarthy, "Sick Are in the Frontline as Supplies and Hope Drain Away for Isolated Gazans" (*The Guardian* [London], 27 November 2007); "Gazan Cancer Patient Dies after Being Delayed Entry into Israel for 10 Days" (B'Tselem Web site, http://www.btselem.org/english/Gaza_Strip/20071018_ Gaza_Medical_Care_Cancer_patient_Mhmoud_Abu_Taha.asp).

Dr. Bushra Lubbed quotation regarding **medical crisis in Gaza**: from Rory McCarthy, "Sick Are in the Frontline as Supplies and Hope Drain Away for Isolated Gazans" (*The Guardian* [London], 27 November 2007).

On **Gaza fishermen**: see "IDF Prohibits Fishing off Gaza Coast and Abuses Fishermen" (B'Tselem, 23 February 2007); "Gaza Fishing: An Industry in Danger" (UN-OCHA, April 2007).

Story of **Ismail Basleh**: testimony given to B'Tselem and published in "IDF Prohibits Fishing off Gaza Coast."

On **food aid to Gaza population** and quotation from **World Food Programme** regarding food aid: see Avi Issacharoff, "International Aid Agency: 80 Percent of Gazans Now Rely on Food Aid" (*Ha'aretz*, 7 March 2007).

John Dugard quotation regarding the **"controlled strangulation"** of Gaza: from John Dugard, *Report of the Special Rapporteur on the Situation of Human Rights in the Palestinian Territories Occupied Since 1967* (U.N. Human Rights Council, 29 January 2007).

Dov Weisglas quotation regarding the **"diet"** imposed on Gaza: from Conal Urquhart, "Gaza on Brink of Explosion as Aid Cut-Off Starts to Bite" (*The Observer* [London], 16 April 2006).

Alex Fishman quotation regarding territorial **"cells"**: from Tanya Reinhart, *The Road Map to Nowhere: Israel/Palestine Since 2003* (London: Verso Books, 2006).

On postredeployment **Israeli bombardment** of **Gaza**: see *Gaza Strip: State of Disaster* (Israeli Physicians for Human Rights, September 2006); "Statement on Gaza by United Nations Humanitarian Agencies Working in the Occupied Palestinian Territory" (United Nations, 3 August 2006); "Israeli Human Rights Organizations Call for Respect of Human Rights and International Humanitarian Law in the Gaza Strip" (B'Tselem and others, Autumn 2006); John Dugard, *Report of the Special Rapporteur on the Situation of Human Rights in the Palestinian Territories Occupied Since 1967* (U.N. Human Rights Council, 29 January 2007); Donald Macintyre, "Gaza: The Children Killed in a War the World Doesn't Want to Know About" (*The Independent* [London], 19 September 2006).

On **Gaza beach massacre**: Chris McGreal, "The Battle of Huda Ghalia: Who Really Killed Girl's Family on Gaza Beach?" (*The Guardian* [London], 17 June 2006).

Quotation from **Amnesty International** regarding **beach massacre**: "Call for International Investigation of Gaza Strikes" (Amnesty International, 21 June 2006).

On **Israeli sonic booms** over **Gaza**, see Chris McGreal, "Palestinians Hit by Sonic Boom Air Raids" (*The Guardian*, 3 November 2005); "Israeli Sonic Booms Terrify Palestinian Children" (Agence France Press, 29 September 2005); Donald Macintyre, "Palestinians 'Terrorised' by Sonic Boom Flights" (*The Independent* [London], 3 November 2005); "Sonic Booms Constitute Collective Punishment" (B'Tselem, 3 July 2006); "Gaza Community Mental Health Program medical report on sonic booms" (30 October 2005); "GCMHP and Al Mezan joint press release condemning sonic booms" (3 July 2006); "Sonic Booms in the Sky Over Gaza" (B'Tselem Web site report on sonic booms (http://www.btselem.org/English/Gaza_Strip/Supersonic_booms.asp).

Eyad el-Sarraj quotations regarding **sonic booms**: from GCMHP statement and also Eyad el-Sarraj, "Stunning Gaza" (*Live from Palestine*, 28 September 2005, available on Electronic Intifada Web site: http://electronicintifada.net/v2/article4212.shtml).

B'Tselem quotations regarding **sonic booms**: from "Sonic Booms Constitute Collective Punishment" (B'Tselem, 3 July 2006).

On use of **experimental weapons in Gaza**: see "Gaza Strip: State of Disaster" (Israeli Physicians for Human Rights, September 2006); Meron Rapoport, "Italian Probe: Israel Used New Weapon Prototype in GS" (*Ha'aretz*, 11 October 2006).

On consequences of **power plant bombing in Gaza**, see"Act of Vengeance: Israel's Bombing of the Gaza Power Plant and its Effects" (B'Tselem, September 2006); John Dugard, *Report of the Special Rapporteur on the Situation of Human Rights in the Palestinian Territories Occupied Since 1967* (U.N. Human Rights Council, 29 January 2007).

On **Beit Hanoun massacre**: see John Dugard, *Report of the Special Rapporteur*.

On **2002 Israeli assault** on **Nablus** and **Jenin** and its aftermath, see Amira Hass, "No More Business in Blocked-off Nablus" (*Ha'aretz*, 5 August 2004); Amira Hass, "The Rooftop Youth of Nablus" (*Ha'aretz*, 27 July 2004); Beshara Doumani, "Scenes from Daily Life: The View from Nablus" (*Journal of Palestine Studies*, Autumn 2004); Amir Oren, "The Fire Next Time" (*Ha'aretz*, 26 March 2004); *Jenin: IDF Military Operations* (Human Rights Watch, May 2002); *Shielded from Scrutiny: IDF Violations in Jenin and Nablus* (Amnesty International, November 2002); Tsadok Yeheskeli, "I Made Them a Stadium in the Middle of the Camp" (*Yediot Aharonot*, 31 May 2002, translated into English and published in, among other places, the Gush Shalom Web site: http://gush-shalom.org/archives/kurdi_eng.html); *Operation Defensive Shield: Soldiers' Testimonies, Palestinian Testimonies* (B'Tselem, 2002); Lethal Curfew: The Use of Live Ammunition to Enforce Curfew (B'Tselem, October 2002); "Israel Shows Reckless Disregard for Human Life" (Amnesty International, August 2001; *State Assassination and other Unlawful Killings* (Amnesty International, February 2001); *Killing the Future: Children in the Line of Fire* (Amnesty International, September 2002); Arjan El Fassed, "Nablus, the Meaning of State Terror" (*Live from Palestine*, 28 April 2002, at http://electronicintifada.net/v2/article303.shtml).

Quotations from **Israeli soldiers** regarding **assaults** and **raids** on Palestinian cities: from Israeli soldiers' testimonies published on Shovrimshtika Web site (www.shovrimshtika.org); from *Breaking the Silence: Israeli Soldiers Speak Out about Their Service in Hebron* (Shovrimshtika, 2004); and from "Operation Defensive Shield: Soldiers' Testimonies, Palestinian Testimonies" (B'Tselem, 2002).

Quotations from **Palestinian survivors** of those **assaults**: from "Operation Defensive Shield" (B'Tselem, 2002).

Quotations from **Human Rights Watch** regarding demolition of **Jenin** refugee camp: from *Jenin: IDF Military Operations* (Human Rights Watch, May 2002).

Quotations from **Amnesty International** regarding **Jenin**: from *Shielded from Scrutiny: IDF Violations in Jenin and Nablus* (Amnesty International, November 2002).

Moshe Nissim quotation regarding demolition in **Jenin**: from: Tsadok Yeheskeli, "I Made Them a Stadium in the Middle of the Camp" (*Yediot Aharonot*, 31 May 2002, translated into English and published in, among other places, the Gush Shalom Web site: http://gush-shalom.org/archives/kurdi_eng.html).

Quotation from **Fathiya Suleiman** regarding demolition in **Jenin**: testimony given to B'tselem and published in Operation Defensive Shield (B'Tselem, 2002).

Quotation from **Ala'a Abu Dheer** regarding assault on **Nablus**: testimony given to B'tselem and published in Operation Defensive Shield (B'Tselem, 2002).

Quotation from **B'Tselem** regarding Israeli army prohibition of **medical rescue operations** in 2002: from "Operation Defensive Shield" (B'Tselem, 2002); also see "Wounded in the Field: Impeding Medical Treatment and Firing at Ambulances by IDF Soldiers in the Occupied Territories" (B'Tselem, March 2002).

Story of **Tahani Fattouh**: testimony given to B'Tselem and published in "Operation Defensive Shield" (B'Tselem, 2002); also on B'tselem Web site (http://www.btselem.org/English/Testimonies/index.asp?YF=2002&image.x=16&image.y=7).

Figures on **raids** and **curfews** in **Nablus**: from data published by UN-OCHA, available on OCHA Web site, www.ochaopt.org) and B'Tselem Web site (www.btselem.org).

Story of **Jihad Muhalad** and of **Ghazi Bani Odeh**: testimonies given to B'Tselem and published in Lethal Curfew: The Use of Live Ammunition to Enforce Curfew (B'Tselem, October 2002).

On **curfews** imposed by Israeli army on Palestinian communities: see reports by B'Tselem (http://www.btselem.org/english/Freedom_of_Movement/Curfew.asp) and UN-OCHA (http://www.ochaopt.org/documents/PoC%20Monthly%20tables%20and%20terminology%20notes_July2007.pdf).

Quotations from **Israeli soldiers** regarding **curfew**: from Breaking the Silence: Israeli Soldiers Speak Out About their Service in Hebron (Shovrimshtika, 2004) and from Israeli soldiers' testimonies published on Shovrimshtika Web site (www.shovrimshtika.org).

Majdi Alawna quotation regarding curfew in **Jenin**: from Lethal Curfew (B'Tselem, October 2002).

Stories of **Alam Ghanem**, **Ahmad al-Turki**, **Ahmad Sma'aneh**: testimonies given to B'Tselem and published in Lethal Curfew.

On **Israeli army's open-fire policy**, see B'Tselem report Lethal Curfew.

On **Bethlehem**, see Costs of Conflict: The Changing Face of Bethlehem (UN-OCHA, December 2004).

On impact of **wall** in and around **Qalqilya**, see sources listed for wall in "Outsides," above.

Shaul Arieli quotation regarding the **"seam zone"**: from Amnon Barzilai, "The Fence: A Path to Voluntary Transfer" (Ha'aretz, 18 February 2004).

On **education** in Israel and the occupied territories: "U.N.: Gaza Students Lack Textbooks Because of Shortages from Crossing Closures" (AP, 3 September 2007); "The Education Gap" (Adalah Newsletter, August 2007).

Ahmed Malhi quotation: from Ilene Plusher, "The Long Walk to Class" (Christian Science Monitor, 20 December 2006).

Omar Musallam quotation: from "Palestinian Views on Travel Curbs" (BBC News, 1 June 2006).

Quotation from **twenty-year-old Gazan**: from "Frustrations of Reality" (Birzeit Right to Education Web site, http://right2edu.birzeit.edu/news/article485).

INSIDE OUT

Video of **attack on Palestinian schoolgirls**: from Tel Rumeida Project Web site (www.telrumeida.org); also available on YouTube (http://www.youtube.com/watch?v=5Mp9 DhPamR8).

On **international observers** in **Hebron** and testimonies of their volunteers: see Web sites of Temporary International Presence in Hebron (www.tiph.org) and Ecumenical Accompaniment Program in Palestine and Israel (www.eappi.org).

On the situation in **Hebron**: see *Free Rein: Vigilante Settlers and Israel's Non-Enforcement of the Law* (BTselem, October 2001); *Hebron, Area H-2: Settlements Cause Mass Departure of Palestinians* (B'Tselem, August 2003); "Ghost Town: Israel's Separation Policy and Forced Eviction of Palestinians from the Center of Hebron" (B'Tselem, May 2007); Amira Hass, *Reporting from Ramallah: An Israeli Journalist in an Occupied Land* (New York: Semiotext(e), 2003); "Israeli Settlers Wage Campaign of Intimidation on Palestinians and Internationals Alike" (Amnesty International, October 2004).

Quotation from **Israeli military establishment** and **B'Tselem** regarding situation in **Hebron**: from "Ghost Town" (B'Tselem, May 2007).

Story of **Nidal al-Awiwi**: testimony given to B'Tselem and published in *Hebron, Area H-2* (B'Tselem, August 2003).

On **Baruch Goldstein** massacre: see Leon Hadar, "The Hebron Massacre: Another 'Defining Moment' in the Middle East" (*Washington Report on Middle East Affairs*, April-May 1994); "Graveside Party Celebrates Hebron Massacre" (BBC, 21 March 2000, available on BBC Web site: http://news.bbc.co.uk/1/hi/world/middle_east/685792.stm).

Inscription on **Goldstein's grave**: from Peace Now Web site (http://www.peacenow. org.il/site/en/peace.asp?pi=62&docid=1528).

Amira Hass quotation regarding **Hebron**: from Amira Hass, "The 'Jewish Only' Roads" (*Ha'aretz*, 18 July 2001).

Quotation from **Pessoptimist**: from Emile Habibi, *The Secret Life of Saeed, the Ill-Fated Pessoptimist* translated by Salma Jayyusi and Trevor Le Gassick (New York: Interlink Books, 1999).

For more on **Palestinian towns depopulated and destroyed in 1948**, see Michael Fishbach, *Records of Dispossession: Palestinian Refugee Property and the Arab-Israeli Conflict* (New York: Columbia University Press, 2003); Walid Khalidi, ed., *All That Remains: The Palestinian Villages Occupied and Depopulated by Israel in 1948* (Washington: Institute for Palestine Studies, 1992); Salman Abu Sitta, *The Atlas of Palestine 1948* (London: Saqi Books, 2005); Meron Benvenisti, *Sacred Landscape: The Buried History of the Holy Land* (Berkeley: University of California Press, 2000); Nur Masalha, *The Politics of Denial: Israel and the Palestinian Refugee Problem* (London: Pluto Press, 2003); Nadia Abu el-Haj, *Facts on the Ground: Archaeological Practice and Territorial Self-Fashioning in Israeli Society* (Chicago: University of Chicago Press, 2001); also see the Palestine Remembered Web site, which includes detailed information on each Palestinian town or village lost in 1948 as well as the circumstances of its depopulation and memoirs of the events of 1948 (http://www.palestine remembered.com/index.html).

On the history of **Zionism** and the **1948 War**: see, in addition to sources cited above, Benny Morris, *The Birth of the Palestinian Refugee Problem Revisited* (Cambridge: Cambridge University Press, 2004); Benny Morris, "On Ethnic Cleansing," interview with Ari Shavit (originally published in *Ha'aretz*, 8 January 2004; republished in *New Left Review* 26, March-April 2004); Norman Finkelstein, *Image and Reality of the Israel-Palestine Conflict* (London: Verso Books, 2003); Edward Said, *The Question of Palestine* (New York: Vintage, 1992); Avi Shlaim, *The Iron Wall* (New York: Norton, 2001); David Hirst, *The Gun and the Olive Branch* (New York: Nation Books, 2003); Eugene Rogan and Avi Shlaim, eds., *The War for Palestine: Rewriting the History of 1948* (Cambridge: Cambridge University Press, 2001); Simha Flapan, *The Birth of Israel: Myths and Realities* (New York: Pantheon, 1987); Ilan Pappé, ed., *The Israel/Palestine Question* (London: Routledge, 1999); Ilan Pappé, *The Ethnic Cleansing of Palestine* (Oxford: Oneworld Publications, 2006); Samih Farsoun and Naseer Aruri, *Palestine and the Palestinians* (New York: Westview Press, 2006); Avi Shlaim's *Collusion Across the Jordan: King Abdullah, the Zionist Movement, and the Partition of Palestine* (New York: Columbia University Press, 1988); Nur Masalha, *Expulsion of the Palestinians: The Concept of "Transfer" in Zionist Political Thought, 1882–1948* (Washington, D.C.: Institute for Palestine Studies, 1992); Benny Morris, *The Road to Jerusalem: Glubb Pasha, Palestine, and the Jews* (London: I.B. Tauris, 2003); Rashid Khalidi, *The Iron Cage* (New York: Beacon, 2006).

Aaron Greenberg and **Palestinian *nakba* survivor**'s quotations: from Michel Khleifi and Eyal Sivan, *Route 181: Fragments of a Journey in Palestine/Israel* (from Part Three: North).

Walid Khalidi quotation: from Walid Khalidi, ed., *All That Remains: The Palestinian Villages Occupied and Depopulated by Israel in 1948* (Washington. D.C.: Institute for Palestine Studies, 1992).

On **unrecognized villages**: see Joseph Schechla, "The Invisible People Come to Light: Israel's 'Internally Displaced' and the 'Unrecognized Villages' " (*Journal of Palestine Studies*, (Autumn 2001); Muhammad Abu al-Hayja, Riad Beidas, and Rachel Leah-Jones, "Ayn Hawd and the 'Unrecognized Villages' " (*Journal of Palestine Studies*, Autumn 2001); *NGO Report: Suggested Issues for Consideration Regarding Israel's Combined 10th, 11th, 12th, and 13th Periodic Report to the U.N. Committee on the Elimination of Racial Discrimination* (Adalah, 15 December 2005); *Parallel Report Jointly Submitted to the U.N. Committee on the Elimination of All Forms of Racial Discrimination, 69th Session, Geneva* (Al Haq and other human rights NGOs in Israel/Palestine, July 2006); *Concluding Observations of the [U.N.] Committee on the Elimination of Racial Discrimination* (International Convention on the Elimination of All Forms of Racial Discrimination, March 2007).

Muhammad Abu al-Hayja quotations regarding **Ayn Hawd**: from al-Hayja, Beidas, and Leah-Jones, "Ayn Hawd and the 'Unrecognized Villages.' "

On **Jaffa in 1948**: see sources for 1948 War, above.

Edwin Montagu quotation regarding **Zionism**: from memorandum submitted to British cabinet by Edwin Montagu (U.K. National Archives, CAB 24/24).

King-Crane Commission quotations: from "King-Crane Commission Report, 1919," available on United Nations Web site http://domino.un.org/UNISPAL.NSF/fd807e46661e 3689852570d00069e918/392ad7eb00902a0c852570c000795153!OpenDocument).

Chaim Weizmann quotations on **Arabs**, and **Edward Said** on Weizmann: from Edward Said, *The Question of Palestine* (New York: Vintage, 1992).

Benny Morris quotation regarding the means of founding **Israel as a Jewish state**: from his essay in Eugene Rogan and Avi Shlaim, eds., *The War for Palestine: Rewriting the History of 1948* (Cambridge: Cambridge University Press, 2001).

Quotations from **Ben-Gurion, Moshe Shertok, Eliahu Dobkin, Eliezer Kaplan, Dov Joseph, Werner David Senator, Shlomo Lavi, Avraham Katznelson, Eliahu Lulu, Chaim Weizmann, Menachem Begin,** and **Joseph Weitz** regarding preparations for **transfer** of the Palestinians and for the **1948 War**: from Benny Morris, *The Birth of the Palestinian Refugee Problem Revisited* (Cambridge: Cambridge University Press, 2004).

Walid Khalidi quotation regarding the **1947 U.N. Partition Plan**: from Walid Khalidi, ed., *All That Remains: The Palestinian Villages Occupied and Depopulated by Israel in 1948* (Washington, D.C.: Institute for Palestine Studies, 1992).

Simha Flapan quotations regarding Zionist pragmatism and the outcome of the 1948 War: from Simha Flapan, *The Birth of Israel: Myths and Realities* (New York: Pantheon, 1987).

Alan Dershowitz quotation encapsulating **Zionist mythography**: from Alan Dershowitz, *The Case for Israel* (New York: Wiley, 2003).

Avi Shlaim quotations regarding the actualities and outcome of the **1948 War** and **Plan D**: from Avi Shlaim, *The Iron Wall* (New York: Norton, 2001).

Ilan Pappé quotations regarding **Plan D and the 1948 War**: from Ilan Pappé, *The Ethnic Cleansing of Palestine* (Oxford: Oneworld Publications, 2006).

Benny Morris quotation regarding the **Palestinian refugee "problem"**: from his essay in Eugene Rogan and Avi Shlaim, eds., *The War for Palestine: Rewriting the History of 1948* (Cambridge: Cambridge University Press, 2001).

Nur Masalha quotation regarding **transfer**: from his essay in Rogan and Shlaim, eds., *The War for Palestine*.

Benny Morris quotation regarding **Plan D**: from Benny Morris, *The Birth of the Palestinian Refugee Problem Revisited* (Cambridge: Cambridge University Press, 2004).

Account of the **capture of Haifa** and other areas and quotations from **Ben-Gurion, Uri Milstein, Ezra Danin, Golda Meir, Meron Benvenisti, Moshe Shertok, Joseph Weitz,** "Retroactive Transfer orders," **Folke Bernadotte, Walid Khalidi,** "American travelers in the 1950s," **Moshe Dayan, Israel Shahak** and **Michael Fishbach**: from Benny Morris, *The Birth of the Palestinian Refugee Problem Revisited* (Cambridge: Cambridge University Press, 2004); Meron Benvenisti, *Sacred Landscape: The Buried History of the Holy Land* (Berkeley: University of California Press, 2000); Michael Fishbach,

Records of Dispossession: Palestinian Refugee Property and the Arab-Israeli Conflict (New York: Columbia University Press, 2003); *All That Remains: The Palestinian Villages Occupied and Depopulated by Israel in 1948* (Washington, D.C.: Institute for Palestine Studies, 1992); Edward Said, *The Question of Palestine* (New York: Vintage, 1992); Ilan Pappé, *The Ethnic Cleansing of Palestine* (Oxford: Oneworld Publications, 2006).

Gideon Levy and **Yair Farjun** quotations regarding present-day remains of **Palestinian villages destroyed in 1948**: from Gideon Levy, "Shards of Memory" (*Ha'aretz*, 2 June 2005).

Lord Justice Smedley quotation: from "Chagos Islanders Return Home" (*The Guardian* [London], 24 June 2007).

CODA

Jerusalem Media and Communications Center poll data: see JMCC Web site (jmcc.org/publicpoll/results/2007/index.htm).

Haggai Alon quotation regarding **Israeli army policy in West Bank**: from interview in *Ha'aretz*, in Meron Rapoport, "The Spirit of the Commander Prevails" (*Ha'aretz*, 27 May 2007).

Extrajudicial killing of **Salah Shehadeh**: see Mark Oliver, "Bush Joins in Condemnation of Israeli Attack" (*The Guardian* [London], 23 July 2002).

Ari Fleischer quotation regarding killing of **Shehadeh**: from Oliver, "Bush Joins in Condemnation."

Dan Halutz quotation regarding killing of innocent victims along with **Shehadeh**: from Akiva Eldar, "Temple Mount Police Are Turning into Tour Guides" (*Ha'aretz*, 1 July 2003).

Chris Hedges quotations on **soldiers shooting children**: from Chris Hedges, "A Gaza Diary" (*Harper's*, October 2001).

David Remnick quotations regarding **Hamas**: from David Remnick, "Letter from Jerusalem" (*New Yorker*, 30 July 2007).

Henry Siegman quotation regarding **violence as a protest of occupation**: from Henry Siegman, "The Middle East Peace Process Scam" (*London Review of Books*, 16 August 2007).

On **right to resist occupation** as enshrined in **international law**: see Richard Falk, "International Law and the al-Aqsa Intifada" (*Middle East Report*, Winter 2000); Richard Falk and Burns Weston, "The Relevance of International Law to Palestinian Rights in the West Bank and Gaza: In Legal Defense of the *Intifada*" (*Harvard International Law Journal*, vol. 32, no. 1, 1991); also see *United Nations General Assembly Resolution 3103* (1973), available on the U.N. Web site (http://daccessdds.un.org/doc/RESOLUTION/GEN/NR0/281/75/IMG/NR028175.pdf?OpenElement), which recognizes the legitimacy of the struggle for self-determination of peoples living under "colonial and alien domination" and says that attempts to suppress such struggles are violations of international law and constitute threats to "international peace and security." Also see Richard Falk, "International Law and the Peace Process" (*Hastings International and Comparative Law Review*, Spring 2005).

Alvaro de Soto quotations: from Alvaro de Soto, "End of Mission Report" (May 2007, available on the *Guardian* newspaper Web site: http://www.guardian.co.uk/israel/Story/ 0,,2101677,00.html); also see Rory McCarthy, "Secret U.N. Report Condemns U.S. for Middle East Failures" (*The Guardian* [London], 13 May 2007).

For more on **Hamas**, the **Palestinian Authority**, municipal **elections** in 2005, and legislative assembly elections in 2006 and their aftermath: see Danny Rubinstein, "Hamas Is the Big Winner These Days" (*Ha'aretz*, 4 April 2005); Akiva Eldar, "Abu Mazen to Israel: Let's Discuss the End of the Conflict" (*Ha'aretz*, 24 March 2006); Lara Marlow, "Palestinians Now Being Punished for Choosing Hamas" (*Irish Times*, 8 April 2006); Ismail Haniyeh, "Peace Can Only Be the Fruit of Justice" (*Al-Ahram Weekly*, 13–19 April 2006); Jimmy Carter, "Punishing the Innocent Is a Crime" (*International Herald Tribune*, 7 May 2006); Avi Issacharoff, "Hamas Arrests Planned Weeks Ago" (*Ha'aretz*, 29 June 2006); Ismail Haniyeh, "Aggression Under False Pretenses" (*Washington Post*, 11 July 2006); Joseph Massad, "Pinochet in Palestine" (*Al-Ahram Weekly*, 9–15 November 2006); Amira Hass, "How the PA Failed" (*Ha'aretz*, 2 November 2005); Ghada Karmi, "With No Palestinian State in Sight, Aid Becomes Adjunct to Occupation" (*The Guardian* [London], 31 December 2005); Mousa Abu Marzouk, "What Hamas Is Seeking" (*Washington Post*, 31 January 2006); Amira Hass, "Missing the Government of Thieves" (*Ha'aretz*, 27 September 2006); Khaled Amariyeh, "Joining Forces" (*Al-Ahram Weekly*, 1 April 2005); Zvi Bar'el, "You Wanted Elections, Huh?" (*Ha'aretz*, 15 May 2005); Avi Issacharoff, "U.N.: Gaza Economy May Crash Soon Unless Israel Reopens Borders" (*Ha'aretz*, 18 July 2007); Ali Abunimah, "Mahmoud Abbas' War Against the Palestinian People," 10 August 2007, available on Electronic Intifada Web site (http://www. electronicintifada.net/v2/article7160.shtml).

Quotations from **Khaled Meshaal** of **Hamas**: from Khaled Meshaal, "We Will Not Sell Our People or Principles for Foreign Aid" (*The Guardian* [London], 31 January 2006).

Hamas political program, 2006: available on Electronic Intifada Web site (http://elec tronicintifada.net/bytopic/historicaldocuments/428.shtml).

On the issue of **Hamas recognizing Israel**: see Saree Makdisi, "In the War of Words, the Times Is Israel's Ally" (*Los Angeles Times*, 22 April 2007).

Quotation from **Jimmy Carter** regarding "criminal" U.S. response to **Hamas electoral victory**: see, among other sources, Democracy Now Web site for 21 June 2007 (http://www.democracynow.org/article.pl?sid=07/06/21/1443211).

On **U.S. and Israeli support for Fateh**: see Amos Harel and Avi Issacharoff, "Israeli Defense Official: Fatah Arms Transfer Bolsters Forces of Peace" (*Ha'aretz*, 28 December 2006); Amos Harel and Avi Issacharoff, "Fatah to Israel: Let Us Get Arms to Fight Hamas" (*Ha'aretz*, 7 June 2007).

On the role of **Elliot Abrams**: see, e.g., Harvey Morris, "Jihadistan?" (*Financial Times*, 27 May 2007); Shahar Smooha, "All the Dreams We Had Are Now Gone" (*Ha'aretz*, 21 July 2007).

Quotations from **Régis Debray** on **end of the two-state solution**: from Régis Debray, "Palestine: A Policy of Deliberate Blindness" (*Le Monde Diplomatique*, August 2007).

Quotations from **Henry Siegman** on **peace process**: from Henry Siegman, "The Middle East Peace Process Scam" (*London Review of Books*, 16 August 2002).

Quotation from **OCHA**: from *The Humanitarian Impact of Israeli Settlements* (UN-OCHA, July 2007).

Birzeit University poll showing support for **one-state solution**: results published on Birzeit University Web site (http://home.birzeit.edu/dsp/opinionpolls/elitepoll/back ground.html).

For more on **Adalah's draft democratic constitution**, and quotations from it, see the text, published on Adalah's Web site (http://www.adalah.org/eng/democratic_constitu tion-e.pdf).

On questions and challenges posed to Israel by the **Committee on the Elimination of Racial Discrimination**, see *Concluding Observations of the [U.N.] Committee on the Elimination of Racial Discrimination* (International Convention on the Elimination of all Forms of Racial Discrimination, March 2007).

For more on the challenges to the continuing discourse of a **two-state solution**, see, e.g., Henry Siegman, "The Middle East Peace Process Scam" (*London Review of Books*, 16 August 2007); Régis Debray, "Palestine: A Policy of Deliberate Blindness" (*Le Monde Diplomatique*, August 2007).

For more on the prospects of a **one-state solution**, see, e.g., Saree Makdisi, "For a Secular Democratic State" (*The Nation*, 20 June 2007); Ali Abunimah, *One Country: A Bold Proposal to End the Israeli-Palestinian Impasse* (New York: Metropolitan Books, 2006); Virgina Tilley, *The One State Solution: A Breakthrough for Peace in the Israel-Palestinian Deadlock* (Ann Arbor: University of Michigan Press, 2005); Meron Benvenisti, *Son of the Cypresses: Memories, Reflections, and Regrets from a Political Life* (Berkeley: University of California Press, 2007); Edward Said, "Truth and Reconciliation" (*Al-Ahram Weekly*, 14 January 1999); Tony Judt, "Israel: The Alternative" (*New York Review of Books*, 23 October 2003); Jeff Halper, "One State: Preparing for a Post–Road Map Struggle Against Apartheid" (available on Z *Magazine* Web site: http://www.zmag.org/content/showarticle.cfm?ItemID=4203); Uri Avnery and Ilan Pappé, "Two States or One State?" (Gush Shalom debate; transcript available online at http://toibillboard.info/Transcript_eng.htm); Meron Benvenisti, "The Case for Shared Sovereignty" (*The Nation*, 18 June 2007); John Rose, "We Need a Post-Zionist Leap of Faith" (*The Guardian* [London], 2 April 2005).

Amos Oz quotation regarding **Zionism**: from Amos Oz, "The Meaning of Homeland," available on the Web site of the World Zionist Organization (http://www.wzo.org .il/en/resources/print.asp?id=1625).

On **Ghassan Kanafani**: see Ghassan Kanafani, *Returning to Haifa and Other Stories*, trans. Barbara Harlow and Karen Riley (Boulder, Colo.: Lynne Rienner, 2000).

Yossi Beilin quotation: from Anthony Cordesman, *The Israeli-Palestinian War: Escalating to Nowhere* (Westport, Conn.: Praeger Security International, 2005).

Vladimir Jabotinsky quotations: see notes to Introduction, above.

Moshe Ya'alon quotation regarding **Palestinians as a defeated people**: quoted in, among other places, Yonatan Mendel, "Diary" (*London Review of Books*, 22 February 2007).

Arnon Sofer quotation on **Gaza**: from Ruthie Blum, "One on One: It's the Demography, Stupid" (interview with Arnon Sofer, *Jerusalem Post*, 20 May 2004).

Benny Morris quotation on **ethnic cleansing**: from Benny Morris, "On Ethnic Cleansing," interview with Ari Shavit (originally published in *Ha'aretz*, 8 January 2004, republished in *New Left Review* 26, March-April 2004).

King-Crane Commission and **Edwin Montagu** quotations, see notes to "Inside Out," above.

Desmond Tutu and **Ian Urbina** quotations: from Desmond Tutu and Ian Urbina, "Against Israeli Apartheid" (*The Nation*, 15 July 2002).

Ehud Olmert quotations regarding the **demographic problem** and **Israel's need for a two-state solution**: from *Ha'aretz* Web site (http://www.haaretz.com/GA/pages/ShArtGA.jhtml?itemNo=360533; Aluf Benn et al., "Olmert to *Ha'aretz*: Two-State Solution, or Israel Is Done For" (*Ha'aretz*, 29 November 2007).

Ehud Olmert quotation regarding the **need for a Palestinian "state"**: from Ehud Olmert, speech to 6th Herzliya Conference, 24 January 2006 (available on Israeli embassy Web site, http://www.israelemb.org).

Uri Dromi quotation: from Uri Dromi, "Full Withdrawal, Full Reoccupation, or Full Deportation (*Jerusalem Report*, 6 May 2002).

Miko Peled quotation: from Miko Peled, "The Next Intifada," 24 August 2007, available on Electronic Intifada Web site (http://www. electronicintifada.net/v2/article8961 .shtml).

Nir Rosen quotations: from interview with Amy Goodman on *Democracy Now*, 21 August 2007.

Ali Abunimah quotations: from Ali Abunimah, *One Country* (New York: Metropolitan Books, 2006).

On **maps "missing" from Israeli textbooks**: see, for example, Akiva Eldar, "PM Olmert Backs Tamir Proposal to Add Green Line to Textbooks" (*Ha'aretz*, 11 January 2007).

Edward Said quotation: from Edward Said, "The Only Alternative" (*Al-Ahram Weekly*, 1–7 March 2001).

John Dugard quotation, from *Report of the Special Rapporteur on the Situation of Human Rights in the Palestinian Territories Occupied Since 1967* (U.N. Human Rights Council, 29 January 2007).

NOTES ON STATISTICS

OCCUPATION BY THE NUMBERS: FIRST SERIES

Length of border: "Crossing the Barrier: Palestinian Access to Agricultural Land" (United Nations Office for the Coordination of Humanitarian Affairs [UN-OCHA], January 2006).

Length of wall: "The Humanitarian Impact on Palestinians of Israeli Settlements and other Infrastructure in the West Bank" (UN-OCHA, July 2007).

Proportion of wall built on border: "Report of John Dugard, Special Rapporteur on the Situation of Human Rights in the Palestinian Territories Occupied Since 1967" (United Nations Human Rights Council, 29 January 2007).

Length of wall in and around East Jerusalem: "The Humanitarian Impact of the West Bank Barrier on Palestinian Communities: East Jerusalem" (UN-OCHA, June 2007).

Length of wall built on internationally recognized border near Jerusalem: "The Humanitarian Impact of the West Bank Barrier on Palestinian Communities: East Jerusalem" (UN-OCHA, June 2007).

Percentage of West Bank surface area cut off: "Movement and Access Restrictions in the West Bank: Uncertainty and Inefficiency in the Palestinian Economy" (World Bank, 9 May 2007).

Amount of land expropriated: "Crossing the Barrier: Palestinian Access to Agricultural Land" (UN-OCHA, January 2006).

Number of gates; number open to Palestinians: "The Barrier Gate and Permit

Regime Four Years On: Humanitarian Impact in the Northern West Bank" (UN-OCHA, November 2007).

Percentage of Palestinian land planted with olive trees: "Humanitarian Update" (UN-OCHA, October 2004).

Percentage of population assisting in olive harvest; number of olive trees; number inaccessible: "The Olive Harvest in the West Bank and Gaza" (UN-OCHA, October 2006).

Number of olive trees destroyed by Israeli army: "Olive Oil Harvest Season in Palestine" (Applied Research Institute, Jerusalem, 18 September 2006).

Families unable to access land in "seam zone": "The Barrier Gate and Permit Regime Four Years On: Humanitarian Impact in the Northern West Bank" (UN-OCHA, November 2007).

Palestinians in "seam zone"; their access to medical care: "Report of John Dugard, Special Rapporteur on the Situation of Human Rights in the Palestinian Territories Occupied Since 1967" (United Nations Human Rights Council, 29 January 2007); "The Barrier Gate and Permit Regime Four Years On: Humanitarian Impact in the Northern West Bank" (UN-OCHA, November 2007).

Palestinians in Jerusalem cut off by wall: "The Humanitarian Impact of the West Bank Barrier on Palestinian Communities: East Jerusalem" (UN-OCHA, June 2007).

OCCUPATION BY THE NUMBERS: SECOND SERIES

Roadblocks and checkpoints in West Bank: *West Bank Closure Count and Analysis* (UN-OCHA, data regularly updated at www.ochaopt.org).

Number of roadblocks army pledged to remove that didn't actually exist: Avi Issacharoff, "IDF Source Admits: 44 'Removed' Barriers Didn't Exist" (*Ha'aretz*, 22 January 2007).

Number of flying roadblocks; number of Israeli raids; number of prisoners: Summary monthly statistics maintained by UN-OCHA, data regularly updated at www.ochaopt.org.

Number of roadblocks army pledged to remove in November 2007; number actually removed: Avi Issacharoff, "Two, Not 24, W. Bank Roadblocks Removed, Watchdog Group Says" (*Ha'aretz*, 16 November 2007).

Israel's travel ban list: "Report of John Dugard, Special Rapporteur on the Situation of Human Rights in the Palestinian Territories Occupied Since 1967" (United Nations Human Rights Council, 29 January 2007).

Number of cars; number with permits to circulate in West Bank: "Forbidden Roads: The Discriminatory West Bank Road Regime" (B'Tselem, August 2004).

Cost to obtain necessary permits: "Restrictions on Movement of People and Goods Within the West Bank" (UN-OCHA, November 2005).

Per capita income data: "Intensified Aid and Urgent Action Needed to Avert Palestinian Economic Collapse" (United Nations Conference on Trade and Development [UNCTAD], 12 September 2006).

Villages severely affected by movement restrictions; their populations: "Restrictions on Movement of People and Goods Within the West Bank" (UN-OCHA, November 2005).

OCCUPATION BY THE NUMBERS: THIRD SERIES

Homes demolished in East Jerusalem: Data from B'Tselem Web site (http://www .btselem.org/english/Planning_and_Building/East_Jerusalem_Statistics.asp).

Palestinians made homeless as a result: Data from B'Tselem Web site (http:// www.btselem.org/english/Planning_and_Building/East_Jerusalem_Statistics.asp).

West Bank homes demolished for lacking permit, 2006: Data from B'Tselem Web site (http://www.btselem.org/english/Planning_and_Building/Statistics.asp).

Palestinians made homeless as a result: Data from B'Tselem Web site (http:// www.btselem.org/english/Planning_and_Building/Statistics.asp).

Palestinian homes in occupied territories demolished for lacking permit: Data from B'Tselem Web site (http://www.btselem.org/english/Planning_and_Building/ Index.asp).

Palestinian homes demolished as punishment: Data from B'Tselem Web site (http://www.btselem.org/english/Punitive_Demolitions/Statistics.asp).

Percentage in which suspect was dead or in prison: *Through No Fault of Their Own: Punitive House Demolition During the al-Aqsa Intifada* (B'Tselem, November 2004).

Average number of people made homeless as a result: *Through No Fault of Their Own: Punitive House Demolition During the al-Aqsa Intifada* (B'Tselem, November 2004).

Number of Palestinian homes demolished since 1967: Data published by Israeli Committee Against House Demolition (ICAHD).

Number of Palestinians stripped of Jerusalem residency: Data from B'Tselem Web site (http://www.btselem.org/english/Jerusalem/Revocation_Statistics.asp).

OCCUPATION BY THE NUMBERS: FOURTH SERIES

Number of Israeli raids, prisoners captured: Summary monthly statistics maintained by UN-OCHA, data regularly updated at www.ochaopt.org.

Days Palestinians and Jewish settlers can be detailed without charge: Data from *Parallel Report Jointly Submitted to the UN Committee on the Elimination of All Forms of Racial Discrimination, 69th Session, Geneva, July-August 2006* (available on the Web site of the United Nations High Commissioner for Human Rights, www.ohchr.org).

Number of Palestinian prisoners held by Israel: "Report of John Dugard, Special Rapporteur on the Situation of Human Rights in the Palestinian Territories Occupied Since 1967" (United Nations General Assembly, 17 August 2007).

Cumulative number held since 1967: Data published by the Palestinian human rights group Addameer (www.addameer.org).

Information and data on children and the law, child prisoners: from *Parallel Report Jointly Submitted to the UN Committee on the Elimination of All Forms of Racial Dis-*

crimination, 69th Session, Geneva, July-August 2006 (available on the Web site of the United Nations High Commissioner for Human Rights, www.ohchr.org)

Occupation by the Numbers: Fifth Series

Number of Palestinians working in Israel, 1987: Data published by European Institute for Research on the Mediterranean and Euro-Arab Cooperation.

Number working in 2000, 2007: Data published by B'Tselem (http://www.btselem .org/English/Workers/Index.asp).

Unemployment data for West Bank and Gaza, 1999–2006: "West Bank and Gaza: Economic Developments in 2006—A First Assessment" (IMF and World Bank, March 2007).

Unemployment, Gaza, summer 2007: Data published by United Nations. See Rory McCarthy, "UN Warns of Economic Collapse in Gaza" (*The Guardian* [London], 18 July 2007).

Poverty in Gaza: "Report of John Dugard, Special Rapporteur on the Situation of Human Rights in the Palestinian Territories Occupied Since 1967" (United Nations Human Rights Council, 29 January 2007).

Food aid to people of Gaza: Avi Issacharoff, "International Aid Agency: 80 Percent of Gazans Now Rely on Food Aid" (*Ha'aretz*, 4 March 2007).

Disease rates: "Two Years After London: Restarting Palestinian Economic Recovery" (World Bank, 24 September 2007).

Occupation by the Numbers: Sixth Series

Children killed by Israeli army: Data from B'Tselem Web site (http://www.btselem .org/English/Statistics/Casualties.asp).

Children living in fear, exposed to violence, displaced, feel vulnerable, value their education: *A Psychosocial Assessment of Palestinian Children* (US Agency for International Development, 2003).

School closures; schooldays lost (2002): Data published by United Nations Children's Fund, UNICEF ("Thousands of Palestinian Children Denied Access to Schools," 2 October 2002).

Assaults on schools; students and teachers killed; schooldays lost (2005): "Trend Analysis: Education Under Occupation" (Palestinian Monitoring Group, published at Right to Education Campaign, Birzeit University, Web site: http://www.right2edu.birzeit .edu).

Number of university age Gazans: "Fact Sheet: Gaza" (Right to Education Campaign, Birzeit University, 25 June 2007).

Capacity of Gaza university system: "Fact Sheet: Gaza" (Right to Education Campaign, Birzeit University, 25 June 2007).

Gazan students at Birzeit: "Fact Sheet: Gaza" (Right to Education Campaign, Birzeit University, 25 June 2007).

Disabled people in Gaza: "Limitations on Access to Higher Education for Palestinian Students" (Legal Center for Freedom of Movement [Israel], December 2006).

Courses on physical rehabilitation in Gaza: "Limitations on Access to Higher Education for Palestinian Students" (Legal Center for Freedom of Movement [Israel], December 2006).

Gazans barred from studying in West Bank: "Limitations on Access to Higher Education for Palestinian Students" (Legal Center for Freedom of Movement [Israel], December 2006).

Hebron universities: Reports published by Right to Education Campaign, Birzeit University Web site (http://www.right2edu.birzeit.edu).

DISPOSSESSION, SEGREGATION, AND INEQUALITY BY THE NUMBERS

All statistics from *Parallel Report Jointly Submitted to the UN Committee on the Elimination of All Forms of Racial Discrimination, 69th Session, Geneva, July-August 2006* (Al Haq and other human rights NGOs in Israel/Palestine, July 2006; available on the Web site of the United Nations High Commissioner for Human Rights, www.ohchr.org); "The Education Gap" (Adalah Newsletter, August 2007); and *NGO Report: Suggested Issues for Consideration Regarding Israel's Combined 10th, 11th, 12th, and 13th Periodic Report to the UN Committee on the Elimination of Racial Discrimination* (Adalah, 15 December 2005).

MAPS

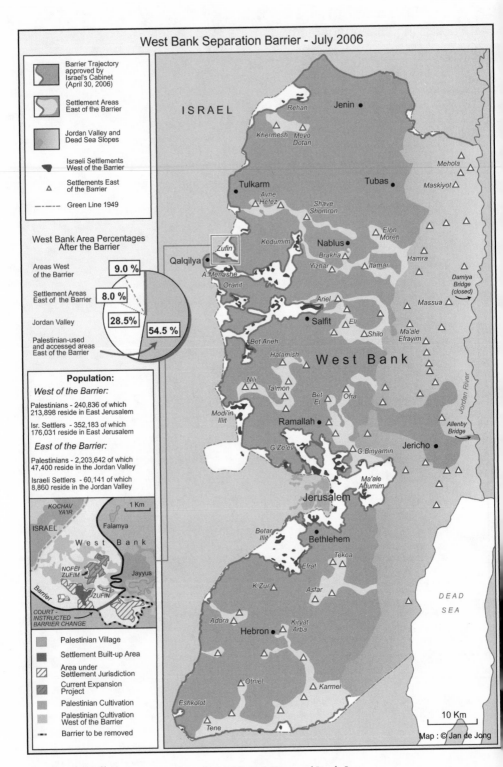

West Bank Separation Barrier - July 2006

Barrier Trajectory approved by Israel's Cabinet (April 30, 2006)

Settlement Areas East of the Barrier

Jordan Valley and Dead Sea Slopes

▾ **Israeli Settlements** West of the Barrier

△ **Settlements East** of the Barrier

----- **Green Line 1949**

West Bank Area Percentages After the Barrier

Areas West of the Barrier — **9.0 %**

Settlement Areas East of the Barrier — **8.0 %**

Jordan Valley — **28.5%**

54.5 %

Palestinian-used and accessed areas East of the Barrier

Population:

West of the Barrier:

Palestinians - 240,836 of which 213,898 reside in East Jerusalem

Isr. Settlers - 352,183 of which 176,031 reside in East Jerusalem

East of the Barrier:

Palestinians - 2,203,642 of which 47,400 reside in the Jordan Valley

Israeli Settlers - 60,141 of which 8,860 reside in the Jordan Valley

KOCHAV YA'IR
ISRAEL
Falamya
West Bank
NOFEI ZUFIM
Jayyus
ZUFIN
Barrier
COURT-INSTRUCTED BARRIER CHANGE
1 Km

■ Palestinian Village
■ Settlement Built-up Area
▨ Area under Settlement Jurisdiction
▨ Current Expansion Project
■ Palestinian Cultivation
■ Palestinian Cultivation West of the Barrier
----- Barrier to be removed

ISRAEL

Rehan · Jenin
Khermesh Mevo Dotan
Tulkarm
Avne Hefez
Shave Shomron
Tubas
Maskiyot
Mehola
Elon Moreh
Kedumim Nablus
Brakha
Hamra
Qalqilya
Zufin
A.Menashe
Oranit
Yizhar Itamar
Damiya Bridge (closed)
Ariel
Massua
Bet Aneh
Salfit Eli
Shilo
Ma'ale Efrayim
Halamish
West Bank
Nili
Talmon
Bet El Ofra
Jordan River
Modi'in Illit
Ramallah
Allenby Bridge
G.Ze'ev
G.Binyamin Jericho
Ma'ale Adumim
Jerusalem
Betar Illit
Bethlehem
Tekoa
Efrat
K.Zur
Asfar
DEAD SEA
Adora
Kiryat Arba
Hebron
Otniel Karmel
Eshkolot
Tene

10 Km

Map : © Jan de Jong

West Bank Wall. Courtesy Foundation for Middle East Peace and Jan de Jong.

Facilitating Disengagement - Israel's West Bank Road Plan - 2004

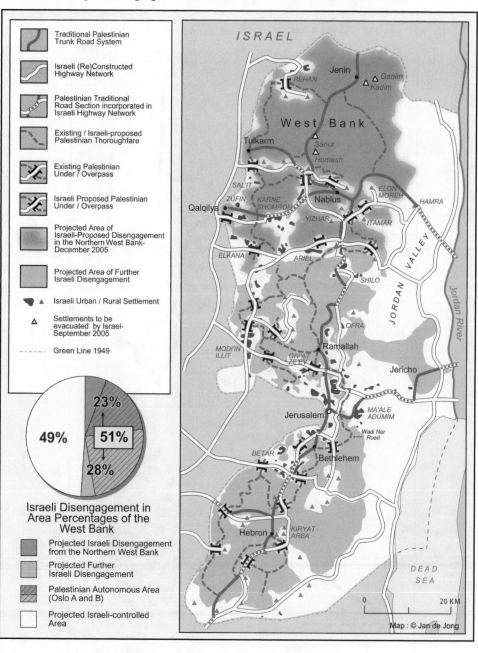

Legend:

Traditional Palestinian Trunk Road System

Israeli (Re)Constructed Highway Network

Palestinian Traditional Road Section incorporated in Israeli Highway Network

Existing / Israeli-proposed Palestinian Thoroughfare

Existing Palestinian Under / Overpass

Israeli Proposed Palestinian Under / Overpass

Projected Area of Israeli-Proposed Disengagement in the Northern West Bank-December 2005

Projected Area of Further Israeli Disengagement

Israeli Urban / Rural Settlement

Settlements to be evacuated by Israel-September 2005

Green Line 1949

Israeli Disengagement in Area Percentages of the West Bank

49%   51%   23%   28%

Projected Israeli Disengagement from the Northern West Bank

Projected Further Israeli Disengagement

Palestinian Autonomous Area (Oslo A and B)

Projected Israeli-controlled Area

Map : © Jan de Jong

Bypass Roads. Courtesy Foundation for Middle East Peace and Jan de Jong.

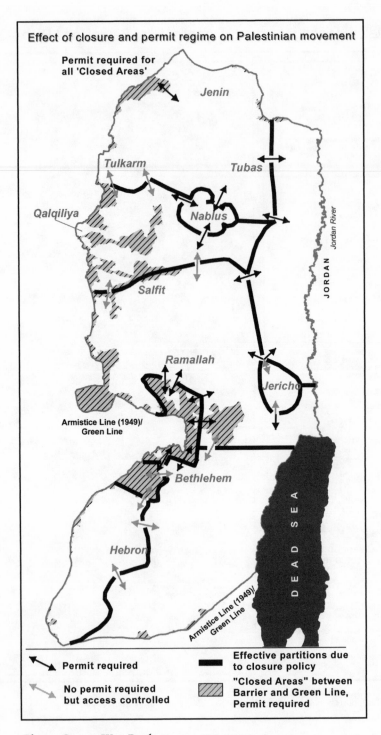

Closure System, West Bank. Courtesy UN-OCHA.

Metropolitan Jerusalem - August 2006

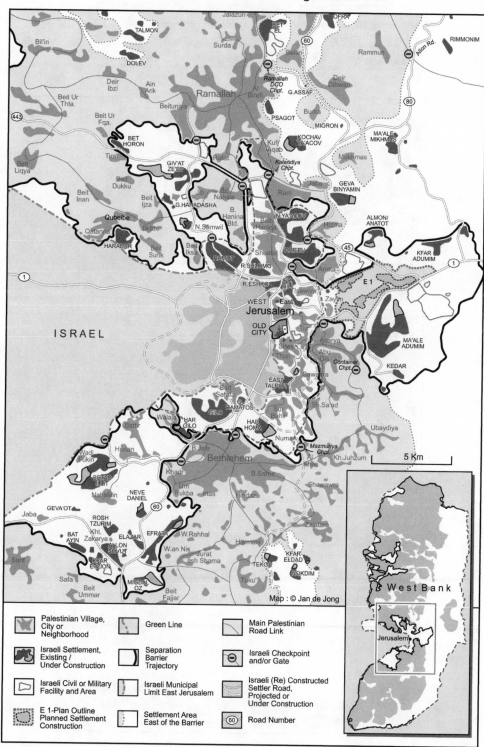

Map : © Jan de Jong

5 Km

Legend

Palestinian Village, City or Neighborhood	Green Line	Main Palestinian Road Link
Israeli Settlement, Existing / Under Construction	Separation Barrier Trajectory	Israeli Checkpoint and/or Gate
Israeli Civil or Military Facility and Area	Israeli Municipal Limit East Jerusalem	Israeli (Re) Constructed Settler Road, Projected or Under Construction
E 1-Plan Outline Planned Settlement Construction	Settlement Area East of the Barrier	Road Number

Jerusalem Area. Courtesy Foundation for Middle East Peace and Jan de Jong.

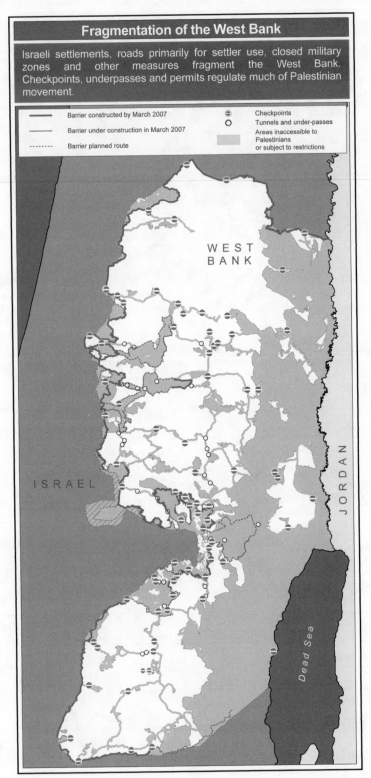

Fragmentation of the West Bank

Israeli settlements, roads primarily for settler use, closed military zones and other measures fragment the West Bank. Checkpoints, underpasses and permits regulate much of Palestinian movement.

Barrier constructed by March 2007
Barrier under construction in March 2007
Barrier planned route

⊜ Checkpoints
○ Tunnels and under-passes
Areas inaccessible to Palestinians or subject to restrictions

WEST BANK

ISRAEL

JORDAN

Dead Sea

Fragmentation of West Bank. Courtesy UN-OCHA.

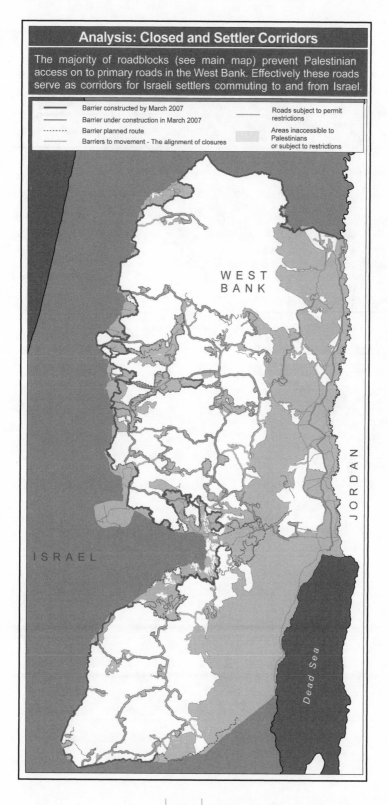

Analysis: Closed and Settler Corridors

The majority of roadblocks (see main map) prevent Palestinian access on to primary roads in the West Bank. Effectively these roads serve as corridors for Israeli settlers commuting to and from Israel.

Barrier constructed by March 2007

Barrier under construction in March 2007

Barrier planned route

Barriers to movement - The alignment of closures

Roads subject to permit restrictions

Areas inaccessible to Palestinians or subject to restrictions

WEST BANK

ISRAEL

JORDAN

Dead Sea

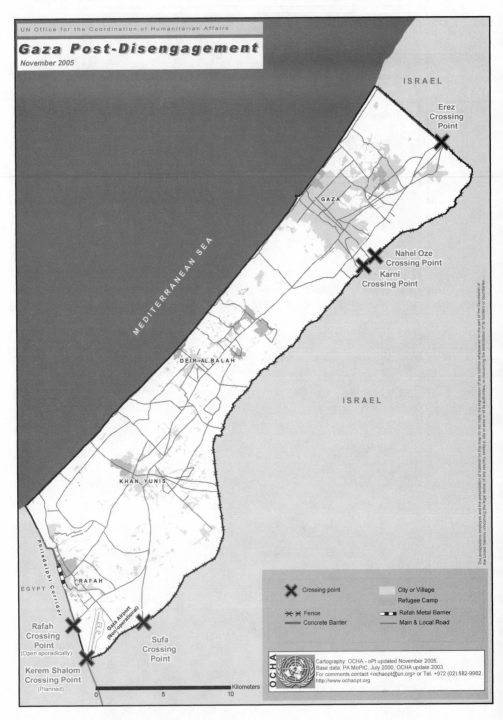

Gaza Strip after 2005. Courtesy UN-OCHA.

Hebron - Depopulation and Separation, May 2007

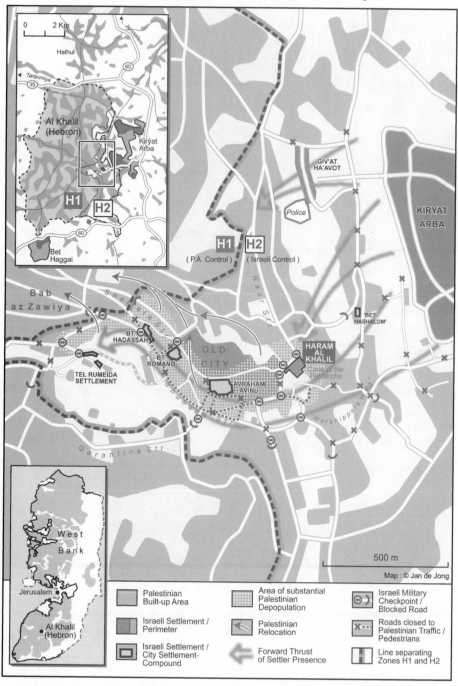

Hebron, 2007. Courtesy Foundation for Middle East Peace and Jan de Jong.

INDEX

Page numbers in *italics* refer to illustrations and maps.